ZEW Economic Studies

Publication Series of the Centre for European Economic Research (ZEW), Mannheim, Germany

ZEW Economic Studies

Further volumes of this series can be found at our homepage:
springeronline.com/series/4041

Vol. 12: W. Smolny
Endogenous Innovations and Knowledge Spillovers
A Theoretical and Empirical Analysis
2000. VIII, 277 pp. ISBN 3-7908-1320-6

Vol. 13: M. Lechner, F. Pfeiffer (Eds.)
Econometric Evaluation of Labour Market Policies
2001. X, 242 pp. ISBN 3-7908-1372-9

Vol. 14: M. Beise
Lead Markets
Country-Specific Success Factors of the Global Diffusion of Innovations
2001. XVI, 305 pp. ISBN 3-7908-1430-X

Vol. 15: O.H. Jacobs, C. Spengel
Effective Tax Burden in Europe
Current Situation, Past Developments and Simulations of Reforms
2002. X, 131 pp. ISBN 3-7908-1470-9

Vol. 16: U. Kaiser
Innovation, Employment, and Firm Performance in the German Service Sector
2002. X, 164 pp. ISBN 3-7908-1481-4

Vol. 17: J. Köke
Corporate Governance in Germany
An Empirical Investigation
2002. VIII, 184 pp. ISBN 3-7908-1511-X

Vol. 18: E. Wolf
What Hampers Part-Time Work?
An Empirical Analysis of Wages, Hours Restrictions and Employment from a Dutch-German Perspective
2003. X, 174 pp. ISBN 3-7908-0006-6

Vol. 19: P. Cecchini et al. (Eds.)
The Incomplete European Market for Financial Services
2003. XII, 255 pp. ISBN 3-7908-0013-9

Vol. 20: C. Böhringer, A. Löschel (Eds.)
Empirical Modeling of the Economy and the Environment
2003. VI, 326 pp. ISBN 3-7908-0078-3

Vol. 21: K. Rennings, T. Zwick (Eds.)
Employment Impacts of Cleaner Production
2003. VIII, 322 pp. ISBN 3-7908-0093-7

Vol. 22: O. Bürgel, A. Fier, G. Licht, G. Murray
The Internationalisation of Young High-Tech Firms
An Empirical Analysis in Germany and the United Kingdom
2003. XII, 291 pp. ISBN 3-7908-0120-8

Vol. 23: F. Hüfner
Foreign Exchange Intervention as a Monetary Policy Instrument
Evidence for Inflation Targeting Countries
2004. X, 175 pp. ISBN 3-7908-0128-3

Vol. 24: E. Lüders
Economic Foundation of Asset Price Processes
2004. XII, 121 pp. ISBN 3-7908-0149-6

Vol. 25: F. Reize
Leaving Unemployment for Self-Employment
An Empirical Study
2004. XII, 241 pp. ISBN 3-7908-0168-2

Vol. 26: Ch. Böhringer, A. Löschel (Eds.)
Climate Change Policy and Global Trade
2004. VIII, 381 pp. ISBN 3-7908-0171-2

Vol. 27: K. Jacob et al.
Lead Markets for Environmental Innovations
2005. XII, 273 pp.
ISBN 3-7908-0164-X

Vol. 28: L. Lammersen, R. Schwager
The Effective Tax Burden of Companies in European Regions
2005. XI, 251 pp. ISBN 3-7908-1562-4

Vol. 29: Ch. Elschner, R. Schwager
The Effective Tax Burden on Highly Qualified Employees
2005. VIII, 123 pp. ISBN 3-7908-1568-3

Vol. 30: Ch. Lauer
Education and Labour Market Outcomes
2005. IX, 286 pp. ISBN 3-7908-1569-1

Vol. 32: O. Heneric, G. Licht, W. Sofka (Eds.)
Europe's Automotive Industry on the Move
2005. XII, 275 pp. ISBN 3-7908-1590-X

Christoph Böhringer · Andreas Lange
(Editors)

Applied Research in Environmental Economics

With 35 Figures
and 13 Tables

Physica-Verlag
A Springer Company

ZEW
Zentrum für Europäische
Wirtschaftsforschung GmbH
Centre for European
Economic Research

Introduction

Christoph Böhringer

Centre for European Economic Research (ZEW), L 7,1, 68161 Mannheim, Germany, and University of Heidelberg, Department of Economics, Hauptstraße 120, 69117 Heidelberg, Germany, boehringer@zew.de.

Andreas Lange

Centre for European Economic Research (ZEW), L 7,1, 68161 Mannheim, Germany, lange@zew.de.

Economic insights are increasingly finding their way into the design of environmental policy. While environmental taxes and permit trading programmes as efficient regulatory instruments play a growing role in environment policies, concerns with the environment are not fading: Sustainable development, climate policy, biodiversity conservation, energy production and consumption – all are examples of issues on the current political agenda in many countries. While these themes are also subject to intensive economic research, both the reception of academic insights by policy makers as well as the timely identification and treatment of policy-relevant questions by researchers often seem to be problematic.

This volume attempts to vitalise the exchange between policy makers and academics. It offers a snapshot of environmental economic research on a range of policy-relevant problems. Academic contributions are complemented by views of policy makers on priority fields in environmental policy, the usefulness of academic research for decision making, and requirements to applied research in the future.

All contributions in this volume are based on presentations given at the Workshop "Frontiers in Applied Environmental and Resource Economics" at the Centre for European Economic Research (ZEW), Mannheim, Germany, in March 2004. They cover the following areas: Sustainability Assessment, Transport and the Environment, Energy Market Regulation, Trade, Environment and Biodiversity, and the Political Economy of Environmental Regulation.

Sustainability Assessment

Sustainable Development (SD) has meanwhile become one of the most prominent catchwords on the world's policy agenda. Nearly all governments and multinational firms have committed themselves to the overall concept of SD. Taking a lead role, the European Union requires Sustainability Impact Assessment in terms of a "careful assessment of the full effects of [any larger] policy proposal ... [that] ... must include estimates of its economic, environmental and societal inputs inside and outside the EU". Yet, SD, which is not just about environment, but also about economy and society, has proven hard to define and rather susceptible for ambiguities. Monitoring progress towards SD requires in the first place the identification of operational indicators that provide manageable units of information on economic, environmental and social (including institutional) conditions. An issue that cannot be clearly measured will be difficult to improve. Therefore, indicator systems that measure sustainability in a meaningful way are a central prerequisite for formulating policy goals.

Against this background, Heinz Welsch, University of Oldenburg, investigates the possibilities and limitations in constructing meaningful sustainability indices. Based on methodological considerations, he defines an index as "meaningful" if it allows unambiguous ordering of the underlying situation, in particular independent of the units in which relevant variables are measured: A sustainability index should allow an unambiguous judgement of whether a situation has improved or worsened. Welsch distinguishes two index categories according to the property of commensurability vis-à-vis incommensurability. In the case of commensurability, the construction of meaningful indices is possible if either monetary welfare measures or bio-physical metrics can be used. In the case of incommensurability, the lack of measures or the desire to aggregate several variables generally leads to the non-existence of meaningful indices.

Despite these fundamental difficulties, indicators are needed in the political arena to monitor and to communicate progress on sustainability issues. Pascal Wolff, Eurostat, provides an overview of how sustainable development indicators are defined for different policy fields in the European Union. Among other criteria, Wolff lays out that the indicators should be consistent, should have an accepted normative interpretation and should be responsive to policy intervention but without becoming subject to manipulation. Most notably, they should allow coherent assessment and comparison of sustainability issues across different countries.

Thilo Goodall, SAM Sustainable Asset Management, Zurich, discusses the problem of measuring corporate sustainability performance and its impact on corporate financial performance. Corporate sustainability is defined as "a business approach to create long-term shareholder value by embracing opportunities and managing risks deriving from economic, environmental and social developments", thereby emphasising a long-term strategy which does not conflict with shareholders' interests. After defining indicators to assess a company's sustainability orientation, Goodall turns to ways and problems of measuring its impact on the financial performance. The hypothesised link between corporate sustainability and shareholder value is, however, still subject to further research.

The integration of different indicators and assessment methods is addressed by Marialuisa Tamborra, European Commission. She describes the efforts of the European Commission to develop an Impact Assessment method which allows a comprehensive analysis of given policy proposals and the identification of trade-offs in achieving different objectives. As ultimate goal it is proposed to combine and integrate assessments of specific policy fields such as business impact assessment, gender assessment, and small and medium enterprises assessment.

Trade, Environment, and Resource Use

Many environmental problems, such as climate change or biodiversity loss, involve transboundary pollution and thereby can only be tackled efficiently at an international level.

Cees Withagen, Free University Amsterdam and Tilburg University, gives an overview on the relationship between environmental policy and international trade. A government which tries to unilaterally implement emission targets, usually faces considerable political pressure from interest groups of different sectors, in particular from those exporting products to other countries and therefore fearing competitive disadvantages on the world market. Withagen demonstrates in a simple theoretical model that a preferential treatment for those sectors might be suboptimal. That is, there is no clear a priori reason to use "over lax" taxation in these sectors. He urges policy makers to be aware of the trade-off between pollution and production, and the impact of environmental policy on trade.

Frank Wätzold, Martin Drechsler, Volker Grimm, and Jaroslav Myšiak, all from UFZ-Centre for Environmental Research Leipzig-Halle, deal with biodiversity loss, a theme which ranks high on the international environmental policy agenda. After an overview of European biodiversity conservation programmes, they address approaches to measure the cost-effectiveness of such policies. In their opinion, adequate approaches involve integrated research between ecologists and economists. Wätzold et al. discuss different state-of-the-art approaches to ecological-economic modeling as well as problems in integrating those two disciplines. They single out important "cultural" differences between ecological and economic models, in particular with respect to the treatment of uncertainty and the resolution of time and space.

Transport and Environment

In contrast to substantial progress in reducing emissions in many sectors of the economy, pollution caused by traffic has increased in the past few years due to a rise of passenger and freight traffic combined with a shift towards motorised road transport. There is a controversial debate on appropriate policy initiatives to promote environmentally compatible transport systems (e.g., based on hydrogen). The interaction between environmental externalities, knowledge spillovers as well as network externalities poses complex challenges to environmental regulation.

The peculiarities of transportation research are deepened by Romain Molitor, Trafico Verkehrsplanung, Wien, and Karl W. Steininger, University of Graz. They point out the spatial structure of transport and its interdependencies with infrastructure, living and working locations. These determinants of traffic generate inertia and explain long-term impacts on transportation system design. Molitor and Steininger start discussing early visions of transport and cities and their impact on today's transport structures before turning to areas of current policy and research needs: interaction of land-use and transport, distributional impacts of transport policy, and behavioral changes.

Armin Schmutzler, University of Zurich, provides an overview of research issues in the field of "transportation and environment". He argues that – different from many textbook approaches – there are good reasons for transportation-specific policies. Policies and associated research problems can be structured by decomposing aggregate emissions from transportation into total amount of transport, modal split, and specific emissions. At each level, normative and positive research questions arise which often require interdisciplinary approaches and exchange between economists, psychologist, engineers, etc.

Wolfgang Schade and Werner Rothengatter, University of Karlsruhe, describe different approaches to perform cost-benefit analyses of transport policies: macro- and micro-economic approaches, computable general equilibrium models, and evolutionary approaches using system dynamics models. Acknowledging that transport policies may evoke reactions inside and outside the transport system, they present a system dynamics approach which allows for dynamic cost-benefit analyses of direct and indirect effects. Finally, they discuss illustrative applications to policy-induced changes in gasoline and diesel taxes.

Günter Hörmandinger, European Commission, comments on the three preceding academic contributions on transportation research and policy. He supports the general findings, but argues that in order to obtain policy-relevant results one has to "take into account the messy details of the 'real' world". Although recognising difficulties in handling complex models, he calls for detailed analyses of transport-specific problems that include network externalities, (natural) monopolies, as well as the spatial structure of traffic.

Energy Market Regulation

Energy utilization plays a central role in solving environmental problems and in implementing sustainable economies in the medium to long term. To promote the transition towards environmentally compatible energy systems, far-reaching policy measures are required. Due to the network-based structure and the transnational dimension of resource use and pollution, the institutional parameters in the national, European and global energy markets must be taken into account when policy recommendations are formulated.

Michael Kraus, University of Applied Sciences Darmstadt, provides an overview of different regulatory principles based on alternative economic paradigms. He then investigates electricity markets thereby highlighting different degrees of regulation along the value-chain from generation, transmission, distribution, to sales and wholesales. Electricity market reforms are distinguished by the degree to which they allow for competition or change the features of regulation at the different levels. Kraus finally addresses difficulties to measure the impacts of regulation and thereby the benefits of regulatory reforms for economic efficiency.

Christoph Weber and Alfred Voß, University of Stuttgart, discuss the specifics of energy-markets in more detail. Characteristics such as peak-load demand, non-storability, and grid-dependency must be considered when describing markets and the impact of changes in their regulation. Weber and Voß portray efficiency and security of supply in the longer run as the "key challenges" for energy policy. In particular, they discuss problems of sufficient investments incentives under uncertainty, i.e., the difficulties to predict revenues and, hence, the refinancing of investment costs. The authors also point out the importance of stochastic market models as supply and demand fluctuate over the day, week, and seasons as well as across locations. Beyond more narrow short-term efficiency issues, one should also consider the robustness of energy systems when designing market reforms.

Eberhard Jochem, ETH Zurich and Fraunhofer Institute for Systems and Innovation Research, Karlsruhe, fits the regulatory issues of energy markets into a broader innovation policy framework designed for sustainable development. In his view, environmental pollution on the one hand and resource scarcity on the other hand call for an active role of government in the stipulation and coordination of innovation activities thereby assessing the large portfolio of technologies and their economic perspectives.

Domenico Rossetti di Valdalbero, European Commission, uses the examples of emissions trading, energy taxation, and renewable electricity targets to show how the European Union backs its policy decisions with research results from academia. The majority of the EU energy-socio-economic research projects addresses links between energy and the environment. The author describes several models and tools which have been used in the EU's policy making process. He argues that EU energy-related initiatives will be more frequent in the future and calls on researchers to elaborate scientifically sound quantitative tools which in particular address energy-related long-term problems like resource depletion, climate change, or waste management.

Political Economy of Environmental Regulation

Political feasibility of environmental policies depends crucially on the specific interest of regulated parties. Stiff opposition by adversely affected influential interest groups explains why regulatory measures suggested by academic research often do not translate into actual policy making.

Friedrich Schneider, University of Linz, and Hannelore Weck-Hannemann, University of Innsbruck, investigate reasons for the gap between theoretical research and actual policy practice by looking into the incentives of key political players. Based on Public Choice Theory, they argue that many incentive-based instruments are neither in the interest of political decision makers nor favoured by the most influential interest groups. Schneider and Hannemann use the examples of an Austrian ecological tax reform and road pricing to demonstrate how Public Choice Theory might guide economists in proposing policy measures that are suboptimal on overall (theoretical) efficiency grounds but increase the political chances of their implementation.

Gebhard Kirchgässner, University of St. Gallen, discusses the discrepancy between economists' policy advice and actual policy implementation from a complementary angle: By applying Public Choice Theory to the advice given by economists themselves, i.e. by looking at economists as interest-driven rather than benevolent scientists, he points out that researchers rarely give unambiguous clear-cut answers but provide rather quite often even contradictory results. Referring to the example of an ecological tax reform in Switzerland, Kirchgässner demonstrates how – hidden behind a myriad of assumptions which often drive the results – economic studies can provide scientific "support for nearly every political position". Given potential self-interest of researchers, Kirchgässner points out the need for a rigorous critical discussion of models and methods before associated results are used in decision making.

Kai Schlegelmilch, German Federal Ministry for the Environment, Nature Conservation and Nuclear Safety, puts the discussion and implementation of an Ecological Tax Reform in Germany into a dynamic policy context. He points out that – during the last decades – academic advice was increasingly used in environmental policy design. Studying the varying position of industrial groups on their preferred policy instruments, Schlegelmilch identifies strategic options to delay or avoid regulation. In his view, the bundling of different political interests is crucial to promote environmental taxation. In this vein, a larger share of revenues of the Ecological Tax Reform in Germany is earmarked to reduce labour costs such that interests of various stakeholders can be satisfied.

Constructing Meaningful Sustainability Indices*

Heinz Welsch

University of Oldenburg, Department of Economics, 26111 Oldenburg, Germany, welsch@uni-oldenburg.de

Keywords. *Environmental Index, Sustainability Index, Preference Ordering, Comparability, Measurability, Environmental Indicator*

JEL. *C4; Q00*

Abstract. This paper surveys and evaluates the possibilities and limitations of sustainability indices from the point of view of meaningfulness. A sustainability index is defined as meaningful if it allows unambiguous orderings of the relevant 'situations' over time independent of the measurement units in which the variables describing the situations are expressed. The cases of commensurability and incommensurability are distinguished. In the former, the comparison of situations is unambiguous be-cause all legitimate choices of measurement units can be accommodated on the basis of exogenously given relationships among the variables. These relationships may define a monetary welfare-metric or a bio-physical effects-metric. In the case of incommensurability, common approaches (both cardinal and ordinal) may fail to yield meaningful indices. A systematic assessment of which indices are meaningful in which circumstances is provided.

1 Introduction

"Don't run down your assets!" – The sustainability imperative can be put as simple as that. There are, however, a variety of assets that may be worth preserving: natural capital, man-made (physical) capital, human capital, not to speak of 'social capital' (governance, trust, and other social institutions). Different notions of sustainability differ with respect to the degree of substitutability which is presumed to exist between the various types of capital. A hypothetical extreme position might entail that each and every asset should be preserved: Not only should the stocks of natural capital, physical capital, human and social capital be non-decreasing but also the different kinds of natural capital, down to individual species, minerals, or fuels.

* Acknowledgement: I am grateful to Udo Ebert, Friedrich Schneider, Armin Schmutzler, Christoph Weber, Cees Withagen and Pascal Wolff for useful comments on an earlier version.

Such a position could be called 'ultra-strong sustainability'. It has a big advantage: To be monitored, it does not need the construction of any 'sustainability index' whatsoever. But ultra-strong sustainability is not a tenable position in the real world, be it only since it would imply that all non-renewable resources remain untouched indefinitely. By contrast, both analysts and policy makers will normally be prepared to tolerate some trade-off between different assets, and this begs the need for sustainability indices, that is, tools for answering the question: "Have the relevant assets been kept intact *overall*?" (weak sustainability of some degree).

Speaking somewhat loosely, a sustainability index should permit an assessment of whether 'the situation' (e.g. the environmental situation) has become better or worse between time t and t+1. This *sustainability problem* is slightly different from the *ranking problem*: How do places (e.g. countries) rank in terms of 'the situation' in question? Though both problems are related, I will mainly focus on the former, touching upon the latter only occasionally.

A basic requirement when constructing a sustainability index is that it should be meaningful, in the sense that the comparison of situations over time should be unambiguous with respect to the choice of measurement units of the relevant variables.

With respect to meaningfulness it is useful to distinguish between the case of commensurability and the case of incommensurability. In the former case, the comparison of situations is unambiguous because all legitimate choices of measurement units can be accommodated on the basis of exogenously given relationships among the variables. This is not the case with incommensurable variables: Here an ambiguity problem may arise, depending on the measurability and comparability properties of the variables involved. The two cases will be addressed in separate sections (Section 2, and Sections 3 and 4, respectively).

The focus of the paper is on methodological issues. Indices actually proposed or applied are mentioned mainly for illustrative purposes. A comprehensive survey of actual indices is not intended.

2 Commensurability

Two types of sustainability indices considered in the literature fall into the category of commensurability: indices based on a monetary welfare metric and indices based on a bio-physical effects-metric, respectively.

2.1 Monetary Welfare-Metric

To illustrate the welfare-based approach to constructing sustainability indices, consider a welfare function defined over consumption C and the stock of natural capital N. Natural capital is an aggregate which comprises various types of exhaustible and renewable resources as well as various dimensions of environmental quality. The welfare function reads

$$W_t = W(C_t, N_t) \tag{1}$$

and is assumed to be twice differentiable, increasing and strictly concave in both arguments. The variable W_t is a monetary measure of per-capita welfare or utility at time t.[1]

A definition of sustainability might involve the following requirements:

(a) $\dot{W}_t \geq 0$ for all t, (b) $W_t > 0$ for all t, that is, welfare should be non-declining and positive. If we accept this definition, W_t is a sustainability index. It can be linked to other, perhaps more popular, notions and indices of sustainability as follows. Consider a well-behaved (per-capita) production function $Y(K,R)$, where K denotes the stock of physical capital and R the flow of natural resources into the production process. Letting S denote savings, we have $C = Y - S$, and requirement (a) can be written as follows (with subscripts denoting partial derivatives and dots denoting time derivatives):

$$\begin{aligned} \dot{W} &= W_C \cdot (Y_K \dot{K} + Y_R \dot{R} - \dot{S}) + W_N \dot{N} \\ &= W_C Y_K \dot{K} + W_N \dot{N} + W_C \cdot (Y_R \dot{R} - \dot{S}) \geq 0 . \end{aligned} \tag{2}$$

If, for simplicity, we disregard the last term before the inequality sign, this corresponds to the well-known concept of weak sustainability (Pearce and Atkinson, 1993) according to which the overall capital stock (man-made and natural) should be non-declining. One way to achieve this would entail that *both* K and N should not decline, a requirement commonly referred to as strong sustainability.

The weaker of the two sustainability concepts presupposes that man-made and natural capital can be aggregated since they are to some degree substitutes for each other. As eq. (2) shows, this aggregation requires weights, which are based on the marginal welfare of consumption and nature (W_C and W_N, respectively) and on marginal products. Of course, even for known welfare and production functions, these marginals can probably take almost all non-negative values. In fact, they will depend on the development path actually taken by the economy. The theoretically appropriate marginals will be those along an optimal sustainable path. Unique values can be obtained by solving the intertemporal optimisation problem

$$\max \int_0^T e^{-\rho t} W(Y(K,R) - S, N)\, dt \tag{3}$$

subject to the appropriate equations of motion, typically $\dot{K} = S - \delta K$, $\dot{N} = G(N) - R$, (δ = depreciation rate, $G(N)$ = growth function of natural capital), and the requirements (a) and (b).

The advantage of this approach with respect to the problem of constructing meaningful sustainability indices is that the weights necessary for aggregation are conceptually well-defined and can accommodate any choice of measurement units for K and N. The difficulty, however, is that the weights are hard to determine in

---

1 The framework presented here has been chosen for simplicity of exposition. More complex set-ups could be considered.

reality. Not all researchers and policy makers would be prepared to specify and solve problem (3), given the prevailing uncertainties.[2] Whether and to what extent weights determined with standard valuation techniques (such as contingent valuation or hedonic regressions) can be used as surrogates is not to be discussed here.

Constructing a meaningful index may appear easier if strong sustainability is considered instead, in which case natural capital, N, is required to be non-declining. But natural capital is a construct, that is, an aggregate of rather diverse components. In other words, natural capital is itself an index. Conceptually, it could be constructed within the framework sketched above by simple re-interpretation of the symbol N, which would then denote a vector rather than a scalar. The difficulties of operationalising the aggregation, however, would probably be almost as severe as in the case of weak sustainability.[3]

2.2 Bio-Physical Effects-Metric

An important alternative to welfare-based sustainability indices is based on bio-physical cause-effect relationships. In this approach, effects are usually classified according to certain 'themes' or 'issues', which often correspond to categories of environmental damage. Issues frequently considered in the literature are climate change, ozone layer depletion, acidification, eutrophication, toxic contamination, and others (Adriaanse, 1993, OECD 1993). Issue indices can plausibly be categorised as a set of strong sustainability indices, that is, they represent sub-aggregates of natural capital. If these dimensions of natural capital are thought to be complementary to each other, rather than substitutable, the aggregation problem mentioned at the end of the preceding sub-section is not relevant.

An example may serve to illustrate the approach. Consider the issue of eutrophication of water and soil. It is caused by an excessive supply of plant nutrients in the form of phosphates and nitrogen compounds. An index of eutrophication is an aggregate of the loads of the two constituents which cause eutrophication: phosphates, expressed in terms of phosphorus, and nitrates, expressed in terms of nitrogen. The two substances differ with respect to their eutrophication effect: A kiloton (kt) of nitrogen can be taken to have a ten-times smaller effect than a kt of phosphorus (Adriaanse, 1993). Given this effect ratio, either of these substances can be used as a 'numeraire' to measure eutrophication. One possibility is to choose phosphorus as the numeraire and to transform nitrogen loads into 'equivalent' phosphorus loads. A 'eutrophication equivalent' then is 1 kt phosphorus = 10 kt nitrogen, and a eutrophication index can be computed using 1 and 10 as weights. It is trivial how to adjust the weights if one of the substances is measured

---

2 Actually, the situation is somewhat paradoxical: Constructing an indicator of sustainability along these lines requires information which the indicator is supposed to deliver, that is, whether the development is sustainable.

3 A more pragmatic approach to implementing indices of both weak and strong sustainability has been pursued by Pearce and Atkinson (1993).

not in kt but in pounds, say, by invoking the proportionality of the two measurement units.

Given the effect ratios and the possibility to convert measurement units for pollutant loads (kt, kg, pounds), the eutrophication index so defined allows an unambiguous comparison of two (or more) situations with respect to the prevailing degree of eutrophication, independent of measurement units. Needless to say, this is also the case if nitrogen is chosen as the numeraire, rather than phosporus.

The same logic applies to the other environmental issues mentioned above. In the case of climate change, for instance, so-called global warming potentials allow to express the various greenhouse gases in terms of global warming equivalents and to construct indices of global warming pressure. These then permit an unambiguous assessment of whether global warming pressure has increased or decreased.

It can thus be concluded that 'issue indices' are meaningful given that they are based on known scientific relationships which allow to accommodate any legitimate choice of measurement units.

3 Incommensurability: The Problem and Common Approaches[4]

We now consider cases in which the situations to be compared are described neither in terms of welfare nor in terms of well-defined bio-physical damage categories or life support functions. These cases often involve concepts that are inherently vague, such as 'air pollution' or 'water pollution'. In contrast to acidification, eutrophication, and other 'issues' mentioned above, these phenomena are ill-defined and, hence, not directly measurable. This circumstance prevents to derive bio-physical relationships between the constituents that contribute to the respective phenomenon.

In addition to ill-defined phenomena, incommensurability may also arise when it is attempted to aggregate several well-defined 'issues' into an encompassing index. Such an aggregation may be desired especially when a one-dimensional index of (weak or strong) sustainability is sought for.

Both cases have in common that some exogenous weights must be applied to the constituents of the index. Weights may be based, e.g., on opinion polls or expert judgements. Sometimes, explicit weighting is avoided for lack of information, but implicitly this means that equal weights are accorded to the constituent variables. The determination of weights is not the subject of this paper. Weights are thus throughout assumed to be given.[5]

---

4 Subsections 3.1 and 3.2 are based on Ebert and Welsch (2002). Subsection 3.3 draws on discussions with Udo Ebert.

5 In aggregating theme indices to an encompassing index, weights may differ from country to country. For instance, if some issue is not relevant in a particular country, it may get a weight of zero.

3.1 The Problem

In order to illustrate the problem, consider a simple example which involves the aggregation of two environmental issues. Similar problems may arise when it is attempted to aggregate several polluting substances into an index of an ill-defined phenomenon like air pollution or water pollution.

Suppose we want to assess whether the joint environmental pressure from acidification (sulphur) and eutrophication (phosphorus) has decreased or increased between t = 1 and t = 2. The data are given in **Table 1**. They are taken from Adriaanse (1993) and refer to the Netherlands 1980 and 1985.

Table 1. Illustrative data for acidification and eutrophication

	Sulphur dioxide in kg per hectare	Phosphorus in kt
t = 1	210	306
t = 2	200	310

For simplicity we assume that the two types of environmental pressure are to be weighted equally. Choosing as an index formula the arithmetic mean yields 258 in t = 1 and 255 in t = 2. Overall environmental pressure has thus *decreased*, or so it seems. However, we could have chosen different units for one or both types of pollution. Suppose that eutrophication were measured in units of 100 kg of phosphorus, instead of kilotons as assumed above. The phosphorus load would then be 3060 and 3100 in t = 1 and t = 2, respectively, and the associated index values would be 1635 and 1650, indicating an *increase* of environmental pressure. We cannot thus be sure whether the state of the environment, composed of acidification and eutrophication, has improved or deteriorated.

A similar ambiguity would have occurred had we chosen to measure eutrophication not in phosphorus equivalents, but in nitrogen equivalents. The level of eutrophication would then be 3060 kt nitrogen in t = 1 and 3100 kt nitrogen in t = 2, and the joint index would again have *increased* from 1635 to 1650. Ambiguity may thus arise not only from trivial choices of units (kilotons, kilograms, pounds etc.) but also from the choice of the substance (the 'numeraire') in which to express some type of environmental pressure.

The question arises whether ambiguity can be avoided by choosing a different index formula (keeping the weighting scheme unaltered). One possibility would be to choose the geometric rather than the arithmetic mean. In this case the index values for t = 1 and t = 2, respectively, are $(210*306)^{1/2}$ = 253.5 and $(200*310)^{1/2}$ = 249.0 under the initial choice of units. Under the alternative choice of units, the values $(210*3060)^{1/2}$ = 801.6 and $(200*3100)^{1/2}$ = 787.4 would be obtained. Independent of measurement units for the individual environmental pressures this kind of index unambiguously indicates a decrease in overall pressure.

This example has shown that some index formulas may give rise to ambiguous comparisons while others allow to avoid these problems. Section 4 will examine systematically which indices are appropriate ('meaningful') in which circumstances.

The problems just illustrated are, to some extent, rather obvious, and there are several ways how they are approached in practice. These can be classified into cardinal and ordinal approaches. The remainder of this section discusses these approaches.

3.2 Cardinal Approaches

The cardinal approach to index construction involves a two-step procedure. It consists of converting the variables from their original (natural) units to 'normalised' (artificial) units and then aggregating the results. The rationale put forward for the first step is that the crude environmental data X_i are considered not suitable for direct aggregation because they may differ with respect to their size (units of measurement) and their variability (range). Obviously, for any given aggregator function and explicit weighting scheme, the *effective* weight of any variable i may depend on the units in which it is measured and on the range it occupies. This may affect the index value in the way illustrated above and imply ambiguous comparisons.

The first step, normalisation, involves in most cases a linear transformation of the crude data, comprising the two elementary operations of translation (addition or subtraction of a constant from all observations of a given variable, thus shifting the origin) and/or expansion (multiplication or division of all values by a constant, thus changing the scale). Following Ott (1978) the normalised variables will be referred to as indicators. The indicator corresponding to the crude data X_i will be denoted by $I_i(X_i)$.

In practice, a variety of normalisation procedures are being applied. Two broad categories can be distinguished: Ranging and standardisation. *Ranging* scales the crude data into the interval 0 to 1. In these approaches, the largest observation has the value 1, but the smallest observation may or may not have the value 0:

$$I_i(X_i) = X_i / X_i^{\max} \quad \text{or} \tag{4}$$

$$I_i(X_i) = \left(X_i - X_i^{\min}\right) / \left(X_i^{\max} - X_i^{\min}\right) \tag{5}$$

where $X_i^{\min}$ and $X_i^{\max}$ denote the minimum and, respectively, maximum of variable i. The first version of ranging (eq. (4)) retains the origin, i.e. zero is mapped to zero. In the second version (eq. (5)) the smallest observation is mapped to zero.

In *standardisation*, indicator values are obtained by subtracting the mean (μ) from the observations and dividing by the standard deviation (σ):

$$I_i(X_i) = (X_i - \mu_i) / \sigma_i \tag{6}$$

Standardised values, hence, give the deviation of the corresponding underlying variable from the mean of observations, expressed in standard deviation units.

Clearly, the standardised variables are mixed in sign even if the crude observations are all positive.

A common problem of these approaches is that the mean, the standard deviation, the smallest and the largest value can all change as additional observations become available. This renders these indices inappropriate for comparisons over time, which are essential to any sustainability assessment. This problem is avoided if, instead of parameters of the observed distribution, exogenous reference values or standards are employed in normalisation. For instance, the X_i^{min} and X_i^{max} in eq. (4) or (5) could be replaced by certain fractions or multiples of environmental standards (or target values). However, even though such indicators and the resulting indices are not plagued with the observation-dependence of the normalisation parameters, the choice of exogenous normalisation parameters is never free of arbitrariness.

Arbitrariness also widely prevails with respect to the aggregation rule applied in the second step. Some authors justify their choices by considerations of presumed substitutability among the environmental variables (see Ott, 1978, Khanna 2000). Widely used aggregation rules are the arithmetic mean, the geometric mean, and the constant-elasticity-of-substitution function (of which the former two are limiting cases). In practice, these aggregation rules are combined with diverse forms of normalisation in a largely unsystematic way, as the examples in **Table 2** illustrate.

Table 2. A selection of environmental indices

Reference	Normalisation	Aggregation
Adriaanse (1993)	$I_i(X_i) = X_i / X_i^*$	$I(X) = \Sigma_i I_i(X_i)$
Den Butter/van der Eyden (1998)	$I_i(X_i) = X_i / X_i^{1980}$	$I(X) = \Sigma_i w_i I_i(X_i)$
ESI (2001)	$I_i(X_i) = (X_i - \mu)/\sigma_i$	$I(X) = \frac{1}{n}\Sigma_i I_i(X_i)$
Hope et al. (1992)	$I_i(X_i) = X_i / X_i^{1980}$	$I(X) = \Sigma_i w_i I_i(X_i)$
Khanna (2000)	$I_i(X_i) = \frac{(X_i - \bar{X}_i^{min})}{(\bar{X}_i^{max} - \bar{X}_i^{min})}$	$I(X) = \left(\frac{1}{n}\Sigma_i I_i(X_i)^{\varepsilon}\right)^{1/\varepsilon}$
Van der Bergh/van Veen-Groot (2001)	$I_i(X_i) = X_i / X_i^{max}$	$I(X) = \frac{1}{n}\Sigma_i I_i(X_i)$

Adriaanse (1993) normalises the values of his 'theme' indices (climate change, ozone layer depletion, acidification etc.) by dividing them by a target value, and adds the normalised values across themes. The pollution index of Hope et al. (1992) uses as its input variables pollutant loads in water, air, and soil, which are expressed as a fraction(or multiple) of their respective values in a base year. These normalised values are then aggregated using the weighted arithmetic mean, with weights derived from opinion polls. Similar normalisations are applied by den

Butter and van der Eyden (1998) and van den Bergh and van Veen-Groot (2001). The 'Environmental Sustainability Index' of the World Economic Forum (ESI, 2001) employs standardisation as a normalisation device. They all use the arithmetic mean to aggregate their normalised data. Khanna (2000) chooses a constant-elasticity-of-substitution aggregator function.

Note that in the case of Adriaanse (1993) and den Butter/van der Eyden (1998) X_i denotes the value of a 'theme indicator' in 'theme equivalent units' and $I_i(X_i)$ the normalised theme indicator value. In all other cases the X_i are in natural units. X_i^* denotes an exogenous target value, and $\overline{X}_i^{\min}$ and $\overline{X}_i^{\max}$ are 50% and 500% of the National Ambient Air Quality Standards in the U.S. w_i denotes the weight of variable *i*.

It is obvious that any two of the normalisation-aggregation configurations in **Table 1** may imply different comparisons of states of the environment since these procedures approach the problem of measurement in rather different, yet arbitrary ways.

3.3 Ordinal Approaches

The ordinal approach deals with the problems implied by the non-uniqueness of the cardinalisation of variables by simply ignoring the cardinal dimension of the data and focusing on the ranking of the objects to be compared.[6] In the case of sustainability assessment, the 'objects' are the environmental situations at $t=1$ and $t=2$, which are described in terms of at least two variables (or attributes).

The ordinal approach consists in aggregating the rank orders of the objects by individual attributes, instead of aggregating the numerical values of the attributes by individual object. A variety of rank aggregation procedures have been proposed (see Chebotarev and Shamis 1998 for an overview and characterisation). They all share a common drawback, namely that they are subject to the impossibility theorem of Arrow (1963) which states that there exists no aggregation rule for rank order preferences that satisfies a set of reasonable axioms. However, one of the Arrow axioms is of little importance in many applications of ranking rules: the 'independence of irrelevant alternatives'. To see this, consider that the 'alternatives' correspond to the objects to be ranked. Whenever the set of objects is fixed (e.g. a fixed list of countries for which a rank order is being sought), the axiom is itself rather 'irrelevant' unless the set of objects is to be changed.[7]

Unfortunately, the axiom *cannot* be discarded if one attempts to apply ranking rules in sustainability assessment. In fact, ranking rules may imply inconsistent assessments. This can be illustrated for the case of the Borda rule, which is the probably simplest and best known ranking rule.

---

6 In fact, ordinal approaches can be applied to data which are ordinal in character, that is, data which lack any cardinal significance.

7 Examples of country rankings include Dasgupta and Weale (1992) and Paul (1997).

The Borda rule is based on simple addition across attributes of the attribute-specific ranks of the objects.[8] More specifically, the Borda score of an object is given by

$$B = \Sigma_k (n - a_k) \tag{7}$$

where n is the number of objects and a_k is the rank number of the considered object in respect of attribute k (higher value of attribute is mapped to higher a_k). The Borda score is 1 for the highest-ranking object and n for the lowest-ranking one.

If we wish to employ the Borda score for sustainability assessment, the objects correspond to time periods t_i and t_j, and $n = 2$. However, there is a sequence of such bilateral comparisons: t_1 vs. t_2, t_2 vs. t_3, etc. Consistency would, of course, require that an improvement in t_2 relative to t_1 and an improvement in t_3 relative to t_2 implies an improvement in t_3 relative to t_1 (transitivity). However, since the 'independence of irrelevant alternatives' is not satisfied, transitivity is not guaranteed.[9]

A numerical example may illustrate this. Assume t_1, t_2, and t_3 are to be compared with respect to 3 pollutants X_1, X_2, and X_3. The (hypothetical) data are given in **Table 3**. The measurement units are ignored since we want to apply an ordinal comparison method.

Table 3. Illustrative pollution data

	X_1	X_2	X_3
t_1	2	6	3
t_1	4	4	4
t_3	1	5	5

At t_2 we can compare t_2 with t_1. The respective Borda scores are $B(t_1) = 2$, $B(t_2) = 1$, that is t_2 ranks first in terms of overall environmental pressure. In other words, environmental pressure has *increased* between t_1 and t_2. As time proceeds, we can compare t_3 with t_2, which yields $B(t_2) = 2$, $B(t_3) = 1$. Thus, there is a *further increase* in environmental pressure. However, a *direct* comparison of t_3 and t_1 yields $B(t_1) = 1$ and $B(t_3) = 2$, indicating a *decline* of pollution.

The Borda ranking rule thus fails to produce unambiguous comparisons of environmental pressure over time. The same is true for all ordinal methods of comparison, the reason being that they violate the axiom of 'independence of irrelevant alternatives'.

---

8 Of course, it would be possible to apply weights to the individual attributes before adding them.

9 This is akin to the Condorcet paradox in social choice theory.

4 Incommensurability: The Social Choice Approach

It may have become clear that common approaches to the construction of sustainability indices involving incommensurable variables all imply the risk of yielding ambiguous (contradictory) assessments. In this sense, these indices are not meaningful. I will now address in a systematic way the question, which indices are meaningful in which circumstances, given that the input variables are incommensurable.[10]

4.1 Basic Framework

We consider $n \geq 2$ environmental variables $X_1,...,X_n$ measuring environmental quality at some point or period of time. Let a vector $X = (X_1,...,X_n)$ denote a quality profile or environmental state. Moreover, we consider a preference ordering *P*. The ordering is defined for all states in the admitted domain $X \in D^n$. It reflects a researcher's or social decision maker's value judgements on states of the environment.

We suppose that the ordering can be represented by an environmental index *I*: $D^n \rightarrow \Re$; i.e. we have

$$X^1 \ P \ X^2 \Leftrightarrow I(X^1) \geq I(X^2) \text{ for all } X^1, X^2 \in D^n. \tag{8}$$

The index is only ordinally unique, i.e., every strictly increasing transformation of *I*(*X*) is also a representation of the preference ordering. This is, of course, sufficient for a sustainability index since we are only interested in whether the environmental situation has improved or deteriorated over time.

As stated above, ambiguous (contradictory) comparisons of environmental states may arise due to the non-uniqueness of measurement scales. Therefore one should take into consideration the possibility of changing the scales by which the variables X_i can be measured.

Changing scales comes down to transforming the quality profile by a corresponding transformation $\Phi = (f_1,...,f_n)$

$$\Phi : (X_1,...,X_n) \rightarrow (f_1(X_1),...,f_n(X_n)) \tag{9}$$

where f_i, $i = 1,...,n$, reflects the respective operation. Let $F := \{\Phi = (f_1,...,f_n) \mid f_i : D \rightarrow D \text{ for } i = 1,...,n\}$ be the set of transformations of D^n into itself which are admitted.

We request that the ranking of environmental profiles must not depend on the choice of scales, i.e. must not be changed by any admissible transformation:

10 This section is based on Ebert and Welsch (2004), to which the reader is referred for details and further references.

$$X^1 \ P \ X^2 \Leftrightarrow \Phi(X^1) \ P \ \Phi(X^2) \tag{10}$$

for all $X^1, X^2 \in D^n$ and $\Phi \in F$. In other words, the ranking has to be invariant with respect to admissible transformations. If an ordering P satisfies (3) it is called invariant with respect to F (or F-invariant).

The invariance condition provides the basis of our definition of a meaningful index, since it can equivalently be stated in terms of any representation I of P:

$$I(X^1) \geq I(X^2) \Leftrightarrow I(\Phi(X^1)) \geq I(\Phi(X^2)) \tag{11}$$

for all $X^1, X^2 \in D^n$ and $\Phi \in F$.

We call an index *meaningful* if it satisfies this condition: An environmental index is meaningful if the underlying preference ordering is invariant with respect to admissible transformations of the environmental variables.[11]

Below we will provide characterisations of classes of indices which are meaningful given that the environmental variables possess certain measurability and comparability properties. To that purpose we will now classify environmental variables into categories of measurability and comparability.

4.2 Measurability and Comparability

Measurability relates to the question what kinds of transformations are admissible for any *single* variable, whereas comparability is concerned with the question whether *several* variables can be transformed independently.

With respect to measurability the classes of interest are interval-scale measurable and ratio-scale measurable variables. A variable X_i is interval-scale measurable if its ordering is unique up to a transformation of the form $f_i(X_i) = \alpha_i X_i + \beta_i$ for $\alpha_i > 0$. In other words, admissible transformations involve translations as well as expansions. Interval-scale measurable variables allow to compare levels and differences independent of transformations of the form stated above, but do not allow to compare ratios. This is different with ratio-scale measurable variables:

A variable X_i is ratio-scale measurable if its ordering is unique up to a transformation of the form $f_i(X_i) = \alpha_i X_i$ for $\alpha_i > 0$. Hence, only expansions but not translations are admissible, that is, the variable has a fixed (natural) origin. The consequence is that levels, differences, and ratios can be compared, independent of transformations of the form stated above.

With respect to comparability, five cases may be relevant for sustainability assessment.

11 The property of 'meaningfulness' is a purely technical one, not suggesting any substantive connotation. The term comes from 'measurement theory', see Pfanzagl (1971), Roberts (1979) or Luce et al. (1990).

(a) Interval-scale noncomparability INC: $f_i(X_i) = \alpha_i X_i + \beta_i$, $\alpha_i > 0$. Under INC, several variables can be translated and expanded separately (independently).

(b) Interval-scale unit comparability IUC: $f_i(X_i) = \alpha X_i + \beta_i$, $\alpha > 0$. Under IUC, several variables can be translated independently, but they can only be expanded jointly.

(c) Interval-scale full comparability IFC: $f_i(X_i) = \alpha X_i + \beta$, $\alpha > 0$. Under IFC, only common translations and expansions are admitted.

(d) Ratio-scale noncomparability RNC: $f_i(X_i) = \alpha_i X_i$, $\alpha_i > 0$. Under RNC, several variables can be expanded independently; translations are not admitted.

(e) Ratio-scale full comparability RFC: $f_i(X_i) = \alpha X_i$, $\alpha > 0$. Under RFC, several variables can only be expanded jointly.

Among these cases, INC and RNC are perhaps the most important ones. INC applies to temperatures: Temperatures in several situations can be measured in Centigrades, Fahrenheit, Réaumur, and Kelvin, which are related to each other as stated under (a). RNC applies to masses (such as pollutant loads): Masses in several situations can be expressed in pounds, kilograms, tons etc., which are related to each other as stated under (d).

4.3 Results

The results for interval-scale measurability and ratio-scale measurability are presented in **Table 4** and **Table 5**, respectively.

Table 4. Results for interval-scale measurability

	C+WM	C+SM	C+SM+SEP
INC	dictatorial ordering	no ordering	
IUC	$\sum_{i=1}^{n} w_i X_i, w_i \geq 0$	$\sum_{i=1}^{n} w_i X_i, w_i > 0$	
IFC	$\sum_{i=1}^{n} w_i X_i, w_i \geq 0$ and more complicated forms	$\sum_{i=1}^{n} w_i X_i, w_i > 0$ and more complicated forms	$\sum_{i=1}^{n} w_i X_i, w_i > 0$

Note: C, WM, SM, and SEP denote continuity, weak monotonicity, strong monotonicity, and separability. These are properties that one may wish to impose on the preference ordering.

It can be seen from **Table 4** that for interval-scale non-comparable (INC) variables at best a dictatorial ordering (dictatorial index) exists, depending on the desired type of monotonicity. The frequently used arithmetic mean requires at least interval-scale unit comparability, that is, the scale of the variables can only be changed jointly (by a common factor); only the origin may be shifted independently.

For ratio-scale measurable variables, the prospects for obtaining a meaningful index are more favourable (see **Table 5**). Most interesting is the case of ratio-scale non-comparable variables, like pollutant loads. In this case, the geometric mean (Cobb-Douglas function) provides a meaningful index

Table 5. Results for ratio-scale measurability

	C+WM	C+SM	C+SM+SEP
RNC	$\prod_{i=1}^{n} X_i^{w_i}, w_i \geq 0$ on $\Re_+^n$ or $\Re_{++}^n$	$\prod_{i=1}^{n} X^{w_i}, w_i > 0$ on $\Re_{++}^n$	
RFC	any homothetic function	any homothetic function	CES function

Note: See **Table 4**.

In the case of mixed measurability, chances to obtain a meaningful index are poor. For instance, if one wishes to define an ordering over an INC variable and a RNC variable the ordering must be dictatorial to be meaningful (free of ambiguity). This then implies that either the INC variable or the RNC variable must be chosen as an index. It is impossible to *combine* them in a meaningful way. This case is, e.g., relevant for water quality indices, which often aim at combining temperature (INC) with pollutant loads (RNC).

5 Conclusions

The paper has surveyed and evaluated the possibilities and limitations of sustainability indices from the point of view of meaningfulness. A meaningful sustainability index is one which allows unambiguous orderings of the relevant 'situations' over time, independent of the measurement units in which the variables describing the situations are expressed. The cases of commensurability and incommensurability were distinguished. In the former, the comparison of situations is unambiguous because all legitimate choices of measurement units can be accommodated on the basis of exogenously given relationships among the variables. These relationships may define a welfare-based monetary metric or an effects-based bio-physical metric. In the case of incommensurability, common approaches (both cardinal and ordinal) may fail to yield meaningful indices.

A systematic assessment of which indices are meaningful in which circumstances has shown that indices in the frequently used form of an arithmetic mean are meaningful only if the variables satisfy (at least) interval-scale unit comparability, i.e. they can be scaled only by a common factor. Important environmental variables like emissions or pollutant loads (masses) do not possess this property. Masses are ratio-scale non-comparable, that is, they can be scaled independently (pounds, kilograms, tons), but have a fixed origin (0 pounds = 0 kilograms etc.). An environmental index which combines masses using the geometric mean is meaningful. Masses (RNC) and temperatures (INC) cannot be combined with each other – as attempted in some water quality indices – in a meaningful way.

The criterion that sustainability indices should guarantee unambiguous comparisons of situations is intuitively plausible. Yet, there may exist a tension with other criteria. For instance, the geometric mean (Cobb-Douglas function) implies that the elasticity of substitution between the constituent variables (e.g. pollutant loads) is unity. This implied elasticity may differ from *a-priori* ideas a researcher or policy maker might have regarding substitutability. A problem may then arise especially when the substitutability that is deemed appropriate is lower than unity. However, the frequently applied arithmetic mean is even worse in this regard: It implies an infinite elasticity of substitution, that is, any deterioration with respect to one pollutant can be neutralised by a finite improvement with respect to another pollutant. In comparison with this case the geometric mean provides a relatively 'prudent' type of index.

If the conditions for meaningfulness are not fulfilled, all one can probably do is to take resort to a statistical approach: One could compute a battery of indices which involve a variety of normalisations and aggregation rules and then show the distribution of improvements vs. deteriorations. This would yield a sort of likelihood that the 'situation' has improved or deteriorated. Possibly, a unanimous answer may be obtained, and hopefully it will indicate that the requirement of sustainability is satisfied.

References

Adriaanse, A. (1993), *Environmental Policy Performance Indicators*, SDU, Den Haag.

Arrow, K.J. (1963), *Social Choice and Individual Values*, New York.

Chebotarev, P.Y. and E. Shamis (1998), Characterizations of Scoring Methods for Preference Aggregation, *Annals of Operations Research* 80, 299-332.

Dasgupta, P.S. and M. Weale (1992), On Measuring the Quality of Life, *World Development* 20, 119-131.

Den Butter, F.A.G. and J.A.C. van der Eyden (1998), A Pilot Index for Environmental Policy in the Netherlands, *Energy Policy* 26, 95-101.

Ebert, U. and H. Welsch (2004), Meaningful Environmental Indices: A Social Choice Approach, *Journal of Environmental Economics and Management* 47, 270-283.

Ebert, U. and H. Welsch (2002), *Meaningful Environmental Indices: A Social Choice Approach*, Discussion Paper V-242-02, Department of Economics, University of Oldenburg.

ESI (2001), *Environmental Sustainability Index 2001*, An Initiative of the Global Leaders of Tomorrow Environment Task Force, www.ciesin.columbia.edu/indicators/ESI.

Hope, C., J. Parker, and S. Peake (1992), A Pilot Environmental Index for the UK in the 1980s, *Energy Policy* 20, 335-343.

Khanna, N. (2000), Measuring Environmental Quality: An Index of Pollution, *Ecological Economics* 35, 191-202.

OECD (1993), *OECD Core Set of Indicators for Environmental Performance Reviews: A Synthesis Report by the Group on the State of the Environment*, Environment Monographs No. 83, Paris.

Luce, R.D., D.H. Krantz, P. Suppes, and A. Tversky (1990), *Foundations of Measurement*, Vol. III, San Diego.

Ott, W. (1978), *Environmental Indices: Theory and Practice*, Ann Arbor.

Pfanzagl, J. (1971), *Theory of Measurement*, 2nd edition, Würzburg.

Roberts, F.S. (1979), *Measurement Theory with Applications to Decision-Making*, Utility and the Social Sciences, Reading.

Paul, S. (1997), The Quality of Life: An International Comparison Based on Ordinal Measures, *Applied Economics Letters* 4, 411-414.

Pearce, D. and G. Atkinson (1993), Capital Theory and the Measurement of Sustainable Development: An Indicator of Weak Sustainability, *Ecological Economics* 8, 103-108.

Van den Bergh, J.C.J.M. and D.B. van Veen-Groot (2001), Constructing Aggregate Environmental-Economic Indicators: A Comparison of 12 OECD Countries, *Environmental Economics and Policy Studies* 4, 1-16.

A Framework for Indicators to Monitor the EU Sustainable Development Strategy

Pascal Wolff

European Commission, Eurostat, 5 Rue Alphonse Weicker, L-2920 Luxembourg, pascal.wolff@cec.eu.int

Keywords. *Sustainable Development, EU Strategy, Indicators*

JEL. *Q56; E61; F18*

Abstract. The European Council will review in 2005 the Sustainable Development Strategy (SDS) which was adopted in Gothenburg in 2001. Indicators for measuring the progress will be needed to assess whether the unsustainable trends identified in 2001 have been overcome and whether international commitments like those taken with the plan of implementation of the 2002 World Summit on Sustainable Development have been translated into facts. This paper presents the contribution of the European Statistical System to the drawing-up of a first set of Sustainable Development Indicators for the purpose of the EU Sustainable Development Strategy.

1 Introduction

One of the main tasks of the Eurostat Task Force on Sustainable Development Indicators is to assist Eurostat in identifying a suitable framework for future work at EU level on Sustainable Development Indicators (SDI). A framework for organising the selection and development of indicators is essential, although it is recognised that any framework on its own is an imperfect tool for expressing the complexities and interrelationships encompassed by sustainable development (SD).

There are many different interpretations of what is meant by 'sustainable development'. It is not the role of Eurostat or the statistical offices to define sustainable development. Two Commission Communications and the related Council Conclusions have set out their interpretation of what sustainable development means in practical terms at EU level, with a number of key objectives, based on the priority themes mentioned below. The EU has also taken a number of commitments following the World Summit on Sustainable Development (WSSD) in Johannesburg in 2002. The framework for indicators must take on board the need to monitor progress in these priority areas.

This paper attempts to set out a framework which could serve as a basis for the development of a list of indicators to be used in evaluating the implementation and effectiveness of the EU Sustainable Development Strategy (SDS). This framework takes account of both the political basis defined by the Commission and the European Council and the technical basis, which has been implemented over the time through many initiatives within and outside the EU.

The fact that this framework and the future indicators have been set up in order to serve for the evaluation of the EU SDS means in particular that the Task Force leaves it to each Member State to determine whether this framework and/or some or all of these SDI are relevant for national purposes or if specific priorities or indicators should be developed at the national level.

The present paper is intended to define a set of rules for the definition and the organisation of the future set of indicators by answering the following questions:

- How should the set of indicators be organised?
- What are the rules to be followed for the selection of indicators?
- How to communicate on the work achieved?
- What is the time frame for this work?

2 The Political and Technical Basis

The priority policy themes, their objectives and measures, as set out in the Commission Communications on SDS and Global Partnership, together with the Conclusions of the European Council Summits in Gothenburg and Seville, form the core features of the framework for SDI. The EU commitments made in the Johannesburg Declaration and the Plan of Implementation (PoI) of the World Summit on Sustainable Development are likely to be integrated into the strategy when it is revised in 2004. Taken together, these documents form the *political basis* for future SDI work.

2.1 The Sustainable Development Strategy

In Gothenburg, the European Council not only added an environmental dimension to the Lisbon Strategy – so putting the environmental dimension on a par with economic and social dimensions – but it also adopted a strategy for sustainable development. The Strategy focuses on six themes[1]:

1. Limiting climate change and increasing the use of clean energy;
2. Addressing threats to public health;
3. Managing natural resources more responsibly;
4. Improving the transport system and land-use management;

---

[1] Commission Communication COM(2001)264 final of 15.05.2001: "A Sustainable Europe for a Better World: A European Union Strategy for Sustainable Development".

5. Combating poverty and social exclusion; and
6. Dealing with the economic and social implications of an ageing society.

For each theme, a number of headline objectives are identified, as well as a set of measures to be introduced in order to meet those objectives. In some cases there are also supplementary objectives linked to the measures, for example, 'alternative fuels should account for at least seven percent of fuel consumption by cars and trucks by 2010'.

2.2 Global Partnership

A second Communication[2], on the external dimension of sustainable development, was endorsed by the European Council in Seville. This complements the first step taken in Gothenburg by proposing that the EU should take a leading role in the pursuit of global sustainable development. It sets out the six priorities listed below:

1. Harnessing globalisation: trade for sustainable development;
2. Fighting poverty and promoting social development;
3. Sustainable management of natural and environmental resources;
4. Improving the coherence of EU policies;
5. Better governance at all levels;
6. Financing sustainable development.

As global partnership refers to both domestic and international actions, some of the issues can be considered as overlapping with the SDS priority themes (e.g. poverty, resource management), while others, such as governance, may add a new aspect also for SD assessments within the EU.

2.3 The WSSD Plan of Implementation

The Johannesburg Declaration and the PoI reaffirmed the Rio commitments and highlighted the issues of poverty and environmental protection, but also strengthened demands in areas such as sustainable production and consumption, water and energy and emphasised the role of the civil society and benefits of partnership. The key commitments refer to the following main issues:

1. Poverty eradication, including water and sanitation;
2. Changing unsustainable patterns of production and consumption, including energy, transport, waste, chemicals, and corporate environmental and social responsibility;
3. Protecting and managing the natural resource base of economic and social development;
4. Health and sustainable development;

---

2 Commission Communication COM(2002)82 final of 13.02.2002: "Towards a Global Partnership for Sustainable Development".

5. Sustainable development of Small Island Developing States (SIDS) and in Africa;
6. Means of implementation (Official Development Assistance, participation).

Several of the priority issues of the PoI have been already included in the EU measures on internal or external SD. The main expansion refers to sustainable production and consumption, corporate social and environmental responsibility, and participation. As the EU will have a leading and decisive role in these, they have been integrated into the proposed framework. This addition will facilitate the integration of more actual considerations of SD into the framework and accordingly, is expected to result in a more policy relevant set of SDI.

2.4 The Technical Basis

With a view to harmonisation and rationalisation with other indicator initiatives, the current work will make maximum use of existing initiatives – both international and national – such as UN Commission on Sustainable Development and Organisation for Economic Co-operation and Development (OECD) lists of SDI, Structural Indicators, Laeken indicators, Environmental Pressure Indicators, etc. This does not mean, however, that the indicators used in these exercises would automatically qualify to become part of the EU set of SDI.

Because one of the major challenges of SDI is to bring out how the economic, social and environmental aspects of SD impinge on each other, accounting frameworks – and particularly the System for integrated Environmental and Economic Accounting (SEEA) – which apply a harmonised approach to the economy and a number of environmental issues, will be favoured as much as possible to describe the interlinks between dimensions. Moreover, the extension of this accounting matrix to include social issues is being explored in a number of Member States.

3 The EU Framework for Sustainable Development Indicators

These themes outlined above, together with the objectives and measures set out in the Communications, will provide the framework for the identification and selection of the indicators. These should be supplemented by some background economic indicators, to provide the context for the other indicators.

The selection of the set of indicators will take into account the technical base of existing sets of indicators and statistical work in related areas. This will ensure consistency between sets of indicators, and should reduce the burden on Member States. However, a further analysis of the themes, objectives and measures may well result in the need for new indicators.

The identification of appropriate indicators is an iterative process. The Commission is required to review the strategy regularly. This may also result in revision of the indicator set to adapt it to new needs, which become apparent following the review.

3.1 Why a Theme Framework?

As discussed during the 9th session of the Commission on Sustainable Development of the UN, the framework employed in the CSD work programme to guide the selection of SDI has evolved from a driving force-state-response approach to one focusing on themes and sub-themes of sustainable development. This change in organisational framework was prompted by the experience of countries that assisted the CSD in testing and developing indicators of sustainable development.

In essence, the rationale for the theme framework is to better assist national policy decision making and performance measurement by focusing on relevant policy issues. The main drawback in this approach is that the set of indicators is not so stable, as priority themes and headline objectives may change over time. However, new priorities and policy targets will also need indicators to monitor their implementation and effectiveness. Indeed, one of the uses of indicators is to monitor if the existing policies are having the desired effect, or whether further measures are needed. So while a stable set of indicators may be desirable from a statistical point of view, for policy makers some flexibility is preferable. This emphasises the importance of a stable base of statistical data, which can be combined in different ways to produce different indicators.

3.2 The Set of Themes

The basis of the framework is, then, the six themes mentioned in the SDS. A theme on *Economic Development* has been added to maintain and visualise the three dimensional nature of sustainable development.

The *Global Partnership* theme refers to the issues of trade, financing for SD etc. and describes the impact (positive or negative) of the EU on the sustainable development of the rest of the world.

As outlined in Section 2.3, two additional themes on *Production and Consumption Patterns* and *Good Governance* have been added. As the EU intends to have a leading and decisive role in the development of both of these, they have been integrated into the proposed framework.

Table 1. Themes

ECONOMIC DEVELOPMENT
POVERTY and SOCIAL EXCLUSION
AGEING SOCIETY
PUBLIC HEALTH
CLIMATE CHANGE and ENERGY
PRODUCTION and CONSUMPTION PATTERNS
MANAGEMENT of NATURAL RESOURCES
TRANSPORT
GOOD GOVERNANCE
GLOBAL PARTNERSHIP

The framework for assessing the EU SDS thus contains the 10 themes presented in Table 1.

3.3 About Sub-Themes

Within each theme a number of sub-themes and 'areas to be addressed' have been identified. The sub-themes encompass the relevant SD issues addressed in the basic policy documents. Generally, the sub-themes are closely linked to the headline objectives, which are also reflected in the labelling of the sub-themes. The 'areas to be addressed', which can be considered as an interface between indicators and policies, are closely linked to the measures announced in both Communications and in the PoI. However, a certain amount of balancing has been done between the sub-themes and the areas to be addressed, to take account of the different levels of importance of the issues and to ensure consistency.

Additional sub-themes have sometimes been included in order to increase the visual clarity of the overall framework and to group the areas to be addressed. In these cases the labelling of the new sub-themes follows the objectives of the common EU policies (see Table 2 in annex 2). The focus is put on the 'slow burning' issues, the things we are doing or failing to do today that may result in future problems (social, environmental or economic) that may be extremely difficult or impossible to reverse. This is the essence of sustainability.

As the policy objectives and measures have not yet been defined in the EU for all aspects of the PoI, the characterisation of *Production* and *Consumption Patterns* and *Good Governance* in the framework is based on aspects singled out in the PoI and the Aarhus Convention.

Under this structure of sub-themes, the selected indicators should contribute to 'telling the story' and for these issues the DPSIR (Driving Force-Pressure-State-Impact-Response) framework may provide useful guidance, depending on the most appropriate message.

3.4 Theme Boundaries and Indicators

The framework for SDI is determined by policy themes that unavoidably overlap partially with each other. Some driving forces such as energy, influence developments in several themes, but cannot be presented several times in the indicator set. Furthermore, the scope of the themes differs considerably as some themes address a very specific domain (e.g. *Climate Change* and *Energy*) and some (e.g. *Production* and *Consumption Patterns*) encompass a wide variety of general socio-economic and environmental issues.

The approach to be taken with these boundary issues, developed in the course of discussions in the Task Force, is presented in annex 1. The main principles for allocation are that the indicator in question:

- complements the overall theme evaluation;
- addresses specific policy objectives in the theme; and
- measures the success/failures of policy actions in that theme.

Accordingly, the framework is based on a strict prioritisation of indicators inside each theme, but with the help of standardised concepts, definitions and classifications, it ensures that information is structured in a manner that facilitates the use of indicators in other themes too.

3.5 Integration

The integration of economic, social and environmental dimensions forms the heart of any assessment of sustainable development. This integration should bring out and present the most relevant interactions, damages, distortions, imbalances etc. taking place in general and with respect to specific themes. As mentioned under Section 2.4, the SEEA is expected to play a major role in the integration of the various dimensions.

The issue of integration can be approached from various perspectives that can be used in several combinations in the final framework. It is proposed to favour the description of integration at the sub-theme or the area level.

The practical integration of the three dimensions of SD has several options. In the optimum case, the integration takes place when one single variable represents the economic, social and environmental aspects of the area/sub-theme/theme in question (e.g. environmental taxes).

The second best case refers to an indicator that is calculated on the basis of several variables, thus combining two or three dimensions together. For instance, eco-efficiency may be considered to be this kind of indicator.

The third option is to present developments in all three dimensions in a single graph. For instance, trends in investments in public transport, incidence of respiratory diseases and emissions of volatile organic compounds (VOC) may be used to indicate different, but simultaneous developments, the concordance of which may require special measures.

The fourth option refers to graphical presentations where two dimensions are combined to a single indicator and the third dimension is presented together with the new, calculated one. An example of this could be to plot resource productivity (two dimensions) and occupational exposure to harmful chemicals (third dimension) describing inter-related developments on a country-by-country basis in the same graph.

These general characteristics for the integration indicators illustrate the possibilities for various practical options.

4 Sustainable Development Indicators: Selection and Coverage

4.1 Selection Criteria

The European Commission and the European Statistical System already have a long experience in the selection of indicators. The proposed set of selection criteria is very close to the one used for the Laeken indicators[3].

The Task Force recommends that each indicator to be selected in the SDI list – and particularly the headline indicators – should respect as far as possible the following criteria, which can be seen, in particular for environmental indicators, as a kind of quality target:

1. An indicator should capture *the essence of the problem* and have *a clear and accepted normative interpretation*. When translating policy goals into indicators there is an unavoidable reduction of the problem. Selected indicators should cover the main concerns of the policy goal without being misleading. Their interpretation should be recognised as meaningful and understandable by a general public.
2. An indicator should be *robust* and *statistically validated*. The data used should be regarded as statistically reliable and should avoid arbitrary adjustments. When data are derived from sample surveys these surveys should comply with the best practices and highest standards of survey research methodology. Indicators should also be reliable over time in the sense that its values are comparable over time and fluctuations can be generally explained.
3. An indicator should be *responsive to policy interventions* but not subject to manipulation. Indicators should reflect the impact of policies, but not be conceived in a way that they can be manipulated in order to show a better score. In general, indicators should reflect outcomes rather than the various alternative ways in which they might be achieved.
4. An indicator should be measurable in a sufficiently *comparable way across Member States*, and *comparable* as far as practicable with *the standards applied internationally by the UN and the OECD*. The aim should be to reach an acceptable level of comparability between the countries involved and to give recommendations, when needed, for an increase of this comparability. Indicators should also not be over-sensitive to structural differences between countries nor pose specific problems of interpretation for some countries.
5. An indicator should be *timely* and *susceptible to revision*. Indicators should be as timely as possible, and should be susceptible to revisions both for data and underlying concepts when necessary.
6. The measurement of an indicator should *not impose* on Member States, on enterprises, nor on the Union's citizens *a burden disproportionate to its benefits*. Wherever possible, the construction of sustainable development indicators

3 Cf. report from the chairman of the indicators Sub-Group to the Social Protection Committee, October 2001, Page 11. Academic research which contributed to the conclusions reached by the ISG can be found in: Atkinson, T., B. Cantillon, E. Marlier, and B. Nolan (2002), Social Indicators: The EU and Social Inclusion, Oxford.

should be based on existing data collections made by Eurostat, the European Environment Agency (EEA) or other recognised international sources.

And the portfolio of indicators should follow the following principles:

7. The portfolio of indicators should be as far as *possible balanced across different dimensions*. The selection of indicators should respect a certain equilibrium across the various SD themes.
8. The indicators should be *mutually consistent* within a theme. Indicators should not deliver contradictory messages, or to the extent that they do so then explanations should be readily available.
9. The portfolio of indicators should be as *transparent* and *accessible* as possible to the citizens of the European Union. Indicators should be easy to read and understand. Dissemination aspects will be treated under Section 4.

Some of the measures announced in both Communications have clear targets and therefore indicators can be readily identified. For others it is less clear and although it has been discussed thoroughly by the Task Force, it has not always been possible to produce meaningful indicators for all sub-themes and areas. In such cases, the Task Force has recommended 'best available' and 'best needed' indicators, the former corresponding to the best indicators in the current state of available information and the latter corresponding to the desired indicators which are not yet feasible for methodological or data availability reasons.

4.2 The Number of Indicators

A large number of indicators are needed to properly assess the multidimensional nature of SD. The Task Force recommends building the set of SDI as a three-level pyramid. If possible, the different levels should form part of a consistent 'story'. For instance, level 1 indicators should be some kind of aggregation of level 2 indicators, while level 2 should constitute a kind of aggregation of level 3 indicators. The use of appropriate breakdowns supports this kind of aggregation between the pyramid levels.

At the top of the pyramid, there should be between 10 and 20 headline indicators focusing on the lead objectives of the SDS. These indicators should contain the essence of the message on SD and cover the most important issues for SD in the EU. It is envisaged that these indicators would be published regularly and made available to a wide audience.

The second level of the pyramid should consist of indicators related to some general policy performance and indicators related to the "areas to be addressed". They should tend to support the message delivered by headline indicators by giving information on more detailed policy aspects. The second level should contain between 30 and 40 indicators.

The maximum degree of comparability will be sought for these headline and second-level indicators. Standard disaggregations of these indicators into key dimensions (e.g. gender, age, branches) will be specified, usually at level three, but these breakdowns will not necessarily feature in all publications.

The third level should contain most of the indicators linked to and allowing for the monitoring of the effectiveness of concrete and specific policy measures, looking in more depth at certain issues. In particular, if the correlation and combination of dimensions (economic/social/ environmental) is not adequately reflected in the headline and second-level indicators, efforts will be made to highlight such links in indicators selected at this level. Clearly, no restriction can be set concerning the number of indicators, except for the question of the availability of resources.

4.3 The Coverage of SDIs

As already stated, the aim of the whole exercise is to give a statistical basis to evaluating the implementation of the EU SDS. Indicators for countries which are not directly concerned with the implementation of this strategy are not really germane. It is thus suggested to limit the calculation of indicators – as far as possible – to the European Union in a broad sense, the EU Member States, the Candidate Countries and the EFTA countries.

The geographical coverage should be limited to the national level without developing indicators at regional (sub-national) level. The spirit of Agenda 21 and later of the Johannesburg Summit was to call for SD initiatives at each level – international, national or regional. These however were bottom-up approaches where local priorities may greatly differ from priorities at national or EU level. In the present context, it appears reasonable not to develop indicators at regional level.

Indicators – at least the headline indicators – should be annual, covering as many time periods as possible in order to show whether political measures have had an impact. They could also include projections to the future (e.g. demography, pensions) and distances to target (e.g. employment, greenhouse gases), where appropriate.

5 The Dissemination of SDIs

The purpose of this exercise is to create a whole system of information on sustainable development. This system should allow for a regular updating of indicators to be made available to the EU institutions, governments and the general public.

The headline indicators – and the information on their validity – should be updated as regularly as possible and at least once a year. The use of regular data collection and existing indicators should allow for quasi-automatic update of most indicators, with the same rhythm as the updating of the basic data. But if separate data collection is needed, indicators in the second and third levels of the pyramid would not necessarily be produced on an annual basis.

A first set of indicators should be available by mid-2004 in order to serve as a basis for the evaluation of the current SDS and its revision. Further refinement of the initial list of indicators will be looked for in order to build a final proposal at the end of the lifecycle of this Task Force.

5.1 Metadata

The Special Data Dissemination Standard (SDDS) developed by the International Monetary Fund (IMF) will be the communication tool used for describing metadata on SDI.

Already used by the EU Member States, most Candidate countries, Norway and Switzerland[4], Eurostat decided to use the SDDS when developing the Structural Indicators and Euro-indicators. The choice of this format will allow more easily the work on SDI to be integrated with other indicator initiatives and other statistical domains where this international standard is compulsory.

The format will be adapted to take into account some additional information linked to SDI (relevance for SD, link to political objectives, limits and precautions when using the indicator). For information, the SDDS templates are annexed to this report.

5.2 Quality Profile

The quality profile process defined for Structural Indicators (SI) will also be used for SDI[5]. The purpose is to attach an overall assessment of the quality to each indicator so as to provide guidance for their interpretation.

In the SI process, the quality profile (see document in annex 4) will be issued by Eurostat in co-operation with the European Statistical System making use of existing working structures. It will be implemented by a questionnaire to be sent to the National Statistical Institutes drawing – as far as possible – from information already available in the various domains, e.g. quality reports.

Most of the information provided with the SI quality profile is immediately applicable to the SDI. Therefore the SI quality profile will be adopted, with additional specifications if needed, for each indicator in common. The quality profile process should be gradually introduced for SDI which are not at the same time SI.

5.3 Data Dissemination

Eurostat intends to set up a specific SDI web page, which will present available information on SDI in the EU as well as links to other relevant websites. Time series will be disseminated through specific data sets in the New Cronos database.

---

4 See http://dsbb.imf.org/country.htm.

5 The concept of quality profile for SI has been accepted by the Statistical Programme Committee in its 51st meeting of November 2003 (document CPS 2003/51/11/EN).

At the end of the Task Force work, Eurostat intends to produce a specific publication in order to present the list of EU SDI.

6 The Timetable for the Development of Sustainable Development Indicators

Eurostat will report back to the Statistical Programme Committee, which created the Task Force on SDI. A first interim report was made in autumn 2003 and a final report is expected on current planning at the end of 2004. This report will describe the achievements of the Task Force, in particular in terms of setting-up and disseminating indicators but will also point out the main difficulties and the main data or conceptual gaps that remain if the European Statistical System is to cover the EU SD policy correctly.

The Commission plans to evaluate the implementation of the EU SDS in 2004. Therefore, a medium-term goal of the Task Force will be to have a first portfolio of SDI ready by mid-2004. This exercise will only constitute a first attempt as the Task Force has also to concentrate on further developments both in terms of data, methodologies and indicators. The final report of the Task Force will give indications on the continuation of the work after the Task Force is dissolved.

Annex 1
Boundaries Between Interlinked Themes in the SDI Framework

By their very nature, many of the issues of sustainable development can be seen as belonging to more than one theme. To avoid duplication a specific issue or indicator should be allocated to only one theme. This allocation should be based on pragmatism and should take into account how the SDS treats these boundary issues.

The following overview describes how the core boundary questions are dealt with in the framework and what have been the main considerations in the allocation of indicators. The following does not aim to be exhaustive, but rather is intended to facilitate a better understanding of the framework of SDI in general.

Employment/unemployment touches the themes *Economic Development*, *Poverty and Social Exclusion* and *Ageing Society*, but is mainly dealt with in *Economic Development*, as it is a key factor for this theme and touches all age groups. However, long-term unemployment is dealt with under *Poverty and Social Exclusion*, as it is a key factor leading to monetary poverty and social exclusion.

Poverty touches themes *Poverty and Social Exclusion* and *Ageing Society*, but is dealt with under the former and broken down by various age groups. Nevertheless, the adequacy of pensions and their influence on the financial sustainability are dealt in *Ageing Society* as they are key issues for this theme.

Health care touches *Ageing Society* (adequacy and sustainability of health care systems), *Poverty and Social Exclusion* (access to health care systems) as well as *Public Health*. Although this issue is singled out as a priority policy issue of *Ageing Society*, health care issues have been all integrated into the *Public Health* theme.

Sectoral contributions to various themes are generally shown as standardised sectoral breakdowns of specific indicators. In some important cases, specific sectors or aspects are singled out in some of the sub-themes like *Climate Change and Energy* (energy/ energy consumption and production), *Public Health* (agriculture/ pesticide residues in food products), *Production and Consumption Patterns* (agriculture/ environmentally friendly farming) and *Transport* (transport growth, fuel use).

Air emissions: All emissions of greenhouse gases (GHG) from EU and acceding countries are primarily allocated to the theme *Climate Change and Energy*. Reductions in the GHG emissions in the non-Annex I countries and under the Clean Development Mechanism of the Kyoto Protocol should be considered under the theme *Global Partnership*. Emissions of particles are treated under *Public Health* and those of acidifying substances and ozone precursors under *Production and Consumption Patterns*. Deposition of acidifying substances and nitrogen affecting the state of vegetation are dealt in the *Management of Natural Resources*. The conceptual inconsistencies between international environmental conventions such as UNFCCC (climate change) and UNECE/LRTAP (air emissions), and the System of National Accounts require a special approach for the assessment of decoupling and eco-efficiency in the framework.

Water issues are addressed in *Public Health* (drinking water quality), *Production and Consumption Patterns* (water use by sectors), *Management of Natural Resources* (water resources and pollution) and possibly in the future also in *Global Partnership* (EU water partnership).

Land use is dealt with under *Management of Natural Resources*, but specific issues, such as fragmentation of ecosystems, due to transport infrastructure belongs more closely to the *Transport* theme.

Management of nuclear waste is relevant for themes *Climate Change and Energy* and for *Production and Consumption Patterns*, but is allocated to the former as the main policy interest is related to the safety of nuclear waste management in energy production.

The impacts of EU consumption on third countries could be addressed under *Production and Consumption Patterns* or in the *Global Partnership.* Due to current methodological difficulties, these issues are addressed now only in relation to imports. Access of developing countries to the EU markets and their resource inputs to the EU economy are assessed in the *Global Partnership.*

Corporate Social Responsibility (CSR) relates both to *Production and Consumption Patterns* and *Good Governance.* The CSR addresses governance issues from the management point of view and on a voluntary basis, while governance in the EU institutions takes place on the basis of strict rules and procedures. Therefore, the sub-theme CSR is allocated to the theme on *Production and Consumption Patterns* where it complements the overall assessment and will thus contribute to the forthcoming global 10 year programme of the Sustainable Production and Consumption.

Good governance issues relate to both internal and external policies. In the framework, the internal governance issues are handled under the theme *Good Governance.* The questions of good governance in third countries or the contribution of the EU to global governance are not taken on board at all.

Annex 2

Theme, Sub-Themes and 'Areas to Be Addressed'

Themes	**Sub-Themes**	**Areas to be addressed**	**Headline objectives in the EU SD Strategy, Presidency conclusions of European Council (EC), Plan of Implementation and the 6th Environmental Action Programme (6EAP)**
Economic development	Investment	Investment in R&D	EC Lisbon2000: An average economic growth rate of around 3% a realistic prospect for the coming years. EC Cardiff1998: Public Sector budgetary deficit to be less than 60% of GDP. The inflation rate of a given Member State must not exceed by more than 1.5 percentage points that of the three best-performing Member States in terms of price stability. EC Barcelona2002: Increase spending on R&D and innovation with the aim of approaching 3% of GDP by 2010.
		Investment in env. friendly technologies	
		Consumption and inflation	
		Saving and borrowing	
	Competitiveness	Labour productivity	
		Unit labour costs	
		Life-long learning	EC Lisbon2000: A substantial annual increase in per capita investment in human resources. Provide new basic skills through lifelong learning of IT skills, foreign languages, technological culture, entrepreneurship and social skills.
	Employment	Employment rate	Raise the employment rate to 67% by January 2005 and to 70% by 2010; increase the number of women in employment to 57% by January 2005 and to more than 60% in 2010. Increase the average EU employment rate among older women and men (55-64) to 50% by 2010.
		Unemployment rate	
Poverty and social exclusion	Monetary poverty	Income inequality	Make a decisive impact on the eradication of poverty
		Non-monetary deprivation	
	Access to labour market	Poverty-in-work	
	Other aspects of social exclusion	Access to education	Halve by 2010 the number of 18 to 24 year-olds with only lower secondary education who are not in further education or training. EC Lisbon2002: Increased social cohesion by 2010.
		Access to health care	
		Access to housing	
		Social participation	

Ageing society	Pensions adequacy	Income of elder generations	EC Stockholm2001: Address the demographic challenge by raising employment rates, reducing public debt and adapting socio-protection systems, including pension systems Ensure the adequacy of pension systems, while at the same time maintaining sustainability of public finances and intergenerational solidarity.
	Demographic changes	Life expectancy	
		Fertility	
		Migrations	
	Financial sustainability	Age of withdrawal from labour market	
		Pension expenditures	
Public health	Human health protection and life styles	Financial sustainability	Ensure the adequacy of health care systems and care of the elderly, while at the same time maintaining sustainability of public finances and inter-generational solidarity
		Disability-free life expectancy	Tackle issues related to outbreaks of infectious diseases and resistance to antibiotics. 6EAP: Contributing to a better quality of life through an integrated approach concentrating on urban areas. PoI2002: Enhance health education with the objective of achieving improved health literacy on a global basis by 2010.
		Premature mortality	
		Life styles	
		Health and safety at work	
		Infectious diseases and resistance to antibiotics	
	Food safety and quality	Pesticide residues	Make food safety and quality the objective of all players in the food chain. 6EAP: Reduce the impacts of pesticides on human health and the environment and achieve a more sustainable use of pesticides as well as a significant overall reduction in risks and of the use of pesticides consistent with the necessary crop production. Achieve quality levels of ground and surface water that do not give rise to significant impacts on and risks to human health and the environment.
		Microbiological contamination	
		Drinking water quality	

	Chemicals management	Chemicals production and consumption	By 2020, ensure that chemicals are only produced and used in ways that do not pose significant threats to human health and the environment. 6EAP: Dangerous chemicals (especially PBTs) should be substituted with the aim of reducing risks to man and the environment (ground and surface water, air quality). PoI2002: in line with SDS & 6EAP
		Exposure to chemicals	
	Health risks due to environmental conditions	Air quality	6EAP: Achieve levels of air quality that do not give rise to significant negative impacts on and risks to human health and the environment.
		Noise exposure	Substantially reduce the number of people regularly affected by long-term average levels of noise.
Climate change and energy	Climate change	GHG emission reduction	Meet the Kyoto commitment. However, Kyoto is but a first step. Thereafter, the EU should aim to reduce atmospheric greenhouse gas emissions by an average of 1% per year over 1990 levels up to 2020. EC Gothenburg2001: Achieve demonstrable progress in the reduction of GHG emission by 2005.
	Energy	Energy taxes	6EAP: Double the overall share of combined heat and power in the Community as a whole to 18% of the total gross electricity generation. EC Brussels2003: *(revised SDS objective)* Increase the share of renewable energy with a EU-wide indicative target for renewable energy of 12% of primary energy needs and 22% of electricity needs by 2010. Promotion of 5,75% target for the use of biofuels in transport by 2010. PoI2002: Remove market distortions, including the restructuring of taxes and phasing out of harmful subsidies. Establish domestic programmes of energy efficiency, with the support of the international community.
		Energy efficiency	
		Renewable energy resources	
		Management of nuclear waste	
		Air pollution from energy use	

	Eco-efficiency	Decoupling economic growth and resource use	Break the links between economic growth, the use of resources and the generation of waste. 6EAP: Ensure that the consumption of resources and their associated impacts do not exceed the carrying capacity of the environment. Achieving a significant overall reduction in the volumes of waste and hazardous waste generated and in the quantity of waste going to disposal while avoiding an increase of emissions to air, water and soil. PoI2002: Encourage and promote the development of a 10-year framework of programmes to accelerate the shifts towards sustainable consumption and production. Renew commitments to the sound management of chemicals and hazardous wastes throughout their life-cycle.
		Decoupling economic growth and emissions	
		Decoupling economic growth and generation of wastes	
Production and consumption patterns	Agriculture	Pesticides use	The Common Agricultural Policy should contribute to achieving sustainable development by encouraging healthy, high quality products, environmentally sustainable production methods, including organic production, renewable raw materials and the protection of biodiversity.
		Nitrogen balances	
		Environmentally-friendly farming	
	Corporate responsibility	Triple bottom line	EC Lisbon2000: A special appeal to companies' sense of social responsibility regarding best practices in lifelong learning, work organisation, equal opportunities, social inclusion and sustainable development. PoI2002: Actively promote corporate responsibility and accountability, including through the full development and effective implementation of intergovernmental agreements and measures, international initiatives and public-private partnerships, and appropriate national regulations.
	Consumer awareness	Consumer information	PoI2002: Develop and adopt, where appropriate, on a voluntary basis, effective, transparent, verifiable, non-misleading and non-discriminatory consumer information tools to provide information relating to sustainable consumption and production, including human health and safety aspects.

Management of natural resources	Biodiversity	Protection of habitats and natural systems and biodiversity	Protect and restore habitats and natural systems and halt the loss of biodiversity by 2010. 6EAP: Conservation of species and habitats with a special concern of preventing habitat fragmentation.
		Maintaining the carrying capacity	Ensure that the consumption of resources and their associated impacts do not exceed the carrying capacity of the environment. PoI2002: Achieve by 2010 a significant reduction in the current rate of loss of biological diversity.
	Marine ecosystems	Over-fishing	EC Gothenburg2001: The review of the Common Fisheries Policies should address the overall fishing pressure by adapting the EU fishing effort to the level of available resources, taking into account the social impact and the need to avoid over-fishing. 6EAP: Conservation, appropriate restoration and sustainable use of marine environment, coasts and wetlands. PoI2002: On an urgent basis, and where possible by 2015, maintain or restore depleted fish stocks to levels that can produce the maximum sustainable yield.
	Fresh water resources	Water extraction and use	6EAP: Ensure that the rates of extraction from water resources are sustainable over the long term. PoI2002: Develop integrated water resources management and water-efficiency plans by 2005.
		Protection of surface and ground water resources	
	Land use	Land use change	
		Soil degradation	6EAP: Conservation and appropriate restoration of areas of significant landscape values including cultivated and sensitive areas. Promotion of sustainable use of the soil, with particular attention to preventing erosion, deterioration, contamination and desertification.
		Forests	PoI2002: Accelerate the implementation of the IPF/IFF proposals for action and by the Collaborative Partnership on Forests, and intensify efforts on reporting to the UN Forum of Forests so as to contribute to an assessment of progress in 2005.
Transport	Transport growth	Decoupling of economic and transport growth	Decouple transport growth significantly from growth in Gross Domestic Product in order to reduce congestion and other negative side effects of transport. 6EAP: Substantially reducing the number
		Road to rail, water and public transport	

		Land use by transport systems	of people regularly affected by long-term average levels of noise. Bring about a shift in transport use from road to rail, water and public passenger transport so that the share of road transport in 2010 is no greater than in 1998 (the most recent year for which data are available).
	Environmental impact of transport activities	Air pollutants	
Good governance	Policy coherence	Citizen's adherence and support to EU actions	EC Barcelona2002: Good governance at the national level is essential for sustainable development and all states should strengthen their government institutions, by promoting the rule of law, improving legal structures and providing access to information. EC Gothenburg2001*(revised in Barcelona2002)*: Ensure that all major internal and external policy proposals include a sustainability impact assessment.
		Sustainability of EU actions and measures	
		Legislative compliance	
	Public participation	Communication and mobilisation	
Global partnership	Globalisation of trade	Market access for least developed countries (LDC)	Ensure that globalisation contributes to sustainable development. EC Barcelona2002: Integrate developing countries into the world economic system notably through the implementation of the Doha Development Agenda and ensure that trade policies and investment flows contribute to sustainable development. 6EAP: Ensure that trade and environment policies and measures are mutually supportive. PoI2002: Improve access by developing countries to alternatives to ozone-depleting substances by 2010, and assist them in complying with the phase-out schedule under the Montreal Protocol.
	Financing for SD	Foreign direct investments to developing countries	Ensure adequate financing to attain the International Development Targets and the Millennium Development Goals. EC Barcelona2002: Reach to UN goal of 0.7% ODA/GNI: MS lacking behind this goal to increase their ODA in the next four years within their respective budget allocation processes, whilst the other MS renew their efforts to remain at or above the target of 0.7% of ODA, so that collectively a EU average of 0.39% is reached by 2006
		Official Development Assistance (ODA)	

		Other official financing	and each MS at least 0.33% ODA/GNI by 2006 (Monterrey2002). EC Barcelona2002: Encourage sustainable foreign direct investments (FDI) in developing countries and export credits consistent with sustainable development.
	Resource management	Resource consumption	Ensure that current trends in the loss of environmental resources are effectively reversed at national and global levels by 2015. Develop sectoral and intermediate objectives in some key sectors – water, land and soil, energy and bio-diversity. 6EAP: The pursuit of ambitious environmental policies at the international level paying particular attention to the carrying capacity of the global environment. The further promotion of sustainable consumption and production patterns at the international level.
		Air emissions & energy	
		Water	
		Waste	

Annex 3

SDDS Format
File 1: Base Page

Domain:
Table: Name and code
Last update: day/month/year (when the text of the metadata file has been updated)

Contact	
Country (Area)	*For instance, "European Union and Euro-zone", or "country x"*
Data category	*Name of indicator, or group of indicators*
Contact person	*Domain manager*
Organisation	*Source for data and metadata, postal address*
Phone Number	*Phone*
Fax Number	*Fax*
Internet Address	*e-mail address*

The Data: Coverage, Periodicity and Timeliness	
Coverage characteristics	*Introductory texts (short presentation of the domain)* *Breakdown available* *Run of data available*
Periodicity	*Frequency of the data*
Timeliness	*Delay between reference period and transmission to Eurostat. Possible delay until dissemination.*
Access by the Public	
Advance dissemination of release calendar	*Release calendar (if any, hyperlink)*
Simultaneous release to all interested parties	*Database update* *News release*

<table>
<tr><th colspan="4">Integrity</th></tr>
<tr><td colspan="2">Dissemination of terms and conditions under which official statistics are produced, including confidentiality of individual responses</td><td colspan="2">Legal basis of the domain
Regulation on Community statistics
Regulation on confidentiality</td></tr>
<tr><td colspan="2">Identification of internal government access to data before release</td><td colspan="2">Access before release (ECB, Commission, ...)</td></tr>
<tr><td colspan="2">Identification of ministerial commentary on the occasion of statistical releases</td><td colspan="2">Official comments</td></tr>
<tr><td colspan="2">Provision of information about revision and advance notice of major changes in methodology</td><td colspan="2">Information about data revisions
Major changes in methodology</td></tr>
<tr><th colspan="4">Quality</th></tr>
<tr><td colspan="2">Dissemination of documentation on methodology and sources used in preparing statistics</td><td colspan="2">References to detailed methodology (direct link to publication of general link to Data Shops)
Bibliographical references</td></tr>
<tr><td colspan="2">Dissemination of information that support statistical cross-checks and provide assurance of reasonableness</td><td colspan="2">Other Eurostat databases and domains containing similar information
Links to other information sources, if applicable</td></tr>
<tr><td colspan="2">Notes:</td><td colspan="2"></td></tr>
<tr><th colspan="4">Dissemination Formats</th></tr>
<tr><td colspan="4">Hardcopy</td></tr>
<tr><td></td><td>( )</td><td>News release:</td><td></td></tr>
<tr><td></td><td>( )</td><td>Weekly bulletin:</td><td></td></tr>
<tr><td></td><td>( )</td><td>Monthly bulletin:</td><td></td></tr>
<tr><td></td><td>( )</td><td>Quarterly bulletin:</td><td></td></tr>
<tr><td></td><td>( )</td><td>Other:</td><td></td></tr>
<tr><td colspan="4">Electronic</td></tr>
<tr><td></td><td>( )</td><td>On-line country bulletin board or database.</td><td>Data-shops contact</td></tr>
</table>

		Internet address:	Hyper-link
	( )	Diskette:	
	( )	CD ROM:	
	( )	Other:	

File 2: Summary Methodology

Indicators:

Summary Methodology provided by Eurostat in conformity with the Special Data Dissemination Standard (SDDS)
Last update: day/month/year (when the text of the metadata file has been updated)

Summary Methodology

1. Analytical framework, concepts, definitions and classifications

Organisation of the data
Statistical concept
Indicators (official definitions)
Classification system adopted, conformity with official standards

2. Scope of the data

Geographical coverage
Time coverage
Sector coverage, including exceptions
Statistical population

3. Accounting conventions

Time of recording
Reference period (period to which the indicator refers)
Valuation principles
Unit of account

4. Nature of the basic data

(Mostly at national level: see IMF prompt points)
Origin of basic data (collection method, e.g. survey, administrative data)
Reporting units, methods and techniques

5. Compilation practices

At EU and Euro-zone level:
Aggregation methods (compilation, estimation, reconciliation)
Treatment of missing values
Adjustments (seasonal, working-day, unadjusted)

6. Other aspects

Limits and precautions when using or interpreting data
Verification of data (elements for a quality assessment)

Annex 4

Structural Indicators Quality Profile

Indicator			
Responsible COM DG:	Eurostat Unit:	Date	..-..-....
European Statistical System Working Group			

1. Objective and relevance of the indicator*: ______________________

If necessary, comments on restrictions of its relevance: ______________________

2. Data availability

		Member States	Candidate Countries	US a. Japan	EEA-EFTA
Target Reference years for SR 200☐	T_1				
	T_2				

Comments (including information on time series): ______________________

3. Overall accuracy Comments

High ☐

Restricted (sources, errors, methodology etc.) ☐ ______________________

4. Comparability across countries Comments

High ☐

Restricted ☐ ______________________

5. Comparability over time Comments

High ☐

Restricted ☐ ______________________

6. Contribution to quality of the set/potential to qualify for an integrated policy analysis* Comments/ Assessment: ______________________

7. Other characteristics which may lead to restriction for using this indicator in the Spring Report: Comments ______________________

8. Overall assessment

☐ AA ☐ A ☐ B ☐ C ☐ Indicator to be developed

9. Development perspective for improving quality of this indicator (including as far as possible an indication of burden on Member States and respondents). ______________________

____

____

____

* Not part of the quality rating.

Description of Quality Grades	
Grade "AA"	An "AA" is given if the indicator fulfils the requirements listed for the "A" grading and in addition (1) time series are available (starting from 1991 for the Member States and 1995 for the Candidate Countries) and (2) data for at least reference year $_{t-2}$ (real data for a majority of countries) is available in time for the Spring Report.
Grade "A"	An indicators is graded "A" if data is available on time for the Spring Report of the year $_t$ for Member States, at least acceding countries, US and Japan. Data cover the years 2000 until at least the reference year $_{t-2}$ (including estimates). The underlying data is collected on the basis of a common methodology for the European Union with the Candidate Countries following the same approach. Data for US and Japan can be considered comparable with any major differences being assessed and documented. Data are comparable over time; impact of procedural or conceptual changes being documented. Data is collected from reliable sources applying high standards with regard to methodology/accuracy and is well documented in line with Eurostat metadata standard.
Grade "B"	An indicator is graded "B" if data is available on time for the Spring Report of the year $_t$ for most Member States and at least most of the acceding countries. Data cover the years 2000 until at least the reference year $_{t-3}$. There are some serious shortcomings with regard to either comparability between Member States/Candidate Countries/US and Japan (including the lack of data) **or** break in series for several countries which seriously hamper comparison over time. Deficiencies with regard to assessing and documenting impact of these shortcomings might be identified. Data is collected from reliable sources applying high standards with regard to methodology/accuracy and is well documented in line with Eurostat metadata standard.
Grade "C"	An indicator is graded "C" if data coverage on time for the Spring Report of the year $_t$ has some severe deficiencies as regards country coverage and/or timeliness. There might be either some serious shortcomings with regard to comparability between Member States/Candidate Countries/US and Japan (including the lack of data) *or* break in series for several countries which seriously hamper comparison over time. Data might have to be interpreted with care as methodology/accuracy does not meet high quality standards.
Indicator to be developed	This indicator is not ready to be used for the Spring Report. Data availability in time for enough countries and/or with a sufficiently high timeliness seems to be unlikely. There might be either some serious shortcomings with regard to comparability between Member States/Candidate Countries/US and Japan (including lack of data) and/or break in series for several countries which seriously hamper comparison over time. Data might have to be interpreted with care as methodology/accuracy does not meet highest quality standards.

Measuring Corporate Sustainability Performance and Its Impact on Corporate Financial Performance

Thilo Goodall

SAM Sustainable Asset Management, Seefeldstrasse 215, 8008 Zurich, Switzerland, thilo@sam-group.com

Keywords. *Sustainability, Sustainability Performance, Financial Performance SRSI Research*

JEL. *G10; G11; G12; G14*

Abstract. Any serious attempt to research impacts of corporate sustainability performance on corporate financial performance has to follow a consistent and thorough research agenda. The research agenda is described in this article. The description may serve as blueprint for any research effort in the SRSI area that is geared towards creating value added, and not just towards serving value sets.

If corporate sustainability orientation and performance can be shown to impact corporate financial performance, a gradual and persistent integration of SRSI research into mainstream investment analysis could evolve. But without any sound evidence, if not proof, that there is indeed a link between corporate sustainability performance and corporate financial performance SRSI research will not be able to serve the investment industry at large. The research and investment approach described in the article lists and addresses a set of recommendations for SRSI research on how to serve the investment industry at large.

1 Introduction

Research on corporate ethical, ecological, socially responsible or sustainability orientation and performance is still conducted by only a small subset of the investment analyst community. Developed to service a very specific niche this small subset of analysts has become highly specialised in its area, because it is driven by the value sets of its analysts or its clients: 'ethical', 'ecological' or 'socially responsible' investors. Unfortunately, this specialisation has hindered general acceptance of SRSI[1] research and investment and has limited its chances of becoming a true market force in the financial markets.

A recent study conducted by the SRSI consultancy firms SustainAbility and onValues, funded by the Swedish Foundation for Strategic Environmental Research (MISTRA) lists opportunities and challenges for SRSI research (Beloe et al., 2004). Opportunities arise because, first, perceived erosion in the quality of mainstream analysis and perceived lack of independence of mainstream analysts may create a market for independent and focused research. Secondly, if corporate sustainability orientation and performance can be shown to impact corporate financial performance, a gradual and persistent integration of SRSI research into mainstream investment analysis could evolve.

Challenges surpass opportunities, however. Ongoing price erosion reduces margins for any investment research activities. New competitors are emerging, contributing to price erosion. And without any sound evidence, if not proof, that there is indeed a link between corporate sustainability performance and corporate financial performance SRSI research will not be able to serve the investment industry at large. If no link can be substantiated, the general investment market will always be impenetrable for SRSI research. To that matter at least SRSI research is confronted with demand for more thorough and scientific analysis and thus more substantial contributions.

Recommendations for SRSI research organisations mentioned in the MISTRA study include

1. to ensure that any research focuses on issues material to corporate financial performance
2. to quantify impacts of corporate sustainability performance on corporate financial performance
3. to integrate more financial and strategic intelligence in the research process.

The research and investment approach described in the following chapters is addressing all these recommendations. Chapter 2 gives the definition of corporate sustainability used by this approach and argues that it is capable of linking corporate sustainability performance with corporate financial performance. The reasoning and the transmission links are described. Chapter 3 describes how such defined corporate sustainability performance can be measured. Chapter 4 describes possible ways of quantifying the hypothesised links between corporate sustainability performance and corporate financial performance and highlights one particularly promising approach. The research agenda is set. Chapter 5 summarises this research agenda and gives an outlook on what needs to be done to make SRSI research a formidable competitor in the field of investment management and research.

---

1 I use the acronym SRSI ('Socially Responsible and Sustainability Investing') to denote the entire range of ethical, ecological, socially responsible, and sustainability research and investment approaches.

2 Corporate Sustainability

2.1 Definition

SAM Sustainable Asset Management has adopted a definition of corporate sustainability that is apt to benefit from the trends and challenges the SRSI investment community has to face. It is positioned to serve not only the value set oriented investors typically targeted by traditional SRSI research, but mainstream investors whose utility function comprises first of all of the parameters 'risk' and 'return'. Corporate sustainability is defined as 'a business approach to create long-term shareholder value by embracing opportunities and managing risks deriving from economic, environmental and social developments'.[2] Sustainability research such defined is geared towards identifying those companies that will seize the opportunities and manage the risks better than their peers and thus create more shareholder value than their peers.

This definition hypothesises a direct link between corporate sustainability and shareholder value. It postulates that there is a value added aspect to sustainability that goes beyond servicing individual investors' value sets. It postulates that sustainability is a viable business approach for companies because it enhances their competitive position. It also postulates that sustainable companies are an attractive investment because they offer superior returns in the form of more sustainable shareholder value creation.

2.2 Reasoning

The reasoning behind the hypothesis is this: Seizing opportunities before others seize them should lead to higher return on invested capital (ROIC), because more profitable investments are made. It should also lead to a higher reinvestment rate (RIR), because more profitable investments are detected, and thus to an increase in free cash flow to the firm (FCFF).[3] Managing risk better than one's peers leads either to lower costs of production, if concerning company specific risks, or to lower risk premiums for financing, if concerning common factor risks. The first will increase FCFF, while the latter will decreases financing costs, defined as weighted average costs of capital (WACC). Since shareholder value is but a function of free cash flow to the firm and weighted average costs of capital, shareholder value is increased.[4]

---

2 See SAM's website at www.sam-group.com.

3 Of course, higher reinvestment rates increase shareholder value only if they are profitable over and above the weighted average costs of capital.

4 This reasoning is independent of the valuation model used. Its only assumption is that the time value of money assumption holds. Stating the hypothesis in terms of a free cash flow to the firm model has the advantage of stressing that there is a beneficial impact of sustainability orientation on the bond risk premium and the risk-return ratio

This kind of reasoning is unique to sustainability investing, because it stresses the competitive environment in which companies operate. Seizing investment opportunities before industry peers do, managing operational risk better than industry peers, and using scarce resources more efficiently are all about competitive advantage. It acknowledges that any competitive advantage is constantly at risk in a market driven economy. The reasoning does not have to rely on changes in the regulatory framework to create competitive pressure.

This perspective on sustainability has not been generally adopted yet. Coming from a different and quite diverse background, the SRSI community has no single view on the role companies are or should be playing for society. Creating shareholder value is not generally accepted as a primary goal. Market economies are not always believed to be the most efficient means of combining resources to satisfy a society's needs, despite all their well documented and analysed shortcomings. So SRSI approaches do not always focus on shareholder value, and if they do, links are either made indirectly via imminent changes in social utility functions, or are left unexplained altogether.

Changing utility functions are believed to result from increasing 'consumer awareness' or 'investor awareness' and are the prime focus of many non-governmental organisations. This requires, however, that utility functions do indeed change or can be made to change over time, while yet remaining uniform enough across market participants to have an impact on prices. A company's preparedness to internalise negative external effects before being forced to do so then determines the degree of SRSI performance. Forced internalisation is assumed to happen either via increasing stakeholder pressure or by changes in the legal framework.

Unfortunately, preparing a company for forced internalisation is usually costly until the internalisation is being imposed. Cost increases reduce FCFF. A positive link to shareholder value can thus only be made via risk premiums and financing costs. If investors think that a prepared company is a less risky investment than an unprepared company, they may demand a lower risk premium for investing in the company's equity or bonds, which reduces financing costs. The 'being prepared' argument thus needs to assume that the market participants that share a common belief of what is 'good' and what is 'bad' are numerous enough to either increase revenues above extra costs or to decrease financing costs to compensate for the extra costs.

This kind of reasoning is both cumbersome and based on assumptions not unanimously accepted. Investor and consumer utility functions may or may not be flexible to this degree. In addition, it ignores the competitive environment companies operate in and the fact that challenges can be met in many different ways. The argument thus usually resorts to changes in legislature, turning awareness groups into lobbying organisations. Of course, being prepared for possible future changes in legislature can be a competitive advantage to companies, but it may not be the prime source.

---

of the company's bonds, too. Corporate sustainability is of interest not only to the equity investor, but also to the bond investor.

Indirect links to shareholder value are also used by SRSI approaches labelled 'sign of skilful management', 'result of prosperity', 'catalyst for change', or 'signalling' (Kurtz and DiBartolomeo, 1996). Proponents of the 'sign of skilful management'-argument see a possibility that socially responsible behaviour is an indicator of better management. This link lacks a definition of 'better', though. The respects in which SRSI oriented management is 'better' than non-SRSI oriented management need to be defined. Proponents of the 'result of prosperity'-argument see SRSI orientation as a by-product of financial success. Successful businesses have more of a reputation to lose, so they try harder to protect their good names. This argument misses the point, though. If companies implement SRSI orientation after having become successful, SRSI has apparently played no role in the companies' success and may not play any in the future. The 'catalyst for change' proponents argue that SRSI programs can stimulate operating efficiencies by increasing the need to innovate and increase capital turnover. A positive impact is far from certain, however, because being forced to adapt is usually costly. Lastly, SRSI behaviour may give a 'signal' towards management's expectations regarding profitability. But again, this argument misses the point. No explanation is given as to why SRSI orientation would increase profitability.

In contrast, positioning sustainability as a way to increase shareholder value by seizing opportunities and by managing risks presented by change is not burdened by indirect and uncertain causalities. It claims that this business approach increases profitability and thus stresses the value added for companies. No assumptions on consumers', suppliers' or investors' value sets are needed. It claims that sustainability investing is an attractive investment approach. No addition to the general two parameter utility function is needed. Value added assures that sustainability research is a viable business beyond serving a small group of individuals. All in all, this definition of sustainability requires few additional assumptions to underline its validity and is not at odds with economic theory.

Unfortunately, defining and positioning sustainability in this manner has disadvantages, too. It requires a much higher research effort than simply screening along negative criteria. Approaches based on value sets simply require a screen that filters out any company not in compliance with a pre-defined value set. This is easily done once a value set has been defined. The data for this kind of screen is easily collected. No weighting scheme is necessary, and no reconciliation with any economic or financial market theory is needed either, since no link to any value added need be claimed. Sustainability research, in contrast, being based on the value added impact of a companies' approach to ecological, societal and economic trends and developments, requires detailed analysis of all companies' strategic positioning within their industry versus the trends and challenges specific to their industry, and their means to seize the opportunities and to manage the risks that arise from these trends and challenges.

This value added approach has no a priori reason for excluding entire industries or sectors. Investing according to ethical and ecological criteria will identify entire sectors that do not or cannot comply with the given value set. They drop from the radar screen altogether and are being treated as if they had no part in society's overall creation of well being. They are, in fact, asked to 'go away'. Sustainability investing, in contrast, has to look for extra value added in every sector and industry, promoting in the end a best-in-class approach. In each industry the sustainability leaders need to be identified, i.e. the companies that seize the opportunities and manage the risks better then their peers and thus create a monopoly niche for themselves in a potentially competitive market. This requires an understanding of how an industry operates and what management practices and processes can be considered best practice.

The knowledge needed to conduct sustainability research and sustainability investing is necessarily much deeper than simply knowing what product and services an industry produces and whether the goods and services are 'good' or 'bad'. To nobody's surprise the value added that sustainability investing promises thus comes at a cost, the cost of collecting and interpreting the right kind of information and turning it into valuable knowledge. It starts with identifying trends and challenges for companies in all industries that are likely to change their competitive environment in the future. It then needs to identify criteria and indicators for the companies' preparedness and ability to seize the opportunities and manage the risks the trends and challenges pose. It further needs to be able to identify the transmission links from these criteria to the factors of shareholder value, free cash flow and weighted average cost of capital. It needs to be able to measure and quantify both the criteria and their impact on shareholder value. Finally, it has to be able to draw the right conclusions from any quantitative results, both from the viewpoint of a company and from the viewpoint of an investor. It is the latter conclusion that is often treated without due respect.

3 Measuring Corporate Sustainability

3.1 Macro Trends and Industry Challenges

In a market economy the competitive position held by a market participant determines his or her share of overall value added. Macro trends may change this framework as well as change the intensity with which competitors challenge the market participant's position. Sustainable companies embrace such changes by seizing the opportunities and by managing the risks that any developments impose on each industry. The first step of sustainability research is thus to identify all shareholder value relevant macro trends and all challenges presented to any industry. Not all of the trends are economic in nature. They stem from different sources; some change the competitive pressure in a given framework, some change the framework itself. Companies that invest time and resources to analyse these trends and the challenges presented to their industry are in the position to benefit from them. They are positioned to make their business model more sustainable and to increase shareholder value. Companies ignoring the trends are not.

Some of the trends worth looking at are listed below, together with a short summary of some of their implications.

- Demographics

  - Changes in consumption and savings patterns lead to an increase in investments and potential growth of income, thus changing the risk-return ratios that can be earned.
- Globalisation and market liberalisation
  - Falling costs of information and transportation services increase competition in product markets and make market flexibility a competitive advantage.
- Environmental change
  - Global climate change, whether man-made or not, imposes market and legislative pressure on carbon-intense industries and suppliers of fuels, a challenge intensified by the demographic developments in emerging economies.
  - Water scarcity increases in sensitive areas globally, partly due to demographic developments.
- Mistrust in production along the food chain
  - Agriculture is the basis of many developing economies but threatens the ecosystems upon which it depends.
- Human capital management
  - Human capital is a key resource in an information based society where innovation drives competition.
- Reputation and brand management
  - Preserving a monopoly niche requires management of intangible assets, including the reputation resting on adequate alignment of interests and of checks and balances regarding management and shareholders.

Challenges deriving from these trends can differ from industry to industry, affect more than one industry, or affect all industries alike. For Example, reputation, brand management and the corporate governance model adopted affect companies in all industries very much alike. Climate change, on the other hand, may affect some industries more than others. Translating macro trends into general, cross-industry and industry-specific challenges, and identifying the opportunities and risks associated with them is the logical next step in assessing a company's sustainability.

Examples for challenges affecting all industries include the need for a workable solution to the principal-agent problem, i.e. the incentives and checks and balances needed to align management's interest with shareholder's interest, and the need to find a way to manage human capital effectively and efficiently. Best practices in these areas are very similar across all industries.

Industry specific challenges depend on the industry's characteristics. The challenges will differ by such characteristics as the degree of regulation, supply and demand structures, and barriers to entry. For Example, challenges for the oil & gas industry are closely related to a general perception of energy resource scarcity and green house gas emissions. Innovations have to be developed for the time when oil and gas resources cease to meet rising demand. New technologies need to be deployed to get the most out of existing reserves. Emerging economies need to balance rapid growth and energy needs with rising import dependence and environmental effects. Growing wealth will lead to increased combustion of fossil fuels and thus GHG emissions, warranting innovations into renewable energy sources and cleaner fuels. Many companies in the oil & gas industry operate globally, requiring strong global business principles and high codes of conduct and labour standards, while addressing local constraints. In addition, the industry must operate under a certain standard of occupational health and safety.

3.2 Criteria and Indicators

Assessing a company's sustainability orientation requires measuring its positioning and degree of preparedness and its ability to seize the opportunities and manage the risks that stem from the challenges. The degree of preparedness and the company's ability can be assessed by evaluating the means implemented by and available to the company and its management. 'Criteria' thus cover aspects of a company's quality of management, process design, and its competence. Competence covers the company's endowment with assets (tangible, intangible and human), their combination and the flexibility of their combination. **Table 1** below list some of the general, i.e. valid for all industries, criteria used by SAM. The criteria are classified as belonging to one of the three dimensions 'economic', 'environmental', and 'societal' and are labelled as relating to either seizing opportunities or to managing risks, or both.[5]

Criteria are still not measurable directly; they are still qualitative in nature. Indicators need to be defined that can serve as proxies for the performance of a company in each of the criteria. For Example, the quality of a company's corporate governance, one of the economic criteria for corporate sustainability, can be measured by indicators like the number of independent board members, the diversity of the board, independence of the remuneration committee, independence of the auditing committee, and the roles assumed by the chairman of the board and the CEO.

Indicators must fulfil common requirements for data for statistical analysis. Each indicator may consist of one or more data points. The data needed to quantify each indicator must fulfil standard requirements for statistical analysis. In particular, they must be observable and measurable. In the area of sustainability research, neither can be taken for granted.

Most indicators for corporate sustainability are not subject to any reporting requirements. Companies maintain different interpretations of what is worth publishing and how to publish it. To fill the voids, data has to be gathered from many different sources other than company documents, like third party surveys and analyses, governmental agencies' and non-governmental organisations' publications, publications of supra-national organisations and various media reports. None of them are likely to cover the entire universe of companies. This is also the case for company interviews, either oral or in writing based on questionnaires. The

5 The relatively low number of environmental criteria on this general level, i.e. the level covering all industries, indicates that environmental issues vary across industries more than economic or societal issues.

response rate is typically too low to ensure data availability across the entire universe.

Table 1. Corporate sustainability criteria for all industries (excerpt)

Dimension	Criteria	To seize opportunity or to manage risk
Economic	Codes of Conduct/Compliance	Manage risks
	Corporate Governance	Manage risks
	Customer Relationship Management	Seize opportunities
	Investor Relations	Manage risks
	Risk & Crisis Management	Manage risks
	Scorecards/Measurement Systems	Seize opportunities
	Strategic Planning	Seize opportunities
	Supply Chain Management	Seize opportunities
environmental	Environmental Management	Manage risks
	Environmental Performance	Both
societal	Employee Satisfaction	Seize opportunities
	External Stakeholder Relations	Both
	Labour Practices Indicators	Manage risks
	Management Attention to Human Resources	Seize opportunities
	Organisational Learning	Seize opportunities
	Public Reporting	Manage risks
	Remuneration, Benefits, Flexible Work Schemes	Seize opportunities
	Workforce Capabilities	Seize opportunities

Source: SAM Sustainable Asset Management

Measurability is another issue. Financial data is at least directly measurable, even if their quality as indicators of a company's profitability and liquidity may at times be questionable. Many sustainability indicators are not directly measurable. Strategic planning, for instance, needs to be assessed using indicators that are not directly measurable. Indicators employing only indirectly measurable data leave room for interpretation both on the transmitting and on the receiving end. They are thus less suitable for objective assessments of corporate sustainability performance. In addition, even directly measurable data cannot be expected to adhere to a single standard of measurement across the many different data sources. Such standards do not exist. Even financial data, although already fairly standardised for globally operating companies, still entertain a large degree of regional differences in definitions, caused by differences in objectives and structures of local legislature.

3.3 Scoring

Quantification of all indicators, whether relating to directly measurable data or not, is necessary in order to be able to make comparisons across companies. Having been defined as a business approach for companies to create more shareholder value than their peers, sustainability requires that results be comparable across companies.

Of course, comparisons can only be made across companies with similar challenges and similar requirements for meeting them. Results are thus comparable only within an industry. Conducting corporate sustainability research and investing as a best-in-class approach is the logical consequence. In each industry the leaders with regards to corporate sustainability are identified and expected to lead the industry in generating shareholder value by seizing opportunities and managing risks that industry challenges present. The best-in-class approach has the advantage of encouraging companies to take up the challenges presented to them. It may be described as positive screening, while negative screening holds no incentives for companies other than to disappear.

For comparing results ordinal scales suffice. Interpretation of the magnitude of differences in scores across companies is not necessary. Still, ordinal scales require a certain degree of data quality and a scoring and weighting system that allows meaningful aggregation of data and scores. On any level of aggregation the scores need to reflect the relative importance of the criteria and indicators in the companies' quest to generate more shareholder value than their peers. Defining a weighting scheme that fulfils this need at any level of aggregation is a magnificent task. Empirical analysis is not always of help, since corporate sustainability research needs to identify not only criteria that have led to an increase in shareholder value in the past, but also to identify criteria that will impact shareholder value in the future. Sustainability analysis is for the most part forward looking. The challenges, criteria, scores and weights are thus also based on the analysts' insights into the future of an industry. Weighting indicator or criteria scores according to past impacts on shareholder value may be seriously misleading.

Aggregation needs differ, of course, depending on usage. Ranking of companies within an industry requires a weighting scheme for total scores across all criteria and dimensions. Lower levels of aggregation require a less elaborate weighting scheme. Weights to aggregate single data points into indicator scores and indicator scores into criteria scores require very few thoughts on weighting schemes.

4 Measuring the Impact on Corporate Financial Performance

4.1 Transmission Mechanisms

Corporate sustainability as defined by SAM hypothesises a link between corporate sustainability performance and corporate financial performance and thus shareholder value. Macro trends and industry challenges set the frame, while criteria and indicators identify and quantify the companies' preparedness and ability to benefit from these trends and challenges.

Simply hypothesising a link between corporate sustainability performance and corporate financial performance via free cash flow and weighted average cost of

Fig. 1. Transmission links

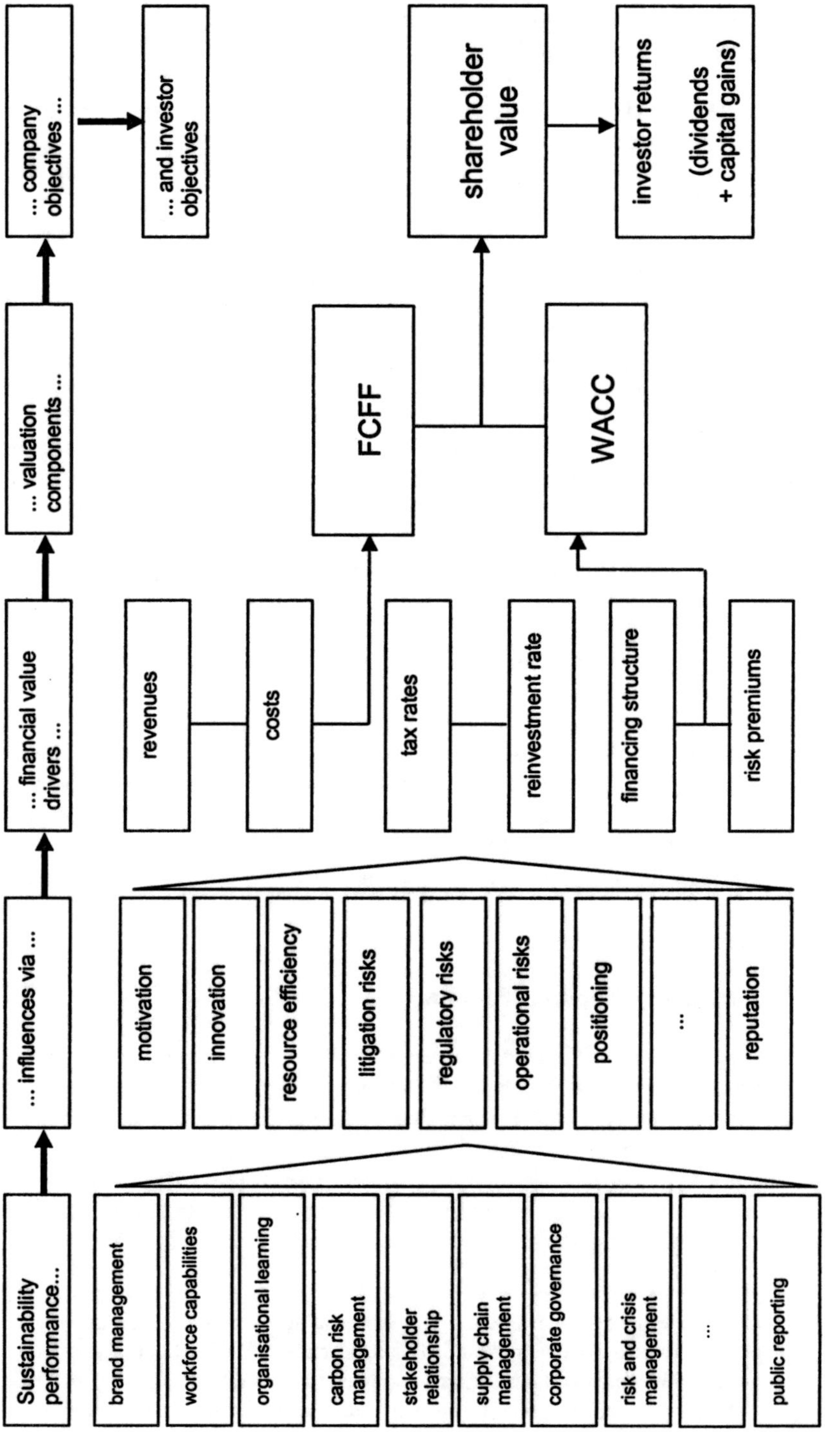

capital is neither thorough nor scientific, of course. Hypothesising transmission mechanisms adds detail and thoroughness.

The transmission mechanisms are quite simply formulated by breaking down the two determinants of shareholder value, free cash flow to the firm and weighted average cost of capital, into their components.[6] Free cash flow to the firm is a function of revenue, costs, taxes and reinvestment rates. Weighted average costs of capital are a function of short term interest rates and the company's risk premiums on equity, bonds, and cash.[7] Corporate sustainability performance needs to impact shareholder value via at least one of these components.

Each sustainability indicator or criteria must thus be linked to at least one of the components. Corporate governance, For Example, may be linked to the risk premiums a company has to pay on equity or debt. Best practices in corporate governance can be assumed to reduce the level of misalignment between shareholder interests and interests of management, thus reducing the risk of misappropriation of funds. Best practices in occupational health and safety may be assumed to reduce costs by reducing staff turnover, insurance premiums and perhaps litigation claims. Best practices in human capital management may be linked to revenues, cost efficiency, and reinvestment rates due to increasing the level of innovation. These examples may suffice to show that management decisions regarding corporate sustainability may be assumed to impact shareholder value via its components.

Fig. 1 depicts the transmission mechanisms. Management decisions regarding sustainability criteria are assumed to impact value drivers like the company's efficiency, the motivation of its workforce, its innovative potential, its reputation with stakeholders, and the company's exposure to a variety of risk factors, both internal and external. The assumed positive influence should sooner or later be measurable in the company's financials, which are identical to the components of shareholder value. Finally, if shareholder value is affected positively, so are the returns investors will reap from an investment in a sustainable company, be it via equity or via debt.

4.2 Categories of Existing Studies

Thorough and scientific research requires at least three steps. First, a hypothesis needs to be built. This has been done here in chapters 2 and 3. Second, the hypothesis must be cast into a form that makes it falsifiable. Third, the hypothesis has to be tested against empirical observation.

A rigorous way of casting a hypothesis into a falsifiable form is to build a mathematical model. The above hypothesis that the sustainability orientation of a company has an impact on its shareholder value would formally be given as a

---

6 I use generic terms here, rather than specific accounting terms. Both the accounting occupation and the occupation of financial analysts deal with an abundance of definitions for the generic terms. There is no need to add more detail here, however.

7 In this definition risk premiums are measured against risk free cash rates.

mathematical function where shareholder value is a function of commonly used ordinary variables (like assets) and sustainability indicators or criteria. If the transmission links are modelled instead, the financial components of shareholder value (like sale, costs, taxes, etc.) are modelled as a mathematical function of commonly used ordinary variables and sustainability variables. In mathematical form

$$y_{j,k} = f\left(\underline{b}_{m,k};\underline{c}_{n,k}\right) \tag{1}$$

where $y_{j,k}$ stands either for shareholder value or for the jth shareholder value component of company k, where $\underline{b}_{m,k}$ stands for a vector of m ordinary variables affecting $y_{j,k}$ and where $\underline{c}_{n,k}$ stands for a vector of n sustainability variables affecting $y_{j,k}$.

Empirical testing of such models comes in several forms. Commonly used are case studies, correlation analyses, surveys, simulations, and econometric multifactor models. All of these methods can be and have been applied to either shareholder value or its components. Shareholder value is more often used than its components, however. Some of methods take recourse to portfolios of companies or their securities while others have been and can only be applied to single companies.

Case studies, or event studies, analyse the impact of singular events on the shareholder value of companies stricken by that event.[8] Unfortunately, event studies are of limited use because of heavily biased sampling and because rigorous attribution and quantification of the impact is impossible.[9]

Correlation analyses probably enjoy widest use in this field of research. Numerous studies try to find and report correlations of one SRSI indicator with some variable linked to corporate financial performance.[10] Correlation studies are problematic in as much as they have to rely on a single explanatory variable, may fall prey to spurious correlation, and cannot detect or distinguish causal relations.

Surveys try to quantify links between SRSI orientation and corporate financial performance by asking investment markets participants 'how much more' they would be willing to pay for a company that fulfils certain indicators of sustainability performance.[11] They are thus limited in the number of indicators that can be used simultaneously. They are also burdened with a distinct lack of comparability across criteria and are furthermore highly subjective and time dependent.

Simulations can be used to quantify impacts of changes in the legal and economic framework a company operates in. The impact of any such change on companies' profitability can be translated into what it is worth to be prepared for the change, which can then be judged against the costs of getting prepared.[12] Comparison across several firms can give a general picture of the costs and benefits in-

---

8 E.g., Jones and Rubin (1999), Karpoff and Lott (1993), or Dowdell et al. (1992).

9 See McWilliams and Siegel (1999) for an analysis of event studies.

10 For an overview and a meta-analysis of correlation studies see Orlitzky et al. (2003).

11 E.g., Coombes and Watson (2000).

12 E.g., Austin et al. (2004).

volved. Unfortunately, simulations are not empirical observations and are thus not positioned to validate[13] or falsify any hypotheses.

The most stringent way is to test the hypothesis simultaneously for impacts of all variables, of course. This is the task of multi-factor econometric models.[14] The data set would ideally comprise cross-company sustainability data and financial data over several points in time. A panel regression, or pooled data regression, would allow quantification of the impacts of several sustainability indicators on any selected exogenous variable.[15] In mathematical form, a possible version of such a model looks like this

$$\underline{y}_j = A_j \cdot \underline{\alpha}_j + B_j \cdot \underline{\beta}_j + C_j \cdot \underline{\gamma}_j + \underline{\varepsilon}_j \quad (2)$$

The vector $\underline{y}_j$ consists of the chosen exogenous variable for every company k in every period t. The matrix A_j holds dummy variables. The vector $\underline{\alpha}_j$ holds the constants which vary across j and across k. The matrix B_j holds commonly used variables not linked to sustainability. The matrix C_j holds sustainability criteria linked to the exogenous variable $\underline{y}_j$. The vector $\underline{\varepsilon}_j$ holds residuals.[16]

Unfortunately, the data requirements are enormous. Only if data on corporate sustainability performance and on corporate financial performance or stock price performance is available over several periods is a panel regression feasible. Financial data is usually available, but data on sustainability performance needs to be collected as described above. In addition, financial data needs to be adjusted for differences in accounting rules and reporting requirements across regions. To comply with the best-in-class approach the data needs to be specified as deviations from industry averages, meaning that unbiased estimates have to be found for industry averages for all variables in vector $\underline{y}_j$ and matrices B_j and C_j.

4.3 Interpretation of Results

When interpreting any results derived from empirical testing of the above hypothesis, it must be remembered that sustainability is much about future trends and challenges and thus forward looking. It observes which companies are positioned to benefit from trends and challenges posed to their industry. Empirical findings can only relate to the past. Positive empirical findings would indicate that

---

13 I should perhaps mention that I use the term 'to validate' in the sense of 'not yet falsified': I subscribe to Karl Popper's reasoning regarding 'proving' hypotheses.

14 See, e.g., Konar and Cohen (1997), Russo and Fouts (1997), Butz und Plattner (1999), King and Lenox (2001), or Ziegler et al. (2002).

15 The data need to be consistent, of course. If level data on sustainability indicators are used, the data on corporate financial performance needs to be given as levels, too. Regressing corporate sustainability data on stock price returns, a much used proxy on shareholder value generation, is inconsistent. For explaining level change data, like stock price returns, level changes in sustainability performance must be used.

16 This is perhaps the simplest pooled data model. For an overview of models and their interpretation and underlying assumptions see Judge et al. (1985).

the companies analysed were prepared with regards to a specific issue that has already become a challenge in the past or is a challenge today. Whether or not they are prepared for the future is another matter. Future impacts can only be quantified either by simulations or by assuming that past impacts can be expected to have an impact also in the future. However, this hypothesis, the hypothesis that leadership in any one sustainability aspect leads to repeated impacts on shareholder value, may be far fetched. The value of sustainability performance may even diminish over time, if the challenge is taken up by the entire industry or if the challenge changes.

This is especially important with respect to claiming any future excess security returns. If corporate sustainability indicators are regressed on security returns, a positive impact found must not lead to claiming that corporate sustainability performance leads to excess security returns in the future. And yet it is this link, the link from a company's shareholder value to the performance of its securities, that lies at the heart of sustainability investing or any other kind of SRSI investing that promises superior security performance. This link seems so self-evident that the claim 'SRSI investing generates alpha' is often made with little further consideration. Unfortunately, the link is not quite as evident as it may seem. Investment performance depends very much on which components of shareholder value are positively affected and whether the effect is a singular one or repeatable. Furthermore, the claim needs to be specified with regards to whether risk-adjusted returns are referred to or not. If risk-adjusted returns are referred to, i.e. if it is claimed that SRSI investing generates excess security returns, then market inefficiency is implicitly assumed. These caveats must not be overlooked when claiming that securities of companies that perform well with regards to any SRSI criteria will outperform securities of their peers. Applying modern portfolio and financial market theory unveils the caveats.

Fig. 2 compares the time paths of three companies' shareholder value per share, otherwise known as the fair value path of the companies' stock. The horizontal axis depicts time; the vertical axis depicts shareholder value or the fair value of the company's stock. It is given in logarithmic scale, so the slopes are equivalent to the expected rate of return on the companies' equity, which is a function of the risk premium the companies are burdened with. The solid line, denoted 'company 1', depicts the fair value path of a company whose future prospects remain unchanged by internal or external events.

The dotted line, denoted 'company 2', depicts a company that decides to strengthen its corporate governance significantly, reducing the risk of misalignment of interests and misappropriation of funds. Under the assumption that good corporate governance reduces non-diversifiable risk, shareholder value is increased at the time of implementation of the new corporate governance practice, because the company should now be burdened with a lower risk premium on equity. Its future cash flows should be burdened with a lower discount rate as a consequence. The time path after implementation has a lower slope than before, though, because the risk premium on equity and thus the rate of return required by investors have been reduced. Assuming efficient markets and share prices to be in equilibrium at all times, investments in company 2 will outperform investments in company 1, but only if the investment has happened before company 2 strengthens its corporate governance. Investments made afterwards will underperform investments in company 1 on a non-risk-adjusted basis. On a risk adjusted basis, their performance will be equal, of course. This is the core result of asset pricing theory.

Fig. 2. Shareholder value path

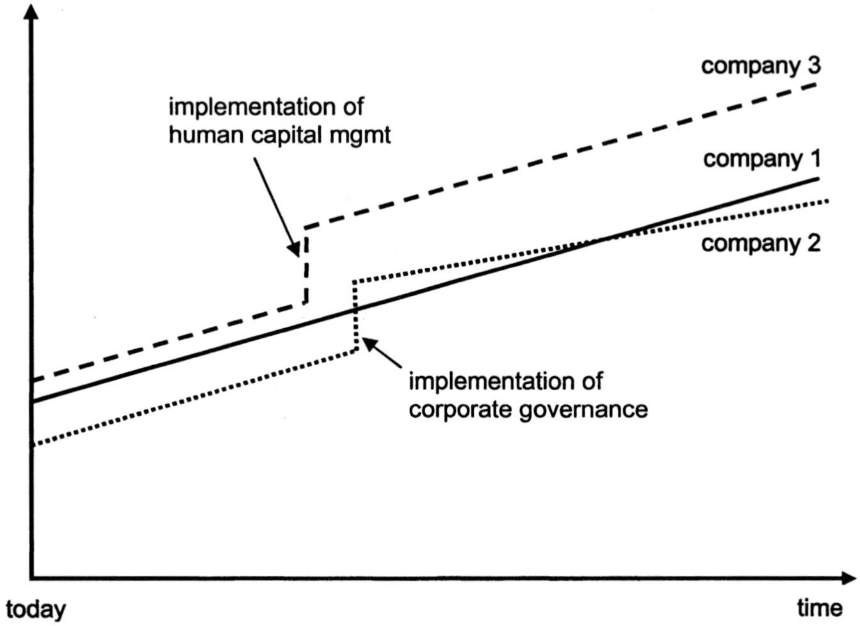

The dashed line, denoted 'company 3', depicts the shareholder value path of a company that increases its free cash flow via investing in more profitable projects than company 1, perhaps because best-in-class human capital management has increased its level of innovation. Its shareholder value jumps at the time of implementation as well, but the slope of the future path of shareholder value remains the same, assuming human capital management does not reduce non-diversifiable risk. In efficient capital markets, investments in company 3 will outperform investments in company 1, but only if conducted before company 3 implements best-in-class human capital management. After the fact, their performance will be equal both on a risk-adjusted and on a non-risk-adjusted basis.[17]

Relaxing the assumption of efficient capital markets changes the picture only slightly. If share prices need some time to adjust to any changes in the level of

17 In this light the definition of corporate sustainability used by SAM may in fact be misleading. The phrase 'to create long-term shareholder value' insinuates that excess shareholder value continues to be created. This is not the case. It must be clearly stated that corporate sustainability is a business approach to fundamentally increase shareholder value, whether in one instance or in several steps.

shareholder value, investments in sustainable companies can be profitable for some time after the measures have been implemented. The question arises of how much time. Perhaps share prices will adjust only after the effects of implementing sustainability are visible in the financial data. This would leave a period of one quarter to several years for sustainability investing to reap an excess return. Ironically, all the research conducted by the SRSI community to show that SRSI investing pays an excess return even on a risk-adjusted basis will lead to shortening this period. The current strong call for transparency and standardised SRSI reporting will have the same effect.

For all SRSI investing that is geared towards investment performance and that claims to achieve an excess risk-adjusted return thus one has to admit that the claim can be upheld only as long as the market efficiency is not at its highest level, and only as long as the impact on shareholder value is not yet reflected in share prices. Increasing research efforts in the SRSI area and calling for more transparency will increase market efficiency. If markets are inefficient, there is an opportunity to reap some extra return, of course. A relative valuation approach, where shareholder value and current prices are compared, can reveal such excess returns. But claiming that ethical, environmental socially responsible or sustainable companies will always outperform under any circumstances is simply false. Continuous outperformance on a risk-adjusted basis would necessitate SRSI leaders to continuously surprise investors on the upside by continuously detecting investment opportunities that continuously increase free cash flow beyond what was expected. Unfortunately, this assumption contradicts basic economic theory.

Of course, all this is purely hypothetical. It assumes that an impact of corporate sustainability performance on corporate financial performance and security performance is reality and can be quantified and demonstrated. The jury is still out. Studies showing some kind of impact are just as numerous as studies questioning their methodology, and as numerous as studies showing no impact whatsoever.[18] A final conclusive answer to this question cannot be given at this point, and cannot be given in any case. Results depend, as always, on the data set used. Different data sets will yield different results. Claims that there is or is not any impact is conditional on the data set used. Not only the methodology but also the data need to be questioned. This creates a competitive environment for the SRSI research and investment houses. The ones capable of showing an impact may have designed the right methodology and be collecting the right data, substantiating their claim. Those that do not find anything may or may not disprove the case. They may simply not have collected good indicators for SRSI performance.

---

18 An overview of some of the existing studies is given in Schäfer and Stederoth (2002). Another good overview is given in Ziegler et al. (2002).

5 Research Agenda and Outlook

Any serious attempt to research the impacts of corporate sustainability performance on corporate financial performance and to use the results in a sensible manner has to follow a consistent and thorough research agenda. Parts of this agenda have been describes above. The agenda is given below in full and in more detail. The description may serve as blueprint for any research effort in the SRSI area that is geared towards creating value added, and not just towards serving value sets.

This research agenda comprises three broad areas. The first area covers the theoretical backing of any claim made, the hypotheses. The hypotheses need to be researched well enough to ensure that any claims made are not at odds with economic and financial market theory.[19] The second area covers empirical testing of the claims made. The third area covers all necessary steps to assure that the way in which SRSI indicators and criteria are selected and designed comply with empirical findings and assure that empirical findings are not distorted or invalid. The third area thus serves as a feedback loop.

The first area, building the hypothesis, needs to answer the following questions:

1. Can there be a possible link between corporate sustainability and shareholder value?
2. Does this link comply with economic theory?
3. Does the link extend to excess security returns?
4. Are there special assumptions needed to extend the link to excess security returns?
5. Do these specific assumptions comply with financial market theory?

Whether such links can reasonably be assumed or not depends on the definition of sustainability adopted. Ethical, ecological, and socially responsible research and investment approaches have difficulty in postulating links to corporate financial performance. They need to rally support in form of pressure groups to make happen what they claim to happen. Sustainability can rely on companies acting in their self-interest. Still, links to excess security returns require special assumptions, like partial capital market inefficiency.

The second area, empirical analysis and validation of the hypotheses made, needs to answer the following questions:

6. How can sustainability performance be measured?
7. Do the data at hand and the data generated fulfil basic requirements for statistical analysis?
8. Which econometric model and estimation procedure are the most powerful?
9. How must the results be interpreted given that impacts of corporate sustainability performance on corporate financial performance may be singular events?

Again, sustainability is at an advantage over other SRSI approaches, because it is based on positive screening and not on negative screening. Positive screening,

[19] Although I tend to view financial market theory as part of economic theory I mention both separately here.

the best-in-class approach, should correlate with better-than-average financials and occasional better-than-average security returns. Positive screening is about who's leading the competition, not about who should be added to a blacklist.

The third area of the research agenda deals with how to interpret the estimation results for refining the analysis. It needs to answer the following questions.

10. Are there any indications that the indicators used are not apt to measure corporate sustainability performance?
11. Are the weights used to aggregate indicators into criteria validated by empirical findings?
12. Are there any indications that the indicators or criteria capture spurious correlations because they correlate with common risk factors (like 'size' or 'value/growth')?
13. How must the results be interpreted given that a visible impact may still lie ahead some time in the future?

This last question is especially important for sustainability analysis because sustainability is for the most part about future industry challenges and the way in which companies prepare themselves to seize the opportunities and manage the risks they create. Indicators and criteria used to capture future aspects will not receive any empirical validation before the impact on financials or shareholder value can be measured. Yet they capture the very essence of sustainability. Validating them without any clear empirical indication is impossible. Scenario analysis and simulations need to be employed to quantify the impacts, but this cannot be accepted as empirical validation. Of course, defending criteria that have not had any impact in the past on the premise that they will have an impact in the future may cause some overconfidence and self-delusion.

It is true that SRSI research and investment is at a crossroads. The not so distant future will determine whether it will remain a niche, appealing to those with certain value sets, or whether it will make its way into mainstream research and investment approaches. To achieve the latter, three things are needed. The SRSI research community will have to improve its understanding of common competitive forces and common trends and challenges that haunt market participants every day. SRSI research and investment will also have to find a way to integrate its findings in commonly used investment processes. Processes based on relative value investing offer the possibility to do just that. There may be others. Whatever process is used, unless the value added generated by SRSI research can be translated into investor value added, the market for SRSI research will remain small. Most importantly, the link between corporate sustainability performance and corporate financial performance and security performance needs to become visible. Without being able to show that there is value added beyond servicing value sets, SRSI will remain an appeaser at best.

What is needed to achieve this is simply transparency. The link will never be found if the data needed to find it is not generated or made available. The link, if it exists, will never be accepted, if the research approach is not transparent. The first kind of transparency calls on all data providers, companies, NGOs, state agencies et cetera to collect and publicise, or to induce to collect and publicise, all necessary data needed to show that here is indeed a self-interest for all market participants to become sustainable in their business approach. The second kind of transparency calls on the SRSI research and investment community. If serious about the business approach they call for, they must apply it to themselves, and must be open about the findings they may or may not have made. It is interesting to note the conundrum they thus face. Being transparent about their findings to support their and the SRSI community's case will at the same time endanger the monopoly niche they have to create for themselves to succeed in their own competitive environment.

References

Austin, D. et al. (2004), *Changing Drivers, The Impact of Climate Change on Competitiveness and Value Creation in the Automotive Industry*, The World Resource Institute, Washington D.C.

Beloe, S. et al. (2004), *Values for Money, Reviewing the Quality of SRI Research*, SustainAbility, London.

Butz, C. and A. Plattner (1999), *Nachhaltige Aktienanlagen, Eine Analyse der Rendite in Abhängigkeit von Umwelt- und Sozialkriterien*, Sarasin, Basel.

Coombes, P. and M. Watson (2000), Three Surveys on Corporate Governance, *The McKinsey Quarterly* 4.

Dowdell, Th. et al. (1992), The Tylenol Incident, Ensuing Regulation, and Stock Prices, *Journal of Financial and Quantitative Analysis*, June, 238-301.

Jones, K. and P. Rubin (1999), *Effects of Harmful Environment Events on Reputations of Firms*, Working Paper, Emory University, Atlanta.

Judge, G.G. et al. (1985), *The Theory and Practice of Econometrics*, 2nd ed., New York.

Karpoff, J.M. and J.R. Lott (1993), The Reputational Penalty Firms Bear from Committing Criminal Fraud, *Journal of Law and Economics* 36, 757-803.

King, A. and M. Lenox (2001), Does It Really Pay to Be Green? An Empirical Study of Firm Environmental and Financial Performance, *Journal of Industrial Ecology* 5 (1), 105-116.

Konar, S. and M.A. Cohen (1997), *Does the Market Value Environmental Performance?*, Working Paper, Vanderbuilt University, Nashville.

Kurtz, L. and D. DiBartolomeo (1996), Socially Screened Portfolios: An Attribution Analysis of Relative Performance, *Journal of Investing* 5, 35-41.

McWilliams, A. and D. Siegel (1999), Event Studies in Management Research: Theoretical and Empirical Issues, *Academy of Management Journal* 42, 43-59.

Orlitzky, M. et al. (2003), Corporate Social and Financial Performance: A Meta-Analysis, *Organization Studies* 24, 403-441.

Russo, M.V. and P.A. Fouts (1997), A Resource-Based Perspective on Corporate Environment Performance and Profitability, *Academy of Management Journal* 40, 534-559.

Schäfer, H. and R. Stederoth (2002), Portfolioselektion und Anlagepolitik mittels Ethik-Filtern – ein Überblick zum Stand der Kapitalmarktforschung, *Kredit und Kapital* 1, 101-148.

Ziegler, A. et al. (2002), *Der Einfluss ökologischer und sozialer Nachhaltigkeit auf den Shareholder Value europäischer Aktiengesellschaften*, ZEW Discussion Paper No. 02-32, Mannheim.

Impact Assessment and Sustainability

Marialuisa Tamborra

European Commission, Directorate General Research, SDME 2/85, 1049 Brussels, Belgium, marialuisa.tamborra@cec.eu.int

Keywords. *Impact Assessment, Sustainable Development, EU Research Framework Programme*

JEL. *H23; O38; Q51; Q56*

1 Background: Introducing Impact Assessment

With its Communication on Impact Assessment (European Commission, 2002a) the European Commission committed itself to perform an Impact Assessment of all major policy proposals, in order to improve their sustainability and to ensure consistency among different policy initiatives. The application of the Impact Assessment in policy-making is expected to become a key instrument for the EU to respond to its Göteborg commitments to implement Sustainable Development, as well as to its Lisbon commitments.

This Communication is one of a series of initiatives on "Better Regulation". Its aim is to improve the quality and coherence of the policy development process. It will contribute to an effective and efficient regulatory environment and to a more coherent implementation of the European Strategy for Sustainable Development.

With this Communication, the Commission responds to its Göteborg commitments to implement Sustainable Development and to establish a tool for Impact Assessment for achieving Sustainable Development objectives. Moreover, at the Laeken Council the Commission made commitments to implement better regulation principles including a regulatory Impact Assessment mechanism. This followed the Commission's own White Paper on European Governance.

Its aim is to improve the quality and coherence of the policy development process. It is intended to contribute to an effective and efficient regulatory environment and to a more coherent implementation of the EU Strategy for Sustainable Development.

There is a strong demand on the part of decision makers for "reliable and applicable" indicators and tools to identify ways towards Sustainable Development, to measure and to communicate the direction of change towards Sustainable Development.

The new Impact Assessment method integrates all existing specific assessments of the direct and indirect impacts of proposed measures, that were traditionally used at he Commission (i.e. business Impact Assessment, gender assessment, environmental assessment, small and medium enterprises assessment, trade Impact Assessment, regulatory Impact Assessment etc.) into one global instrument. This single instrument will replace the existing situation of a number of partial and sectoral assessments, and is intended to integrate, reinforce, streamline and replace all the existing sectoral Impact Assessment mechanisms for Commission proposals.

The ultimate goal of the Impact Assessment is to analyse the positive and negative impacts associated with a given policy proposal, enabling informed political judgements to be made and identifying trade-offs in achieving different objectives.

Impact Assessment is an aid to decision-making, not a substitute for political judgement. An Impact Assessment does not necessarily generate clear-cut conclusions or recommendations. It does, however, provide an important input by informing decision makers of the consequences of policy choices.

The Impact Assessment is also an effective and valuable communication tool. Consultations with interested parties generate useful discussion and bring in valuable information and analysis that are required by the Communication on general principles and minimum standards for consultation (European Commission, 2002b).

The process of "Impact Assessment" started in 2003 with the first few 43 policies under scrutiny for the Extended Impact Assessment. The following year 46 policy proposals were selected for the Extended Impact Assessment. This process consists of a two-stage approach: The preliminary impact assessment is a filtering exercise that justifies the choice of going or not for an Extended Impact Assessment. The extended one will imply an in-depth assessment, both qualitative and quantitative, and there is a strong demand for methodologies and tools that are able to cope with Sustainable Development challenges.

European research in Sustainable Development needs to support this process. Moreover, the Communication on "Impact Assessment" encourages Member States to re-think their way of making policies in the light of the requirements of the Commission "Impact Assessment".

Fig.1 shows that the assessment and the decision-making process are two separate but mutually influencing activities and that the assessment needs to start at an early stage of the decision-making process in order to be effective. It also illustrates that impacts related to the three dimensions of Sustainability are not captured completely by Impact Assessment. As **Fig.1** depicts, such an assessment will provide a set of quantitative and qualitative assessment variables on both positive and negative impacts, that will guide and support policy makers in taking decisions.

The identification of impacts implies the definition of the links from cause (the policy proposal) to effect (the impacts), and addresses the questions of who is affected by the identified impacts and over what timescale (causal chain analysis). The analysis of the causal links allows for a subsequent qualitative analysis of the

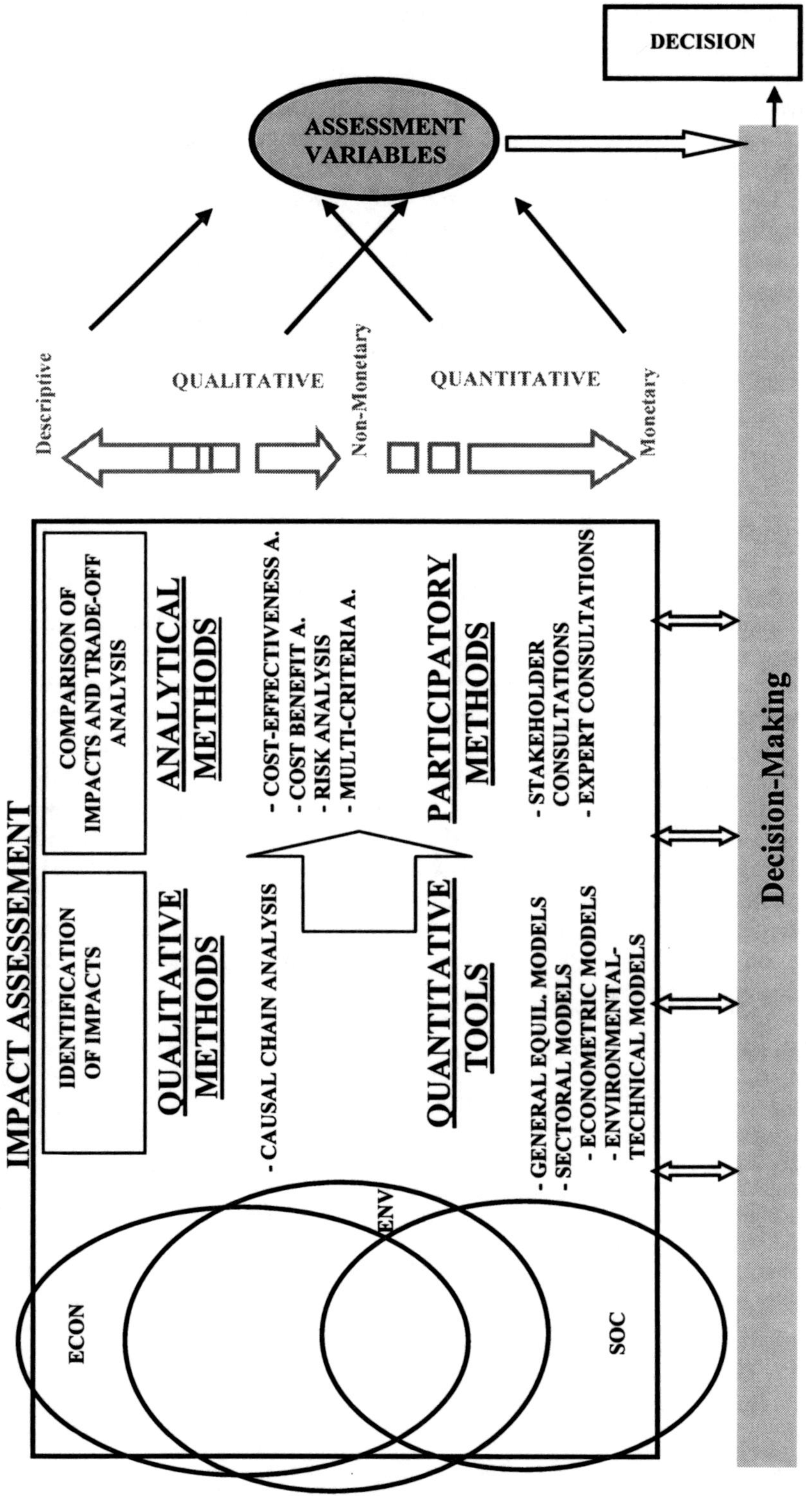

Fig. 1. Diagram of tools and methods used for Impact Assessment

impacts identified and then for a quantitative analysis, where appropriate. Some of the tools for calculating those impacts have been developed within the EU research programmes. These tools are well suited for devising impacts in a quantitative way, so that they can be analysed in physical terms if multi-criteria analysis is applied in policy appraisal, or translated into monetary terms if cost effectiveness and cost-benefit analysis are to be used[1].

The comparison phase does not only involve the use of analytical methods ranging from a full cost-benefit analysis to a multi-criteria analysis, but also the consultation of interested parties. In fact, quantitative variables derived from analytical tools would be of little use without the right process tool to bring it to action. Social sciences are asked to develop methodologies, tools for better communication and social learning processes to manage large multi-disciplinary groups of stakeholders.

2 A Tentative Classification of Quantitative Tools and Some Achievements of EU-Funded Research

In this section a possible classification of quantitative tools is provided with some examples from EU research projects and models. A more detailed description of these projects is available in a EU publication (Tamborra, 2002). Most relevant and well-developed quantitative tools for impact analysis purposes consist in models that can be classified into:

(1) Computable General Equilibrium (CGE) models: CGE models calculate a vector of prices such that all the markets of the economy are in equilibrium, implying that resources are allocated efficiently. They are based on economic theory and theoretical coherence (i.e. the Walrasian representations of the economy). Therefore, parameters and coefficients are calibrated with mathematical methods and not estimated as in econometric modelling. They can be static – comparing the situation at one or more dates – or dynamic, showing developments from one period to another. CGE models require an input-output table to model interrelations between sectors.

Examples of EU-funded CGE models

GEM-E3 is an example of a successful CGE model developed with European Commission (DG Research) funds. It is an applied general equilibrium model for the European Union Member States, taken individually or as a whole, which provides details on the macroeconomy and its interaction with the environment and the energy system. The model is being used to evaluate policy issues for the European Commission. Applications of the model have been (or are currently being) carried out for several Directorate Generals of the European Commission (economic affairs, competition, environment, taxation, research). At present, the model is operational for EU-15 Member States, while further development is under way.

[1] Other methods are available such as risk analysis, cost assessment, risk-risk assessment, cross-risk analysis, etc.

The *CCGT*[2] project was financed by the European Commission under the Energy, Environment and Sustainable Development programme within the Fifth Framework Programme. The project aimed at providing quantitative insights into the impacts of two important international policy initiatives: (i) multilateral agreements on climate protection strategies, and (ii) trade agreements towards global trade liberalisation. The main part of the CCGT project consists of the development of an appropriate analytical framework and its parameterisation. Starting from a multi-regional, multi-commodity computable general equilibrium (CGE) model several extensions are introduced such as imperfect competition on commodity markets and scale economies, and different degrees of trade liberalisation, i.e. the representation of (non)tariff barriers.

By introducing increasing returns to scale on the plant or firm level, the *GEM-CCGT* model is able to capture pro-competitive industrial organisation effects of trade policy reforms (such as EU enlargement). Besides the model can analyse how EU emission abatement policies will change under efficiency and equity considerations in response to different developments of world trade.

(2) Sectoral models: These models are constructed on the equilibrium of one specific sector of the economy. These models are often very detailed since they are sometimes complemented by more specific (e.g., engineering economic) bottom-up models. On the other hand they are not able to capture the effects on other markets.

Examples of EU-funded sectoral models

PRIMES is a simulation model focusing on EU energy markets and as such is very useful in analysing in detail the impacts of various forms of carbon emission trading on energy markets, although its focus on the EU means that it cannot capture some of the impacts of carbon emission trading in the wider economy (e.g., exchange rate effects, trade balances). PRIMES generates results for each of the 14 Member States (Luxembourg excluded), and has also been used to investigate the effects of carbon emission trading being limited to a subset of Member States. Because of the detailed sectoral breakdown it also allows the analysis of the effects of carbon emission trading being restricted to a number of economic sectors. The equilibrium is static (within each time period) but repeated in a time-forward path, under dynamic relationships. PRIMES is specially conceived for scenario construction and policy impact analysis.

POLES is a partial equilibrium worldwide energy market model. Its geographical coverage is different to that of PRIMES, as it covers the whole world but has a less detailed breakdown of EU Member States. This renders it an excellent tool to shed light on the consequences for international energy markets of EU carbon emission trading. On the other hand, POLES is less suited to illuminate in detail the effects of sectorally and geographically limited permit markets, because of its wide scope. Also PRIMES does not capture general economy-wide effects like changes in international trade.

TREMOVE is a sectoral simulation model developed by DG Environment. It allows the simulation of consumer behaviour with regard to the choice of modes of transport and vehicle types (i.e. size and technologies). The demand for each mode is determined by taking into account the interactions between the various modes of transport. This model allows an analysis of the extent to which policies can affect these choices and the subsequent atmospheric emissions. Moreover, it calculates the cost of policies to society. The cost components modelled in TREMOVE are the cost to transport users, transport produc-

---

2 CCGT: The Climate Change Policy and Global trade (EVK2-CT-2000-00093).

ers, and governments. The output of TREMOVE includes, inter alia, annual forecasts of transport flows, vehicle stock size and composition, costs to society from transportation, and emissions from transport both in the base case and in any variant thereof. More information on this model can be found on: http://europa.eu.int/comm/environment/air/tremoveassessment.htm

(3) Macroeconometric models: These models are empirical and are therefore developed using coherent datasets. The parameters of the equations are estimated with econometric methodologies. They are fundamentally designed to evaluate macro-sectoral impacts of economic policies, although they have been extended to incorporate environmental dimensions.

The strength of macroeconomic models relies on the validation of the equations of the model with statistical methods and on the model's ability to provide short-medium term forecasting and to evaluate the impact of policies. Moreover, these models ensure a coherent framework of analysis for analysing inter-linkages between variables.

Examples of EU econometric models

NEMESIS[3] is a very detailed econometric model estimated on the basis of long time series. It includes 30 productive sectors and 27 consumption categories. A detailed energy/environment module allows energy prices, volumes and subsequent pollutant emissions (CO_2, SO_2, NO_X, etc.) to be calculated. Moreover, it describes sectoral dynamics with interdependencies among activities. Another important characteristic of this model is the introduction of endogenous R&D and innovation decisions that allows for a new assessment of policies, such as energy, environmental, fiscal, R&D ones.

The NEMESIS model can be used for several policy applications. First of all, it can be used to run forecasts on short and medium term. Then, it enables energy and environment-related policies and economic, fiscal, R&D policies etc. to be assessed. Moreover, the model can assess the effects of EU RTD policy on competitiveness, employment, innovation and Sustainable Development. All results for simulations are available for each EU country or Europe as a whole both at macro and sectoral level.

(4) Environmental-technical models: These models intend to measure and to evaluate the environmental impact of economic activities or policy measures. An established approach within these models is the so-called impact pathway analysis. This is a bottom-up approach for estimating external costs starting from a particular process and its emissions, and moving through their interactions with the environment to a physical measure of impact (the main component being health), and eventually a monetary valuation. In the Dose-Response step of analysis, data from the physical, biological sciences and epidemiology are used to link a particular pollutant at different levels (the dose) with different levels of physical damage to human health and ecosystems. The calculation process is highly site-sensitive, as the aggregate impact is determined by the geographical distribution of victims or receptor ecosystems.

[3] NEMESIS: New Econometric Model for Environment and Strategies Implementation for Sustainable Development (EVG1-CT1999-0014).

The impact pathway analysis has allowed the Commission to review many of its decisions in the environmental sphere, in order to reach a better compromise between economic and environmental objectives. There have been many applications of the methodology where it has helped, through a quantification of the environmental and health damages, to make policy decisions that are better-informed and more consonant with the goals of Sustainable Development.

Impact Pathway Analysis in EU-funded projects
The most well known example of implementation of the Impact Pathway Analysis is the project *EXTERNE*. This is the first comprehensive attempt to use a consistent 'bottom-up' methodology to evaluate the external costs associated with a range of different fuel cycles in different locations in Europe. Local, regional and global impacts are calculated with the *ECOSENSE* model, although uncertainty attached to global impacts is still very high. Uncertainties are treated with a systematic application of the sensitivity analysis. This methodology has proved its potential also in the transport sector, in industrial technologies and in the waste sector.

Externalities analysis has a wide number of policy applications, when environmental costs borne by society need to be taken into account, such as in the definition of environmental taxes.

One offshoot from EXTERNE that is beginning to guide policy makers in following a sustainability pathway is *GREENSENSE*[4], which looks both at the national/global impacts of economic activity as well as the costs, including external costs, associated with different thresholds of sustainability. By comparing the two, and taking account of future impacts and uncertainty in a careful way, it will provide some guidance on how adequate current policies are and where they need to be strengthened.

3 Looking Forward: The Contribution of the Sixth Research Framework Programme

There is a strong demand for methodologies and tools able to contribute to the definition and assessment of the Sustainable Development Strategy. The Climate Change issue has led to significant developments of new methods and tools during the nineties. The tools for facing the Climate Change challenge are today operational and they constitute with the necessary adaptations the starting point for assessing the impacts of policies and measures to be implemented as part of the EU Strategy for Sustainable Development. It is hoped that the EU Sustainable Strategy will allow similar major developments and best practices to be developed as it was for the Climate Change Strategy design.

The new Framework Programme supports the development of quantitative and qualitative methods and tools for Impact Assessment. In the work programme of Priority 6.3 "Climate Change and Ecosystems", several inter-related topics are relevant for Impact Assessment:

---

[4] GREENSENSE: An Applied Integrated Environmental Impact Assessment Framework for the European Union (EVG1-CT2000-00022).

- *Estimating thresholds of sustainability and externalities*: One key issue for Impact Assessment to be realistic relies in the identification and quantification of externalities, so that economic instruments can be used to steer society on a Sustainable Development pathway. Whereas substantial results have already been achieved in the field of energy and transport, the challenge is still open for areas such as agriculture or forestry.
- *Developing tools for integrated sustainability assessment and for the incorporation of sustainability in decision-making processes*: The aim is to explore new approaches and tools for Sustainability Impact Assessment embedding and integrating environmental, economic and social aspects in the analysis of policies.

The objective of these two areas is precisely to provide those tools and models that can be used to perform Impact Assessments using an analytical approach.

Also the so-called Priority 8 for "Specific Support to Policies" states in its objectives the support to the implementation of the EU Strategy of Sustainable Development, especially in the area 3.4 "Forecasting and Developing Innovative Policies for Sustainability in the Medium and Long Term". The research topics are identified by DG Research in co-operation with other DGs of the Commission and are aimed at supporting their own policies.

The Sixth Framework Programme for Research is funding a number of research projects that are relevant to the Impact Assessment implementation. Their aim is to make stock of past research results and explore new approaches and socio-economic tools for Sustainability Integrated Assessment allowing to integrate and quantify environmental, economic and social aspects (e.g. I.Q. TOOLS and SustainabilityA-Test[5]). Additional projects (e.g. METHODEX, ESPREME[6]) are on the identification and quantification of externalities that will allow taking into account the actual and full cost of policy actions, including their external cost. Ongoing and future calls for proposals will strengthen and complement significantly this research area.

These are the most relevant projects (traditional instruments) that have already started: I.Q. TOOLS is a Priority 8 Project ("Specific Support to Policies") and is aimed at directly supporting the Impact Assessment Implementation in the Commission, whereas Sustainability A-Test is part of Priority 6.3 "Global Change and Ecosystems".

---

5 I.Q. TOOLS: Indicators and Quantitative Tools for Improving the Process of Sustainability Impact Assessment (SSP1-CT-2003-502078); SustainabilityA-Test: Advanced Techniques for Evaluation of Sustainability Assessment Tools (GOCE-CT-2003-505328).

6 METHODEX: Methods and data on environmental and health externalities: harmonising and sharing of operational estimates (GOCE-CT-2003-505368); ESPREME: Estimation of willingness-to-pay to reduce risks of exposure to heavy metals and cost-benefit analysis for reducing heavy metals occurrence in Europe (SSP1-CT-2003-502527).

I.Q. TOOLS

This project is directly relevant to the European Commission, as its aim is to provide a decision-support tool for desk-officers of the European Commission who are in charge of developing a policy proposal. The tool will help to provide the users with qualitative and quantitative tools such as indicator sets, and checklists for a practical appraisal of Community policies, as well as a model analysing in a quantitative manner inter-linkages among different policy areas or sectors and indirect effects across specific impacts. Besides, an electronic Handbook of best practices will be produced.

SustainabilityA-Test

This project will assist in improving both impact assessments and the Sustainable Development strategy definition, by high level validation of existing tools using a consistent and comprehensive evaluation framework. This evaluation framework will indicate how the tools relate, the merits of each tool, the circumstances under which they can be used, the constraints, the pros and cons and the extent to which they integrate externalities of policies. Moreover, the evaluation framework will show which tools are useful for answering which key aspects of Sustainable Development and will identify the trade-offs of using the different tools for addressing the three pillars of Sustainable Development (economic, environmental and social).

A preliminary overview of the methodologies and tools used in the first few Impact assessments done in 2003 by the European Commission confirms that the European research community has an important role to play in providing tools for the assessment of the environmental, economic and social impacts of policy initiatives, and in strengthening the quantitative and analytical analysis used in Impact Assessments. From an overview of 2003 IAs based partly on the preliminary results of the project I.Q. TOOLS it turns out that the main areas of improvement concern:

- the choice of the options that hardly includes more than only one viable option;
- the comprehensiveness of the analysis that is sometimes almost exclusively restricted to the analysis of one type of impacts, i.e. the economic ones;
- the use of quantitative analysis along with the qualitative one; this includes the use of indicators that are often difficult to identify and calculate in a transparent and consensual way.

Much is expected from research in the coming years in view of developing the appropriate support tools for policy-making. Strengthening the methodological and scientific base for Impact Assessment will eventually strengthen the Impact Assessment process itself.

References

Blanchard, O., P. Criqui, A. Kitous, and L. Viguier (2003), Combining Efficiency with Equity: A Pragmatic Approach, in: Kaul, I., P. Conceicao, K. Le Goulven, and R. Mendoza (Eds.), *Providing Global Public Goods: Making Globalization Work for All*, New York.

Blanchard, O., P. Criqui, M. Trommetter, and L. Viguier (2001), *Equity and Efficiency in Climate Change Negotiations: A Scenario for World Emission Entitlements by 2030*, IEPE, Cahier de Recherche n° 26, http://www.upmf-grenoble.fr/iepe/Publications/cahiers.html.

Böhringer, C. (2002), Climate Politics from Kyoto to Bonn: From Little to Nothing?, *The Energy Journal* 23 (2), 51-71.

Böhringer, C. and A. Löschel (2002), Assessing the Costs of Compliance: The Kyoto Protocol, *European Environment*, 12 (1), 1-16.

Böhringer, C. and A. Löschel (2002), Economic Impacts of Carbon Abatement Strategies, in: C. Böhringer, M. Finus, and C.Vogt, *Controlling Global Warming*, Cheltenham, 105-179.

Böhringer, C. and T.F. Rutherford (2002), Carbon Abatement and International Spillovers, *Environmental and Resource Economics* 22 (3), 391-417.

Böhringer, C. (2002), Sustainable Impact Analysis: *The Use of Computable General Equilibrium Models in Methodological Tools for SIA*, Report of the CEPII Workshop held on 7-8 November 2002 in Brussels, No. 2003-19.

Böhringer, C. (2001), *Climate Politics from Kyoto to Bonn: From Little to Nothing?!?*, ZEW Discussion Paper No. 01-49, Mannheim, http://www.zew.de/de/publikationen/neuepublikationen.php3?action=article_show&id=0000000813.

Böhringer, C. et al. (2000), *European Emission Mitigation Policy and Technological Evolution: Economic Evaluation with the GEM-E3-EG Model (GEM-E3-ELITE)*, Final Report to the EC, Contract No. JOS3-CT97-0017.

Boulanger, P.M. and T. Bréchet (2002), *Setting Concepts into Motion. Improving Scientific Tools in Support of Sustainable Development Decision-Making*, http://www.belspo.be/belspo/home/publ/pub_ostc/AS/dddobo_en.pdf.

Capros, P., N. Kouvaritakis and L. Mantzos (2001), *Top-Down Analysis of Greenhouse Gas Emission Reduction Possibilities in the EU*, Final Report to EC – DG ENV.

Capros, P. (2000), Technology Evolution and Energy Modelling, special issue of *the International Journal of Global Energy Issues* (IJGEI) 14, 1-4.

Capros, P., L. Mantzos, D. Petrellis, V. Panos, K. Delkis, J-F. Guilmot, and E.L. Vouyoukas (1999), European Union Energy Outlook to 2020, special issue of *Energy in Europe*, European Commission Directorate General for Energy.

Capros, P., P. Georgakopoulos, D. Van Regemorter, S. Proost, T. Schmidt, H. Koschel, K. Conrad, and E.L. Vouyoukas (1999), *Climate Technology Strategies 2 – The Macro-Economic Cost and Benefit of Reducing Greenhouse Gas Emissions in the European Union*, ZEW Economic Studies, Vol. 4, Heidelberg.

Capros, P., P. Georgakopoulos, D. van Regemorter, and D. Willenbockel (1998), Aggregate Results of the Single Market Programme, in: *General Equilibrium Macro-Economic Ex-Post Evaluation of the EU Single Market Programme*, Office for Official Publication of the European Communities, Luxembourg.

Criqui, P. and N. Kouvaritakis (2000), World Energy Projections to 2030, *International Journal of Global Energy Issues* 14, 116-136.

Criqui, P., N. Kouvaritakis, and C. Thonet (2000), World Post-Kyoto Scenarios: Benefits from Accelerated Technology Progress, *International Journal of Global Energy Issues*, 14, 184-203.

Criqui, P., S. Mima, and L. Viguier (1999), Marginal Abatement Costs of CO2 Emission Reductions, Geographical Flexibility and Concrete Ceilings: An Assessment Using the POLES Model, *Energy Policy*, 27 (10), 585-602.

Eckermann, F., A. Hunt, T. Taylor, and M. Stronzik (2003), *The Role of Transaction Costs and Risk Premia in the Determination of Climate Change Policy Responses*, ZEW Discussion Paper No. 03-59, Mannheim, ftp://ftp.zew.de/pub/zew-docs/dp/dp0359.pdf.

European Commission (2002), *Communication on Impact Assessment*, COM(2002)276 final.

European Commission (1996), *POLES 2.2*, DG XII, EUR 17358, Brussels.

European Commission (1995/1999), *EXTERNE: Externalities of Energy*, volumes 1-10, Brussels.

European Commission (1995), *Computable General Equilibrium Model for Studying Economy-Energy-Environment Interactions GEM-E3*, DG XII, EUR 16714, Brussels.

European Commission (1995), *PRIMES*, DG XII, EUR 16713, Brussels.

Friedrich, R. and P. Bickel (Eds.) (2001), *Environmental External Costs of Transport*, Heidelberg.

HM Treasury (1997), *The Green Book. Appraisal and Evaluation in Central Government*, London.

Löschel, A. and M. Mraz (2002), EU Enlargement and Environmental Policy, in: Böhringer, C. and A. Löschel (Eds.), *Empirical Modeling of the Economy and the Environment*, ZEW Economic Studies, Vol. 20, Heidelberg.

Navrud S. (2000), *Strengths, Weaknesses and Policy Utility of Valuation Techniques and Benefit Transfer Methods*, Invited paper for the OECD-USDA workshop "The Value of Rural Amenities: Dealing with Public Goods, Non-Market Goods and Externalities", Washington D.C., June 5-6.

Navrud, S. and O. Bergland (2000) Value Transfer and Environmental Policy, *Policy Research Brief Series* 8, Cambridge Research for the Environment, http://www.mluri.sari.ac.uk/serp/research/eve/publ.html#PRB).

Navrud, S. and G.J. Pruckner (1997), Environmental Valuation – To Use or Not to Use? A Comparative Study of the United States and Europe, *Environmental and Resource Economics* 10, 1-26.

OECD (1997), *Regulatory Impact Analysis – Best Practices in OECD Countries*, Paris.

Rotmans, J. (1998), Methods for IA: The Challenges and Opportunities ahead, in: Rotmans, J. and P. Vellinga (Eds.),*Challenges and Opportunities for Integrated Environmental Assessment, Environmental Modeling & Assessment*, Bussum, The Netherlands.

Rotmans, J. and H. Dowlatabadi (1998), Integrated Assessment of Climate Change: Evaluation of Methods and Strategies, in: Reyner, S. and E. Malone (Eds.), *Human Choice and Climate change: An International Social Sciences Assessment*, Washington.

Rotmans, J. and P. Vellinga (Eds.) (1998), *Challenges and Opportunities for Integrated Environmental Assessment, Environmental Modeling & Assessment*, Bussum, The Netherlands.

Spash, C. (2000), The Concerted Action on Environmental Valuation in Europe (EVE): an Introduction, *Policy Research Brief Series* 1, Cambridge Research for the Environment, Cambridge, United Kingdom (http://www.mluri.sari.ac.uk/serp/research/eve/publ.html#PRB).

Stirling, A. (Ed.) (1999), *On Science and Precaution in the Management of Technological Risks, A ESTO Project Report* – IPTS, EUR 19056 EN, Luxembourg.

Tamborra M. (2003), *Developing Tools for Sustainability Impact Assessment: The Role of Socioeconomic Research in the EU*, paper presented at the conference "New Directions in Impact Assessment for Development: Methods and Practice", 24-25 November 2003, http://www.enterprise-impact.org.uk/conference/Abstracts/Tamborra. shtml.

Tamborra, M. (2002), *Socio-Economic Tools for Sustainability Impact Assessment, the Contribution of EU Research to Sustainable Development*, European Commission, EUR 20437.

Viscusi, W.K. (1997), Improving the Analytical Basis for Regulatory Decision-Making, in: OECD, *Regulatory Impact Analysis. Best Practices in OECD Countries*, Paris.

Should Environmental Policy Discriminate Between Exposed and Sheltered Sectors?

Cees A. Withagen

Free University Amsterdam, Department of Spatial Economics, Faculty of Economics, De Boelelaan 1105, 1081 HV Amsterdam and Tilburg University, Department of Economics, Warandelaan 2, 5000 LE Tilburg, The Netherlands, cwithagen@feweb.vu.nl

Keywords. *Strategic Environmental Policy, International Trade*

JEL. *Q10; F18*

Abstract. The present paper demonstrates that with imperfect competition on world markets, a government acting as a Stackelberg leader should impose stricter environmental policy on the exposed sector of the economy than on the sheltered sector, if it pursues the maximisation of social welfare. This is illustrated by means of a model covering a large class of economies.

1 Introduction

The relationship between environmental policy and international trade offers several interesting perspectives. To mention just a few: Does trade liberalisation lead to more or to less pollution? Is there a case for using environmental policy as an instrument of trade policy? Is there a theoretical and empirical foundation of the Porter hypothesis? Under what circumstances will there occur a relocation of firms as a consequence of strict environmental policy? What can we learn from the theory on international environmental agreements? When does carbon leakage occur? What kind of tradable permits system should be implemented in a federal state? Apart from the fact that these issues are interesting from a theoretical point of view, they are also compelling and extremely relevant from an empirical and policy point of view. It is tempting to provide an overview of the issues involved, in order to sketch a broad outline and to indicate where future research should focus on. However, excellent surveys already exist (see e.g. Copeland and Taylor 2004, Sturm 2002, and Ulph 1999), and, moreover, it seems to me that all questions raised above have not yet been dealt with completely, and deserve further attention. Therefore, in this paper I would like to make a modest original contribution to just one of the fields of the link between international trade and environmental policy.

I will deal with the question whether in the design of environmental policy making there is case for treating the exposed exporting sector of an economy differently than the sheltered sector. This is a relevant question, since we observe, for example in the Netherlands, that the exporting sector has on several occasions been exempted from environmental taxation, arguably by an appeal on the importance of its competitiveness. Presently the debate revives with the upcoming introduction of a European system of tradable CO_2 permits. Recently an advisory council to the government proposed to install a system where the exposed sector would be treated more leniently than the sheltered sector[1].

From a theoretical perspective a lot has already been done in this area. The theoretical results depend largely on the market structures being studied. In the case of perfect competition on world markets and absence of international spill-overs, the standard result is that there is no case for differential treatment (Rauscher, 1994, Neary, 2003). Hoel (1994), however, shows that preferential treatment of exposed sectors may be justified, particularly if trade policy is impossible and transboundary pollution occurs. Rauscher (1994) suggests that in the case of a large country, it may be optimal to be more stringent for the exporting sector, in order to improve the terms of trade. The theory on optimal environmental policy in an oligopolistic world market is inspired by the strategic trade literature pioneered by Spencer and Brander (1983), Brander and Spencer (1985), and Helpman and Krugman (1985). Following this line of research, the strategic environmental policy literature addresses the issue whether an "over-lax" environmental policy can be used as an alternative to providing subsidies to domestic exporting firms. Barrett (1994) and Neary (2003) show in a partial equilibrium framework with Cournot competition that welfare maximisation indeed dictates an "over-lax" environmental policy: The home firm pays less than the Pigouvian tax corresponding to the marginal damage of pollution. This result is reversed in the case of Bertrand competition. Rauscher (1994) and Elbers and Withagen (2002a,b) consider the issue in a general equilibrium setting. Their analyses go beyond the question whether or not environmental policy yields Pigouvian outcomes, by considering discrimination in the stringency of environmental policy between the domestic and the export sectors. Elbers and Withagen (2002a,b) show by numerical examples that the partial equilibrium recommendation may not hold in the case of a general equilibrium approach. Mulatu et al. (2004) employ a somewhat different framework, inspired by international agreements on emissions, where there is an exogenous upper bound on emissions. They find that in that case it might be better not to be lenient with regard to the exposed sector.

In the present paper I aim to fill some gaps in this literature. In particular I want to show that preferential treatment of the exposed sector is suboptimal for a large class of large economies and for a class of Cournot competition models, rather than showing it for a set of numerical examples. In doing so I extend the applicability of policy recommendations made earlier. At the same time I intend to provide a rather up-to-date survey of the literature in this specific field.

1 Probably political economy considerations are important here too. We will not address this in the present paper.

The remainder of this paper is organised as follows. In Section 2, I introduce the basic model with features largely identical to the models discussed above. I also derive some preliminary results on perfect competition and the large country case. Section 3 investigates the issue in an oligopolistic structure of the world market. Section 4 concludes.

2 The Model and First Results

The model is strongly related to the model employed by Rauscher (1994) in his seminal work on ecological dumping. The economy has three consumer commodities and employs two factors of production, capital and raw materials. The first consumer commodity is consumed and produced domestically only. Production takes place in the sheltered sector with many price-taking firms. The aggregate production function F_1 is neoclassical, and has capital k_1 and raw material y_1 as inputs. Domestic consumption is denoted by c_1. The second class of consumer commodities is produced in the exposed sector. There are n $(n \geq 1)$ varieties, indexed by $i = 1, 2, ..., n$. On aggregate variety i is produced by a neoclassical production function F_2^i, again using capital k_2^i and raw material y_2^i. Output is partially consumed domestically (c_2^i), whereas the remainder is exported (x_2^i). The third consumer commodity is imported, and its consumption is denoted by c_3. Utility from consumption is represented by a neoclassical utility function $U(c_1, c_2, c_3)$ with $c_2 = (c_2^1, c_2^2, ..., c_2^n)$. The imported commodity is used as the numéraire by taking its world market price equal to unity. We require equilibrium on the current account of the balance of payments.

Capital is mobile domestically, but immobile internationally.[2] Gordon and Bovenberg (1996) provide empirical as well as theoretical support for the assumption of international immobility of capital.[3] The economy's endowment of capital (owned by the consumers) is given by $\bar{k}$, with a rate of return r. The raw material can be conceived of as a fossil fuel. The possible exhaustibility of the resource from which the raw material is extracted, is neglected. Pollution is normalised such that using one unit of the raw material entails one unit of polluting emission. No abatement technology is available. With regard to pollution two variants will be considered:

---

2 The immobile factor is referred to as capital, but if applicable one can also think of labour as the immobile factor.

3 In an attempt to explain the empirical evidence on international immobility of capital, Gordon and Bovenberg (1996) single out asymmetric information between domestic investors and foreign investors as the most important factor. They argue that foreign investors are at a disadvantage due to lack of information regarding issues such as purchase prices of assets and inputs, output markets, and future government policies.

1. Due to international environmental agreements, there is an upper bound $\bar{y}$ on emissions.
2. Pollution brings along damage, which is of a domestic nature only. The damage function is given by $D(y_1 + \sum_{i=1}^{n} y_2^i)$ with D increasing and strictly convex.

So, in the first variant there is no domestic damage inflicted by pollution, or the optimal emission level is a priori captured by the upper bound on pollution. We will refer to this situation as the global pollution case, assuming that the international agreement deals with a global pollutant such as CO_2. The alternative case occurs when domestic damage is caused by domestic emissions only. In the sequel this will be referred to as the local damage case. The government levies emission taxes τ_1 and τ_2^i $(i = 1,2,...,n)$ per unit of raw material input in the sectors of the economy. Tax revenues are recycled to consumers in a lump sum fashion. Alternatively, the government implements a system of tradable emissions permits. Such a system is called uniform if trade is possible among all domestic parties involved. The system is differentiated if individual sectors have their own system, with trade limited to those firms belonging to the individual sectors.

This completes the description of the model. Its simplicity allows for a rather thorough analytical approach, but obviously so at the cost of some realism. In particular the assumption that the polluting commodity is freely available, except for the tax, is restrictive, because one could think here of energy that is usually imported. However, it is my conjecture that an alternative model taking this into account would not alter the main results of the analysis.

I now characterise the first-best optimum and study if and how it can be implemented in a decentralised setting. The first-best optimum in the economy is the allocation that maximises social welfare,

$$W = U(c_1,c_2,c_3) - \delta D(y_1 + \sum_{i=1}^{n} y_2^i)$$

subject to:

$$c_1 = F_1(k_1, y_1) \tag{2.1}$$

$$c_2^i + x_2^i = F_2^i(k_2^i, y_2^i), \ (i = 1, 2, ..., n) \tag{2.2}$$

$$c_3 = \sum_{i=1}^{n} p_2^i(x_2^i)x_2^i \tag{2.3}$$

$$k_1 + \sum_{i=1}^{n} k_2^i = \bar{k} \tag{2.4}$$

$$y_1 + \sum_{i=1}^{n} y_2^i = (1-\delta)\bar{y} \tag{2.5}$$

where $p_2^i = p_2^i(x_2^i)$ denotes the inverse world demand functions, and where $\delta = 1$ in case of local damage and $\delta = 0$ in case of global pollution. Note that equation (2.3) incorporates the equilibrium condition on the current account. Several results regarding the implementation of the first-best optimum in a decentralised economy are straightforward modifications of earlier work by, for instance, Hoel (1996) and Rauscher (1997). In particular, regardless of the type of damage, the following holds:

- If the country under consideration is small, meaning that the exposed sector has no market power on aggregate, it is optimal for the government to impose a uniform emission tax or to install a uniform system of tradable permits that makes no distinction between sheltered and exposed sectors.
- If the country under consideration is large, meaning that the exposed sector has some market power on aggregate, the first-best solution will be implemented by imposing export taxes, together with uniform emission taxes or a uniform tradable permits system, provided the individual firms in the exposed sector behave competitively.
- If the country under consideration is large, meaning that the exposed sector has some market power, the first-best solution will be implemented by imposing uniform emission taxes or a uniform tradable permits system, provided the individual firms in the exposed sector behave as larger players by themselves.

So, in all three cases, trade policy can either be implemented by assumption, or is just not needed. However, if trade policy is ruled out and if the country has market power on aggregate but none of the individual exposed firms has, the first-best optimum cannot be reached. We sketch an example where it is second-best optimal to confront the exposed sector with a stricter environmental policy than the sheltered one. Suppose there is just one exported commodity $(n = 1)$, and:

$$D(y_1 + y_2) = \tfrac{1}{2}(y_1 + y_2)^2 \tag{2.6}$$

$$U(c_1, c_2, c_3) = \ln c_1 + \ln c_2 + \ln c_3, \tag{2.7}$$

$$F_1(k_1, y_1) = k_1^{\alpha} y_1^{1-\alpha}, \tag{2.8}$$

$$F_2(k_2, y_2) = k_2^{\beta} y_2^{1-\beta}, \tag{2.9}$$

$$p_2(x_2) = x_2^{1/\varepsilon}, \tag{2.10}$$

where $0 < \alpha < 1$, $0 < \beta < 1$ and $\varepsilon < 0$ are constants. Since there are no trade tariffs, income of the representative consumer equals $p_1F_1 + p_2F_2$. Utility maximisation subject to the budget constraint implies $p_1c_1 = p_1F_1 = \tfrac{1}{3}[p_1F_1 + p_2F_2]$. Hence $p_2F_2 = 2p_1F_1$. Demand for capital follows from profit maximisation: $rk_1 = \alpha p_1 F_1$, $k_2 = 2\beta\bar{k}/(\alpha + 2\beta)$. Therefore, the respective capital inputs are independent of environmental policy parameters. Taking into account that $p_2c_2 = c_3 = \tfrac{1}{3}[p_1F_1 + p_2F_2] = \tfrac{1}{2}p_2F_2$ we have

$$W = U(c_1, c_2, c_3) - \delta D(y_1 + y_2) = \ln k_1^{\alpha} y_1^{1-\alpha} + \ln \tfrac{1}{2} k_2^{\beta} y_2^{1-\beta} + \ln(\tfrac{1}{2} k_2^{\beta} y_2^{1-\beta})^{1+1/\varepsilon} - \delta \tfrac{1}{2}(y_1 + y_2)^2 \quad (2.11)$$

For the case of local damage ($\delta = 1$) we have to maximise the expression in (2.11) with respect to y_1 and y_2. This yields

$$\frac{y_1}{y_2} = \frac{1-\alpha}{(1-\beta)(2+1/\varepsilon)} \quad (2.12)$$

For the case of global damage ($\delta = 0$) we have to maximise (2.11) with respect to y_1 and y_2 subject to $y_1 + y_2 = \bar{y}$. This yields:

$$y_1 = \frac{(1-\alpha)}{(1-\alpha)+(1-\beta)(2+1/\varepsilon)}\bar{y},\ y_2 = \frac{(1-\beta)(2+1/\varepsilon)}{(1-\alpha)+(1-\beta)(2+1/\varepsilon)}\bar{y}. \quad (2.13)$$

It follows from the factor demand equations, $\tau_1 y_1 = (1-\alpha)p_1 F_1$ and $\tau_2 y_2 = (1-\beta)p_2 F_2 = 2(1-\beta)p_1 F_1$, that in both cases:

$$\tau_2 = \frac{2}{2+1/\varepsilon}\tau_1.$$

The price elasticity of world demand is negative, implying that the exposed sector should be taxed more heavily than the sheltered sector. This is a novel result, for the class of large country models. Alternatively, a tradable permits system should be dual, allowing for a separate permits market in each sector. In an unconstrained tradable permits system the exposed sector would demand more emission permits and supply more in the world market than is optimal. In the case of more than one export sector, multiple separate permits markets should be established. This policy is generally more difficult to implement, and it will be intricate to ensure perfect competition as well. A policy design based on differentiated emission taxes is therefore likely to be more appropriate.

3 Cournot Oligopoly

The preceding section considered the issue of strategic environmental policy in the case where world markets are perfectly competitive or exhibit monopolistic features. In many instances, markets are however better described by an oligopolistic structure, giving rise to strategic interaction among firms as well as among governments.

In this section I consider a two-country world. Superscripts f and h refer to the foreign and home country, respectively. I consider the usual case of a single domestic producer ($n = 1$) of the exportable acting as a Cournot duopolist on the world market. The commodity produced in the exposed sector is not consumed domestically, implying $c_2 \equiv 0$. The inverse world demand function is written as

$p_2(x_2) = p_2(x_2^h + x_2^f)$. Profit maximisation in the exposed sector, taking foreign supply as given, yields:

$$[\frac{dp_2}{dx_2}x_2^h + p_2]F_{2k} = r, \tag{3.1}$$

$$[\frac{dp_2}{dx_2}x_2^h + p_2]F_{2y} = \tau_2. \tag{3.2}$$

To examine the welfare effects of a policy, totally differentiate the welfare function $W = U(c_1, c_3) - \delta D(y_1 + y_2)$ and make use of utility maximisation ($U_{c_1} = p_1 U_{c_3}$), profit maximisation and equations (2.3) – (2.5). This yields:

$$\begin{aligned} dW &= p_1 U_{c_3}[F_{1k}dk_1 + F_{1y}dy_1] + U_{c_3}[p_2 dx_2^h + x_2^h dp_2] - \delta D'[dy_1 + dy_2] \\ &= U_{c_3}[rdk_1 + \tau_1 dy_1] + U_{c_3}[p_2 dx_2^h + x_2^h \frac{dp_2}{dx_2}[dx_2^h + dx_2^f]] - \delta D'[dy_1 + dy_2] \\ &= [U_{c_3}\tau_1 - \delta D']dy_1 + [U_{c_3}\tau_2 - \delta D']dy_2 + U_{c_3}x_2^h \frac{dp_2}{dx_2}dx_2^f. \end{aligned} \tag{3.3}$$

Suppose, the home government takes foreign supply as given $(dx_2^f = 0)$. Then the policy recommendations follow straightforwardly. In the case of local pollution ($\delta = 1$) it is optimal to set emission taxes equal to marginal damage: $\tau_1 = \tau_2 = D'/U_{c_3}$ or to install an undifferentiated system of permit trading. In the case of global pollution ($\delta = 0$) it is optimal to have $\tau_1 = \tau_2$ as well, because $dy_1 + dy_2 = d\bar{y} = 0$. Alternatively, a system of uniform emission trading is in order.

However, things change if by manipulating the domestic emission tax rates foreign supply can be manipulated. The interesting case is therefore the case where the foreign country is a Stackelberg follower, and the home country is the Stackelberg leader.

Each firm is a Nash player on the world market and takes supply by its rival as given. I model the game at the level of the governments by assuming that the foreign government takes world market supply by the home firm as given, and subsequently determines its own optimal tax structure. So, for any given x_2^h, the foreign government sets uniform emission taxes that maximise social welfare. Therefore, the foreign government is the Stackelberg follower. These taxes also generate foreign supply written as $x_2^f(x_2^h)$. Subsequently, the home government takes the overall reaction function of the foreign country into account in determining its own optimal taxes. So, the home country is the Stackelberg leader. If the foreign reaction function is upward sloping, then, starting from a situation of undifferentiated emission taxes, the home government wants to decrease its own supply to the world market, implying a welfare increase, since

$$dW = U_{c_3} x_2^h \frac{\partial p_2}{\partial (x_2^h + x_2^f)} dx_2^f \tag{3.4}$$

The welfare increase is then accomplished by increasing the tax rate on the exposed sector. On the other hand, if the foreign reaction function is downward sloping, a decrease of the tax rate imposed on the exposed sector is in order.

Collie and De Meza (1986 and 2003) address the slopes of the reaction functions in a partial equilibrium model. If demand is isoelastic they show that the reaction functions in a Nash equilibrium are downward sloping if and only if demand is elastic. However, in a general equilibrium setting the sign may be reversed. This is illustrated by Mulatu et al. (2004) for the case of global pollution when the functional forms are given by (2.6)–(2.9) for both countries. I address the case of local damage here. This case is more difficult to analyse because total emissions are not fixed, but vary with the tax rate. I will therefore simplify even more, by assuming that $\alpha = \beta = ½$. Point of departure is a Nash equilibrium, in which both countries have undifferentiated emission taxes. The system of general equilibrium conditions *for the foreign country* is given by

$$rk_1 = \tau y_1 \tag{3.5}$$

$$rk_2 = \tau y_2 \tag{3.6}$$

$$p_1 = 2r^{1/2}\tau^{1/2} \tag{3.7}$$

$$p_2 = (x_2^h + x_2^f)^{1/\varepsilon}, \ \varepsilon < -1 \tag{3.8}$$

$$p_2 \left[1 + \frac{x_2^f}{\varepsilon [x_2^h + x_2^f]} \right] = 2r^{1/2}\tau^{1/2} \tag{3.9}$$

$$y_1 + y_2 = \frac{\tau}{p_1 k_1^{1/2} y_1^{1/2}} \tag{3.10}$$

$$k_1 + k_2 = \bar{k} \tag{3.11}$$

$$p_1 k_1^{1/2} y_1^{1/2} = p_2 k_2^{1/2} y_2^{1/2} = p_2 x_2^f \tag{3.12}$$

Equations (3.5) and (3.6) follow from cost minimisation. The right hand side of equation (3.7) is the unit cost function in the sheltered sector. Hence the equation follows from perfect competition in the sheltered sector. Equation (3.8) defines the market price for the exposed sector and (3.9) follows from profit maximisation in that sector. Equation (3.10) says that, in the Nash equilibrium from which the analysis starts, the tax rate τ equals marginal damage $U_{c_3} D' = \frac{y_1 + y_2}{c_3}$ where use has been made of the fact that $c_3 = p_1 c_1$. Equation (3.11) is just (2.4). Equation (3.11) follows from $p_2 x_2^f = c_3 = p_1 c_1 = \frac{1}{2}[p_1 F_1 + p_2 F_2] = \frac{1}{2}[p_1 F_1 + p_s x_2^f]$ and represents the condition that there is an equilibrium on the current account.

Define $z = x_2^h$, $x = x_2^f$, $v(z/x) = 1 + \frac{1}{\varepsilon[1 + z/x]}$. Eliminate k_1, k_2, p_1 and p_2 to obtain

$$(x+z)^{1/\varepsilon} v = 2r^{1/2}\tau^{1/2} \tag{3.13}$$

$$y_1 + y_2 = \frac{1}{2y_1} \tag{3.14}$$

$$\tau[y_1 + y_2] = r\bar{k} \tag{3.15}$$

$$(x+z)^{1/\varepsilon} x = 2\tau y_1 \tag{3.16}$$

$$x = \left(\frac{\tau}{r}\right)^{1/2} y_2 \tag{3.17}$$

By elimination of y_1, y_2, r and τ I arrive at

$$x^4 = \frac{1}{2}\bar{k}^2 \frac{v^4}{(1+v)^3} \tag{3.18}$$

Now suppose that z (supply by the home country) increases and x (supply by the foreign country) decreases. This implies that v increases, since $\varepsilon < 0$. The right hand side of (3.17) then increases, but this contradicts that the left-hand side increases too. Hence, the reaction function of the foreign country is increasing. Therefore, this establishes an example where a Stackelberg leader will find it optimal to tax emissions in the exposed sector more than emissions from the sheltered sector.

4 Conclusions

In this paper I have addressed the problem of preferential treatment of exposed sectors in environmental policy making. It has been demonstrated that in the large country case it is second-best optimal to tax the exposed sector more heavily than the sheltered one. This has also been demonstrated for a model of strategic environmental policy making with Cournot competition between firms. The policy recommendation from this analysis is clear: There is no case in general or a priori to use 'overly lax' taxation for the exposed sector. This does not mean that it is always suboptimal to do so. There might be instances where preferential treatment of the exposed sector is to be preferred. But policy makers should be aware of the trade-off between pollution damage and production, and the effect of environmental policy on the terms of trade.

References

Barrett, S. (1994), Strategic Environmental Policy and International Trade, *Journal of Public Economics* 54, 325-38.

Brander, J. and S. Taylor (1997), International Trade Between Consumer and Conservationist Countries, *Resource and Energy Economics* 19, 267-97.

Brander, J. and B. Spencer (1985), Export Subsidies and International Market Share Rivalry, *Journal of International Economics* 18, 83-100.

Collie, D. and D. de Meza (2003), Comparative Advantage and the Pursuit of Strategic Trade Policy, *Economics Letters* 81, 279-283.

Collie, D. and D. de Meza (1986), Inadequacies of the Strategic Rationale of Export Subsidies, *Economics Letters* 22, 369-373.

Copeland, B. and S. Taylor (2004), Trade, Growth and the Environment, *Journal of Economic Literature 42*, 7-71.

Elbers, C. and C. Withagen (2003), Environmental Policy and International Trade: Are Policy Differentials Optimal?, in: Marsiliani, L., M. Rauscher, and C. Withagen (Eds.), *Environmental Policy in an International Perspective*, Dordrecht, 173-191.

Elbers, C. and C. Withagen (2002a), Environmental Regulation and International Trade: A General Equilibrium Approach, in: List, J. and A. de Zeeuw (Eds.), *Recent Advances in Environmental Economics*, Cheltenham, 98-118.

Elbers, C. and C. Withagen (2002b), Environmental Policy and Bertrand Competition: A General Equilibrium Approach, in: Hommes, C., R. Ramer, and C. Withagen (Eds.), *Equilibrium, Markets and Dynamics*, Heidelberg, 183-195.

Gordon, R. and L. Bovenberg (1996), Why Is Capital so Immobile Internationally? Possible Explanations and Implications for Capital Income Taxation, *American Economic Review* 86, 1057-75.

Helpman, E. and P. Krugman (1985), *Market Structure and Foreign Trade,* Cambridge, MA.

Hoel, M. (1996), Should a Carbon Tax Be Differentiated Across Sectors?, *Journal of Public Economics* 59, 17-32.

Mulatu, A., R. Florax, and C. Withagen (2004), *Optimal Environmental Policy Differentials Under Emissions Constraints*, mimeo Free University Amsterdam.

Neary, P. (2000), *International Trade and the Environment*, University College Dublin (mimeo).

Rauscher, M. (1997), *International Trade, Factor Movements, and the Environment,* Oxford.

Rauscher, M. (1994), On Ecological Dumping, *Oxford Economic Papers* 46, 822-840.

Spencer, B. and A. Brander (1983), International R&D Rivalry and Industrial Strategy, *Review of Economic Studies* 50, 707-722.

Sturm, D. (2003), Trade and the Environment: A Survey of the Literature, in: Marsiliani, L., M. Rauscher, and C. Withagen (Eds.), *Environmental Policy in an International Perspective*, Dordrecht, 119-149.

Ulph, A. (1999), Environment and Trade, in: Folmer, H. and L. Gabel (Eds.), *Principles of Environmental Economics II,* Cheltenham, 479-528.

Ecological-Economic Models for Improving the Cost-Effectiveness of Biodiversity Conservation Policies

Frank Wätzold

UFZ-Centre for Environmental Research Leipzig-Halle GmbH, Department of Economics, Sociology and Law, P.O. Box 500136, 04301 Leipzig, Germany, frank.waetzold@ufz.de

Martin Drechsler, Volker Grimm

UFZ-Centre for Environmental Research Leipzig-Halle GmbH, Department of Ecological Modelling, P.O. Box 500136, 04301 Leipzig, Germany, martin.drechsler@ufz.de, volker.grimm@ufz.de

Jaroslav Myšiak

UFZ-Centre for Environmental Research Leipzig-Halle GmbH, Department of Ecological Modelling, P.O. Box 500136, 04301 Leipzig, Germany and Fondazione Eni Enrico Mattei, Palazzo Querini Stampalia, Campo S. Maria Formosa, Castello 5252, 30122 Venezia, Italy, jaroslav.mysiak@feem.it

Keywords. *Biodiversity, Conservation, Ecological-Economic Modelling, Cost-Effectiveness*

JEL. *Q20*

Abstract. Compared to other areas of environmental policy there has been little research addressing the cost-effectiveness of biodiversity conservation policies. One important reason is that meaningfully applying the traditional neoclassical analysis of environmental policy instruments to conservation issues often requires combining it with ecological knowledge. The paper gives an overview of existing research which analyses cost-effectiveness issues of conservation policies integrating ecological and economic knowledge in models and outlines some research opportunities where ecological-economic models could be usefully applied in the future. Furthermore, the paper reflects on the integration of ecological and economic knowledge in models with a particular focus on a topic that certainly complicates co-operation between ecologists and economists but has received little attention so far and needs to be better understood if integration is to be improved: different modelling cultures in economics and ecology.

1 Introduction

For many years there has been growing concern over the accelerated loss of biodiversity all over the world. The European Union has responded with a number of policy initiatives and by passing legislation. Prominent examples include the decision of the EU Heads of State at the Gothenburg Summit in 2001 to commit themselves to the goal of halting the loss of biodiversity in Europe by 2010, the Habitats Directive[1] and agri-environmental programmes targeted at biodiversity conservation. A substantial amount of research has addressed the issue of how the conservation goals expressed in the various policy initiatives and legislation can best be achieved. More recently, research has also tackled the issue of how acceptability of conservation policies can be raised, since the implementation of such policies has frequently encountered considerable levels of resistance. By contrast, very little research has dealt with the cost-effective design and implementation of conservation policies. This is surprising as conservation policies in Europe impose substantial opportunity costs on society in terms of foregone production and consumption (cf. Strijker et al., 2000, OECD, 2001). Research into the cost-effectiveness of environmental policies aimed at fields other than biodiversity also suggests that it may well be worthwhile analysing the potential for cost-savings. One prominent example is the US Environmental Protection Agency's policy to reduce SO_2-emissions by using allowance trading, which could save 700-800m USD annually compared to a command and control programme based on a uniform emission standard (Carlson et al., 2000).

Why has environmental economic research so far neglected the cost-effectiveness analysis of conservation policies? One important reason is doubtless that meaningfully applying the traditional neoclassical analysis of environmental policy instruments to conservation issues often requires combining it with sound ecological knowledge. For many important issues central to the economic analysis of policy instruments, the necessary thorough understanding of the ecological effects of conservation measures can only be gained from ecologists. However, although interdisciplinarity has become a buzz word, genuinely integrated research between economists and ecologists is still rare. This is somewhat surprising as both disciplines share some common ground.

1. They address the similar question of how to deal with scarcity. Plant and animal species try to maximise their reproductive success in the face of limited food resources while humans try to maximise their wants under a budget constraint (Settle et al., 2002).
2. Both disciplines use mathematical models which ought to facilitate communication and the integration of knowledge between them.
3. Economists and ecologists both aim to give decision support to policy makers and conservation managers.

Very recently, the opportunities and potential benefits of co-operation between these two disciplines have been increasingly recognised, and a small but growing

[1] Council Directive 92/43/EEC of 21 May 1992 on the conservation of natural habitats and of wild fauna and flora.

body of literature has emerged which analyses cost-effectiveness issues of biodiversity conservation policies integrating ecological and economic knowledge in models (referred to as ecological-economic models hereafter).

The aim of this paper is twofold. Based on an analysis of selected challenges of European biodiversity conservation policy its first aim is to provide an overview of the literature on ecological-economic models as far as they are relevant to the two main policy instruments in Europe[2] (viz compensation payments for conservation measures and reserves) and to outline some research opportunities where ecological-economic models could be usefully applied in the future to support conservation policies. However, for ecological-economic modelling to play an important role in the future a better understanding of the barriers that have hindered its development so far is required. Therefore, the second aim of the paper is to reflect on the integration of ecological and economic knowledge in models and analysis concentrating in particular on why this integration has not taken place on a broad scale. The focus will be on a topic that certainly complicates co-operation between ecologists and economists but has received little attention so far and needs to be better understood if integration is to be improved: different modelling cultures in economics and ecology. While our analysis of the different modelling cultures focuses on research related to biodiversity conservation, the results may also be relevant to other fields such as climate and water policy where co-operation between economists and natural scientists seems to be potentially beneficial.

The paper is structured as follows: Section 2 provides some background information about European biodiversity conservation policy while Section 3 gives an overview of existing ecological-economic models relevant to the cost-effectiveness of this policy. This provides the basis for an analysis of future policy challenges and resulting research requirements in Section 4. Section 5 discusses problems of integrated research focusing on differences between modelling traditions in economics and ecology.

2 European Biodiversity Conservation Policy[3]

The purpose of this section is to provide some background information about European biodiversity conservation policy. It starts by outlining the threats to biodiversity which have led to the policy responses of compensation payments and reserves. Then, the main policy developments at the EU level related to these instruments are outlined and the challenges that these two instruments face in terms of their cost-effective design are briefly considered.

---

2 An example of research that integrates ecological and economic knowledge but is not directly relevant to European conservation policy is Pethig and Tschirrhart (2001).

3 This section is based on Wätzold and Schwerdtner (2005).

2.1 Threats to Biodiversity

Most parts of Europe have been transformed by humans into what is often called cultural landscapes. This process began a few thousand years ago when humans started to clear the landscape for farming. In the Middle Ages, the area used for agricultural production was larger than it is today, and agricultural production was carried out in many different ways (three-field crop rotation, monasterial horticulture, fish farming, various forms of animal husbandry, etc.). This development transformed a landscape originally largely covered with forests into a highly diversified structured landscape with the consequence that by the 19th century biological diversity in terms of habitat types and the number of species had substantially increased (cf. Cox et al., 1973, Hampicke, 1991, Kaule, 1996).

This trend was completely reversed during the course of the 20th century, when technological progress led to a change in agricultural production methods which transformed most of the diverse cultural landscapes into uniform agricultural landscapes. Intensive use of fertiliser and pesticides, the levelling of water levels and the destruction of natural and man-made landscape structures such as wet sinks, hedges and stone walls led to the destruction of many habitats, a process which is still ongoing (Hampicke, 1991). Halting this destruction is essential for European biodiversity. Given the above mentioned development agricultural land use has a key influence on biodiversity in Europe, and important parts of the biodiversity-rich land in the EU continue to depend on low-intensity farming (Wiseman and Hopkins, 2001, Howe and Perkins, 2001). In other words, in order for a high number of endangered species to be conserved, farmers must regularly carry out certain traditional and biodiversity-friendly land-use practices to ensure the continuing existence of habitats necessary for the survival of these species.

There are, however, many other endangered habitats and species that need reserves for their protection where human influence is limited. The extent of such limitations depends on the habitat or species to be conserved. An example of a species that requires undisturbed forest patches to breed is the black stork (*Ciconia niger*), while an example of a habitat that is negatively affected by human disturbance is raised bog. However, it should be noted that for the conservation of many endangered habitats and species, designating reserves is not sufficient by itself but has to be complemented by certain land-use measures. Thus, while in actual conservation management, the two policy options of designing reserves and carrying out biodiversity-enhancing land-use measures often complement each other, a clear distinction is drawn between them in the reminder of this paper for the sake of analytical clarity.

2.2 Policy Responses from the EU

Altering agricultural land-use for the benefit of biodiversity conservation is usually costly due to foregone agricultural production. Since the political will often exists that farmers should not be forced to make their land-use practices more conducive to biodiversity conservation, they have to be compensated for doing so

(Bromley and Hodge, 1990, Hanley et al., 1998). Furthermore, experience with the USA Endangered Species Act has shown that forcing owners of land with endangered species to undertake conservation measures may be counterproductive. It provides landowners with an incentive to undertake measures to eliminate these species on their land in order to avoid the burden of conservation costs rather than to undertake measures to conserve the species (Brown and Shogren, 1998, Innes et al., 1998). To induce farmers to carry out their production in a more environmentally sensitive way, the EU has developed 'agri-environmental schemes' in which farmers are paid to adapt the management of (parts of) their farms to benefit biodiversity, the environment or the landscape while allowing a wide range of measures depending on the specific aim and the country/region (cf. Kleijn et al., 2001). Agri-environmental schemes have been developed under Regulations 2078/92[4] and 1257/99[5] and are mostly voluntary management agreements taking the form of state-farmer contracts (Van Huyelenbroek and Whitby, 1999).

The main important instruments to protect Europe's natural habitats and endangered species are the Birds Directive[6] and the Habitats Directive. The Birds Directive focuses solely on the protection of birds and their natural habitats, and calls for the establishment of protected areas to ensure their conservation. The Habitats Directive aims to protect European natural habitats and endangered species as a whole. Taken together, the two directives are designed to create a coherent network of protected areas in Europe (NATURA 2000). Both directives had to be transposed into national law and implemented by each member state. The criteria for the selection of protected areas are based solely on ecological aspects, though measures taken pursuant to these Directives must take into account economic, social and cultural requirements.

2.3 Cost-Effectiveness of Conservation Policies

One important criterion that should be taken into account when implementing conservation policies such as NATURA 2000 and agri-environmental schemes is cost-effectiveness. Cost-effectiveness requires compensation payments for conservation measures to be designed such that the combination of individual conservation measures is chosen which achieves a given conservation aim (for example ensuring a certain survival probability of an endangered species) at least cost. Similarly, cost-effectiveness requires the selection of individual areas and their designation as reserves such that for a given conservation aim the costs are mini-

4 Regulation (EEC) No 2078/92 of 30 June 1992 on agricultural production methods compatible with the requirements of the protection of the environment and the maintenance of the countryside.

5 Regulation (EC) 1257/1999 of 17 May 1999 on support for rural development from the European Agricultural Guidance and Guarantee Fund (EAGGF) and amending and repealing certain Regulations.

6 Council Directive 79/409/EEC of 2 April 1979 on the conservation of wild birds.

mised.[7] [8] The reason why the costs of achieving a certain conservation aim may vary is that both costs and benefits may be subject to spatial and temporal variations. The cost of conservation measures and of areas to be designated as reserves may differ in space, because opportunity costs do (e.g. due to the spatial variation of soil quality for agriculture). Spatial differentiation of (ecological) benefits may be caused by variations in habitat quality (e.g. food abundance or the existence of safe nesting sites) for the species concerned. Costs may vary over time due to changing opportunity costs of foregone economic development. Variations in benefits arise if the ecological effects of a conservation measure depend on exactly when the measure is carried out (e.g. the fauna and flora of a mowed meadow depend strongly on the exact mowing date).

The knowledge of the ecological effects of conservation measures and reserve designation needed by economists to meaningfully make recommendations regarding the cost-effectiveness of conservation policies requires the economic analysis of environmental policy instruments to be combined with ecology. Mathematical models (ecological-economic models) are a promising tool for this integration.

3 Ecological-Economic Models to Analyse the Cost-Effectiveness of Conservation Policies

In this section we provide an overview of ecological-economic models developed to analyse the cost-effectiveness of conservation policies relevant to a European context. To our knowledge, only a few ecological-economic models relevant for this purpose exist. We distinguish between two types of models: conceptual models aimed at generating general insights into the interplay between ecological and economic systems and the importance of the various parameters that determine the cost-effectiveness of conservation policies and applied models developed for specific situations which are more directly relevant to the implementation of particular conservation policies.

7 Given the paper's focus on ecological-economic models we are interested here only in the 'production costs' of biodiversity. A more comprehensive definition of cost-effectiveness may also take into account monitoring, enforcement and decision making costs (see Birner and Wittmer, 2004 and Wätzold and Schwerdtner, 2005).

8 An equivalent definition of cost-effectiveness is that for given costs a conservation aim is maximised. Which definition is appropriate depends on the political circumstances. For example, in a situation where a conservation aim is given and we are interested in the least cost option to achieve this goal, the definition in the main text is appropriate.

3.1 Conceptual Models

Research addressing the cost-effective allocation of conservation measures and reserves in space and over time on a conceptual level integrates ecology into the economic analysis in a variety of ways: (1) it takes up ideas and concepts developed in ecology to build an ecological benefit function which then is integrated into an economic model; (2) is the same as (1) with the exception that the benefit function is explicitly deduced from ecological theory or from ecological modelling; or (3) it integrates economic parameters into an approach developed in ecology for conservation management.

One prominent example of the first approach is the research by Wu and Bogess (1999) who adopt the idea of ecological thresholds (caused by cumulative effects) from ecology and analyse how an ecological benefit function that takes thresholds into account influences the spatial allocation of conservation funds[9]. One important result of their analysis is that given the existence of thresholds and a limited budget, the optimum approach is to concentrate funds in one region in order to exceed the threshold instead of allocating funds evenly among different regions.

The second approach is chosen by Drechsler and Wätzold (2001) who derive the ecological benefit function from general quantitative ecological models (e.g. for the relationship between species survival and habitat area depending on species-specific parameters). In a model with two regions they systematically examine how the budget size, the shapes of the cost functions and the shapes of the benefit functions affect the cost-effective spatial allocation of a conservation fund. Their findings include that if in both regions the benefit function increases with habitat area slightly more than proportionally and if marginal costs only rise slowly, a small increase in conservation funds may require a significant reallocation of funds between the two regions. The reason is that if the total area that can be used for conservation is below a certain threshold, it should be allocated to the region with the larger initial amount of habitat area, but as soon as one additional unit of land can be transformed into habitat, even allocation between the two regions becomes cost-effective.

In an extension of their model, Wätzold and Drechsler (2002) examine the efficiency losses that arise if the criterion of cost-effectiveness requires spatially heterogeneous compensation payments but other aspects such as equity concerns or legal barriers prevent a differentiation. Although the question of efficiency losses of spatially uniform environmental policy instruments had been addressed previously by Kolstad (1987) and Babcock et al. (1997), the applicability of this research to biodiversity conservation is limited as their benefit functions cover only a fraction of the possible benefit functions relevant to biodiversity conservation. Wätzold and Drechsler examine efficiency losses of uniform compensation payments for different types of cost and benefit functions and show that such losses can vary from 0 to almost 100%.

---

9 Although Wu and Bogess (1999) do not explicitly address compensation payments, their research is still relevant for this instrument as it improves our understanding of the relevant factors that determine the spatial allocation of conservation measures.

Ando et al. (1998) integrate economic costs into an ecological approach to select reserve sites and thus choose the third above-mentioned way of integrating ecological and economic knowledge. A typical approach in ecology of selecting reserves is to cover the maximum number of species given a constraint on the total number of sites that can be included. Implicit in this selection procedure is the assumption that establishing a reserve at each potential reserve site costs the same. Taking into account costs Ando et al. applied a budget-constrained reserve selection approach where a set of selected sites is only a feasible reserve system if the sum of the costs of the selected sites (average land value by county for the United States was used as cost indicator) is less than or equal to the conservation budget. Ando et al. compared the costs of covering the same number of species under both the budget-constrained and the site-constrained approaches and found that the costs of achieving a given level of species coverage were far lower with the budget-constrained approach.

Conceptual research on the temporal aspects of the cost-effective design of conservation policies has received less attention than research on their spatial aspects. Drechsler and Wätzold (2003) analyse a situation where the survival of an endangered species depends on carrying out certain types of conservation measures on a regular basis, yet due to uncertain political commitment, the possibility of an economic downturn or fluctuating donations to NGOs active in conservation management, the periodical availability of a budget to compensate landowners for such measures cannot be guaranteed. An option to insure against future underfunding is to save money for conservation in later periods. Given the aim of maximising the long-term survival of an endangered species, it has to be decided in each period whether the money available should be spent now or saved for future use. The results indicate that the optimum course of action is to spend the same amount of money in each period if possible. This requires a certain amount of precautionary saving to insure against future underfunding. Similar to the other research mentioned by these authors, the ecological benefit function, i.e. the relationship between the population extinction risk and conservation measure in a particular period, is derived from an ecological model.

The conceptual ecological-economic models described provide valuable insights into the interaction of ecological and economic factors relevant to the cost-effectiveness of conservation policies and the relative importance of the various parameters on an abstract level. However, providing decision support for actual conservation policies requires the development of more applied models.

3.2 Applied Models

One of the most challenging questions to be addressed when developing applied ecological-economic models to support conservation policies is how to generate and integrate quantitative knowledge of the relevant economic and ecological parameters. Oglethorpe and Sanderson (1999) combine an ecological and an economic model to assess the conservation benefits and costs of various agri-environmental policies. The ecological model determines the effect of changes in agricultural management on various plant communities depending on site-specific characteristics such as soil type, rainfall, gradient and altitude, while the economic model is able to calculate the costs of the management changes for farmers. Although the combined ecologic-economic model illustrates how a simultaneous evaluation of costs and benefits of conservation measures can be achieved, it does not address the issue of how to allocate conservation measures cost-effectively.

Hanley et al. (1998) go one step further in this direction by calculating compensation payments to protect Scottish heather moorland from degeneration into grassland through overgrazing by sheep. For this ecosystem an ecological model predicts the site-specific (depending for instance on altitude) amount of vegetation produced as well as the amount of biomass taken up by the sheep. For a selection of farms in the Shetland Islands this is used to determine the site-specific maximum stocking rate that will prevent overgrazing and is thus compatible with moorland conservation. To calculate the costs of the necessary stocking rate reductions on a farm-by-farm basis and hence the necessary compensation payments, a linear programming model is constructed. One result of the analysis is that the necessary compensation payments significantly differ from one farm to the next, suggesting that the spatial differentiation of compensation payments may be important in terms of cost-effectiveness.

To quantitatively determine cost-effective compensation payments for species protection, Johst et al. (2002) develop a numerical optimisation procedure. How this procedure functions is illustrated through the development of a compensation payment scheme to protect the white stork (*Ciconia ciconia*). The effects of conservation measures (mowing of meadows at certain pre-specified dates) on the stork population are calculated with an ecological simulation model and the costs are assessed via a survey of farmers. The quantitative data on costs and benefits are used as input parameters in the optimisation procedure, which calculates the cost-effective payments (differentiated in space and over time) in a hypothetical landscape for a range of conservation budgets.

To increase the practical applicability of the described approach, considering a conservation problem in a real landscape and replacing the economic survey by a model-based cost assessment are desirable. Drechsler et al. (2004) develop a landscape-based ecological-economic model for the conservation of an endangered butterfly species of the genus Maculinea near the town of Landau in the Rhine Valley, Germany. The butterfly resides on meadows whose suitability for them depends on the mowing regime (characterised by the frequency of mowing and the mowing week). A total of 112 different mowing regimes are considered and their effect on the *Maculinea* population assessed via an ecological simulation model. The costs of each mowing regime per meadow are calculated with a linear programming model. The required landscape information is gathered through expert interviews and satellite images and stored in a Geographic Information System (GIS). The model is able to determine the cost-effective mowing regime and the corresponding compensation payment as a function of the available conservation budget.

Wu and Skelton-Groth (2002) use a case study to illustrate the extent to which conservation funds may be misallocated when threshold effects are ignored. Their example is investment in riparian vegetation that reduces the stream temperature necessary for salmon restoration in the Pacific Northwest. They find that significant environmental benefits may be lost if conservation funds are distributed equally and not primarily directed at those streams where thresholds exist, i.e. where a small reduction in the stream temperatures is enough to produce a suitable habitat for the cold-water fish targeted.

The conceptual framework developed by Ando et al. (1998) to integrate economic and ecological aspects in the selection of reserves was applied by Polasky et al. (2001) to the problem of terrestrial vertebrate conservation in Oregon, United States. Focusing on one single state rather than on a nationwide level enables more detailed data to be gathered and patterns to be analysed at a finer geographic scale, which allows a more realistic picture of the possible cost-savings to be obtained than with the approach proposed by Ando et al. (1998). The results support the notion that significant cost-savings can be achieved by applying the budget-constraint approach rather than the site-constraint approach. For example, for a certain range of species coverage cost savings of up to 90% may be achieved with the budget-constraint approach compared to the site-constraint approach.

4 Selected Policy Challenges and Future Research

The research described in Section 3 has significantly improved our understanding of how the cost-effectiveness of compensation payments and reserves can be enhanced in various respects. However, a number of important issues and challenges have not been addressed. In the following we look at a selection of such issues and challenges that arise from (I) developments in environmental policy, (II) economic development and (III) scientific research.

1. Over the last decade, the development and implementation of a growing amount of environmental policies can be observed. An important challenge for policy making and thus research arises through the fact that these policies interact, complement and sometimes contradict each other (Loske, 2004). This development is also relevant for biodiversity conservation and here, particularly to the instrument of compensation payments. So far, research on the cost-effectiveness of compensation payments has mostly been concerned with the conservation of a single or two species on a regional scale. This was a useful initial step to develop an understanding of how ecological and economic knowledge can be combined to analyse the cost-effectiveness of compensation payments. However, conservation policies in one region are rarely limited to the conservation of an individual species but are aimed to protect many different species and/or habitats. Furthermore, in the context of agriculture, many compensation payment schemes directed at environmental targets other than biodiversity exist, that nevertheless have a positive or negative effect on biodiversity. Examples include policies to support the production of plants for biofuel and policies to improve the quality of groundwater through a reduction in fertilizers and pesticides. So far, our knowledge about the cost-effectiveness of

compensation payments to conserve biodiversity in the context of policy instruments targeted at other environmental goals but affecting biodiversity is very limited and needs to be improved.
2. One important policy challenge with respect to the designation of reserves is that in a dynamic world with spatially heterogeneous economic development the opportunity costs of reserves may change over time. This implies that a reserve site selection that was cost-effective at one point in time may not necessarily be cost-effective later on. It would be interesting to explore whether a mechanism such as a tradable habitat system can be found that enables the potential cost-savings that arise in a dynamic world as the opportunity costs of reserves change to be exploited. Obviously, such research can only be carried out in collaboration with ecologists, as only ecologists can identify the conditions that ensure that reserves are of equal value in terms of conservation and can thus be traded. A starting-point for fruitful research may be the concept of dynamic ecological networks, which has been developed in ecology. Ecological networks are a spatially arranged set of ecosystems of the same type which are linked within a spatially coherent system. The key feature of the networks is that they can have different spatial configurations and still be of the same value for conservation (Opdam et al., 2004). This allows flexibility in terms of the spatial structure and, therefore, a potential for trading exists.
3. Further need for future research may come not from political and economic developments but from innovations in ecological research. The essential element that led to improvements in understanding cost-effectiveness issues of conservation policies was the integration of neoclassical analysis of policy instruments with state-of-the-art ecological knowledge. This has only been done to a limited extent so far, and continuing this approach may generate new knowledge which will enable us to further improve our understanding of the cost-effectiveness of conservation policies. For instance, the metapopulation concept is extensively discussed in ecology (see e.g. Hanski, 1999) but we know little how it affects the cost-effectiveness of conservation policies. It remains to be explored which other new findings in ecology ought to be integrated in the economic analysis of policy instruments to enhance our understanding of the cost-effectiveness of conservation policies. However, such integration can only take place on a broader scale, if we know what barriers exist for the integration of ecological and economic knowledge in models.

5 Different Modelling Cultures as a Barrier for Ecological-Economic Modelling

In discussions about the integration of research from the natural and social sciences, a number of reasons have been listed that make such integration difficult. They include the lack of publication opportunities for integrated research and limited career opportunities for those involved in integrated research (c.f. Klepper, 2004). However, one reason that complicates co-operation between ecologists and economists has so far received little attention: different modelling cultures in economics and ecology. This reason is analysed in more detail below.

5.1 Different Modelling Cultures in Economics and Ecology

Economics and ecology use mathematical models as a tool for their analysis. At first glance, this would appear to facilitate the integration of knowledge from both disciplines. However, while some collaborative research has clearly been fruitful, other researchers report significant problems of communication and difficulties in finding a common approach when it comes to co-operating with colleagues from the other discipline. One important reason behind these difficulties seems to be different modelling cultures. When economists talk about a 'model' they generally have something else in mind than ecologists. Of course, some overlaps exist between modelling traditions in economics and ecology, and it should not be forgotten that within each discipline there are also often different perceptions of modelling. However, as far as the majority of modellers and models are concerned, there seem to be differences which allow a distinction between the 'typical' modelling approaches of the two disciplines. These differences concern (1) the way the models are formulated and solved; and (2) different consideration of real world phenomena such as time, space and uncertainty.

5.2 Analysing the Differences

To better understand these differences, we carried out a literature survey and compared predominantly economic and predominantly ecological models as well as models that integrate knowledge from economics and ecology (ecological-economic models).[10] In ecology, the following four leading conservation journals were evaluated: *Biological Conservation*, *Conservation Biology*, *Ecological Applications*, and *Journal of Applied Ecology*.[11] From the years 1998-2003, all papers with the words 'model' or 'model(l)ing' in either the title, abstract or key word list were filtered. From the resulting approximately 800 papers, 30 were selected randomly for detailed evaluation. Papers presenting descriptive, statistical models were not selected because similarities in statistical methods might mask differences between ecological and economical models. Of the economics journals *Ecological Economics*[12], *Environmental and Resource Economics*, *Journal of Environmental Economics and Management*, and *Land Economics* were chosen.

---

10 A comprehensive description of the evaluation can be found in Drechsler et al. (2004).

11 Please note that models in applied and theoretical ecology are different and that we have chosen journals that focus on applied ecology.

12 *Ecological Economics* considers itself to be a transdisciplinary journal rather than an economic one. It was nevertheless chosen because it contains a large number of purely economic models related to biodiversity conservation.

From the years 1998-2003, all papers quoting biodiversity, conservation, nature protection or species in the abstract or title and applying a mathematical modelling approach were selected. A total of 162 articles were found. As with the ecology journals, 30 were selected at random, with statistical and econometric models being ignored. All 60 selected papers were evaluated according to criteria which are explained below. The criteria were chosen to identify the disciplinary approach of the models and to capture essential differences in their structure, design and orientation.

With respect to disciplinary approach, we distinguish three different types: predominantly ecological, predominantly economic, and ecological-economic. The problem with this classification is that it is difficult to draw a line between a 'disciplinary' model and an 'ecological-economic' model. A certain number of the papers reviewed are clearly dominated by one discipline but contain some elements from the other (e.g. an ecological paper which contains a cost analysis as a sub-component of an otherwise ecological model). However, classifying such a model as 'ecological-economic' would be inappropriate as knowledge from the non-dominant discipline is only taken into account to a very limited extent. Instead of a clear distinction between disciplinary and ecological-economic models, there is evidently a continuum and an arbitrary line has to be drawn somewhere. Bearing this in mind, we chose a two step approach to distinguish between the different types of models. In the first step, we differentiated between purely disciplinary models which do not contain any knowledge from the other discipline and other models. In the second step, we screened the papers containing models of the latter type and classified those as ecological-economic when references were made to journals from both disciplines. We excluded references to general journals such as Science or Nature, as well as to journals which are mixed by their very nature such as Ecological Economics. According to these criteria our sample consists of 30 ecological, 12 economic and 18 ecological-economic models.

5.3 Model Formulation, Solution and Complexity

One important difference between ecological and economic approaches to modelling may be the way the model is formulated and how the model results are obtained. We make the following distinctions: The formulation may be analytical (the model is completely described by equations), or algorithmic (flow charts or if-then rules are needed to describe the model). The results of analytical models are obtained either analytically (e.g. by solving equations for equilibrium solutions), numerically (e.g. by determining eigenvalues in a matrix model), or through simulation (e.g. by simulating the dynamics of a population time step by time step); algorithmic models are always run on a computer, i.e. they are solved through simulation. Numerical methods are distinguished from simulations by the fact that simulations try to mimic a real process whereas numerical methods approximate analytical solutions of analytical models.

Fig. 1. Percentage of reviewed economic and ecological papers that have an analytical or algorithmic formulation (a) and are solved analytically, numerically, or via simulation (b)

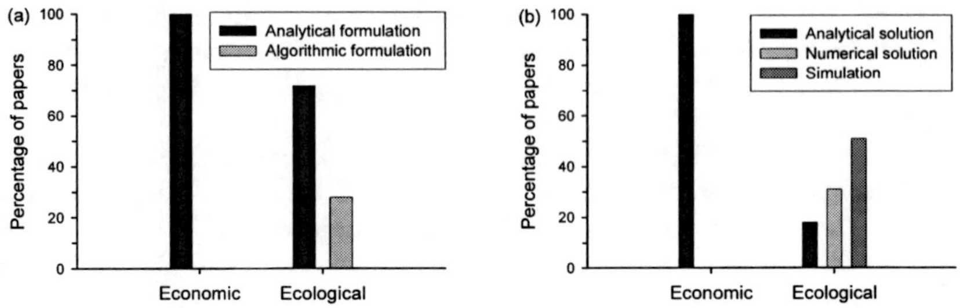

Fig. 1 shows the approach of the two disciplines in formulating and solving models. Whereas all economic models in our sample are formulated analytically, a significant proportion (28%) of the ecological models is formulated algorithmically. This means that there is some common ground between ecology and economics in the form of analytical modelling, but that one approach – algorithmic modelling – that is quite common in one discipline seems to be non-existent in the other. Even larger differences exist regarding the solution techniques applied in the two disciplines. The papers sampled with the economic models are solved exclusively analytically, whereas only a comparatively small fraction of the ecological models (18%) choose this approach. The large majority of the ecological models are solved either numerically (31%) or through simulation (51%).

The reason for the use of algorithmic models in ecology may be that ecological processes can often be more conveniently modelled and communicated by rules rather than mathematical equations. The high proportion of simulations in ecological models may be explained by the explicit consideration of stochasticity and spatial location in ecological models (see below). These are crucial elements in the understanding of ecological processes and usually make a model analytically intractable, such that ecologists have to refer to simulation. An alternative explanation for the different types of model formulation and solution might be that economic models tend to be of a general nature (see below), designed to answer questions in a general manner, while ecological models tend to be more specific which again makes models analytically intractable. Altogether, be it attributable to a difference between the systems studied or a difference in the modelling purpose, there are significant differences in how models are formulated and solved between the two disciplines of ecology and economics.

Closely related to how the models are formulated and solved is the level of generality that the models aim at. We distinguish between models that try to explain general phenomena and models designed for specific situations. We classify the models by the data used in them: General models may be completely hypothetical or use observations and data to exclude unrealistic settings, but the models are not parameterised for specific cases; by contrast, specific models use data related to specific situations. Both of these criteria are evaluated independently, because some papers include both, a general model and an application of it to a specific situation.

Fig. 2. Percentage of reviewed economic, ecological and mixed (i.e. ecological-economic) models that address general or specific problems. Note that a model may address both kinds of problems

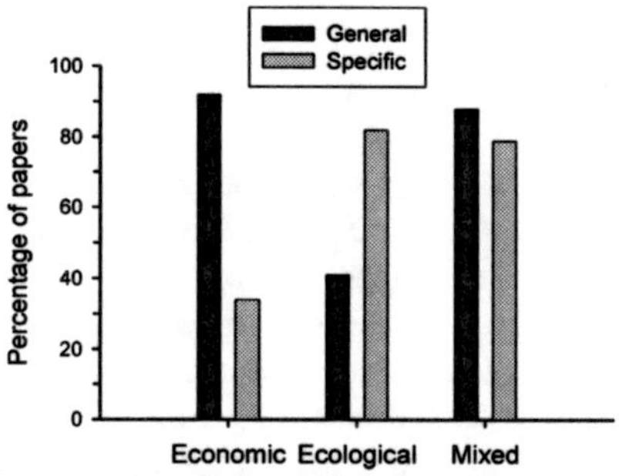

Models that are formulated and solved analytically usually imply a rather general approach. The emphasis on such models in economics is therefore reflected by the fact that nearly all economic models (92%) are of a general nature (**Fig. 2**). However, approximately one third of the models (34%) are also specific. Here, some real world data are usually inserted in the model and the model is used to explain, predict or analyse a certain empirical phenomenon. By contrast, in ecology only 41% are general models, whereas a large majority (82%) have a specific character. A large majority of ecological-economic models have a general (88%) but a large majority have also a specific character (79%). Once again, we see that the prevalent modelling approach is different in economics and ecology.

Table 1. Mean and standard deviation of parameters in different model types

Model Type	Mean	Standard Deviation
Ecological	16.5	16.2
Economic	8.8	2.1
Ecological-Economic	11.9	7.7

Modelling approaches in economics and ecology may differ in terms of the model's complexity. An obvious indicator of model complexity is the number of parameters. A parameter may be defined as a number mediating the relationship between state variables. Parameters are constant during the run of a model or for the analysis of a certain model scenario. We found that the number of parameters is on average higher in ecological (16.5) than in ecological-economic (11.9) and economic (8.8) models (**Table 1**).

The main reason for the difference between ecological and economic models regarding the mean number of parameters is that the sample contains some very complex ecological models with a huge number of parameters (8 out of the 30 ecological models have more than 30 parameters and 6 more than 50 parameters, whereas none of the economic models has more than 15 parameters). But as a significant proportion of the ecological models have a relatively small number of parameters (14 ecological models have no more than 10 parameters) it would be wrong to conclude that the complexity of ecological and economic models is different from the outset. Instead, a certain class of complex models with a high number of parameters is used in ecology which is not common in economics.

5.4 Modelling Uncertainty, Time and Space

Often, modelling faces the challenge of having to deal with uncertainties of various types. These can be modelled and considered in a number of ways. While a detailed review and comparison of these approaches is beyond the scope of the present paper, differences between the two disciplines already emerge when we look at whether uncertainty is taken into account at all. This is the case for 50% of the economic models sampled. By contrast, in a clear majority of ecological-economic models (66%) and in nearly all ecological models (97%) uncertainty is considered explicitly. Besides uncertainty, the consideration of time and space are decisive characteristics of a model.

We differentiate between dynamic and static models. In a dynamic model, time is explicitly introduced as a variable, whereas this is not the case in a static model. In order to classify a model as a dynamic model the state variable(s) has/have to be calculated for different points in time in a single model run. Half of the economic models (50%) are static. In all the other models dynamic aspects are taken into account using abstract time scales such as periods. A different picture emerges when the ecological models are considered with 10% of these models being static and 90% dynamic. Only 6% of the ecological models use an abstract time scale but 84% a physical one (e.g. days, years).

We distinguish between three classes of models where space is taken into account to varying degrees. For a model to be considered as 'spatially explicit', state variables must exist which explicitly refer to space, i.e. coordinates in the landscape. This includes topological relations (e.g. neighbourhood), distances and distance-dependent interactions between state variables at different locations being explicitly taken into account. Typical examples include cellular automata with for example next neighbour interaction. In a 'spatially differentiated' model, parameters differ between patches of land. However, the location of the patches is not considered. Examples include economic models with two or more regions, whose locations are irrelevant in the analysis, and in particular, whose interactions are not distance-dependent. Models that do not consider space explicitly belong to the third category. Most of the economic models (83%) do not explicitly consider space. If space is considered, only spatially differentiated models are applied. By contrast, a significant share of ecological models (34%) is spatially explicit. A smaller percentage is spatially differentiated (13%) while 53% of the models do not explicitly consider spatial aspects. Again we observe that although some overlap exists between economic and ecological modelling approaches, in ecology there is a certain approach which is obviously not common in economics.

To sum up, while some common ground exists significant differences are to be observed in the modelling approaches of the two disciplines of economics and ecology. Generally speaking, economic models tend to be general and are formulated and solved analytically whereas ecological models tend to be specific and, – while the majority of models are formulated analytically – a significant minority is formulated algorithmically. In addition, the ecological models that are formulated analytically are largely solved numerically and through simulation. Another important difference between the two disciplines is that ecological models explicitly take into account time, uncertainty and space to a much larger extent than economic models. The way time and space are taken into account is also different in economic and ecological models. In contrast to economic models, ecological models use a physical time scale more often than an abstract time scale. Moreover, ecological models are often spatially explicit, an approach which does not exist in the economic models of our sample. The differences between ecological and economic models found in the literature survey may well explain why it is often difficult for economists and ecologists to communicate and co-operate. It remains a task for further research to explain why these differences exist and the extent to which they can be overcome with a view to further stimulating ecological-economic modelling.

6 Summary

The first aim of this paper was to provide an overview of the state-of-the art of ecological-economic modelling regarding the cost-effectiveness of biodiversity conservation policy and to outline some research opportunities relevant to European conservation policy where ecological-economic modelling may be usefully applied in the future. We found that ecological-economic modelling has already significantly improved our knowledge about the cost-effectiveness of compensation payments for conservation measures and reserves as the two main instruments of European biodiversity policy. Other useful applications of ecological-economic models could concern analysing the cost-effectiveness of compensation payments to conserve biodiversity in the context of policy instruments targeted at other environmental goals but affecting biodiversity, and the development of policy instruments that are able to ensure the cost-effectiveness of reserves in a dynamic environment. Additional challenges for the application of ecologic-economic models may come from innovations inside ecology which could improve our understanding of the cost-effectiveness of conservation policies if they are integrated in the economic analysis of policy instruments. The second aim of the paper was to reflect on the integration of ecological and economic knowledge in models with a particular focus on different modelling cultures in economics and ecology. We found that economic and ecological models do indeed differ in important respects implying that more research is needed to understand why these differences exist and what can be done to overcome them.

References

Ando, A., J. Camm, S. Polasky, and A. Solow (1998), Species Distribution, Land Values and Efficient Conservation, *Science* 279, 2126-2128.

Babcock, B.A., P.G. Lakshminarayan, J. Wu, and D. Zilberman (1997), Targeting Tools for the Purchase of Environmental Amenities, *Land Economics* 73, 325-339.

Birner, R. and H. Wittmer (2004), On the "Efficient Boundaries of the State" – The Contribution of Transaction Costs Economics to the Analysis of Decentralization and Devolution in Natural Resource Management, *Environment and Planning C: Government and Policy*, 22/5, 667-685.

Bromley, D.W. and I. Hodge (1990), Private Property Rights and Presumptive Policy Entitlements: Reconsidering the Premises of Rural Policy, *European Review of Agricultural Economics* 17, 197-214.

Brown, G.M. Jr. and J.F. Shogren (1998), Economics of the Endangered Species Act, *The Journal of Economic Perspectives* 12, 3-20.

Carlson, C., D. Burtraw, M. Cropper, and K. Palmer (2000), Sulphur Dioxide Control by Electric Utilities: What Are the Gains from Trade?, *Journal of Political Economy* 108, 1292-1326.

Cox, C. B., I. N. Healey, and P. D. Moore (1973), *Biogeography: An Ecological and Evolutionary Approach*, Oxford/UK.

Drechsler, M., V. Grimm, J. Myšiak, and F. Wätzold (2004), *Ecological and Economic Models: Mindsets and Traditions*, unpublished manuscript.

Drechsler, M., K. Johst, F. Wätzold, J. Settele, and H. Bergmann (2004), *Developing Cost-Effective Compensation Payments for Maculinea Conservation in Germany*, unpublished manuscript.

Drechsler, M. and F. Wätzold (2003), *Species Conservation in the Face of Political Uncertainty*, UFZ-Diskussionspapiere 4/2003, Leipzig.

Drechsler, M. and F. Wätzold (2001), The Importance of Economic Costs in the Development of Guidelines for Spatial Conservation Management, *Biological Conservation* 97, 51-59.

Hampicke, U. (1991), *Naturschutzökonomie*, Stuttgart.

Hanley, N., H. Kirkpatrick, I. Simpson, and D. Oglethorpe (1998), Principles for the Provision of Public Goods from Agriculture: Modelling Moorland Conservation in Scotland, *Land Economics* 74, 102-113.

Innes, R., S. Polasky, and J. Tschirhart (1998), Takings, Compensation and Endangered Species Protection on Private Lands, *The Journal of Economic Perspectives* 12, 35-52.

Johst, K., M. Drechsler, and F. Wätzold (2002), An Ecological-Economic Modelling Procedure to Design Compensation Payments for the Efficient Spatio-Temporal Allocation of Species Protection Measures, *Ecological Economics* 41, 37–49.

Kaule, G. (1996), *Arten- und Biotopschutz*, Stuttgart.

Kleijn, D., F. Berendse, R. Smit, and N. Gilissen (2001), Agri-Environment Schemes Do Not Effectively Protect Biodiversity in Dutch Agricultural Landscapes, *Nature* 413, 723-725.

Klepper, G. (2004), Umweltökonomische Politikberatung – Reflexionen zu dem Symposium: "Umweltpolitik und umweltökonomische Politikberatung in Deutschland", *Zeitschrift für angewandte Umweltforschung*, special issue, forthcoming.

Kolstad, C.D. (1987), Uniformity Versus Differentiation in Regulating Externalities, *Journal of Environmental Economics* 14, 386-399.

Loske, R. (2004), Instrumentenmix und Zielkonflikte: Zukünftige Aufgaben der Umweltpolitik und der ökonomischen Politikberatung, *Zeitschrift für angewandte Umweltforschung*, special issue, forthcoming.

OECD (2001), *Working Party on Economic and Environmental Policy Integration – Working Group on Economic Aspects of Biodiversity: Direct Payments for Biodiversity Provided by Swiss Farmers: An Economic Interpretation of Direct Democratic Decision*, Paris.

Oglethorpe, D. and R. Sanderson (1999), An Ecological-Economic Model for Agri-Environmental Policy Analysis, *Ecological Economics* 28, 245-266.

Polasky, S., B. Csuti, C.A. Vossler, and S.M. Meyers (2001), A Comparison of Taxonomic Distinctness Versus Richness as Criteria for Setting Conservation Priorities for North American Birds, *Biological Conservation* 97, 99-105.

Settle, C., T.D. Crocker, and J. Shogren (2002), On the Joint Determination of Biological and Economic Systems, *Ecological Economics* 42, 301-312.

Strijker, D., F.J. Sijtsma, and D. Wiersma (2000), Evaluation of Nature Conservation. An Application to the Dutch Ecological Network, *Environmental and Resource Economics* 16, 363-378.

Pethig, R. and J. Tschirrhart (2001), Microfoundations of Population Dynamics, *Journal of Bioeconomics* 3, 27-49.

van Huyelenbroek, G. and M. Whitby (1999), *Countryside Stewardship: Farmers, Policies and Markets*, Oxford.

Wätzold, F. and K. Schwerdtner (2005), Why Be Wasteful when Preserving a Valuable Resource? – A Review Article on the Cost-Effectiveness of European Biodiversity Conservation Policy, *Biological Conservation*, forthcoming.

Wätzold, F. and M. Drechsler (2002), Spatial Differentiation of Compensation Payments for Biodiversity-Enhancing Land-Use Measures, UFZ-Diskussionspapiere 3/2002, Leipzig.

Wiseman, R. and L. Hopkins (2001), *Sowing the Seeds for Sustainability. Agriculture, Biodiversity, Economics and Society*, Proceedings of the eighth interactive session, IUCN, Gland, Switzerland and Cambridge, UK.

Wu, J.J. and K. Skelton-Groth (2002), Targeting Conservation Efforts in the Presence of Threshold Effects and Ecosystem Linkages, *Ecological Economics* 42, 313-331.

Wu, J.J. and W. Boggess (1999), The Optimal Allocation of Conservation Funds, *Journal of Environmental Economics and Management* 38, 302-321.

Vision, Analysis, and Future Pathways in Transport Research

Romain Molitor

Trafico Verkehrsplanung, Fillgradergasse 6/2, 1060 Wien, Austria, romain.molitor@trafico.at

Karl W. Steininger

University of Graz, Department of Economics, Universitätsstraße 15, 8010 Graz, Austria, karl.steininger@uni-graz.at

Keywords. *Access Service, Land Use Patterns, Spatial Computable General Equilibrium, Transport System Development, Transport Policy*

JEL. *D58; O2; R11; R14; R4; R52*

Abstract. Congestion, environmental and health problems are all rising in the transport sector. This article focuses on the contribution of economics, particularly environmental economics, to the analysis, and in particular to the quantitative analysis of transport systems and transport policy in tackling such problems. Starting out with a historical review of transport perspectives, the importance of both overall coherence as well as the time period it may take for a particular vision to materialise are then illustrated. Promising current research issues are identified, and related developments in quantitative modelling and data availability are discussed.

1 Introduction

"In contrast to substantial progress in reducing emissions in many sectors of the economy, environmental damages caused by traffic have increased in the past few years due to a rise of passenger and freight traffic combined with a shift towards motorised road transport."[1]

In explaining why this has occurred, we take a step back to analyse grand, basic trends in transport, which are found to originate in the interlinkage between spatial

---

1 Programme of the Workshop „Frontiers in Applied Environmental and Resource Economics", from which the present volume originated, Session *Traffic and Environment*.

planning and transport systems. Transport demand is derived demand, and changes arising in reaction to policy are thus often more complex than those arising in the consumption of other goods of more direct interest. Our analysis of the transport *system framework,* and of people's early visions for transport development, takes account of such complexity.

The objective of this article is to investigate which types of research input can illuminate policy design and thus facilitate the development of solutions and promote improvements for the future.

The structure of this article is as follows. In Section 2 we investigate in very basic terms how the science of (environmental) economics can illuminate transport policy analysis in general.

Historically, specific transport visions and – in pre-TV and pre-internet times – their respective presentations, particularly at World Fairs, have proven to be strong indicators for future development. In Section 3 we look into these visions, and analyse how they came about and why they came to dominate. One question turns out to be why spatial planning, and even more so city planning, developed so as to accommodate car use so extensively.

Section 4 takes up this line of thought and applies it more directly to the science of economics again: What can economics contribute to the generation of a more consistent vision – now – for *our* future? What can it contribute to policy instrument analysis?

In examining specific policy design and implementation, for the remainder of the article we turn our attention to questions of quantitative analysis. Our outline of future quantitative transport policy modelling proceeds in three steps. First, in Section 5 we identify some promising research areas. Second, in Section 6, we relate recent model developments, with a focus on (spatial) computable general equilibrium modelling, to each of these issues. Third, we identify the major issues in data (non)availability. A final section summarises the main conclusions.

2 Environmental Economic Analysis in Transport Research

The economic analysis of transport systems and transport policy is increasingly drawing on environmental economics. Both main strands in the historical development of environmental economics, the neoclassical approach, with its focus on the concept of externalities and reshaping of incentive systems by price correction, and the material balance approach, with its focus on physical flows of energy and material inputs and emission outputs, lend themselves easily to analysis in the field of transport.

One forum of analysis simply entails extending the standard environmental-economic approach to include transport goods, and then modelling the latter's production and consumption characteristics, and the physical flows they are connected to.

The question soon arises, however, as to whether the field of transport differs substantially from other fields of application in environmental economics, say energy. The authors of this article argue below that considerable differences do in fact exist.

2.1 Degrees of Freedom and Time Horizon in Transport Systems

In the "first" field of environmental economics, *energy* economics, we learned the importance of considering the service perspective of energy, i.e. that we are not interested in consuming primary energy itself, but rather in the heat services it provides, e.g. keeping a certain room volume at a specified temperature. The latter can be achieved by a large array of technological options, including insulation and other demand side adjustments.

A similar change in perspective is happening in *transport* economic analysis. Ultimately it is the service of access that humans look for in consumption and production. It is not a particular amount of physical movement ("transport flow"), but rather access to goods, services, and people, that is in actual demand.

What seems considerably different between these two examples is the "degrees of freedom" that determine the extent to which physical flows are connected to one service unit of consumption. With respect to energy services, the following factors basically determine the amount of physical input flows and emission levels of the energy system:

- the parameters that determine how much energy is needed to provide a specific energy service (e.g. level of insulation),
- efficiency of the technological energy transformation process,
- the choice (or mix) of the primary energy source(s), and
- overall production and consumption level.

Similarly, with respect to access services, we find that the following factors determine the physical (and energy) input flows and emission levels of the transport system:

- the parameters that determine the amount of physical transport needed in gaining access, such as
  - spatial distribution of home relative to work
  - spatial distribution of production sites
  - spatial distribution of home relative to consumption locations
- efficiency of the transport system
- the choice (or mix) of transport mode(s), and
- overall production and consumption level.

We see that in both cases the last three issues may be of roughly identical complexity, but not so the first category stated for each field. Here, the parameters that determine how much (physical) *transport* is needed for the establishment of a particular access level are considerably more complex. The whole spatial structuring of activities, governed by land-use regulations, land rents, historical availability of infrastructure etc. determine how much physical mobility is necessary to ensure access.

There also seems to be a bias towards a longer time horizon for investments determining transport for unit access (housing location, mode shares in transport infrastructure) compared with those needed for energy services, e.g. type of housing energy systems, or insulation. Energy systems within a given residential building are renewed over a roughly 20-year cycle, whereas the development of e.g. housing and residential areas involves a much longer time horizon.

We thus have a stronger "stock effect" in the transport field, where the term "stock" is used to refer to the interdependent systems of transport infrastructure, spatial structure of land use, and spatially bound investments by households and firms.

2.2 The Access Service Perspective Reconsidered

Normative economic analysis uses an ordinal or even cardinal scale to measure the relative superiority of one state of the world over another. With reference to this scale policy suggestions can then be given. In energy policy analysis, the scalar definition of heat services seems straight forward: Service supply is sought to be supplied with as little detriment to the environment and health as possible, with a clear trade-off existing between these factors.

In transport, the definition of access service is the most basic approach to be used in measuring benefits, where a similar trade-off, this time between access service and detrimental impacts of transport production, is seen. The difference, however, lies in the number of ways available for providing access, which are further determined in a broader and more long-term way than is the case for energy service supply.

For example, one could think of transport systems where each household uses only private cars for consuming "access", and the corresponding sprawl in housing areas necessary to ensure sufficient and cheap parking space. The motorised transport volumes required to ensure access to work, daily supply, and leisure facilities would then turn out to be very high.

One could also think of a densely populated area where access to work, daily supply and leisure locations is (only) possible by walking or public transport. The total transport volumes necessary to ensure access would easily turn out to be much lower than in the first case.[2]

---

2 The reader interested in a fuller discussion of the transport service concept may also wish to consult Steininger (2002a).

3 Visions in Transport – A Historical Review

3.1 Visions in Transport

Experience gained over the last century and beyond tells us that some early visions of the future did in fact have a significant impact on actual outcome. In the analysis below, we examine a few such visions for transport and attempt to present meaningful conclusions.

Changes in the mobility structure, i.e. increasing car traffic, new transport technologies etc., took place first of all in the (big) cities and only later gained ground on a more general scale. New (transport) technologies usually develop in agglomerations, where the respective financial and intellectual resources are more easily at hand. The drivers of change in mobility structures include changes in the spatial structure (e.g. industrialisation, suburbanisation) and in life style, to mention only the most important.

The bad hygienic conditions prevailing in the often densely populated city areas of the 19th and early 20th century inspired urbanists, economists and hygienists to ameliorate living conditions by improving technology (e.g. in transport technology, the shift from horse to car, in energy technologies and housing) and in changing the spatial structure (separating industrial and residential areas).

Thus, historically speaking, town planning, discussed by the Congrès International d'Architecture Moderne (CIAM) and leading to the so-called Charta of Athens in the early 1930s, may be seen as one point of focus in the discussion of transport development. Utopian pictures (see **Fig. 1**) showing new and modern infrastructure for car and air traffic can also be seen as one theoretical basis for the subsequent town planning of the 20s and 30s. The CIAM might also be viewed as a compilation/concentration of the ideas relating to a new, modern and livable city discussed in the preceding decade.

The messages stated in the Charta of Athens (published in 1933) are based on the experience gained in densely populated cities, with a mix of different functions in each district (e.g. §§ 9 and 10). The problems experienced in the cities at the beginning of motorisation (e.g. noise and a high number of accidents) led to the statement that locating residential buildings beside heavy traffic had to be prohibited (§ 27). The separation of pedestrian and car traffic was also demanded due to the difference in their respective speeds of 4 km/h and 50 or even 100 km/h. Separate areas for pedestrians were also requested (§ 27). Further noteworthy demands include a reduction of distances between home and work to a minimum (§ 46) and the construction of industrial zones near railways, inland waterways or trunk roads (§ 48). The discussion of traffic in the Charta concentrated on the inadequacy of roads for car traffic (§§ 52-58). Solutions recommended include grade-separated junctions, a hierarchy of roads based on their specific function and separate traffic areas reserved for different transport modes – mainly for pedestrians and car traffic (§§ 59-64) (Hilpert, 1984: 115ff.).

Fig. 1. Le Corbusier – Airport, Plan Voisin, Paris 1925.

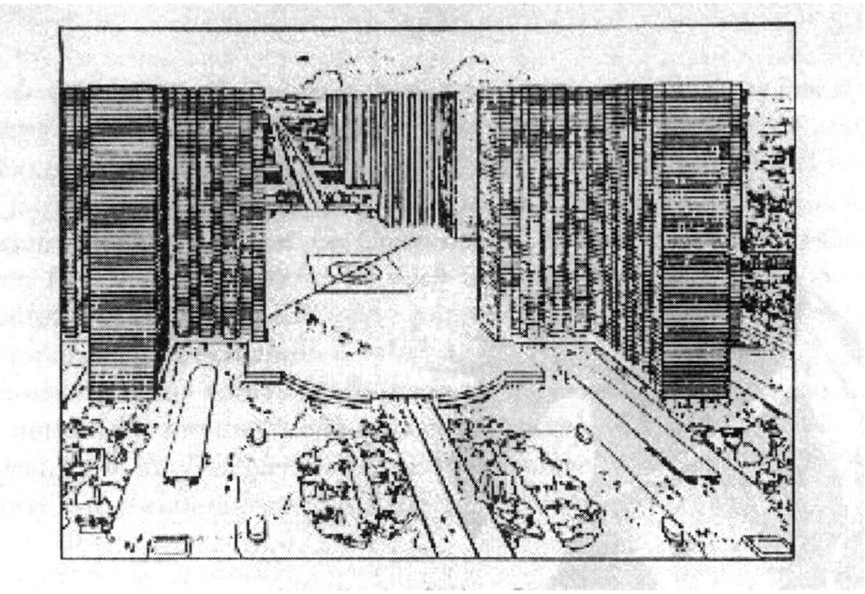

Source: Hilpert (1984)

The architect, Le Corbusier, who was considerably involved in the preparation of the Charta, and who later became active worldwide in city planning, presented the idea of a city as 'mesh civilisation', a finite city, which should be made controllable and subservient as a system. Here the city system is divided into elementary zones, interlinked or meshed together by the "mechanical speed" of the car, which produces the "daily cycle of functions" (Hilpert, 1984: 60). However, even at the time of Le Corbusier cities were no longer mere finite entities, but city-regions, polycentric, interlinked areas. The idea of a finite city was also promoted by Le Corbusier in his plan for the "ville radieuse" in 1929-30. Here, the monofunctional areas of the city are linked with each other by traffic bands (multilane roads designed for speeds from 50 to 100 km/h) (**Fig. 2**).

At about the same time Marcel Breuer (1929) developed a new design for Potsdamer Platz in Berlin, including a grade-separated junction for car traffic. Breuer was of the opinion that the "square in the city should not be viewed as a park, not as a given or desirable form and also not as point de vue". He expected that the capacity of car traffic on the Potsdamer Platz would soon reach its limits and therefore proposed solutions with overbridges and underpasses. Underpasses for pedestrians should also serve as access to the underground. Bicycle traffic is not mentioned. Public transport is run beneath the square (underground) and in the middle of the streets (tramway). He proposed tramway stops along the sidewalks, so the passenger still has to cross the traffic lanes. The carriageways are partially divided by central barriers. The main objective was to handle car and pedestrian traffic separately without junctions so as not to reduce capacity of car traffic (Breuer, 1929).

Fig. 2. Plan 11 of the 17 plans of the Ville Radieuse presented at the CIAM congress in Brussels 1930 (Le Corbusier).

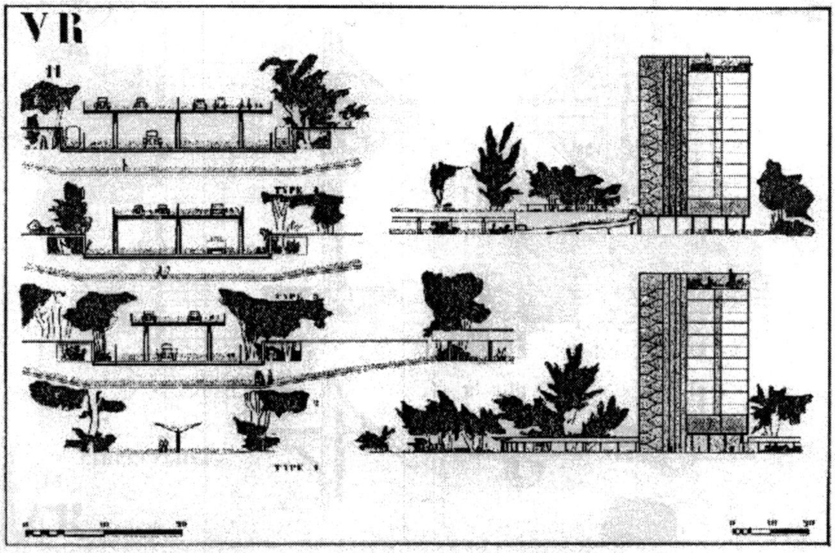

Source: Hilpert (1984)

Both visions cited here as examples of future city planning and future traffic management probably became the theoretical basis for the creation of an image of a modern city.

3.2 First Experience of the Vision of a Modern City Life

Using his experience in theatre architecture and stage design, Norman Bel Geddes was able to concentrate the developing images of city life into a specific vision which was presented at the General Motors pavillion at the World Fair in New York 1939/40. The vision he created was so powerful and easily comprehensible that General Motors managed to dominate the World Fair. The model of a future city in the 60s, conceived, built and presented by Norman Bel Geddes was named "Futurama" (**Fig. 3** and **Fig. 4**). 24 million visitors out of a total of 45 million over two seasons visited the 'Futurama'. The visitors were transported on comfortable sound-chairs by a conveyor belt along the model of a landscape with a futuristic "Motorway of 1960", "a 14-lane, two-directional limited access highway with separate speed lanes for 50-mph, 75-mph, and 100-mph traffic. Entrance onto the highway from feeder roads, transfers from one speed to another and even the distance between cars were controlled by radio from traffic towers situated every five miles along the Motorway." (Hauss-Fitton, 1994: 57-58). The ride took 16 minutes. During the ride information was conveyed to visitors via an impressive sound and lightning system. At the end of the ride, a model of the city of tomorrow with a close-up view of the city's downtown section was shown. After viewing the intersection the "chairs turned away from the model, and the visitor stepped into a full-scale version of the street intersection he had just seen." (Hauss-Fitton, 1994: 59). Among the four main buildings on the intersection, an Auto Salon with the exhibit of the General Motors products was located. The reactions of the public were mostly enthusiastic. In fact, in all likelihood, the utopian pictures produced by the car industry had no inconsiderable impact on individual thinking and on the development of future transport patterns. The 14-lane motorway actually became reality, e.g. in Los Angeles with its 2000 mile freeway net (cf. Bratzel, 1995) **(Fig. 5)**.

Fig. 3. Final scene of animated traffic exhibit, model and intersection with replicas of General Motors exhibit buildings 1939 (Geddes).

Source: Hauss-Fitton (1994)

For Bel Geddes "fast transportation was the means for solving problems, for opening up possibilities on two fronts: that of urban structure and that of the style of the century's objects" (V. Gregotti, Editorial, in: Hauss-Fitton, 1994: 4). As a designer, Bel Geddes drew streamlined aircraft, trains, automobiles and household equipment and he can also be seen in the same vein as other well known contemporaries, such as the designer Raymond Loewy.

Fig. 4. Futurama building, actual street intersection with display vehicles and visitors on elevated sidewalks 1939 (Geddes).

Source: Hauss-Fitton (1994)

Fig. 5. Futurama Motorway intersection with 14-lane, two directional traffic and high speed entrance/exit ramps 1939 (Geddes).

Source: Rassegna (1994)

The Geddes model shows a vision of future life in an air-conditioned city, where inhabitants only leave the city by car to see some landscape. There is a new mobility structure, where futuristic, streamlined cars are driven by remote-control and where pedestrians – should it be necessary to leave the air-conditioned buildings – have their own dedicated traffic areas. Thus, 'Futurama' can be seen as a model for future life (Krasny, 1996: 329). The World Fair in New York was prototypical, not only with respect to the utopias shown, but also in terms of the adventure world presented. Edgar Lawrence Doctorow described in his novel the effect of the exhibit on visitors in general and on himself as a child in particular. He calls it the "most fascinating moment of my life". Doctorow paints a picture of – characteristic of the staging by Norman Bel Geddes – his impressions, "all those wonderful things moving past, the rain-drop-shaped cars, the air-conditioned cities. And then came the stunning finish, seeing a certain junction in the model, and the show was over, and with your I-have-seen-the-future-sticker in your hand you stepped out into the sun and stood exactly at the junction you had just seen, the future was exactly where you were standing and what had been small had become big, the scale had increased, and you were not looking on the crossing of the future any more, you were standing on it, here, at the World Fair!" (Krasny, 1996: 330-331). The fascination was unbroken despite the transparency of model and reality.

World Fairs were "experimental fields" in many respects. They were often used to present new transport technologies or new systems of transport management to the public for the first time.

At the World Fair in Paris 1900, for example, an elevated railroad and a "trottoir roulant" in the Champ-de-Mars were installed – new transport technologies for public transport users and pedestrians. "Trottoirs roulants" (also known as "plateforme mobile") were first implemented and used in 1900, but similar ideas had already been discussed for the World Fair in 1889. A capacity of 26,000 users per hour, a speed of 4 to 8 km/h and a length of 3.36 km was reported.

The "trottoirs roulants" were considered to guarantee a "superior gliding-by, a strolling perception without disturbance on the level of the objects themselves" (Krasny, 1996: 319). Perhaps the ideals of the flaneur, strolling down the boulevards of the Belle Epoque, went some way in promoting the development of such visions.

3.3 From Visions to Reality

Comparing the mobility structures presented at the World Fairs in Paris and New York, we see that on the one hand, a considerable change in transport technology had taken place between 1900 and 1939, and on the other hand preferences had also changed. This radical change in the idea of a modern city took place within only 40 years. Considering these historical examples, we observe that ideas, visions and utopias of a modern mobility structure were formulated, specific images emerged during a phase of further consideration and social discussion, and finally they became reality. Given the huge effort necessary to build the present motorway network and other transport infrastructure the period between utopian vision, and actual realisation, is remarkably short.

Underlying Breuer's design for the city of Berlin in 1929, was the belief in the optimal solution for car traffic. Considering that at the time only few cars compared to today were registered in Berlin, this concept has to be interpreted – like Le Corbusier's ideas – more as a vision than a concrete plan. Mobility structure in a large city like Berlin in 1929 was dominated by non-motorised and public transport. 50% of public transport was carried out by tramways. This means that the Breuer concept also was used to introduce archetypal ideas and visions, which were implemented in cities some decades later.

The vision of an ideal city, as proposed in the Charta of Athens and as discussed by other bodies, led to functional and social segregation within urban areas. The city is divided into mono-functional areas (e.g. only residential), linked with each other through traffic bands, but also clearly separated. This functional segregation can only be overcome with the help of mechanical mobility, i.e. the areas in such a city are only accessible by car or public transport (bus, underground, railway etc.). A supply-oriented policy for motorised traffic, as demanded in the Charta of Athens and defined in the plans for the "Ville Radieuse", leads – as we know today – not to a finite city, but rather to an atomised city.

Within the space of a mere 40 years a total change in societal preferences in mobility took place as a result of such policies. World Fairs are fairly good indicators of future or near-future developments. Bel Geddes compressed the theoretical and technical utopia of leading urbanists and architects into a comprehensive, atmospheric vision of how the future might look.

Le Corbusier, Breuer and Bel Geddes have been referred to here as they are deemed to be representative of certain social developments taking place between World War I and II, in particular of a modernistic approach in urban planning. While similar ideas had been discussed on a larger scale before, the imaginative power of the images produced by these three individuals exerted considerable influence on the ongoing discussion of the time. The visions and atmospheric pictures they presented served to influence future town planning by taking into account new forms of mobility – e.g. the car and plane – and to influence decisions on future developments and the allocation of financial resources.

4 Economics and the Development of a Vision for Transport and Land Use

4.1 A Coherent Depiction

In dealing with the current shortcomings of existing transport systems (congestion, environmental pressure, or regularly denied access for the elderly and children), which in part have arisen as a result of town planning on the basis also of these town planning perspectives just discussed, the transport vision drawn up for the future today will probably look different to the one reviewed above. But what will it look like?

Initial ideas and building blocks for such a vision do exist: e.g. high density living with simultaneous high availability of close-by open space, polycentric structures with agglomerations of different size that serve mixed functions each, car-free environments served by public transport, and the like.

What seems to be an open question, however, is whether such diverse concepts offer sufficient coherence for the development of a new vision. We have to ask questions such as: How do such spatial structures interact with the achievement of objectives such as high rates of innovation or labour productivity? Where are the trade-offs? What makes the vision in its full and coherent form a better world than today's? Is it a better world at all?

Economics can contribute a lot to answering such questions. Many of the above issues centre on the interaction of land-use structures and transport. Thus, further work in new economic geography, a field that inherently focuses on both these aspects, could prove illuminating. Although core theories and modelling roads in new economic geography have already been developed (Fujita et al. 1999), the empirical applications to date remain largely within the area of experimental simulations.

A research agenda starting with the objective of developing and testing a transport and land use vision could substantially enhance both the fields of economic geography and transport policy research.

It seems very characteristic in this respect, that in a recent ECMT (European Conference of Ministers of Transport) survey on the expertise developed within transport economics (Bonnafous, 2003), only one area is identified where there is a substantial deficiency across all modes and transport categories (passenger/freight): "concerning the impact of [...] transport supply on the structuring of space, transport economics has not yet developed models of capturing these structuring effects adequately." (Bonnafous, 2003: 38).

We accept Bonnafous' statement on the existing shortcomings in transport economics, and argue that future research must aim to provide a bridge between economic geography and transport policy by supporting the development of a coherent vision for the future.

4.2 Areas of Current Policy Action

One could tackle shortcomings in transport by adopting a completely different approach to that described above. Instead of beginning with a grand vision one could begin on a micro-scale by looking at specific policy instruments. Usually we do have a pretty good idea which instruments we would need to use, and where, in order to improve a specific situation. For example, in transport pricing, fuller accounting of actual marginal costs is one of the major issues. It is taken as a basic tenet in economics that the right prices will bring about an adequate spatial structure in the long run anyway, whatever this structure may be. Therefore, within this approach, the analysis of the ultimate state of affairs is not a pressing issue, since this state will arise anyway, once the proper transport policy instruments are employed.

Usually the areas of policy action are seen to be threefold (compare e.g. Viegas, 2003):
- supply-side instruments
- regulatory instruments
- pricing and taxation instruments.

For each of the three we may identify a current research agenda. Concerning supply-side instruments, it is no longer the supply of infrastructure, and not so much the supply of technology, but the organisation and management of transport that is highlighted as a crucial starting point for defining the agenda.

In terms of regulatory instruments, it is primarily institutional design which ranks high on the agenda. The (self-)interests of public agencies may interfere with an efficient regulation of private agents.

With respect to taxation (or subsidies in this case) issues of counterproductive support measures in transport are the object of analysis, while in terms of efficient pricing the main research focus is shifting more and more from the analysis of freight to that of passenger transport.

5 Some Areas of Extended Future Research

Reflecting the above comments, the authors here wish to point out three areas to which in their mind, crucial future research effort will (have to) be devoted. These are briefly described in Sections 5.1, 5.2 and 5.3 below.

5.1 Interlinkage of Land-Use and Transport

Choices in land-use and in transport are mutually dependent. Any given pattern of activity location induces a specific trip pattern, and, reversely, the location choice for each activity is dependent on the transport system and the opportunities it offers, since it is the transport system which defines the cost associated with all future activities at any specific location.

Most modelling has chosen one of the above approaches of primary causation. Only few efforts at integration have been made, e.g. Martinez (2000). The developments within new economic geography, triggered by Krugman (1991, 1995), however, have provided a number of new theoretical modelling devices and possibilities for simulation which need to be employed in suitable areas of empirical application beyond illustrative modelling.

5.2 Distributional Impacts of Transport Policy

While most effort in modelling transport economics focuses on the evaluation of transport efficiency, researchers engaged in policy advising tell a different story of priorities. In the introduction to their *Handbook of Transport Modelling*, Hensher and Button (2000: 3) put it this way: "in detailed research work by Bruno Frey in Zurich, amongst others, it was found that policy-makers are much more interested in the impacts of various transport actions on different societal groups and that this distributional consideration far outweighs matters of technical efficiency."

Although this experience is echoed repeatedly by several others engaged in policy research, empirical modelling work focusing on questions of distribution is still rather rare (for a theoretical discussion and model and its numerical illustration see Mayeres and Proost, 2001).

5.3 Change in Behaviour Due to Significant Transport Price Changes

Marginal changes in transport pricing have been amply observed and modelled in the past. At the same time, in both academic circles and among the public at large, it has become evident especially for roads that the gap between the price of transport activities and overall costs, is not marginal, but substantial. Nevertheless, experience in empirically analysing the implications of substantial price changes is at best rudimentary.

Even worse, most pre-launch studies of transport pricing (even for "small" changes) have produced results that strongly mismatched with the experience actually gained after real-world implementation of the respective pricing schemes. The bias was almost always in the direction of predicting too little behaviour change, and thus too much revenue. "Let us confine ourselves to a single example that aptly illustrates traffic forecasting errors. A report was recently issued by Standard & Poor's ['Credit Implications of Traffic Risk in Start-Up Toll Facilities', Rating Direct, Standard & Poor's, 15 August, 2002] on investment in toll roads on different continents. Out of the 32 cases studied, four showed that traffic was slightly higher than had been forecast, while in all the other cases traffic was lower than originally forecast and in twelve cases more than 40% lower!" (Bonnafous, 2003: 39). The literature has only recently begun to focus on why this one-sidedness occurs. One reason given in Hensher and Goodwin (2004) is that a skewed distribution of time value causes the mean value to diverge (significantly) from the median value. While the former is usually used in pricing impact forecasts, it is the latter that determines actual behaviour change. With a positively skewed distribution a larger share of people reacts to price changes than indicated when considering the mean time value.

6 CGE Transport Policy Analysis: Models and Data

The three research issues identified above are becoming increasingly important. All three issues have a significant long-term and structural component, with one exhibiting in addition an explicit pricing component. They thus lend themselves to quantitative analysis by means of computable general equilibrium, and for this reason we focus exclusively on this method here, highlighting the questions of recent model developments and data availability. This is not to deny that crucial input can be gained by other quantitative modelling techniques. Nevertheless, the selection of one method serves to somewhat deepen the analysis and to supply a coherent framework within the confines of a single article.

6.1 Models

For the first of the three issues outlined above, interlinkage of land-use and transport, spatial computable general equilibrium (SCGE) models serve as basic starting point. Implementing the monopolistic competition models of the Dixit-Stiglitz (1977) type into multi-region CGE-models, the few empirical examples available start from one of two ends: broad regional coverage with few economic sectors (Bröcker, 1998); or from a fully fledged sectoral structure, with regional diversity restricted to within a single country (Knaap et al., 2001, or in a later state of progress of the same model Tavasszy et al., 2003). In both cases the transport cost component is exogenously given by companion-models. The future issue, therefore, is to transfer transport cost to an inherently endogenous variable.

With respect to the second issue, several arguments have been presented which underline the importance of further analysis (besides the work cited earlier, see for example Oberholzer-Gee and Weck-Hannemann, 2002)), but hardly any quantitative modelling work exists. While Mayeres and Proost (2001) provide a theoretical model, real world data has been used in a four-income-class CGE transport model by Friedl and Steininger (2004), in this case for Austria. The latter show that road pricing is in fact very likely to have a *progressive* impact. The ongoing adjustment of models to the structure of distributional data that is to become available, seems to be the major challenge here.

Concerning the third issue, transport price changes of significant magnitude, modelling has so far focused on partial (transport) equilibrium, and often at the regional level (e.g. Jansen and Denis (1999), or Proost and Van Dender (2001), both building on the TRENEN model) or on truck transport (e.g. Steininger, 2002b). Computable *genera*l equilibrium models for analysing a significant price change in passenger transport have been developed only recently, e.g. to the knowledge of the present authors, Boeters et al. (2003) still represent a relatively rare example here. New lines of modelling reactions to substantial price changes, also taking so-called "captives" into account, i.e. those agents unable to adjust in terms of transport behaviour, still have to be developed with respect to this issue.

6.2 Data

Numerous problems exist in economic transport modelling with respect to data. First, and most importantly, classifications in terms of goods transported (in transport statistics) and in terms of economic sectors (in national accounting) simply do not match. The resulting gaps in the data are difficult to bridge in modelling terms. This is true for both the European Union as well as for individual countries. Second, transport mode differentiation is not available in any economic statistics, which is why the above mentioned mismatch in classifications matters all the more. Third, differentiated freight transport statistics for within-country (and within-EU) trips are generally poor, the same is true for passenger transport statistics, when trip purpose or income is a required trip characteristic. Fourth, and finally, international trade transport data is not available in consistent terms. One of the most commonly used economic databases for this end, GTAP, for example, uses the label 'transport' to just reflect all statistical differences between export and import values by sector in bilateral trade statistics.

7 Conclusions

Promising theoretical developments in transport economic modelling have been made. Ultimately, however, much more work has to be done before adequate quantitative analysis can be achieved in the following areas:

- the interaction of land-use and transport,
- distributional impacts of transport policy, and
- behavioural changes due to significant transport price changes.

Present research is inadequate for a number of reasons. To begin with, a mismatch exists between available data and a first-best modelling requirement. We have discussed the latter with respect to access services. While transport CGE models have been creative in depicting transport services, e.g. in a dynamic setting Boeters et al. (2003) isolate an automotive capital stock, the technical parameters of car fleet vintage relating to environmental policy, but none of the models so far has explicitly focused on access service.

A further reason lies in the difficulties faced when attempting to meaningfully transfer monopolistic competition mark-ups to *dynamic* spatial CGE models. While calibration can be successfully achieved and allows for the generation of base cases, modelling the dynamics, including the interactions of land-use and transport systems is a totally different story.

One final reason for inadequate research stems from the often poor integration of economic variables in transport statistics (or a poor integration of transport variables in consumption statistics). For most countries, for example, not even the most basic economic indicators, such as – for passenger transport – person (or household) income, are available within trip structure statistics, or – for freight transport – the value of goods transported.

Nevertheless, the pressure of transport burdens in terms of health and environmental impacts is significant and still growing. Lack of data and data quality will thus have to be overcome. In order to ensure that adequate demand statistics be identified a all, quantitative transport modelling needs to be further developed and nurtured even if for the time being it means using rather rough and ready data.

References

Breuer, M. (1929), Verkehrsarchitektur – ein Vorschlag zur Neuordnung des Potsdamer Platzes, in: Wagner, M. and A. Behne. (Ed.), *Das neue Berlin* (7), reprint 1988, Basel, Berlin, Boston, 136-141.

Boeters, S., C. Böhringer, and A. Löschel (2003), How to Regulate CO_2 Emissions of Passenger Cars in Europe?, paper contributed to the Annual Meeting of the European Association of Environmental and Resource Economists, Bilbao.

Bonnafous, A. (2003), Assessing Our Expertise, in: ECMT (Ed.), *Fifty Years of Transport Policy*, European Conference of Ministers of Transport, Paris, 33-40.

Bratzel, S. (1995), *Extreme der Mobilität – Entwicklung und Folgen der Verkehrspolitik in Los Angeles*, Basel, Boston, Berlin.

Bröcker, J. (1998), Operational Spatial Computable General Equilibrium Modelling, *The Annals of Regional Science* 32, 367-387.

Dixit, A. and J. Stiglitz (1977), Monopolistic Competition and Optimum Product Diversity, *American Economic Review* 67, 297-308.

Friedl, B. and K.W. Steininger (2004), Economic and Distributional Impacts of Nationwide Car Road Pricing: A CGE Analysis for Austria, paper presented to the Umweltökonomischer Ausschuss des Vereins für Socialpolitik, Annual Meeting 2004, St. Gallen.

Fujita, M., P. Krugman, and A.J. Venables (1999), *The Spatial Economy*, Cambridge MA.

Hauss-Fitton, B. (1994), Futurama, New York World's Fair 1939-40, in: Rassegna Vol. XVI, no. 60, IV/1994, Issue on: Bel Geddes, N. 1893-1958.

Hensher, D.A. and P. Goodwin (2004), Using Values of Travel Time Savings for Toll Roads: Avoiding Some Common Errors, *Transport Policy* 11/2 (April), 171-181.

Hensher, D.A. and K.J. Button (2000), *Handbook of Transport Modelling*, Amsterdam.

Hilpert, T. (Ed.) (1984), *Le Corbusiers "Charta von Athen"* – Texte und Dokumente – Kritische Neuausgabe, Braunschweig, 115ff.

Jansen, H. and C. Denis (1999), A Welfare Cost Assessment of Various Policy Measures to Reduce Pollutant Emissions from Passenger Road Vehicles, *Transportation Research Part D* 4, 379-396.

Knaap, T., J. Oosterhaven, and L. Tavasszy (2001), *On the Development of Raem: The Dutch Spatial General Equilibrium Model and It's First Application to a New Railway Link*, mimeo/ERSA conference paper, University of Groningen.

Krasny, E. (1996), Zukunft ohne Ende – das Unternehmen Weltausstellung, in: Felderer, B. (Ed.), *Wunschmaschine Welterfindung*, Wien, New York, 314-338.

Krugman, P.R. (1995), *Development, Geography, and Economic Theory*, Cambridge MA.

Krugman, P.R. (1991), *Geography and Trade*, Cambridge MA.

Martinez, F.J. (2000), Towards a Land-Use and Transport Interaction Framework, in: Hensher, D.A. and K.J. Button (Eds.), *Handbook of Transport Modelling*, Amsterdam, 145-164.

Mayeres, I. and S. Proost (2001), Marginal Tax Reform, Externalities and Income Distribution, *Journal of Public Economics* 79, 343-363.

Oberholzer-Gee, F. and H. Weck-Hannemann (2002), Pricing Road Use: Politico-Economic and Fairness Considerations, *Transportation Research Part D* 7, 357-371.

Proost, S. and K. Van Dender (2001), The Welfare Impacts of Alternative Policies to Address Atmospheric Pollution in Urban Road Transport, *Regional Science and Urban Economics* 31, 383-411.

Robert, J. (1974), *Histoire des transports dans les villes de France*, Paris.

Steininger, K.W. (2002a), Transport, Access and Economic Growth, *World Economics* 3, 75-91.

Steininger, K.W. (2002b), The Foreign Trade and Sectoral Impact of Truck Road Pricing for Cross-Border Trade: A CGE Analysis for a Small Open Economy, *Environmental and Resource Economics* 23, 213-253.

Steininger, K.W. (2001), *International Trade and Transport*, Cheltenham.

Tavasszy, L.A., M.J.P.M. Thissen, A.C. Muskens, and J. Ooserthaven (2003), *Pitfalls and Solutions in the Application of Spatial General Equilibrium Models for Transport Appraisal*, mimeo, University of Groningen.

Transportation and the Environment – Perspectives for Future Research*

Armin Schmutzler

University of Zurich, SOI, Hottingerstr. 10, 8032 Zurich, Switzerland, arminsch@soi.unizh.ch

Keywords. *Transportation, Environment, Modal Split*

JEL. *Q28; R40; R48*

Abstract. The paper sketches potential research topics concerning "Transportation and the Environment", emphasising those questions to which economists can contribute. It also briefly discusses to which extent these topics have been addressed in earlier literature.

1 Introduction

I have been asked to outline perspectives for future research on transportation and the environment. Given my professional background, I will necessarily argue from an economist's point of view. Transportation is not a big topic for mainstream economists. While environmental economics has established itself as a subdiscipline of economics, transportation research is an interdisciplinary enterprise. For better or worse, most economists do not appear to take much notice of transportation research, and vice versa. Perhaps surprisingly, "Transportation and the Environment" is not even a big issue within environmental economics. Even though environmental economics journals and even general audience journals occasionally address transportation-related environmental issues, such cases are extremely rare: For instance, in the course of the last ten years, only five articles in the Journal of Environmental Economics and Management have dealt explicitly with transportation-related issues. At first glance, this appears bizarre: After all, the transportation sector is rightly seen as an important culprit, and often the main culprit for many serious environmental problems. Why then do environmental economists not care about transportation research?

Most conceivable answers are related to the fact that (academic) economists in general, and environmental economists in particular are often reluctant to delve deeply into specific sectors. There are two reasons for such reluctance.

* Acknowledgement: I am grateful to Dennis Gärtner for helpful comments.

First, in some sense abstraction is the main strength of economic research. By ignoring messy details, important general mechanisms can be exposed that are relevant in many different industries. Arguably, however, to really understand what is going on in a specific sector, the institutional or technological knowledge of specialists is at least as important as the knowledge of general principles that economists hopefully possess. Thus, in the relatively rare cases where leading mainstream economists have made notable contributions to research in specific sectors, they usually have committed to becoming specialists in the particular field as well, which involves very high costs.

Second, there are justified reasons for being wary of "sectoral environmental economics". For instance, from an efficiency point of view, targeting specific environmental goals for the transportation sector is already problematic. In most cases, the only important issue is if pollution is reduced, not in which sector it is reduced. From an economic point of view, however, it is often extremely important in which sector pollution is reduced. In some cases, for instance it may be very easy to reduce emissions in the transportation sector; in other cases, it will be a lot cheaper to do this in the chemical industry, the paper industry, etc. One of the main tenets of environmental economics is that environmental policy should be designed in a way that minimises abatement costs. A consequence of this principle is that economists dislike sectoral policy targets: Based on the conviction that the market is usually better at discovering the most efficient ways of reducing pollution than policy makers, economists usually prefer policy instruments that leave the allocation of emission reductions across sectors to the market. Pollution taxes or tradable permits that are based on emissions, but are independent of the source of the emissions are typical examples of such instruments. A substantial part of transportation research, however, is based on the implicit assumption that emissions should be reduced within the transportation sector.

Nevertheless, there are plenty of reasons for economists to dispense with their reluctance and deal with transportation and the environment, the obvious problems notwithstanding.

First, whether economists like it or not, policy instruments are often sector-specific. Public transport is subsidised, not least because of environmental concerns. The development of alternative fuels is encouraged by government policies such as the Californian Zero Emissions Program. Of course, one could make the point that such policies should be substituted for by broader based policies such as economy-wide pollution taxes and pollution permits, because these policies allow the market to adapt, thereby leading to the cheapest paths towards pollution reduction. Considering the political reality, however, it may be a reasonable alternative strategy to take the existence of transportation-specific instruments as given, and to ask how these different sector-specific instruments compare.

Second, in a world that differs from the simplest textbook models, there may be good reasons for transportation-specific policies. For instance, public transportation is characterised by economies of scale, and by a need for co-ordination. As a result, there is substantial state intervention in this sector, even where private companies are active. Such intervention is likely to have substantial environmental effects. Therefore, thinking about reasonable ways of organising the public transport is an important aspect of environmental policy which may well benefit from the expertise of economists.

Third, the contribution of transportation to some environmental problems is so important that little is lost by targeting this sector only. This is true (or at least was true until recently) for pollutants such as carbon monoxide and lead. Even more obviously, there are some problems where there is simply no way of tackling the problem without tackling transportation related issues directly: For instance, noise pollution in many areas is almost exclusively caused by transportation. Hence, there is no issue of cross-sectoral substitution of pollution reduction efforts.

Fourth, environmental legislation with respect to transportation is simply an important case of environmental legislation in general. From the perspective of Political Economy, insights that emerge from the study of legislation relating to transportation can therefore be helpful for a more general understanding of environmental policy.

Armed with this set of excuses, I shall now sketch actual and research topics in "Transportation and the Environment" from an economist's point of view.

2 Classification of Research Topics

In this section, I provide a classification system for the relevant research topics. The classification starts from a simple identity.

Environmental policy is a multi-dimensional enterprise. For a start, there are many different substances polluting air, soil and water. In addition, there are noise emissions, the destruction of landscape, etc.[1]

Thus, the scope of environmental policy in general, and "environmental transportation policy" in particular, is to deal with a multitude of environmental problems $i=1,...,I$.

For simplicity, suppose the contribution of transportation to problem i can be summarised by a real number e_i. For instance, this could be interpreted as emissions from transportation in a particular time period.[2]

Then, we consider the following decomposition of e_i:

$$e_i = e_{iF} + e_{iP}$$

$$e_i = \sum_m e_{miF} + \sum_m e_{miP}$$

1 Further, whenever a particular environmental problem is not entirely global, one needs to distinguish according to where the problem occurs. Thus, emissions of carbon monoxide in cities A, B, C... are different problems, as compared to noise emissions in neighbourhoods x, y, z, and so on.

2 For problems such as landscape destruction, the interpretation in terms of a measurable quantity is less obvious.

$$e_i = f \cdot \sum_m \mu_{mF} \eta_{miF} + p \cdot \sum_m \mu_{mP} \eta_{miP} \tag{1}$$

where the variables have the following meanings:

e_{iF}	total emissions of type *i* in freight transportation
e_{iP}	total emissions of type *i* in passenger transportation
m	mode of transportation (rail, bus, car, air, ferry, etc.)
e_{miF}	total emissions of type *i* by transportation mode *m* in freight transportation
e_{miP}	total emissions of type *i* by transportation mode *m* in passenger transportation
f	total amount of freight transportation
p	total amount of passenger transportation
μ_{mF}	mileage share of mode *m* in freight transportation
μ_{mP}	mileage share of mode *m* in passenger transportation
η_{miF}	specific emissions of mode *m* with respect to problem *i* in freight transportation (e.g. CO_2-emissions of trucks per freight tonne kilometer)
η_{miP}	specific emissions of mode *m* with respect to problem *i* in passenger transportation (e.g. CO_2-emissions of cars per passenger-kilometer)

Decomposition (1) has a trivial, but useful implication: Changes in transportation emissions e_i must be brought about by a change of one of the following quantities:

1. Total freight transport *f* or passenger transport *p*.
2. Modal-split coefficients μ_{mF} or μ_{mP}.
3. Specific emissions η_{miF} or η_{miP}.

This simple statement will turn out to be useful for organising research questions that arise in environmental transportation economics. In addition, I shall distinguish between "Positive Environmental Transportation Economics" (PETE) and "Normative Environmental Transportation Economics" (NETE), though the distinction between the two areas is not clear-cut. PETE attempts to explain the behaviour of actual emissions e_i. NETE asks which future patterns for e_i are most desirable and how they should best be brought about.

3 Positive Environmental Transportation Economics

3.1 The Issue

3.1.1 Understanding the Evolution of Emissions: The Role of Total Transportation, Modal Split and Specific Emissions

The evolution of transportation emissions differs strongly across pollutants. For instance, carbon monoxide emissions from transportation have been falling in most Western industrialised countries for at least two decades, whereas carbon dioxide emissions have been increasing almost everywhere. Furthermore, there are important cross-country differences. In Switzerland, for example, carbon monoxide emissions began to fall earlier than in the other European countries, and the increase in carbon dioxide emissions has been less pronounced. **Fig. 1** and **Fig. 2** illustrate this for emissions from automobiles (rather than total transportation).

Fig. 1. CO emissions of road transport.

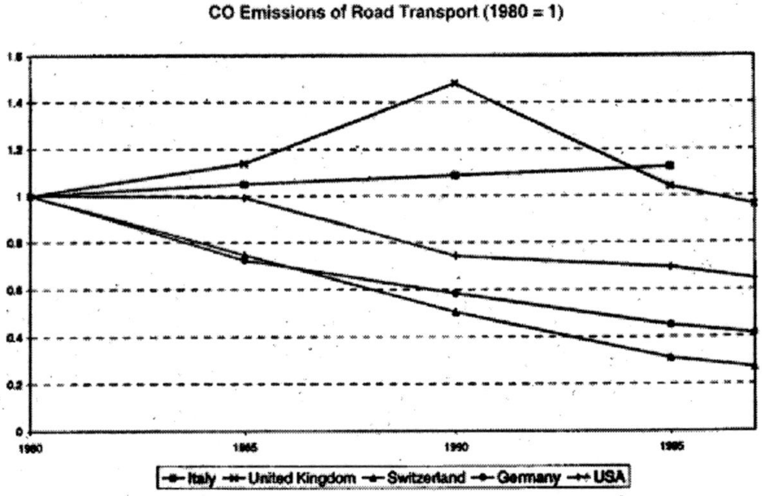

Thus, PETE should address questions such as:

- *Why did carbon monoxide emissions start to fall in the 1980s?*
- *Why did they fall earlier in Switzerland than elsewhere?*
- *Why did carbon dioxide emissions continue to grow?*

Decomposition (1) helps to provide a first, very rough, step towards an answer by highlighting the role of total transportation, modal split and specific emissions.

First, total transportation (freight and passenger) has increased almost everywhere, which, other things being equal, would result in an increase of all pollutants.

Second, over the last few decades, the modal split in passenger transportation has shifted from rail, busses and ships to cars and aeroplanes, and similarly for freight. With respect to most environmental problems (and, in particular, with respect to the two pollutants under consideration), the latter modes are more polluting than the former. Thus the change in modal split is another force towards increasing emissions of both pollutants. **Fig. 3** illustrates the joint effect of the increase in total (passenger) transportation and the growing share of road transportation: a substantial increase in road transportation.

Fig. 2. CO_2 emissions of road transport.

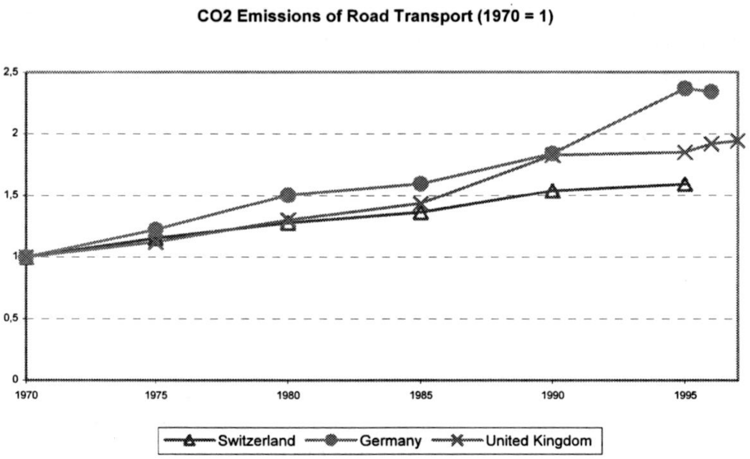

Fig. 3. Passenger kilometers.

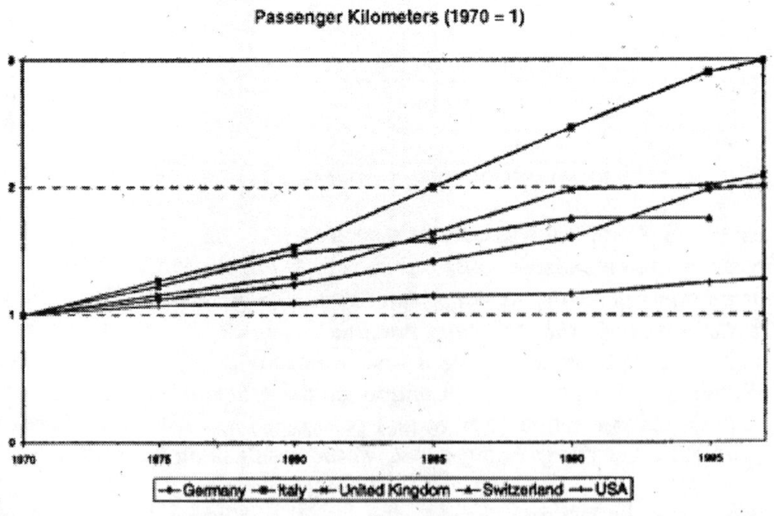

Third, however, specific emissions have behaved differently for both pollutants, at least for automobiles. Specific emissions of carbon monoxide have fallen dramatically since the 1980s, thanks to the diffusion of catalytic converters. Specific emissions of carbon dioxide, however, have shown little or no change. **Fig. 4** and **Fig. 5** show the development of specific emissions from passenger transportation by automobiles.

Fig. 4. CO_2 emissions per passenger kilometer.

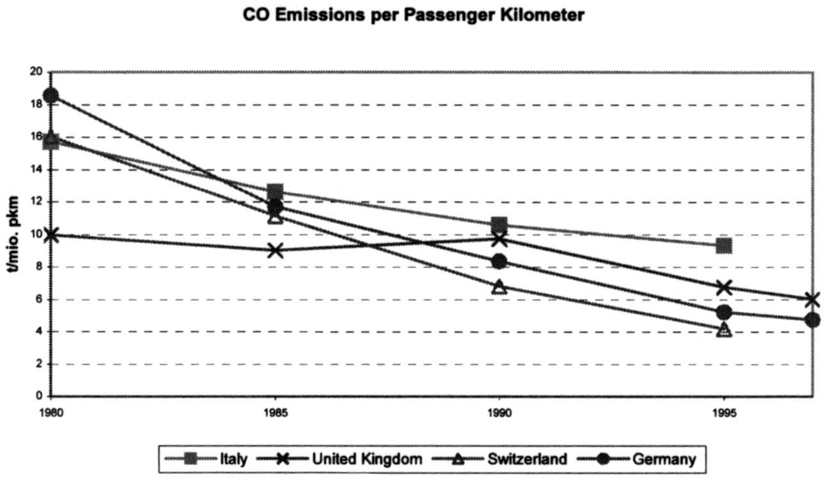

Fig. 5. CO_2 emissions per passenger kilometer.

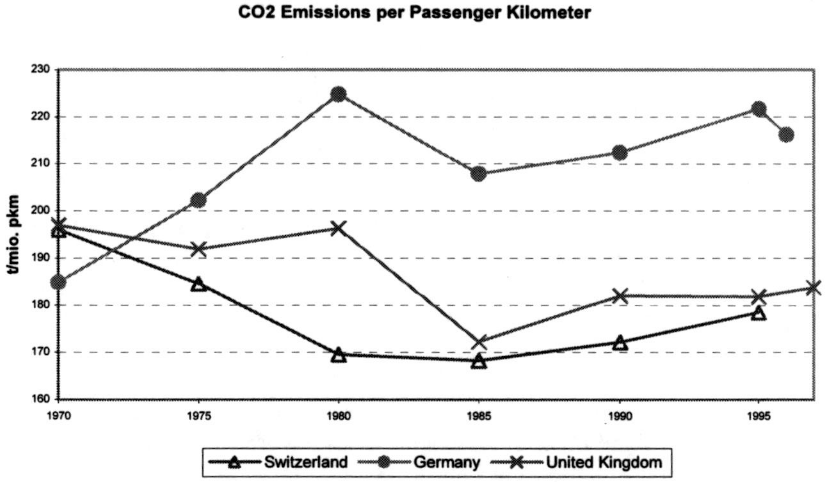

The national differences also become more transparent thanks to (1). For instance, Switzerland is the rare example of a country where (passenger) road transportation has only increased very slightly over the last two decades, and the share of railroads has actually increased. This goes some way towards explaining the relatively favourable behaviour of emissions in Switzerland. In addition, Switzerland was among the earliest countries to introduce the catalytic converter (see **Fig. 6**), which is why carbon monoxide emissions started falling earlier than elsewhere.

Fig. 6. Cars with catalytic converters.

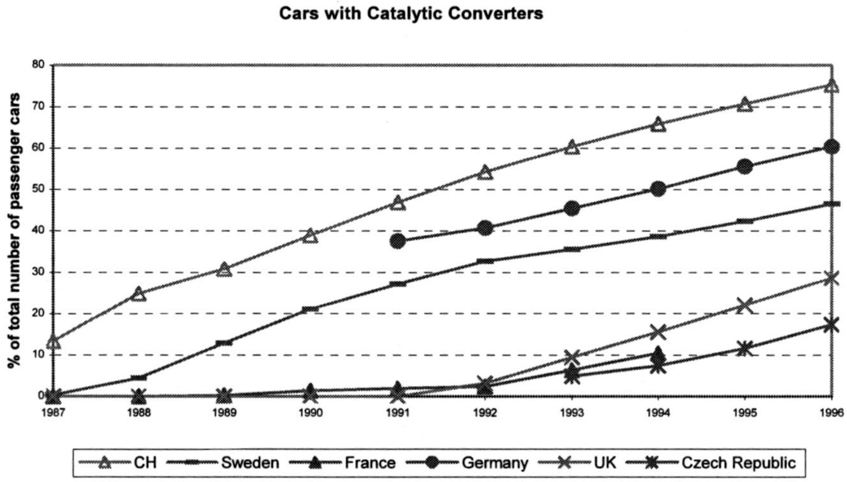

3.1.2 More Fundamental Explanations

At a superficial level, we can thus "explain" changes in emissions by reference to changes in the components total transportation, modal split and specific emissions. Obviously, one must dig deeper. The next step of analysis would involve figuring out why the components have behaved in the way they have behaved. Which policy and/or economic conditions lie behind the evolution of total transportation, modal split and specific emissions?

Consider specific emissions: With respect to carbon monoxide, the big picture is fairly obvious. Substantial changes in specific carbon monoxide emissions were the result of dramatic changes in emission norms for this local pollutant (and some others), compliance with which could only be achieved with the catalytic converter. While this is not the only source of change in specific emissions behaviour, it is certainly the dominant source.

For carbon dioxide, the answer is much more complex: Specific carbon dioxide emissions have changed much less, in spite of considerable dynamics in boundary conditions: Most importantly, the joint forces of oligopolistic price setting behaviour and, in many countries, fuel taxation have led to substantial swings in fuel prices. Further, increasing incomes made larger cars affordable for more people. On the other hand, specific policies directed at increasing fuel efficiency have worked in the opposite direction. The Corporate Average Fuel Economy Standard in the US is one example; other countries have used tax incentives and subsidies to induce a change in the vehicle fleet. Apparently, the net effect of these changes on fuel efficiency has been small.

From the economic point of view, this description of factors influencing the evolution of specific emissions is still not entirely satisfactory, as it does not address the underlying issues of Political Economy:

Why have emissions norms for local pollutants been introduced that were the basis for the diffusion of the catalytic converter? Why has Switzerland been faster to introduce such laws than most other countries? Why were there no equally effective measures to reduce carbon dioxide emissions?

In summary, PETE should deal with the following three sets of issues.

- (P1) At the most basic level, we need to understand the extent to which the changes in emissions were brought about by changes in total transportation, modal split and specific emissions, respectively.
- (P2) Beyond that, we need to know which economic developments, which policies and which other conditions were responsible for the changes in these quantities.
- (P3) Finally, PETE should aim at understanding why certain policies were introduced while others were not.

3.2 Existing Literature

The questions raised in the last section have, to some extent, been addressed in the literature. I shall first consider research on transportation and modal split, then move to specific emissions.

3.2.1 Total Transportation and Modal Split

Many researchers have attempted to understand the factors underlying the evolution of total transportation and modal split, using studies about observed real-world transportation behaviour as well as questionnaires about individual attitudes towards transportation. Most of the work has dealt with (P2) above.

Real-World Studies

1. A large group of authors attempt to explain the dynamics of transportation in specific countries. Most of the studies under consideration are concerned with modal split rather than just total transportation.[3] The central questions are: *Why did shifts from rail to road occur in most countries? Why is the share of public transportation usually so small?* Relevant studies include Ginther and

[3] An exception is Stead (2001) who deals with transport intensity in Europe.

Schmutzler (1996) for Germany, Hook (1999) for Hungary, Hensher (1998) for Australia, Kulsreshta and Nag (2000) for India, Xie et al. (2002) for China.

2. A related set of papers deals with the relatively rare cases that were not consistent with this trend, asking: *Why were there some cases where public transport did not lose much of its market share?* For instance, Fitzroy and Smith (1998) analyse the factors behind a doubling of public transport patronage in Freiburg in Germany within one decade. Bratzel (1999) also considers Freiburg, but beyond that he addresses cities such as Amsterdam, Groningen, Basel and Zürich. Asensio (2000) explains a 30% growth in patronage for the Spanish suburban railways between 1991 and 1998. Babalik-Sutcliffe (2002) compares urban railsystems in different countries, including Turkey as a developing country.

Individual Behaviour

A complementary strand of literature uses questionnaires to gain insights about individual travel behaviour, and in particular about mode choice. Unlike the real-world studies mentioned earlier, this literature does not analyse the development of transportation in specific countries or cities. Stradling et al. (2000), Kingham et al. (2001) and Cullinane (1992) attempt to estimate the potential for "moving people out of cars". Mackett (2003) deals specifically with reasons to use cars for short trips. Wardman et al. (1997) concentrate on the alternative of cycling.

Of specific interest is recent work that examines the role of habits for mode choice (Gärling and Axhausen, 2003, Garvill et al., 2003, Fujii and Kitamura, 2003, Bamberg et al., 2003). Though the outcomes of this research are somewhat ambiguous, it suggests that habits may reduce the elasticities of transportation demand with respect to changes in exogenous variables substantially.

3.2.2 Specific Emissions

Perhaps surprisingly, the literature that explains the behaviour of specific emissions is much smaller than the literature explaining modal split. An exception is a relatively large set of papers dealing with the relation between geographic factors and energy consumption. Such a relation could exist because urban structure might affect both total road transportation and specific energy consumption.

Starting with Newman and Kenworthy (1989), several authors have therefore explored the hypothesis that low urban density and high energy consumption should coincide: A reason for such a coincidence would be an increased need for automobile transportation as the initial simple correlation analysis of Newman and Kenworthy suggests. On the other hand, urban density should also increase specific emissions (if it leads to more stop-and-go traffic). Thus, it is unsurprising that the results are ambiguous.

3.3 Perspectives for Future Research

3.3.1 Modal Split

As already indicated, a large body of research deals with the explanation of modal split. These studies are very heterogeneous. They apply different methods, relate to different countries, different periods. Also, they deal with a wide variety of policy instruments. In some sense, the most important task for future research may be a consolidation of existing contributions. Are there any general lessons that emerge from this vast literature?

Beyond that, some special issues warrant particular attention.

Understanding Counterexamples to Historic Trends

The decreasing significance of public transport is an almost universal trend. Nevertheless, there are notable examples where the trend has been reversed or at least slowed down considerably at a local or even national level.

Swiss railways have increased their share of passenger transport slightly over the last 20 years. Why did this happen? Was it the result of pricing strategies? Was it largely due to service improvements? How important were income increases?[4] Did legislation favouring public transport play a crucial role? If so, why did such legislation come into place in Switzerland and not in most other European countries?

In Germany, in spite of an overall decline in the importance of railways, the reorganisation of the railroad sector in the nineties has led to substantial increases of patronage on many rural lines, often coinciding with a change in ownership, with patronage often at two or three times the original level. Which aspects of service improvement were responsible for such developments? Which institutional changes lay behind such improvements?

Developing Countries

From a global perspective, the most significant recent shifts in modal split are taking place outside of what used to be the Western Hemisphere. Superficially, the patterns are very similar across countries. In Eastern Europe, motorization has increased at an unprecedented speed over the last few decades. In emerging economies such as China, there are similar tendencies. It would be important to see whether there are significant deviations from this trend in individual countries, and how they can be explained. Are there cases where the combination of the decreasing role of the state and increasing incomes for non-negligible parts of society did not go hand in hand with increasing motorization? Or are there at least cases where the shift in modal split was moderate? If so, why?

---

4 In Switzerland, there is a high share of people who own cars, but nevertheless are very regular train users. This is of course much more likely in high income countries than elsewhere.

Habits

Until recently, most economic research was based on the assumption of perfectly rational behaviour. One of the many aspects of this approach was the exogeneity of preferences: Individuals are hard-wired to want particular things and then choose behaviour accordingly. Strange as such an assumption may seem to non-economists, there are good reasons for using it in benchmark models. For many purposes, however, it may be extremely important to understand how preferences are influenced both by other individuals and by own past behaviour. To really understand the mode choices of individuals, for instance, I believe that the analysis of habits for driving patterns is of utmost importance. Such an analysis is not only important to understand observed mode choice, but also as part of an informed policy discussion: If habits are so important, then policy measures aiming at behavioural change must make sure that they can break habits. I therefore hope that the research program sketched at the end of Section 3.2.1 will be pursued vigorously in the future.

3.3.2 More General Topics

Specific Emissions

To repeat, the dynamics of pollution differ widely across substances. Existing literature has done very little to explain this phenomenon, as it has concentrated on the evolution of total transportation and modal split rather than specific emissions. I believe that this is not a small oversight: So far, at least substantial improvements in environmental quality, even at a local level, have almost always involved reductions in specific emissions. Understanding why such reductions came about in the past may therefore be an important prerequisite for future improvements.

Political Economy

There can be little debate that special interests play a substantial role in the transportation sector. A more systematic understanding of how they influence legislation would most likely be a very promising research goal. There are many facets to this topic, including the role of the automobile industry in influencing the share of infrastructure budgets that is used for road projects. The distribution of public transport subsidies across projects is also a subject worthy of studying: Casual empiricism suggests that there may be a bias towards using money for prestige projects on the one hand, and for supporting desolate rural railway lines with limited economic and ecological value, but clearly defined interest groups who benefit from their existence.

Political economy considerations are also of great interest with respect to environmental policy in the transportation sector. Public support for alternative fuels, for instance, takes very different forms across different countries. Why are different policies pursued in different countries? Who benefits from the policies that are introduced and why?

4 Normative Environmental Transportation Economics

4.1 Overview

The ultimate motivation for most research in transportation economics is to find "good" transportation policy. This is even true for the literature dealt with in the section on PETE: In most cases, these studies emphasise the need to reduce road transportation or to improve environmental quality by other means. In addition, of course, there is a wide range of research questions that are explicitly normative. In addition to the issues just discussed, the following interrelated sets of issues warrant attention.

(N1) Which changes in transportation-related emissions e_i are desirable?

In particular, which types of environmental problems related to transportation should be addressed? Or, looking back, was it a good policy choice to emphasise the reduction of local pollutants such as carbon monoxide rather than paying more attention to global pollutants such as carbon dioxide?

Of course, the questions relate closely to the desired level of total emissions e_i, which depends on the valuation of environmental quality. Understanding more about this valuation is not an issue that is specific to transportation. Whatever insights can be achieved about the benefits of environmental improvements, these insights are independent of a particular sector.[5] A vast literature deals with this task; I shall not address it in this paper.[6]

However, choosing the right path for transportation emissions not only involves understanding the benefits of emissions reduction, but also the costs. In particular, it is important to know at least approximately how costly it is to reduce total emissions in the transportation sector rather than elsewhere. This knowledge is also a prerequisite for understanding to which extent total emissions themselves should be reduced.

(N2) How should the components of e_i evolve to achieve the desired change of total transportation emissions?

This question has several aspects: Which changes in total freight transportation f and passenger transportation p should be targeted? To which extent should changes in modal split (μ_{mF} and μ_{mP}) be pursued? How about the desired evolution of specific emissions (η_{miF} and η_{miF}) respectively?

Again, one can look backwards: Did policy put too much emphasis on changes of specific emissions rather than changes of modal split, or vice versa?

5 Exceptions concern the valuation of aspects of environmental quality that are entirely transportation-specific. For instance, several authors investigate the costs of aircraft noise or, equivalently, the benefits of noise reduction (e.g. Collins and Evans, 1994).

6 See Smith (1996) for a collection of influential papers in this area.

(N3) Which policy instruments should be used to achieve the desired changes in total transportation, modal split and specific emissions?

Obviously, the relation to questions (N1) and (N2) is close: Both the types of instruments chosen and the level at which they are set will depend strongly on the targeted emissions and the extent to which the targets are to be achieved by changes of modal split or by reductions in specific emissions. For instance, discussions on the right level of environmental taxes are closely related to discussions on the right level of emissions. Similarly, attempts to reduce emissions by way of subsidies for railways should be based on an argument that affecting the modal split is a more efficient way of improving environmental quality than reducing specific emissions (or at least a useful complement).

4.2 Existing Literature

Some aspects of questions (N2) and (N3) have been addressed in the literature.

4.2.1 Modal Split

In Which Direction Should Modal Split Change?

Much of the research on policy towards modal split is based on the understanding that lowering the share of cars and trucks, and of air transportation is an appropriate policy goal. Two assumptions are implicit in these arguments. First, there are environmental benefits of a shift in modal split, and second, the benefits outweigh the costs.

Most literature I am familiar with considers only the benefits, concluding that, for most pollution problems, changes in modal split would be desirable. For instance, Hughes (1990) shows that buses and railways are more energy-efficient than cars and planes.[7]

Influencing Modal Split: Policy Instruments

Supposing that the benefits of changing modal split so as to reduce automobile transportation outweigh the costs, question (N3) has to be addressed with respect to modal split policies. *How should such changes in modal split best be brought about?* How do different policy instruments differ with respect to (i) political feasibility; (ii) the effect on the environment, (iii) efficiency and (iv) distributional impacts?

A large group of papers attempts to obtain some idea about the potential effects of policy measures by looking back at the effects of policies that were introduced in the past. Eskeland and Feyzioglu (1997a,b) emphasise the undesired side-effects of a policy of prohibiting the usage of each car in Mexico City on a particular day of the week. Similarly, Phang et al. (1996) identify unintended consequences of car quotas in Singapore. Parkhurst (2000) considers the ambiguous ef-

7 In a similar vein, Kahn-Ribeiro and Balassiano (1997) demonstrate that buses are more energy efficient than cars in Rio de Janeiro.

fects of park and ride systems in the UK on car transportation. Brown et al. (2001) emphasise the positive effects of free public transportation schemes for students at US universities. Several papers discuss the effects of road pricing experiments. For instance, Ison (1998) explains why an attempt to introduce congestion metering did not proceed beyond the trial stage in Cambridge.

Apart from such policy measures that are clearly designed with the intention to "move people out of cars", the literature has also dealt with policies whose purpose is to foster road transportation, such as road infrastructure investments. A resounding argument in this discussion is that such investments not only have a positive effect on the amount of road traffic, but that this effect may be so strong that congestion increases rather than decreases.[8]

In addition to this "backward-looking" literature, there are some authors who use simulations and/or theoretical ideas to investigate the likely effects of policy instruments. Several authors consider road pricing (e.g. Viegas, 2001, Hyman and Mayhew, 2002, Santos and Rojey, 2004). Tsamboulas (2001) deals with the effects of parking fares. Walton (1997) sketches ideas as to how a system of auctioned permits for car ownership could be used to reduce car ownership.

Finally, a considerable number of authors deals specifically with issues of feasibility. They use surveys to understand why some policy instruments have better chances of being introduced than others. They do so by dealing explicitly with attitudes towards specific policies. For instance, Bhattacharjee et al. (1997) deal with commuters' attitudes toward a variety of demand management policies; Holding and Kreutner (1998) discuss the support for measures designed to foster public transport in a Bavarian National Park. Rye (1999) uses survey data from the UK and the Netherlands to explore the attitude of employers to transport plans designed to induce their employees to shift away from cars. Attitudes towards road pricing have met with particular interest (Odeck and Brathen, 1997, Jakobsson et al., 2000, Ison, 2000).

4.2.2 Specific Emissions

Some authors have dealt with the impacts of actual policy programs on specific emissions. Dill (2003) analyses the impact of accelerated vehicle retirement programs in California on emissions. Sperling (2001) discusses the effects of public-private partnerships in the United States for the development of energy efficient vehicles. Hubbard (1997) explains why inspection and maintenance programs have often failed to lead to low in-use emissions of motor vehicles.

Numerous studies deal with the potential for future changes in specific emissions. Johansson (1998) asks whether future technological improvements can compensate for an expected increase in traffic. Other authors discuss whether there are suitable policies to unleash this technological potential, that is, to achieve a change in the vehicle stock that leads to lower overall emissions. Obvious candidates include vehicle characteristic taxes favouring low-pollution cars. Kavalec and Setiawan (1997) and Johnstone and Karousakis (1999) come to positive con-

---

8 See Mogridge (1997) for a review.

clusions, using simulations and theoretical arguments, respectively. Similarly, Fullerton and West (2002) use a theoretical model to compare the merits of different types of automobile and fuel taxes. Kazimi (1997) considers the effects of price reductions for alternative-fuel vehicles in the Los Angeles area.

4.3 Perspectives for Future Research

4.3.1 Basics: A General Framework

I suspect that many colleagues think that the basic normative principles for doing environmental transportation policy are well understood: Just internalise external costs, preferably using market-based instruments. I am unconvinced that this settles the issue, even from a theoretical perspective. Several aspects of the transportation sector imply that an optimal policy is non-trivial to derive. These aspects include:

1. the importance of emissions from consumption activities rather than from production;
2. the severe monitoring issues resulting from the large number of polluters
3. the importance of scale economies in public transportation.

In spite of some attempts to characterise optimal policy, I am unconvinced that these complications have already been adequately addressed. There still is a need for a comprehensive theoretical framework for environmental transportation economics from which clear optimality conditions can be devised.[9]

Apart from this task, there are many other important topics for future research. Rather than attempting to be exhaustive, I shall point to a few issues that deserve particular attention. In brief, they relate to the right level of pollution, the right modal split and the right policy instruments.

4.3.2 Priorisation of Environmental Goals

Given the finite amount of political attention that is paid to transportation and the environment, it is clearly important to prioritise policy issues. How much attention should be paid to improving air quality in cities relative to preventing global warming? Should policy address road noise pollution in agglomerations first, or is it more important to reduce the adverse effects of transportation on the landscape in more rural areas?

Of course, an informed answer to these questions would presuppose an answer to the question outlined in Section 4.1, namely, which development of e_i is desirable for each type of environmental problem. As argued earlier, however, finding the right policy targets for the various environmental problems is an issue that transcends transportation economics, because it involves estimations of the bene-

---

9 A useful step in this direction is Fullerton and West (2002) who analyse the relative efficiency of different types of taxes as substitutes for emission taxes. See also Innes (1996).

fits of environmental improvements. Given the tremendous uncertainties surrounding the damages from environmental pollution, the scientific basis for such estimates will necessarily be shaky, and therefore a prioritisation of environmental goals will involve a lot of gut feeling. Unfortunately, it is indispensable nevertheless.

4.3.3 Which Changes of the Modal Split Are Desirable?

While I agree with the general assessment that changes in modal split are potentially useful means of improving environmental quality, there are several non-trivial issues that need to be addressed.

First, existing research on the relative environmental performance of different modes needs to be improved. Relative performance depends in a very complex way on the type of environmental problem, the type of traffic (freight vs. passenger, intercity vs. rural vs. intra-agglomeration), and so on. Knowing where the relative advantages of, say, railway transportation over road transportation are most pronounced is extremely important in order to set the right priorities for a change in modal split.

Second, in most European countries, railways have an extremely low share of transportation (at least for passenger transportation, where the share is typically around five percent). Even a substantial increase of passenger transportation (in the order of magnitude of 20 or 30%) would, in itself, have very little impact on environmental quality. Therefore, a notable contribution of railways and of public transport in general to the solution of environmental problems is unlikely, except in specific regions or in the very long run. This suggests at least two research questions. (i) Is there a potential for really big changes in the long run? In brief, can other European countries copy Switzerland? (ii) Might it be more effective to concentrate activities to support public transport on specific areas where the chances of obtaining a significant increase are high?

Third, the relative environmental performance of different modes is subject to change. In several dimensions, automobiles have become less polluting than they used to be. It is likely that this trend will continue. To assess to which extent changes in modal split should be pursued in the future, it is therefore important to have estimates about the relative environmental performance of the different modes in the future.

Fourth, the emphasis of NETE has been on reducing environmental problems from road pollution. Pollution by aircraft, which is also extremely problematic in many ways, has met with relatively little attention. This was justified as long as air transportation was relatively unimportant. The recent turbulence notwithstanding, air transportation has increased its share of transportation and its significance as an environmental nuisance at a dramatic speed over the last three decades. NETE should therefore put more attention on "how to get people out of aeroplanes".

4.3.4 Policy Instruments

Of the many issues arising in this area, I shall pick two examples that are of particular importance.

Railway Reform

Modal split is not only affected by policies that are explicitly designed for this purpose, but also by policies that were introduced for very different reasons. A case in point is provided by the railway reforms that have been taking place all over Europe for more than a decade. These reforms are changing the organisational structure of the industry. They differ in many ways that are almost certainly extremely important for the performance of the railway sector, and thereby for modal split. An extremely important research question is therefore: Which boundary conditions for the railroad sector are conducive to a substantial increase in rail transportation (at reasonable economic costs)?

Incentives for Low-Energy Vehicles and Alternative Fuels

Over the next few decades, the share of vehicles which use alternative fuels or are at least extremely energy efficient is likely to increase. Various kinds of policy measures might support this process. The conceivable forms of such measures include different types of subsidies, prizes for successful innovations and many other options. Very little is known about the optimal design of such policies, not even in theory. Understanding which policies may be fruitful is an important theoretical question. Analysis of this question can build from a huge literature on innovation incentives, which has addressed environmental innovations as well as more general innovations. Importantly, however, existing literature must be modified to deal with innovations in the transportation sector. Crucially, innovators (automobile firms) and polluters (consumers) are not identical. This differs from standard environmental economics approaches to innovation.

5 Concluding Remarks

There are many open questions that research on "Transportation and the Environment" should address. Personally, I believe that the most important question is whether changes in modal split or reductions in specific emissions are more appropriate paths for future transportation policy. The answer is by no means obvious, as it depends on most of the questions addressed in this paper. Whether useful contributions can be made, will depend on several factors.

1. Researchers must take a long-term perspective. Some progress notwithstanding, the remaining problems in the relation between transportation and the environment will take decades of hard work to solve. At the same time researchers must take into account that important decision makers are subject to constraints that are incompatible with a long-term perspective.
2. The right division of labour between different disciplines must be found. Economists can make there contributions to some topics. On other issues raised he-

re, psychologists and engineers will have more to say. Transportation research has always involved interdisciplinary communication – but there still seems to exist room for improvement.

References

Asensio, J. (2000), The Success Story of Spanish Suburban Railways: Determinants of Demand and Policy Implications, *Transport Policy* 7 (4), 295-302.

Babalik-Sutcliffe, E. (2002), Urban Rail Systems: Analysis of the Factors Behind Success, *Transport Reviews* 22 (4), 415-447.

Bamberg, S., D. Rölle, and C. Weber (2003), Does Habitual Car Use Not Lead to More Resistance to Change of Travel Mode?, *Transportation* 30 (1), 97-108.

Bhattacharjee, D., S.W. Haider, Y. Tanaboriboon, and K.C. Sinha (1997), Commuters' Attitudes Towards Travel Demand Management in Bangkok, *Transport Policy* 4 (3), 161-170.

Bratzel, S. (1999), Conditions of Success in Sustainable Urban Transport Policy – Policy Change in 'Relatively Successful' European Cities, *Transport Reviews* 19 (2), 177-190.

Brown, J., D.B. Hess, and D. Shoup (2001), Unlimited Access, *Transportation* 28 (3), 233-267.

Collins, A. and A. Evans (1994), Aircraft Noise and Residential Property Values, an Artificial Neural Network Approach, *Journal of Transport Economics and Policy* 28 (2), 175-197.

Cullinane, S. (1992), Attitudes Towards the Car in the U.K.: Some Implications for Policies on Congestion and the Environment, Transportation Research Part A, *Policy and Practice* 26 (4), 291-301.

Dill, J. (2003), Estimating Emissions Reductions from Accelerated Vehicle Retirement Programs, Transportation Research Part D, *Transport and Environment* 9 (2), 87-106.

Eskeland, G.S. and T. Feyzioglu (1997a), Rationing Can Backfire: The "Day Without a Car" in Mexico City, *The World Bank Economic Review* 11 (3), 383-408.

Eskeland, G.S. and T. Feyzioglu (1997b), Is Demand for Polluting Goods Manageable? An Econometric Study of Car Ownership and Use in Mexico, *Journal of Development Economics* 53, 323-445.

Filho, J.M.A., A. Lenzi, and P.H.T. Zannin (2003), Effects of Traffic Composition on Road Noise: A Case Study, Transportation Research Part D, *Transport and Environment* 9 (1), 75-80.

FitzRoy, F. and I. Smith (1998), Public Transport Demand in Freiburg: Why Did Patronage Double in A Decade?, *Transport Policy* 5 (3), 163-173.

Fujii, S. and R. Kitamura (2003), What Does a One-Month Free Bus Ticket Do to Habitual Drivers? An Experimental Analysis of Habit and Attitude Change, *Transportation* 30 (1), 81-95.

Fullerton, D. and S. West (2002), Can Taxes on Cars and on Gasoline Mimic an Unavailable Tax on Emissions?, *Journal of Environmental Economics and Management* 43, 135-157.

Gärling, T. and K.W. Axhausen (2003), Introduction: Habitual Travel Choice, *Transportation* 30 (1), 1-11.

Garvill, J., A. Marell, and A. Nordlund (2003), Effects of Increased Awareness on Choice of Travel Mode, *Transportation* 30 (1), 63-79.

Ginter, D. and A. Schmutzler (1996), Die Aufteilung des Güterverkehrs auf Bahn, Schiff und LKW – eine dynamische Analyse, *Zeitschrift für Verkehrswissenschaft* 67, 49-68.

Hensher, D.A. (1998), The Imbalance Between Car and Public Transport Use in Urban Australia: Why Does It Exist? *Transport Policy* 5, 193-204.

Holding, D.M. and M. Kreutner (1998), Achieving a Balance Between "Carrots" and "Sticks" for Traffic in National Parks: the Bayerischer Wald Project, *Transport Policy* 5 (3), 175-183.

Hook, W. (1999), The Political Economy of Post-Transition Transportation Policy in Hungary, *Transport Policy* 6 (4), 207-224.

Hubbard, T.N. (1997), Using Inspection and Maintenance Programs to Regulate Vehicle Emissions, *Contemporary Economic Policy* 15, 52-62.

Hughes, P. (1990), *Transport and the Greenhouse Effect*, Energy and Environmental Research Unit, Open University, Milton Keynes.

Hyman, G. and L. Mayhew (2002), Optimising the Benefits of Urban Road User Charging, *Transport Policy* 9 (3), 189-207.

Ison, S. (2000), Local Authority and Academic Attitudes to Urban Road Pricing: A UK Perspective, *Transport Policy* 7 (4), 269-277.

Ison, S. (1998), A Concept in the Right Place at the Wrong Time: Congestion Metering in the City of Cambridge, *Transport Policy* 5 (3), 139-146.

Jakobsson, C., S. Fujii, and T. Gärling (2000), Determinants of Private Car Users' Acceptance of Road Pricing, *Transport Policy* 7 (2), 153-158.

Johansson, B. (1998), Will New Technology Be Sufficient to Solve the Problem of Air Pollution Caused by Swedish Road Transport?, *Transport Policy* 5 (4), 213-221.

Johnstone, N. and K. Karousakis (1999), Economic Incentives to Reduce Pollution from Road Transport: The Case for Vehicle Characteristics Taxes, *Transport Policy* 6 (2), 99-108.

Kavalec, C. and W. Setiawan (1997), An Analysis of per Mile Pollution Fees for Motor Vehicles in California's South Coast, *Transport Policy* 4 (4), 267-273.

Kazimi, C. (1997), Evaluating the Environmental Impact of Alternative-Fuel Vehicles, *Journal of Environmental Economics and Management* 33, 163-185.

Kingham, S., J. Dickinson, and S. Copsey (2001), Travelling to Work: Will People Move out of Their Cars, *Transport Policy* 8 (2), 151-160.

Kulsreshtha, M. and B. Nag (2000), Structure and Dynamics of Non-Suburban Passenger Travel Demand in Indian Railways, *Transportation* 27 (2), 221-241.

Mackett, R.L. (2003), Why Do People Use Their Cars for Short Trips?, *Transportation* 30 (3), 329-349.

Mindali, O., A. Raveh, and I. Salomon (2004), Urban Density and Energy Consumption: A New Look at Old Statistics, Transportation Research Part A, *Policy and Practice* 38 (2), 143-162.

Mogridge, M.J.H. (1997), The Self-Defeating Nature of Urban Road Capacity Policy: A Review of Theories, Disputes and Available Evidence, *Transport Policy* 4 (1), 5-23.

Newman, P.W.G. and J.R. Kenworthy (1989), Gasoline Consumption and Cities: A Comparison of U.S. Cities with a Global Survey, *Journal of the American Planning Association* 55, 24-37.

Odeck, J. and S. Bråthen (1997), On Public Attitudes Toward Implementation of Toll Roads – the Case of Oslo Toll Ring, *Transport Policy* 4 (2), 73-83.

Parkhurst, G. (2000), Influence of Bus-Based Park and Ride Facilities on Users' Car Traffic, *Transport Policy* 7 (2), 159-172.
Phang, S-Y., W-K. Wong, and N-C. Chia (1996), Singapore's Experience with Car Quotas: Issues and Policy Processes, *Transport Policy* 3 (4), 145-153.
Pucher, J. (1999), The Transformation of Urban Transport in the Czech Republic, 1988-1998, *Transport Policy* 6 (4), 225-236.
Ribeiro, S.K. and R. Balassiano (1997), CO_2 Emissions from Passenger Transport in Rio de Janeiro, *Transport Policy* 4 (2), 135-139.
Rye, T. (1999), Employer Attitudes to Employer Transport Plans: A Comparison of UK and Dutch Experience, *Transport Policy* 6 (3), 183-196.
Santos, G. and L. Rojey (2004), Distributional Impacts of Road Pricing: The Truth Behind the Myth, *Transportation* 31 (1), 21-42.
Smith, V.K. (1996), *Estimating Economic Values for Nature – Methods for Non-Market Valuation*, Cheltenham.
Sperling, D. (2001), Public-Private Technology R&D Partnerships: Lessons from US Partnership for a New Generation of Vehicles, *Transport Policy* 8 (4), 247-256.
Stead, D. (2001), Transport Intensity in Europe – Indicators and Trends, *Transport Policy* 8, 29-46.
Stradling, S.G., M.L. Meadows, and S. Beatty (2000), Helping Drivers out of Their Cars Integrating Transport Policy and Social Psychology for Sustainable Change, *Transport Policy* 7 (3), 207-215.
Tsamboulas, D.A. (2001), Parking Fare Thresholds: a Policy Tool, *Transport Policy* 8 (2), 115-124.
Viegas, J.M. (2001), Making Urban Road Pricing Acceptable and Effective: Searching for Quality and Equity in Urban Mobility, *Transport Policy* 8 (4), 289-294.
Walton, W. (1997), The Potential Scope for the Application of Pollution Permits to Reducing Car Ownership in the UK: Some Preliminary Thoughts, *Transport Policy* 4 (2), 115-122.
Wardman, M., R. Hatfield, and M. Page (1997), The UK National Cycling Strategy: Can Improved Facilities Meet the Targets?, *Transport Policy* 4 (2), 123-133.
Xie, R., H. Chen, and C. Nash (2002), Migration of Railway Freight Transport from Command Economy to Market Economy: The Case of China, *Transport Reviews* 22 (2), 159-177.

Research Issues in Transport Economics: Dynamics, Integration, and Indirect Effects

Wolfgang Schade, Werner Rothengatter

University of Karlsruhe, Institute for Economic Policy Research (IWW),
Kollegium am Schloß Bau IV, 76128 Karlsruhe, Germany,
wolfgang.schade@iww.uni-karlsruhe.de, rothengatter@iww.uni-karlsruhe.de

Keywords. *Integrated Assessment, Indirect Economic Effects, Transport Policy, System Dynamics*

JEL. *E27; L91; O21*

Abstract. Transport policy assessment is usually based on a comparative static Cost-Benefit Analysis (CBA) using a transport network model. However, transport policies exert impacts also outside the transport system. These impacts exhibit different dynamic characteristics and affect other systems than the transport system itself like the economic system or vehicle purchase decisions. Hence to improve transport policy assessment it would be required to integrate those systems into the analysis and to model the dynamic interactions between them. Following these suggestions transport policy assessment could be based on or accompanied by measuring indirect effects (e.g. change of GDP or employment). The paper describes a dynamic integrated system model to measure indirect effects of transport policies.

1 Introduction

This paper addresses improvements in the field of transport policy assessment with respect to the long-term macro-level impacts of transport policies. That means the emerging fields of micro-simulation of traffic or agent-based modelling of activity patterns including transport are outside the scope of the paper.

The point of departure for transport policy assessment is constituted by cost-benefit analysis (CBA) that is based on measuring the changes of transport costs and transport times calculated by using a transport network model. This rigid microeconomic framework of impact analyses has dominated the cost-benefit methodology in the transport sector for some decades such that the comparative static approach is most frequently used as a standard evaluation scheme. It is based on a comparison between a situation with and without the considered transport initiative (transport investment project or general transport policy) for a defined year of the future. For the transport sector this approach has a clear computational advantage. The forecasting algorithm, which usually includes the socio-economic development, the change of traffic behaviour, the change of industrial location and logistics, the traffic generation, distribution, modal split and assignment on a network scale, has only to be performed for one year of the past (for calibration purposes) and one year of the future (for forecasting and impact analyses). Also the assessment and the appraisal analyses can be done by applying standard static welfare concepts such that the complex dynamics stemming from the feedback mechanisms within the transport sector and between the transport sector and other economic sectors as well as the difficult construction of a dynamic, intergenerational welfare concept are not necessary. If dynamics are introduced then in most cases they are based on very simple assumptions to avoid the complexity mentioned above. For instance in the German standard scheme for the evaluation of investments in the Federal transport system it is assumed that the yearly benefits, which have been calculated for the year of forecasting, remain constant over the life time of the investment projects.

While the estimation failures stemming from this static procedure might be small if small independent projects are considered, which produce only marginal changes of the initial situation, in the case of large scale projects or interdependent project bundles, which heavily influence the transport sector and other sectors of the economy, large errors are possible. Therefore the intention of this paper is to show ways forward to improve transport policy assessment in such cases.

The paper is structured into four sections. The first section describes alternative modelling approaches to provide the impact measurement for transport policies. This section is followed by three sections each addressing one of the three most challenging issues in transport policy assessment: *dynamics*, *integration* and *indirect effects*.

2 Approaches for Impact Measurement to Perform CBA

There are well-known deficiencies of CBA that were identified some decades ago. In 1972 Dasgupta and Pearce in *Cost-Benefit-Analysis – Theory and Practice* stated that after some 20 years of experience with Cost-Benefit-Analysis (CBA) one should expect that a common consensus about the proper methodology and its application has been developed. However, they concluded that this was not the case. They listed a set of issues over which there was disagreement like the problem of evaluating non-market goods; and if they have been evaluated then a hypothetical static configuration of the economy was a prerequisite; the point that CBA is based on welfare economics, which is a normative theory and therefore not testable; and finally the big discussion on the appropriate social discount rate. Despite all that they concluded that *"whether these problems constitute insuperable objections to the use of CBA, bearing in mind the objections which can easily be raised against the alternative decision procedures, is for the reader to judge".*

Looking at the criticism mentioned by Dasgupta/Pearce the situation of CBA has improved in the last 30 years. This concerns the establishment of more or less agreed valuations for a set of non-market goods like the value of environmental impacts e.g. emissions or noise, the value of life or the value of time spent for transport. However, all other critics still hold and it looks, as if they cannot be resolved because they are inherent to the methodology. Nevertheless, CBA today is widely applied in practice and this demonstrates that it is a useful tool for at least a vast range of policy decisions including transport policy-making.

No doubt, the current practice of applying microeconomically founded transport network models for CBA in transport policy-making, provides a useful and decent methodology that will play an important role in the future, too. The question is whether this state-of-the-art CBA is already a comprehensive methodology for all kinds of decisions that have to be taken in the field of transport policy. In this paper we identify three directions in which CBA or in wider terms transport policy assessment is developing: modelling dynamics, integration of models and measuring indirect effects. Before explaining these three directions the next section describes potential theoretical approaches to perform a CBA of transport policies.

2.1 Macroeconomic Approaches

Macroeconomic approaches are usually either Keynesian or Neo-classic. Keynesian approaches presuppose that price mechanism does not work efficiently such that important markets are permanently constrained. If this holds for instance for the supply sides of the goods market and the labour market then a permanent situation of unemployment accompanied with an under-utilisation of the labour and capital resources of the economy follows. Public investments, including investments in networks, then can produce a multiplier effect, which relaxes the constraining situation on the markets and moves the economy to a higher equilibrium position.

Neo-classical approaches start from the assumption that the supply side is governing the economic development. Consequently the production function is in the focus of analyses. To analyse the influence of infrastructure on economic development it is possible to specify a production function in a way that the transport infrastructure represents one of the endogenous factors of economic growth. Econometric estimation of the production function eventually disaggregated by sectors and inserting the "with and without" figures of transport infrastructure capital into the functional gives an aggregate estimate for the influence of the transport infrastructure capital on the economy. Aschauer (1989) followed this approach, but the results are questioned very much (for an overview see Pfähler et al., 1996).

In both cases, the Keynesian or the Neo-classical, figures of national accounting such as gross domestic product (GDP), domestic consumption or domestic employment are used as measures of welfare. We will see in the following section that this is not conforming to the microeconomic concept of welfare.

2.2 Microeconomic Approaches

The microeconomic approaches are in general based on the Kaldor-Hicks criterion, which states that a public measure brings a net benefit to society if the advantaged parties are able to compensate the disadvantaged parties and still enjoy a net advantage after compensation. Starting from this general criterion one can work out the theoretical foundation either on the base of utility or on the base of demand theory.

The welfare concepts based on demand theory date back to Marshall (1920), Hicks (1941) and Henderson (1941). Marshall has introduced the concept of consumers and producers surplus into the welfare discussion. Separating the considered market from the interrelationships with other markets he depicted the situation on this market by introducing demand and supply functions and their equilibrium position. The equilibrium position is characterised by a price, which does not exhaust the consumers' total willingness to pay. The sum of all willingness-to-pay measures of the consumers, which exceed the equilibrium price is denoted as the consumers surplus. On the suppliers side the equilibrium position can be characterised by the surplus of revenues over costs. The change of the welfare position, then, can be measured by the sum of the variations of the consumers' and the producers' surplus (see the reformulation of surplus theory by Hicks (1941) and Henderson (1941)).

As the quantification of the demand and supply curves is a non-trivial exercise most of the standard evaluation schemes assume that prices are constant over the interval considered. In this case one can separate the cost-benefit analysis in two parts: the quantification of impacts (forecasting) and the appraisal of impacts using constant willingness-to-pay measures (appraisal). Usually, these willingness-to-pay measures are taken from surveys, i.e. they are inserted as constant values into the appraisal part. This approach allows for a very differentiated benefit measurement, beginning with the generalised costs (operating and time costs) and including accident costs, costs of the environment and eventually spatial effects. Although computation of costs and benefits is – applying these simplifying rules – comparatively easy and transparent it incorporates a number of caveats:

- Willingness-to-pay measures abstract from income distribution, which means that people with a higher income usually express the higher willingness to pay for a good.
- The Kaldor-Hicks test is not actually performed but only implicitly done through calculating the surplus of benefits over costs. Therefore, it can happen, that in a sequence of state actions the same social groups are always losers in the public policy game.
- The rigid assumptions of microeconomic analysis hold, which means that dynamic interactions are not considered.
- If the spatial competition or the sectoral interlinkages are incomplete then the partial surplus measures give wrong indications on welfare changes.

2.3 Computable General Equilibrium (CGE) Models

Computable equilibrium models for transport have become popular through the work of Krugman (1991), Venables (see SACTRA[1], 1999) and Venables and Gasiourek, (1998). The main difference to the standard microeconomic approach is that spatial CGE (SCGE) models start from the assumption that demand and supply are distributed over space and that spatial competition exists, which is distorted by market imperfections (monopolistic competition in at least one sector; regional barriers to trade). Public activities, which remove restrictions to interregional trade then can be assessed by applying constraint equilibrium modelling and comparative static analysis. Obviously this spatial approach has big advantages over the microeconomic approach based on the simple partial market analysis of Marshall. But again this method suffers from the very rigid assumption of equilibrium theory and the computational problems, which arise in the real economy. The analyses of Krugman (1991) and Venables (see SACTRA, 1999) have shown, that in order to simulate realistic reaction mechanisms in the regional economic system imperfect markets have to be assumed.

However, a quantitative CGE analysis of interdependent regions with incomplete markets in a sectorally disaggregated economic system is very tedious and has not been successful until now. Therefore the SACTRA Committee of the U.K. department of transport has decided – after detailed discussion of the approach of Venables and Gasiourek (1998) – to confine itself to a purely qualitative interpretation of the outcomes of this type of models. These outcomes are clearly dependent on the constraints, which are assumed for interregional trade, the flexibility of prices, the spatial organisation of the industry, and the regional equipment with private and public production sectors. The SACTRA Committee concludes that investments in roads can have positive economic effects beyond the effects measured by the standard microeconomic approach. However, these effects could be positive or negative, this means that there cannot be given a general rule for the deviation of the actual benefits and costs in the regions from the results which have been computed based on traditional microeconomics. Lakshmanan and Anderson (2002), dealing with the same question as SACTRA in a White Paper on behalf of the US Department of Transportation, suggest, though raising some fundamental doubts about CGE, to further develop CGE for the assessment of indirect effects of transport policies.

2.4 Evolutionary Approaches Using System Dynamics Models

Since the work of Schumpeter (1934) this branch of economic dynamic theory has been developed in cycles. The name results from its parallels to biological evolution, which is governed by processes of selection and mutation of species. The agents do not decide on the base of maximisation calculus, but rather on the base of learning schemes. They behave according to routines, which they only change

[1] Standing Advisory Committee on Trunk Road Assessment, United Kingdom.

if failures force them to rethink their attitudes. Satisfying behaviour replaces optimal behaviour because in an uncertain world the agents never know what the exact parameters for an optimality calculus are (Simon, 1984).

Evolutionary development is backed by a history, but historical events never repeat in the same form. Also equilibria, if they occur, are never of the same structure. The notion of equilibrium is much different from neo-classics. This is because the economic system is permanently driven by endogenous and exogenous changes. Business cycles are not dampened over time. In the process of growth periods of recessions are not only occurring repeatedly, they are intrinsically moving forces of the capitalist dynamics. Schumpeter has called this the process of creative disruption: Old technology, inappropriate routines are questioned, innovations for products and production processes discovered. Firms, which are not successful with this change, disappear from the market and the next upturn is governed by the successful adopters of the change. According to Schumpeter such a system of permanent creation and disruption can grow more dynamically than a system in which the neoclassical rules are followed at every point of time.

The main focus of dynamic analysis is whether the time path of the development is sustainable or whether conflicts are expected to occur. Schumpeter for instance was interested in the question whether capitalism can survive despite the occurrence of heavy business cycles or whether in a phase of deep crisis socialism would win and change the economic system. Presently evolutionary modelers are more interested in long-term environmental and social sustainability – which does not mean a stationary world or a world with constant growth rates.

The economic theory of evolution has a direct link to the theory of synergy, developed in physics (Haken, 1983), and the theory of self-organisation, which has been influenced by findings in physics, biology and information science. Agents are interacting in an uncertain environment, i.e. the activity of one individual is responded by others. As soon as the responses go to the same direction they move the system to a new state. This process is formulated in a very general way by Weidlich's master equation system, which is the basis for a number of approaches in economic and social science. Koblo (1991) for instance analyses the investor's/consumer's interaction and reformulates the Samuelson/Hicks paradigm of a business cycle generated by multiplier/accelerator settings. Schuster et al. (1981) have shown that game theory can be integrated in such a dynamic approach such that strategic behaviour can be analysed. Weidlich and Haag (1984) have applied the master equation to migration phenomena and contributed to a better understanding of mobility in space. Both authors (Weidlich and Haag, 1999) have edited a volume on an Integrated Transport and Evolutionary Model. Schreckenberg (1998) and Helbing (2001) have developed a reformulation of traffic flow theory on the base of self-organisation and agent-modelling, which gives powerful explanations for congestion phenomena.

When it comes to the measurement of impacts for CBA the main building blocks of evolutionary theory can be used by employing System Dynamics Modelling (SDM). The use of system dynamics for giving decision support to transport policy makers has been presented in Schade and Rothengatter (2001) and Schade (2004). This tool is able to handle a high complexity of interactive subsystems such that it is appropriate to analyse long-term impact mechanisms within the transport sector and between the transport sector and other sectors of the economy.

With system dynamics it is also possible to include the regional dimension. In the European project SCENARIOS (Scenarios for the Trans-European Network) the regional analysis with quasi-production functions (see Biehl, 1991) considering agglomeration, space for industrial settlement, transport infrastructure, natural resources and infrastructure for education has been successfully combined with a system dynamics model to analyse the long-term effect of transport investments on European NUTS[2] II regions of different type (IWW, 1998). Depending on the bottleneck situation of the quasi-production factor "transport infrastructure" this instrument diagnoses strong or weak affinities of regions to transport infrastructure. Therefore in some cases transport infrastructure investments even can lead to negative results for the regional economy ("backwash effects"). In other cases such investments are the conditio sine qua non for regional development.

It is possible to integrate a number of welfare criteria into the framework of a system dynamics model. This can include microeconomic (individuals), mesoeconomic (groups, sectors) and macroeconomic indicators. In particular it is feasible, to define a standard CBA indicator which measures the change of aggregate willingness-to-pay. The difference compared with the microeconomic approach is then, that transport system changes and the interactions between regions and sectors as well as the evolution of variables over time is considered in a consistent way. Compared with SCGE approaches the system dynamics model has the advantage that it is not bound to the equilibrium concept. The development can be completely evolutionary, i.e. it has a history but it does not necessarily repeat itself. In the transport sector there is some evidence that this type of dynamics is more appropriate to the development, which we can observe, than the equilibrium theory. To summarise, system dynamics is a most flexible instrument to cope with complex systems in an evolutionary environment and therefore provides an excellent platform for a dynamic assessment of political actions including CBA, as will be shown in the next section.

3 Dynamics

Transport policies, comprising either infrastructure policies and any kind of regulation or pricing policy, may evoke many reactions inside as well as outside the transport system. These reactions will have different time profiles i.e. some reactions will occur immediately after implementation of the transport policy while others incorporate lags between policy implementation and policy impacts. These time profiles constitute one element of dynamics relevant for transport policy assessment. Another element is given by the interaction between the different reactions to the policy. It makes a difference if one assumes, like in the comparative static CBA, that all policy reactions occur simultaneously at the forecasting

---

2 Nomenclature of territorial units for statistics.

time horizon, or if some reactions occur immediately while others emerge with a delay leading to further reactions. As an example one could consider a transport pricing policy for road leading immediately to modal shift away from road to competing modes. With some lag load factors of road freight will increase due to improved logistics to counterbalance the cost increase. Furthermore regions that depend less on road transport e.g. concerning their trade relationships or economic sectors that show a higher affinity to non-road modes will improve their competitiveness e.g. leading to faster growth than for other regions or sectors. However, these reactions exhibit different time profiles than e.g. the modal shifts or the change of load factors such that these earlier reactions cause further adaptations to later reactions. To capture all these dynamics caused by the variance of response times and the interactions of responses should be an objective of improved transport policy assessment such that a shift away from the comparative static CBA towards dynamic CBA seems to be required. However, this does not alter that much the structure of the CBA approach but it affects the choice of model that is used for the impact measurement of policies. Out of the approaches described in the previous sections one approach providing these capabilities would be evolutionary economics applying SDM. Therefore the following paragraphs present an example of a dynamic CBA using the system dynamics model ASTRA[3].

3.1 Description of the ASTRA Model

The ASTRA model consists of eight modules that are all implemented within one Vensim system dynamics software file. One scenario simulation between 1990 and 2020 with yearly saving intervals of results generates 270 Mega-Byte of output data. About 12.000 time series are used to calibrate ASTRA for the period 1990 until 2000. Model variables are grouped into the following eight modules shown in **Fig. 1**.

A detailed description of the ASTRA model is provided by Schade (2004). The following paragraphs briefly describe the concepts of the eight ASTRA modules. The Population Module (POP) provides the population development for the 15 European countries[4] with one-year age cohorts. The model depends on fertility rates, death rates and immigration into the EU15 countries. Based on the age structure, given by the one-year age cohorts, important information is provided for other modules like the number of persons in the working age or the number of persons in age classes that permit to acquire a driving license. POP is calibrated to EUROSTAT population predictions (Ponti et al., 2002).

---

[3] Assessment of Transport Strategies. Originally developed on behalf of the European Commission in 4th Research Framework Programme.

[4] For simplicity reasons we are speaking of 14 European countries, though this always means the 15 member states of the EU as of March 2004, of which 13 are represented as single countries and two, Belgium and Luxemburg, are aggregated to form one region.

Fig. 1. Overview on the ASTRA model.

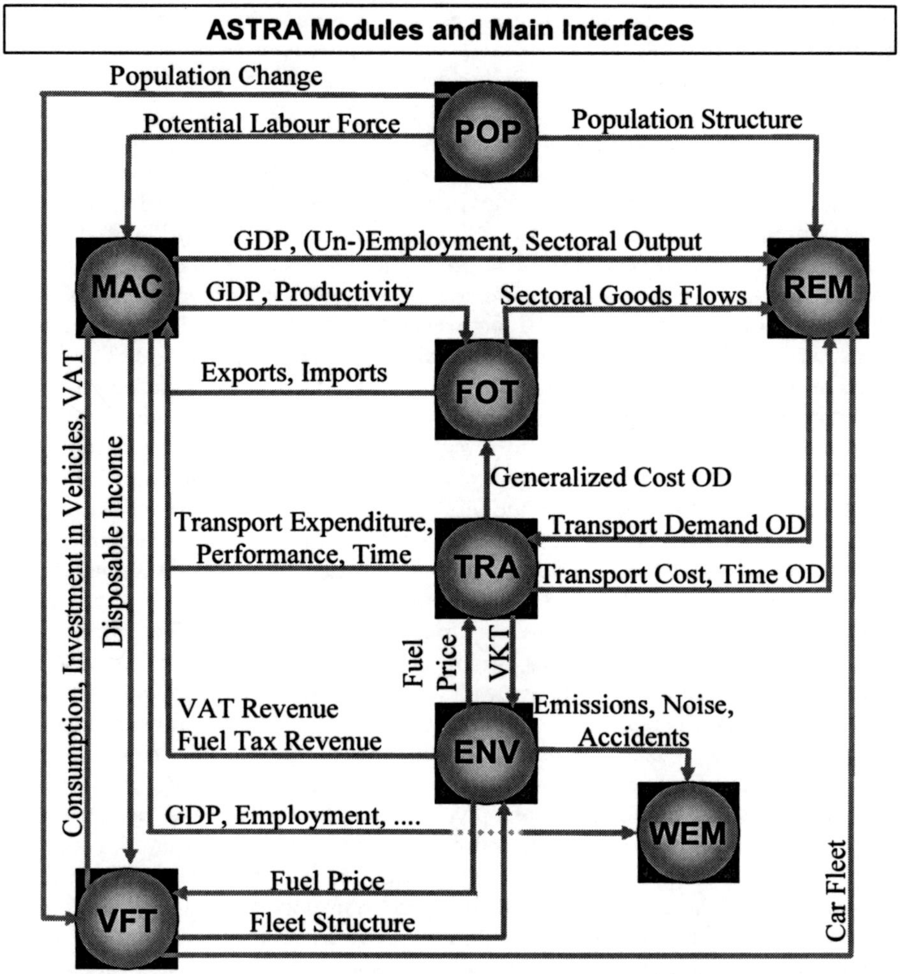

Abbreviations:

POP = Population Module	**TRA = Transport Module**
MAC = Macroeconomics Module	**ENV = Environment Module**
REM = Regional Economics Module	**VFT = Vehicle Fleet Module**
FOT = Foreign Trade Module	**WEM = Welfare Measurement Module**

The Macroeconomics Module (MAC) provides the national economic framework, which imbeds the other modules. The MAC could not be categorised explicitly into one economic category of models for instance a neo-classical model. Instead it incorporates neo-classical elements like production functions. Keynesian elements are considered like the dependency of investments on consumption extended by some further influences on investments like exports or government debt. Or elements of endogenous growth theory are incorporated like the implementation of endogenous technical progress as one important driver for the long-term economic development.

Six major elements constitute the functionality of the macroeconomics module. The first is the sectoral interchange model that reflects the economic interactions between 25 economic sectors of the national economies. Demand-supply interactions are considered by the second and third element. The second element, the demand side model, depicts the four major components of final demand: consumption, investments, exports-imports and government consumption. The supply side model reflects influences of three production factors: capital stock, labour and natural resources as well as the influence of technological progress that is modelled as total factor productivity. Endogenised total factor productivity depends on investments, freight transport times and labour productivity changes. The fourth element of MAC is constituted by the employment model that is based on value-added as output from input-output table calculations and labour productivity. Employment is differentiated into full-time equivalent employment and total employment to be able to reflect the growing importance of part-time employment. In combination with the population module unemployment could be estimated. The fifth element of MAC describes government behaviour. As far as possible, government revenues and expenditures are differentiated into categories that can be modelled endogenously by ASTRA and one category covering other revenues or other expenditures, respectively. Categories that are endogenised comprise VAT and fuel tax revenues, direct taxes, import taxes, social contributions and revenues of transport charges on the revenue side as well as unemployment payments, transfers to retired persons and children, transport investments, interest payments for government debt and government consumption on the expenditure side.

The sixth and final of the elements constituting the MAC are the micro-macro bridges. These link micro- and meso-level models, for instance the transport module or the vehicle fleet module, to components of the macroeconomics module. That means, that expenditures for bus transport or rail transport become part of final demand of the economic sector for inland transport within the sectoral interchange model. The macroeconomic module provides several important outputs to other modules. The most important one is certainly the GDP. This is for instance required to calculate sectoral trade flows between the European countries. Employment and unemployment are two influencing factors for passenger transport generation. The sectoral production value drives national freight transport generation. Disposable income exerts a major influence on car purchase affecting finally the vehicle fleet module and even passenger transport emissions.

The Regional Economics Module (REM) mainly calculates the generation and distribution of freight transport volume and passenger trips. The number of passenger trips is driven by employment situation, car-ownership development and number of people in different age classes. Trip generation is performed individually for each of the 53 zones of the ASTRA model. Distribution splits trips of each zone into three distance categories of trips within the zone and two distance categories crossing the zonal borders and generating OD-trip matrices with 53x53 elements for three trip purposes. Freight transport is driven by two mechanisms: Firstly, national transport depends on the sectoral production value of the 15 goods producing sectors where the monetary output of the input-output table calculations are transferred into volume of tons by means of value-to-volume ratios. For freight distribution and the further calculations in the transport module the 15 goods sectors are aggregated into three goods categories. Secondly, international freight transport i.e. freight transport flows that are crossing national borders are generated from monetary intra-European trade flows of the 15 goods producing sectors. Again transfer into volume of tons is performed by applying value-to-volume ratios that are different from the ones applied for national transport. In that sense the export model provides generation and distribution of international transport flows within one step on the base of monetary flows.

The Foreign Trade Module (FOT) is divided into two parts: trade between the EU15 member states of the year 2003 (INTRA-EU model) and trade between the EU15 countries and the rest-of-the world (RoW) that is divided into 12 regions (EU-RoW model). Both models are differentiated into 25 economic sectors and bilateral relationships between country pairs. The INTRA-EU trade model depends on three endogenous and one exogenous factor. World GDP growth exerts an exogenous influence on trade. Endogenous influences are provided by GDP growth of the importing country of each country pair relation, by relative change of sectoral labour productivity between the countries and by averaged generalised cost of passenger and freight transport between the countries. The latter is used as a kind of accessibility indicator between the countries. The EU-RoW trade model is mainly driven by relative productivity between the European countries and the rest-of-the-world countries. Productivity changes together with GDP growth of the importing RoW-country and world GDP growth drive the export-import relationships between the countries. Since, transport cost and time are not modelled for transport relations outside EU15 transport is not considered in the EU-RoW model. The resulting sectoral export-import flows of the two trade models are fed back into the macroeconomic module as part of final demand and national final use respectively. Secondly, the INTRA-EU model provides the input for international freight generation and distribution within the REM module.

Major input of the Transport Module (TRA) constitutes the demand for passenger and freight transport that is provided by the REM in the form of OD-matrices. Using transport cost and transport time matrices the transport module is performing the modal-split for five passenger modes and three freight modes. Cost and time matrices depend on influencing factors like infrastructure investments, structure of vehicle fleets, transport charges, fuel price or fuel tax changes. For road transport network capacity and network loads are considered for four different road types such that congestion effects may affect the road transport time matrices in a simplified way. For other modes rough capacity models and capacity constraint functions are developed such that interactions between load and travel times can also be taken into account. Depending on the modal choices, transport expenditures are calculated and provided to the macroeconomic module. Changes in freight transport times are also transferred to the macroeconomic module such that they may influence total factor productivity. Considering load factors and occupancy rates respectively, vehicle-km are calculated. These represent an important input for the ENV module where emissions or accidents are calculated and for the VFT module, which estimates the new purchase of road vehicles besides cars.

Major output of the TRA provided to the Environment Module (ENV) are the vehicle-kilometres-travelled (VKT) per mode and per distance band and traffic situation, respectively. Based on these traffic flows and the information from the vehicle fleet model on the different vehicle fleet compositions and hence on the emission factors, the environmental module is calculating the emissions from transport. Besides emissions, fuel consumption and, based on this, fuel tax revenues from transport are estimated by the ENV. Traffic flows and accident rates for each mode form the input to calculate the number of accidents in the European countries. Expenditures for fuel, revenues from fuel taxes and value-added-tax (VAT) on fuel consumption are transferred to the macroeconomics module and provide input to the economic sectors producing fuel products and to the government model.

The Vehicle Fleet Module (VFT) is describing the vehicle fleet composition for all road modes. Vehicle fleets are differentiated into different age classes based on one-year age cohorts and into different emission standard categories. Additionally, car vehicle fleet is differentiated into gasoline and diesel powered cars with different cubic capacity categories. Car vehicle fleet is developing according to income changes, development of population and of fuel prices. Vehicle fleet composition of bus, light-duty vehicles and heavy-duty vehicles mainly depends on driven kilometres and the development of average annual mileage per vehicle of these modes. The purchase of vehicles is translated into value terms and forms an input of the economic sectors in the MAC that cover the vehicle production.

Finally, in the Welfare Measurement Module (WEM) major macroeconomic, environmental and social indicators can be compared and analysed. Also different assessment schemes that combine indicators into aggregated welfare indicators, for instance an investment multiplier, are provided in the WEM. In some cases e.g. to undertake a CBA the functionality is separated into further tools to avoid excessive growth of the core ASTRA model by including the full CBA assessment scheme directly in the model.

The integrated modular approach of ASTRA reveals the advantage that feedback loops, which commence on the micro- or meso-level in one of the modules (e.g. transport expenditures for one mode and one OD-pair in one distance band in the TRA) and then end up with an effect on the national level (e.g. changes in sectoral consumption and gross-value-added), can influence the originating module such that the feedback loop is closed e.g. in this case by the integration of the MAC module. Closing the feedback loop then implies to establish either macro-micro-bridges (e.g. from GDP and sectoral output to goods flows) or vice versa micro-macro-bridges (e.g. from transport investments into vehicle fleets to overall investments).

System dynamics methodology used to develop ASTRA was first developed during the 1960s by Forrester (1962, 1977). It rests on a few building blocks to construct a model, which are level and flow variables, auxiliary variables, parameters and, if using the graphical representation of a system dynamics model, connectors to describe the structure of the system. Mathematically a system dynamics model consists of non-linear differential equations that are computed by numerical integration since usually analytic solutions for the system of equations cannot be found (Sterman, 2000). The construction of system dynamics models assumes that the behaviour of a system is primarily determined by its feedback mechanisms. "*The central concept that system dynamicists use to understand system structure is the idea of two-way causation or feedback.*" (Meadows, 1980: 31).

3.2 Approach for Dynamic CBA with ASTRA

In principle most of the necessary indicators to be considered for a transport CBA (TCBA) are already implemented in ASTRA. Hence, to develop the dynamic CBA only the standard calculation scheme for a CBA has to be added to the ASTRA model. The dynamic CBA in ASTRA follows the approach of the German Federal Transport Infrastructure Planning procedure (BVWP), which is similar to other European, Japanese or US evaluation schemes in terms of the core categories of considered benefits. To derive the net present value the costs and benefits are discounted with a rate of 3% that also stems from the German BVWP (BMV, 1993). In total seven categories of (dis-)benefits are considered in the ASTRA TCBA:

- Variable transport costs: Considering all modes for passenger and freight (except pipelines) in all distance bands.
- Transport times: Considering all modes for passenger and freight (except pipelines) in all distance bands. The number of trips that are used for the calculation of time savings is revised by a subtraction of the induced trips per corridor.
- Induced transport: Considering all modes for passenger and freight (except pipelines) in all distance bands. To estimate the number of induced trips the total over all modes per corridor (is equivalent to an OD-pair in ASTRA) from the base scenario is compared with the number of trips in the policy scenario. If number of trips and trip length increase in the policy scenario the difference is estimated to be induced trips. These are then distributed to the modes proportionally and their benefits are monetised with the generalised cost of a trip (analogously for freight).
- Transport investments: Considering all modes for passenger and freight (except pipelines). There are two options to consider investments: The usual way is to calculate only the investments in infrastructure. But as ASTRA also estimates all investments in vehicles for all modes changes in those investments can be considered, too.
- Safety: Four categories of consequences of accidents are estimated for all modes: Fatalities, serious injuries, light injuries and material damages. They are all considered in the CBA.
- Environment: CO_2 and NO_x emissions of all modes are estimated with life cycle assessment approach that includes the production stages of vehicles and fuel or electricity, respectively. For particulate matter the potential risk of local

immission concentrations are estimated and put in relation to affected population. Obviously there are several important environmental indicators missing e.g. noise.

- Employment: The change in overall employment in the economy is calculated and monetised by cost values from the German BVWP. This might be a source for double counting. On the other hand employment can be seen as rough proxy for equity or changes in fairness.

Results of the dynamic CBA can either be displayed as benefit-cost-ratio or as benefit-cost-balance. Benefits for the mentioned indicators would be a reduction of (total) transport expenditures, time savings because of a reduction of transport times, induced transport, a reduction of investments needed for transport, a reduction of emissions and accidents and an increase in employment all compared with the base scenario. Benefits that are associated with reduced transport likewise turn into costs or disbenefits for the case of induced transport.

3.3 Results for the Dynamic CBA[5]

For the prototypical demonstration of a dynamic CBA using ASTRA two policies have been tested:

- *Tax for TEN* (Trans-European Networks): Increase of gasoline and diesel fuel tax over a period of 15 years to cover the investment costs of the implementation of the European rail TEN that are part of the priority projects of the TEN. That means tax increases are varying according to the funding needs for the TEN investments and the progress in their construction.
- *Integrated Policy*: The rail TEN are implemented in the same way as in the Tax for TEN policy. Furthermore gasoline and diesel fuel tax are stepwise (i.e. incrementally) increased by 5% every 2 years from 2000 through 2010. Additional tax revenues are used to reduce labour cost. On top of this the tax level of gasoline and diesel taxation is balanced, which leads to a further increase of diesel taxes. New European emission legislation for automobiles are introduced at an earlier point of time (3 years in advance) starting with EURO II. Seat-belt usage of car drivers is increased to a level of 98% for non-urban roads in all countries.

The impact of the two policies on fuel tax revenues for the European Union are presented in **Fig. 2**. In the *Tax for TEN* policy additional fuel taxes are generated in three distinct five-year periods between 2000 and 2015 with the highest increase of about 12% in the first five years. After 2015 the revenues are slightly below the base scenario revenues as car modal share is reduced because of the increased attractiveness of rail. In the *Integrated Policy* the additional fuel taxes reach a peak level with a 50% increase in 2010, when all tax increases are implemented but the implementation of high-speed rail is not completed such that mo-

5 Results in this section refer to an earlier version of ASTRA that incorporates a spatial resolution of the EU15 countries into four macro regions instead of 15 countries and 53 zones.

dal shift towards rail is only partially taking place. Instead, over a 10-years period there is also a strong modal shift towards air that is gradually reduced when the high-speed rail network is completed.

Fig. 2. Changes of revenues and modal split due to the two policies.

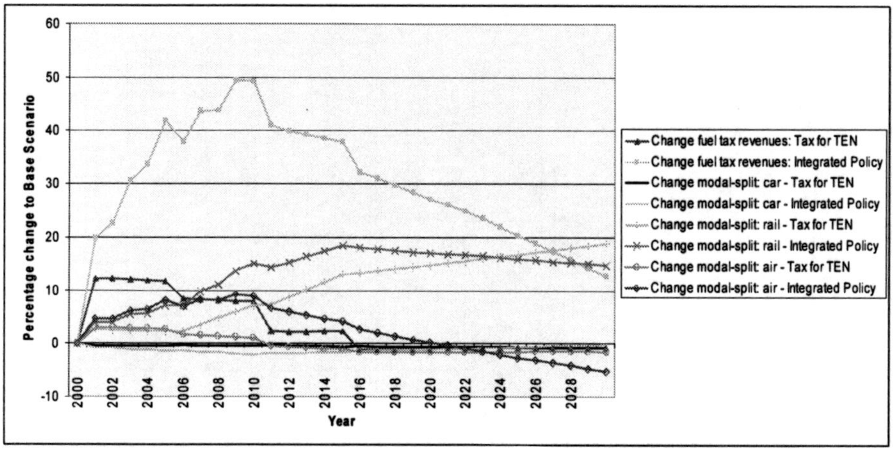

Source: ASTRA model

The results of the dynamic CBA are presented in **Fig. 3**, which shows the evolution of the CBA-ratio between 2005 and 2030. The period before 2005 is considered for the calculation of costs and benefits but is not included in the figure as it has some initial peaks because of the division by small numbers. The results indicate that there is no policy that is superior at all points of time and that the *Integrated Policy* provides higher total benefits.

Table 1 shows the numerical values of CBA-ratios for selected points of time. The bold numbers indicate which policy would have been the best in a comparative static CBA with this specific time horizon. We notice that with a time horizon 2010, 2025 and 2030 the *Integrated Policy* would be most advantageous. But at 2015 it would be the *Tax for TEN*. Hence, we state that the result of a comparative static CBA might be rather arbitrary depending on the time horizon that is chosen. At this stage we leave open how to decide what would have been the "correct" time horizon in this case.

Table 1. CBA-Ratios for selected points of time.

	2010	2015	2025	2030
Tax for TEN	1.27	**2.12**	2.67	2.82
Integrated Policy	**1.88**	2.06	**2.72**	**3.14**

Source: ASTRA model

Fig. 3. CBA-ratio and total benefits for the two policies from 2005 to 2030.

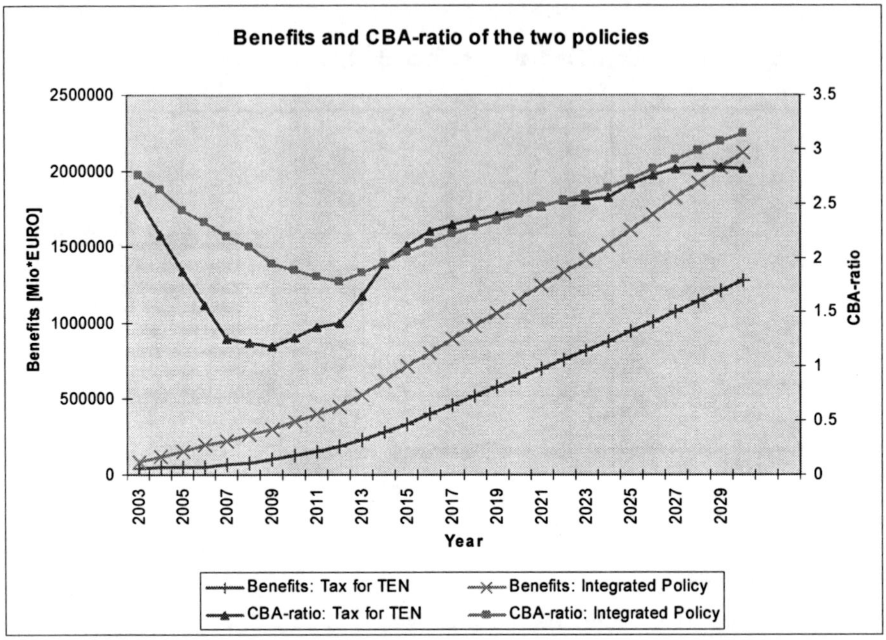

Source: ASTRA model

We complete the picture of the dynamic CBA by an analysis of the distribution of benefits (disbenefits) onto the 9 (7) categories considered. **Fig. 4** shows the distribution of the benefits summing up to 100% over all nine categories for the *Tax for TEN* policy and the *Integrated Policy*. In the *Tax for TEN* policy time savings plus induced transport for passenger and freight contribute more than 85% of the total benefits of which about two thirds is induced transport.

However, for the *Integrated Policy* time savings plus induced transport contribute less than 60% of total benefits, which is still a large share. But in this case the benefits of reduced externalities amount to more than one third of all benefits, while those in the *Tax for TEN* policy are close to zero changes in 2030. Reduced externalities in this policy are only significant in the period 2000 to 2015 when the fuel tax is increased to finance the TEN investments. Afterwards, despite modal shift towards rail the overall increased transport activity counterbalances the success of the modal shift.

Looking closer at the size of the shares reveals that in the *Integrated Policy* the passenger time savings play also an accentuated role as they produce the second biggest share of benefits after the externalities, while in the *Tax for TEN* policy they are similar to the benefits of freight time savings and the benefits of induced transport. This can be explained since in the *Tax for TEN* policy less persons shift

Fig. 4. Distribution of discounted gross benefits over the 9 benefit categories for the two policies.

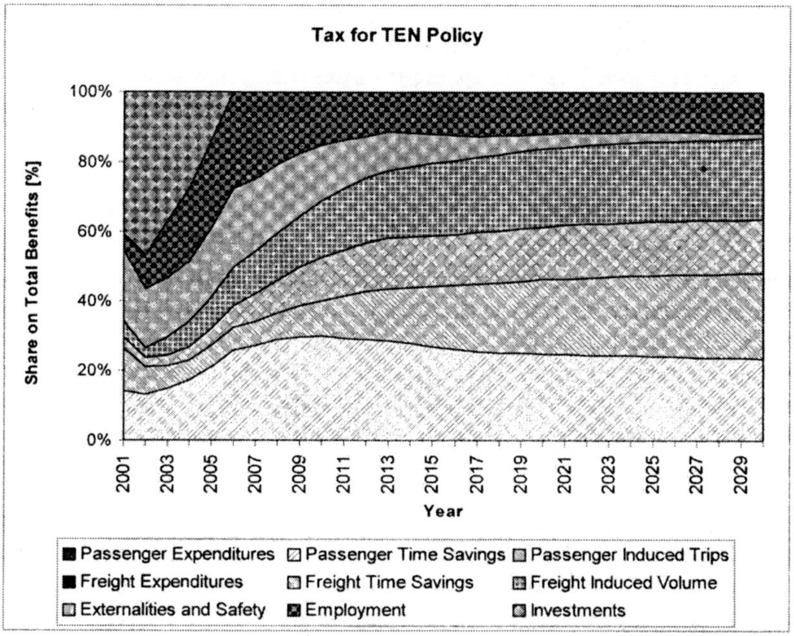

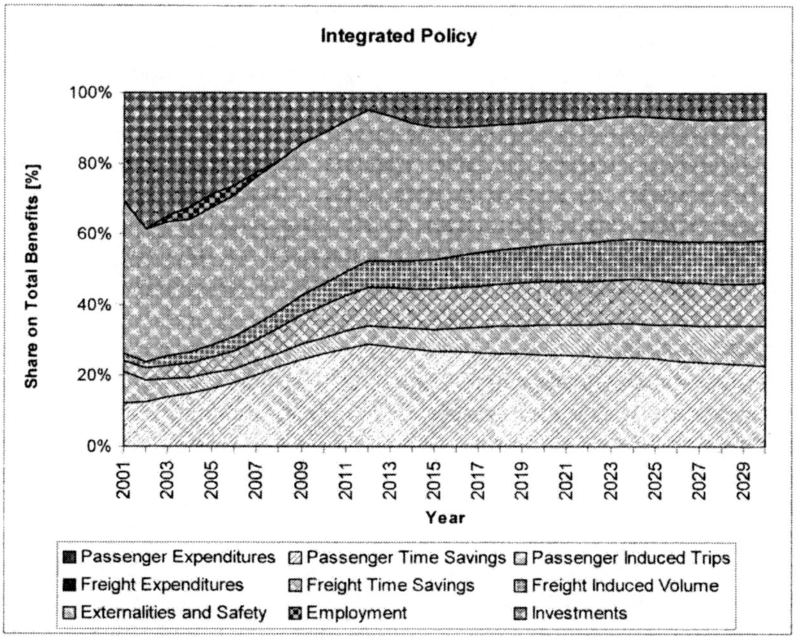

Source: ASTRA model

to train mode since the tax level is back to the base scenario level after the completion of the TEN construction. Therefore less people benefit from the faster train transport and road transport is less released such that transport times by road are higher than in the *Integrated Policy* case in which there remains a significant increase of fuel tax after the termination of the TEN construction. In this case push (tax increase) and pull (rail quality improvement) forces unfold synergies to increase the benefits while in the *Tax for TEN* only the pull forces are substantial.

4 Integration

The transport system is connected with other complex systems like society, economy and environment. In 1995 in the EU15 countries transport services generated 4% of the GDP and 6.2 million employees – that is 4.2% of all employees – are working in the transport sector. These figures exclude the production of infrastructure and vehicles. Transport forms part of the social life of society by providing the basis for personal mobility. This is reflected by the growing passenger transport demand that reached a value of 4,800 billion pkm in the year 1999. On the other hand transport is a major source of environmental burdens that influences sustainability adversely, contrarily to the positive welfare effect and the mobility effects of transport. In 1999 road transport caused 43,000 deaths by traffic accidents within the EU15 countries. The World Health Organization (WHO) estimates that additionally 80,000 people in EU15 are killed by hazardous gaseous emissions of transport per year. The significance of transport for global effects like the greenhouse effect is substantial as CO_2 emissions of transport contribute with a share of 29% to the man made CO_2 emissions of the EU15 (Eurostat, 2001). This imbedded situation of transport is reflected in **Fig. 5**.

Given the situation of transport being imbedded into the other systems as well as the interactions between the other systems, the development of assessment models that consider the impacts in each of the systems and the feedbacks from each change within one of the systems to the other systems is necessary. A key characteristic of such assessment models is the need for integrating the different systems into one integrated model. Three levels of integration can be distinguished:

- Integrated models
  - integrative coded models
  - computer network linked models
- Separate models.

The lowest level of integration is reached with separate models that exchange their results at a few points of time. In most cases the exchange occurs at the final point of time of the assessment time horizon such that the final result of one model becomes an input to the other models. That implies that there is no feedback considered from the latter model to the former model. An example for this type of linkage can be found in the IASON project, which is funded by the European

Fig. 5. Transport and its linkages to the sustainability triangle.

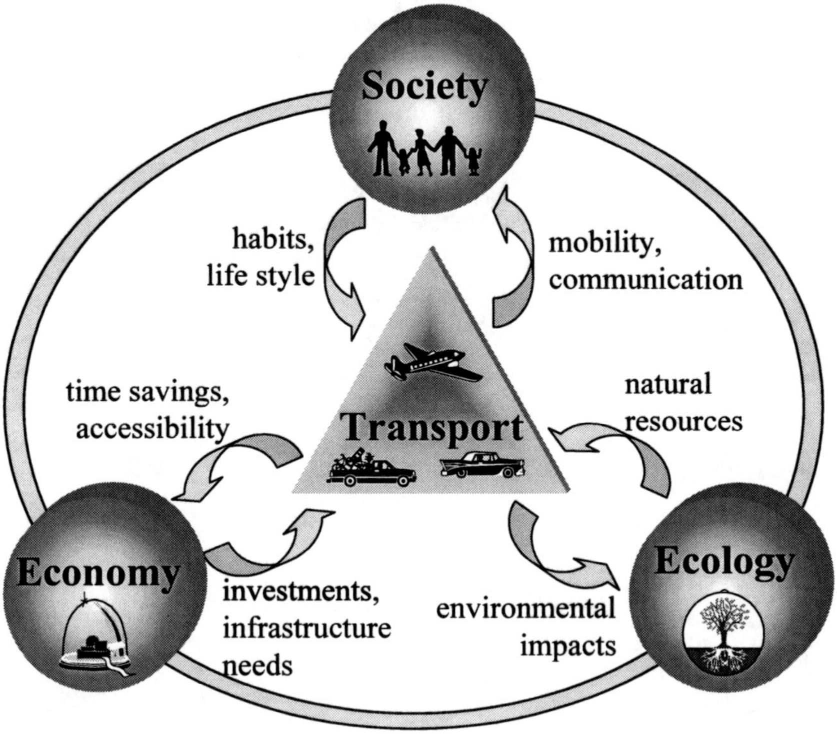

Commission, in which a simulation model for regional analysis (SASI) is linked to a CGE model for distributive spatial analysis (CGEurope) where SASI provides transport cost and time information on NUTS III level for the year 2020 to CGEurope, which is then calculating new market equilibria from which the spatial impact of the policy is derived (Bröcker et al., 2001). An example with increased integration developed in the TIPMAC project, which is funded by the European Commission, is the linkage of an econometric macroeconomic energy-environment model (E3ME) with a transport network model (SCENES), which manually exchange information in both ways at one intermediate point of time in 2010 and at the final point of time in 2020 (Köhler et al., 2003).

Developing integrated models starts with the next level of integration and concerns the field of Integrated Assessment Models (IAM) that follow two approaches: network linked models and integrative coded models. Network linked models can be implemented using different software on spatially separated computers but require a common network interface that integrates the separate models into an integrated systems model. Integrative coded models would be implemented by a single software within the file structure of the software and would run on one computer or computer cluster.

An example of network linked models is developed in the SAT project, which is also funded by the European Commission, where an economy-transport-environment model (ASTRA) is linked via computer networks to a transport network model (VACLAV) and the final result of both models is linked to a separate model for calculation of regional small scale environmental indicators (Regio-SUSTAIN, see **Fig. 6**). In that case the first two models, ASTRA and VACLAV, perform a two-way exchange of results in regular intervals and after any kind of policy implementation.

Fig. 6. Network linked models ASTRA-VACLAV and their integration with Regio-SUSTAIN model.

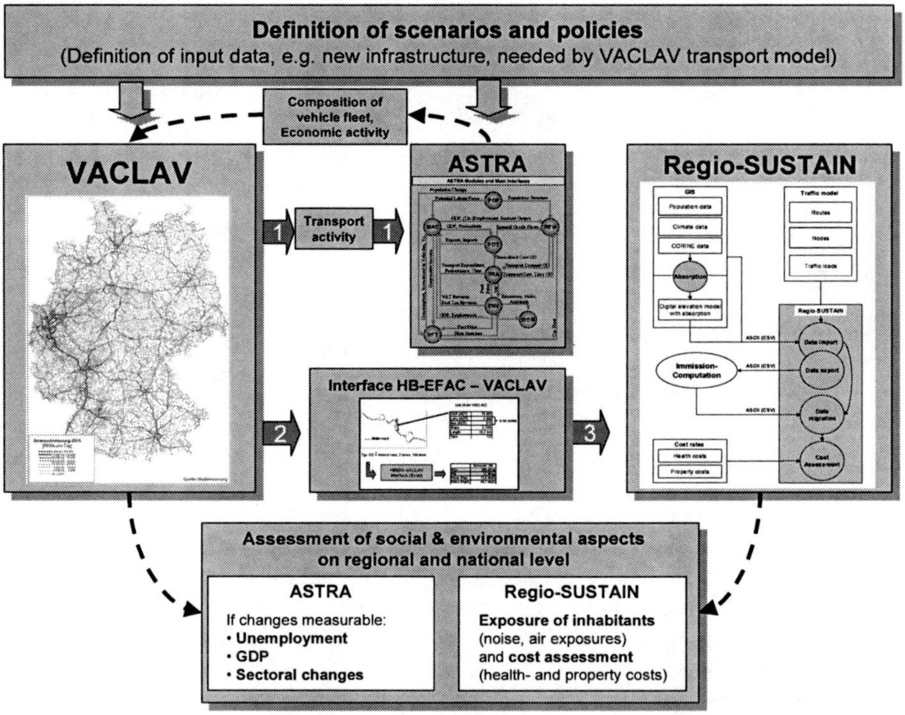

The highest level of integration is reached with integrative coded models that include all implemented systems within one model developed by the same software to enable unlimited connectivity between the system models. The ASTRA model described in Section 3.1 provides an example of an integrative coded model when it comes to assessing the macro- and meso-scale impacts of transport policies.[6] It includes seven models stemming from several scientific disciplines and an

6 As mentioned in the previous paragraph, if detailed analysis e.g. on small-scale regional level should be undertaken then ASTRA has to be linked to a model for regional analysis.

assessment model that are all implemented within one file. At each calculation interval all models exchange their results such that previous and current reactions to transport policies in each of the models could impact any other model. For example, income changes due to taxation policies exert an influence on the car purchase behaviour and hence on car ownership. The latter provides an influence on trip making behaviour and modal-choices, which in turn influences private expenditures for different modes affecting the revenues of the different modes leading to sectoral output and employment changes of the transport service sectors. These impacts include models like macroeconomic model, car fleet model, passenger transport model and modal-split model and any of these models could forward its changes to all other seven models.

The variety of levels of integration and frequency of exchange of results between different systems of integrated models as described by the model combinations in the previous paragraphs are summarised in **Fig. 7**.

Fig. 7. Classification of model integration.

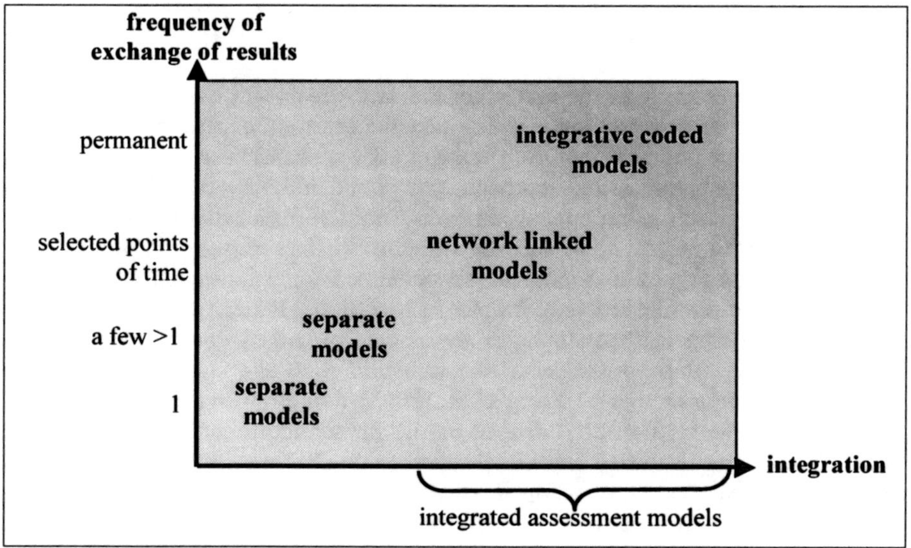

5 Indirect Effects

In general comparative static CBA based on network models is used for transport policy assessment. This approach only measures the *direct effects* of transport policies with the core indicators of volumes, transport times and cost changes that are used to calculate microeconomic welfare indicators. However, what is interesting from the welfare point of view and the requirement to undertake a complete assessment are the *indirect effects*. Indirect effects occur outside the transport system i.e. in other markets like product markets or land and labour markets. Another type of indirect effects would be environmental and health impacts (e.g.

accidents). However, the following discussion concentrates on the economic indirect effects and their effects on non-transport markets and private households. A further term relevant for the discussion are *additional effects* that would be the welfare difference between indirect effects and direct effects, such that:

Indirect effects = Additional effects + Direct effects

In an ideal world with perfect markets and rational behaviour the additional effects would be zero such that direct effects would equal indirect effects and we could go on using the current comparative static assessment scheme for transport policies. However, usually we are far away from this ideal world such that indirect effects are probably different from direct effects and additional effects would exist. At this point it should be clearly stated that the notion 'additional effect' does not imply that these will be positive (>0). They could also become negative (<0) e.g. if some of the direct effects (direct benefits) get lost during the transfer between the different markets. The estimation of potential additional effects has been on the research agenda for quite some time and under different headings, most often with the main purpose to identify the full indirect effects of transport policies (e.g. also appearing as "wider economic effects", "spill-over effects") without comparing it with results of the conventional measurement of direct effects.

One famous example of the search for indirect effects was the Aschauer debate (1989) about a decade ago highlighting that the question of macroeconomic impacts of transport policy at that time was not answered. Aschauer concluded from a rather aggregate regression approach that public infrastructure investment including transport infrastructure investment would significantly foster economic growth expressed as growth of GDP as an indirect effect of transport policy. Critics convincingly argued that the analysis contained some flaws and would therefore exaggerate the impacts (e.g. Pfähler et al., 1996). Hence, common approach for transport policy assessment after the debate remained cost-benefit analysis measuring direct transport impacts like transport time and cost changes on the transport networks though Nijkamp et al. (2003) found out in a meta-analysis of 39 studies on the relationship between public infrastructure and long-run growth that 72% of them identified a positive relationship. But the direction of causality remained unclear i.e. the question if growth comes first and then the money for infrastructure investment to relieve bottlenecks is available or if infrastructure would come first and induces economic growth is unanswered. Probably it accounts for a mutual relationship as Wang (2002) points out.

An important contribution in the late 1990s to the still ongoing debate on additional effects stems from the Standing Advisory Committee on Trunk Road Assessment in the UK (SACTRA, 1999). Using results of a stylised spatial computable general equilibrium (CGE) model developed by Venables and Gasiorek (1998) SACTRA concluded that additional benefits of transport policy would exist, that they could become negative or positive and that they are meant to be small.

Spatial CGE models are used to analyse additional effects and indirect effects of transport policies by Bröcker (2001) and Bröcker et al. (2004), who arrive at similar conclusions as SACTRA with additional effects being small and either positive or negative. Their results are based on CGEurope, a spatial CGE covering all Europe with about 1,300 zones and using a limited sectoral differentiation. Welfare in these CGEs is measured as equivalent variation but can also be translated into GDP changes or changes of disposable income to compare CGE results with other models that do not include equivalent variation.[7]

Oosterhaven and Elhorst (2003) developed a spatial CGE model for the Netherlands, which in contrast to CGEurope includes a finer sectoral differentiation and imperfect labour markets. Applying this model for case studies of new Maglev links led to significantly higher results for additional effects, which again could become negative or positive.

Measurement of additional effects in this paper is performed by applying the system dynamics model ASTRA (see Section 3.1, Schade, 2004). The difference of ASTRA compared to the CGE approaches listed above accounts for the usage of a dis-equilibrium model instead of an equilibrium model and the formulation of a dynamic approach that reveals as results trajectories of reactions to transport policies. Furthermore the iceberg-type consideration of transport cost introduced into economic modelling by Samuelson (1954) and usually applied in spatial CGE models is replaced by an OD-pair-based and modal differentiated transport generalised cost approach.

The question related to indirect effects in ASTRA concerns the way the transport system, modelled on the micro-level of transport decisions of household groups, is linked to the macroeconomic system. For this purpose micro-macro bridges are implemented. Micro-macro bridges have the most important task of connecting ASTRA modules that are modelled on a micro-level e.g. on the base of modal choice decisions for a specific OD-pair with modules modelled on a meso-level like economic sectors or even a macro-level like national aggregates. Implementing micro-macro bridges establishes influences of the transport system on the economic system that so far have not been realised within one integrated model elsewhere. An example would be the link between the transport module (TRA) calculating results on the level of roughly 60,000 origin-destination transport flows for each passenger and freight transport and the macroeconomic module (MAC) finally incorporating these results within variables like consumption or investments on the level of a few sectors per country totalling to 84 input links (14 countries times 6 directly affected economic sectors) for each of these variables.

Two major questions have to be answered designing the micro-macro bridges: First, how could we aggregate the detailed flow-based transport data to feed the results sensibly into the MAC. Second, what would be the appropriate link point for each of the detailed inputs from the micro-level modules to the meso-level and macro-level modules.

The first question most often could be answered easily as obviously the country level is the most relevant level in the macro-level modules. However, sometimes data can be aggregated in different ways to country level e.g. in the case of the

---

7 It should be clearly differentiated between equivalent variation as welfare indicator following welfare economic theory and GDP as an indicator of monetary and material wealth, only.

origin-destination flows one could aggregate all originating flows of a country or all ending flows of a country but optionally one could also consider that most long distance flows pass through several countries on their way between origin and destination such that each of the countries could in principle be affected. By splitting the effects of the trip onto the different countries the latter could be taken into account. We will call the latter point of view the domestic (aggregation) approach while the first approach aggregating all originating transport as belonging to the origin country the origin (aggregation) approach. For instance, the origin approach would be relevant for finding out about the transport expenditures of all residents of a country, which in this case is based on the simplifying assumption that all trips identified by the transport model as originating from a country are made by residents.

The second question represents the more tricky one. In some cases the link points between micro- and macro-level modules might be obvious e.g. the expenditures for fuel burned in private cars is clearly linked to the fuel and power sector in the consumption model of the MAC. However, other links are more difficult and could only be answered by intensive review of the literature, by own investigations or by rules based on expert judgement and rough approximations e.g. the incorporation of time savings into the MAC, which e.g. could influence labour productivity, total factor productivity (TFP) or the capital costs for goods that are transported. Considering these remarks six most important micro-macro bridges are implemented:

- passenger transport expenditure and sectoral consumption,
- transport demand, transport policy and sectoral investment,
- transport per mode and sectoral employment,
- freight transport times and TFP,
- transport cost and intermediate inputs of input-output tables and
- transport generalised cost and exports.

Model analysis revealed that within the fully integrated context the link between freight transport times and TFP, the private transport consumption expenditures and the influences of transport on exports are the most relevant micro-macro bridges for indirect effects.

In total, results of the indirect effects depend on the interactions between short- and long-term dynamics of the ASTRA model. First to be mentioned are the dynamics between transport and the economy themselves let it be changes in transport cost or times that have economic implications or changes in economic activity that exert transport changes. Second, on the transport side dynamics are related to modal shift in the short term and change of generation-distribution in the longer term. Third, on the economic side dynamics concern the interplay between sectors, consumption, exports, investments and TFP. Also government may play a role if a significant increase or decrease of government debt is caused by a policy. Finally, all these effects exert an impact on a country's GDP and the alternative indicators to measure indirect effects.

An extended analysis of transport-economic interactions in ASTRA can be based on the example of testing reactions to a pricing policy i.e. implementing Social Marginal Cost Pricing (SMCP) for all transport modes. **Fig. 8** presents major impact chains that are stimulated by SMCP policy focusing on the dynamic profiles of impacts. Each chain starts with the SMCP implementation on the left hand and ends with change of GDP on the right hand. However, each chain follows different time structures such that in some cases SMCP policy immediately affects GDP. ASTRA performs calculations on a quarterly base. In that sense, immediately could mean in the same quarter or in the subsequent quarter depending on the structure of equations. In other impact chains it takes up to 5 years until the bulk of impacts is reaching GDP. In the figure it is also indicated that there are interactions between different impact chains. And GDP changes feed back into the chains e.g. to income or exports. Nevertheless, the figure shows only a selection of important chains that is by far not exhaustive.

Fig. 8. Impact chains responsible for indirect effects kicked-off by pricing policies in ASTRA (according to Schade, 2004).

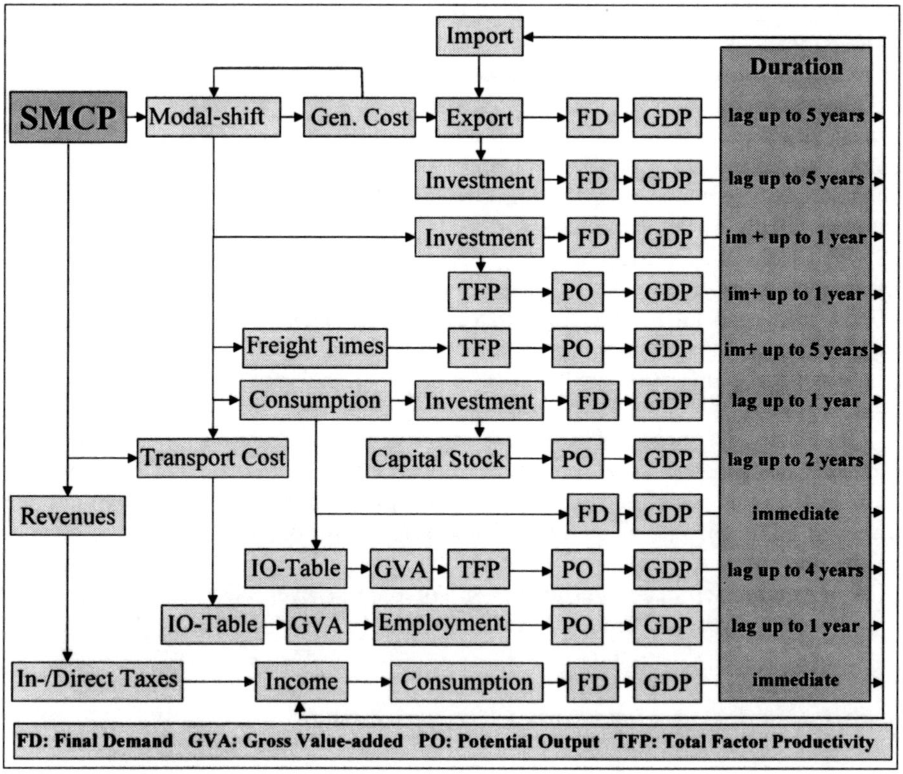

The following paragraph presents a comparison of direct effects with indirect effects for a pricing policy in EU15 as defined in the TIPMAC project (Ponti et al., 2002). The structure of ASTRA incorporating both a transport model and economic models enables to measure direct effects and indirect effects in parallel within one model. Direct effects of transport policy can be measured as consumer surplus considering the rule of half (Mackie et al., 2001) and indirect effects are measured as changes of GDP. Both indicators are discounted by 3% to the year 2002.

Fig. 9 presents results for two variants of the pricing policy. In the standard variant the revenues generated by the pricing policy are recycled by reducing direct taxes of households leading to balanced income. In this case we note a large difference between direct effects (consumer surplus) that indicates on average a loss of 250bn EUR annually compared with nearly neutral indirect effects (GDP). In the scenario variant indicated as worst case the revenues of the pricing policy are not refunded to the households but go into the general government budget reducing the government debt. In this case direct effects (consumer surplus, worst case) do not show any significant difference to the standard scenario while the indirect effects (GDP, worst case) are much different from the standard variant. The two obvious conclusion are: first, that direct and indirect effects can be much different from each other, and second, that it is rather important to analyse complete policies i.e. if revenues are generated by a policy to consider the usage of the revenues or if investments are made to consider their financing.

The surprising ASTRA results concerning the potentially large difference between direct and indirect effects are contradicting the SACTRA (1999) conclusions that additional effects of transport policies are small. ASTRA results are substantiated by analyses in the IASON[8]-TIPMAC[9] projects, in which direct and indirect effects of the same transport policies are analysed with different models (SASI, CGEurope, E3ME-SCENES, ASTRA). In fact, economic mechanisms in the models used to analyse indirect effects seem to dominate and transform the effects measured in the transport system. This conclusion seems to be valid for large infrastructure programmes or national policies. It could be different for single small-scale infrastructure projects e.g. those analysed in the UK SACTRA studies (1999).

Obviously, for large infrastructure programmes or national transport policies current CBA practice based on direct effects only is not sufficient. The final results in terms of social and economic impacts measured as (un-)employment and either as GDP, income or equivalent variation are produced by economic mechanisms that seem to change the result for the direct effects based on consumer surplus or generalised cost significantly in some cases even changing the algebraic sign between direct and indirect effects.

---

8 Integrated Appraisal of Spatial economic and Network effects of transport investments and policies, Project on behalf of the European Commission 5th Research Framework Programme.

9 Transport infrastructure and policy: a macroeconomic analysis for the EU, Project on behalf of the European Commission 5th Research Framework Programme.

Fig. 9. Comparison of direct effects and indirect effects with varying usage of road charge revenues.

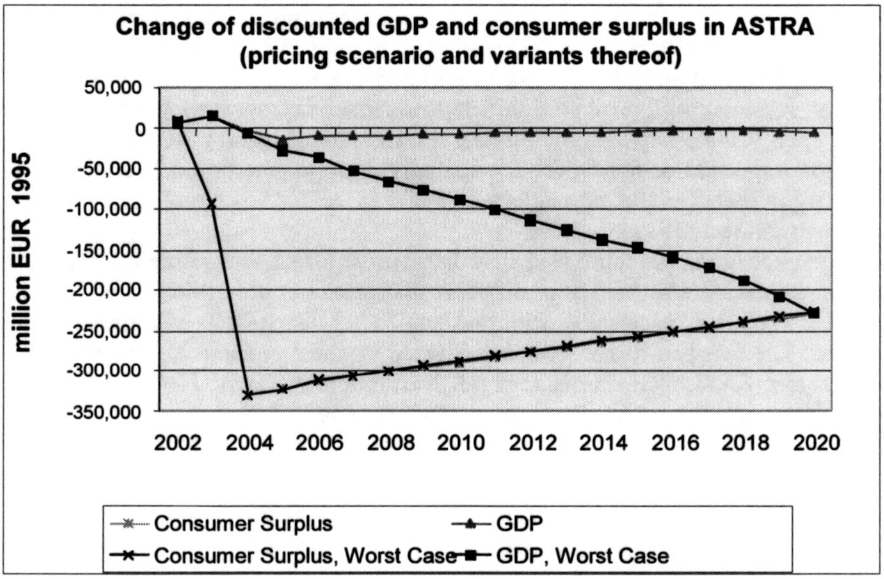

Source: ASTRA results

6 Conclusions and Outlook

Measuring indirect effects of transport policies probably will remain the most demanding topic in transport economics especially if one aspires to assess large scale policies let it be the TEN, European pricing policies or transport policies of national significance. Addressing this question several European models are competing each following its own modelling approach leaving the standard transport network modelling approach. The range of modelling approaches spans from spatial computable general equilibrium models (e.g. CGEurope) over econometric approaches (e.g. E3ME-SCENES) to various dis-equilibrium approaches based on simulation techniques like system dynamics (e.g. ASTRA, SASI). The conclusion derived from ASTRA, supported to some extent by the other models, is that indirect effects can be significant such that economic mechanisms would dominate the benefits measured within the transport system.

It seems that looking at large scale policies it becomes very important to base assessment on or at least to accompany transport policy assessment by a measurement of indirect effects of the policies. Prerequisite for appropriate policy design would be a complete definition of policies including all levers where a policy could have an impact e.g. a transport charge raises transport cost for the users but it also generates revenues that at some point have to enter the economic system.

Important model features to estimate indirect effects of transport policies are to consider dynamics as the time profile of the different impact chains can be rather different and to integrate the relevant systems into the analysis e.g. transport, trade, vehicle fleet and car ownership, population and the economic system since all these systems could provide significant responses to the transport policies.

An open dispute between the models remains the question if sectoral differentiation is important or not where the spatially disaggregated models (e.g. CGEurope) argue that it could be neglected, while in ASTRA sectoral shifts provide important indirect effects.

In general it can be concluded that distributive effects constitute an important part of additional effects. Three different distributional dimensions are relevant: spatial distribution, sectoral distribution and social distribution of impacts of the policies. The first two dimensions are covered by the models listed above (spatial distribution: SASI, CGEurope; sectoral distribution: ASTRA, E3ME), while the third dimension, the social distribution of impacts is lacking adequate representation in the models such that efforts are needed to integrate it better in those models or in models that link transport to a social distribution model.

References

Aschauer, D.A. (1989), Is Public Expenditure Productive?, *Journal of Monetary Economics* 23, 177-200.

Biehl, D. (1991), The Role of Infrastructure for Regional Development, in: Vickerman, R. (Ed.), *Infrastructure and Regional Development*, London.

BMV – German Ministry of Transport (Ed.) (1993), *Gesamtwirtschaftliche Bewertung von Verkehrswegeinvestitionen – Bewertungsverfahren für den Bundesverkehrswegeplan 1992*, BMV Schriftenreihe, Volume 72, Bonn.

Bröcker, J. (2001), Trans-European Effects of Trans-European Networks: Results from a Spatial CGE Analysis, in: Bolle, F. and M. Carlberg. (Eds.), *Advances in Behavioral Economics*, Heidelberg, 141-159.

Bröcker, J., R. Meyer, N. Schneekloth, C. Schürmann, K. Spiekermann, and M. Wegener (2004), *Modelling the Socio-Economic and Spatial Impacts of EU Transport Policy*, Deliverable D6 of IASON project funded by the European Commission 5th RTD framework, Kiel.

Bröcker, J., A. Kancs, C. Schurmann, and M. Wegener (2001), *Methodology for the Assessment of Spatial Economic Impacts of Transport Projects and Policies*, IASON Deliverable 2, funded by 5th Framework RTD Programme, Delft.

Dasgupta, A.K. and D.W. Pearce (1972), *Cost-Benefit Analysis – Theory and Practice*, London.

EUROSTAT (2001), *Panorama of Transport: Statistical Overview of Road, Rail, Inland Waterway and Air Transport in the European Union: Data 1970-1999*, CD-ROM, Luxembourg.

Forrester, J.W. (1977), *Principles of Systems*, Cambridge MA.

Forrester, J.W. (1962), *Industrial Dynamics*, 2nd edition, New York.

Haken, H. (1983), *Synergetics – An Introduction*, 3rd edition, Berlin.

Helbing, D. (2001), Traffic and Related Self-Driven Many-Particle Systems, in: *Review of Modern Physics*, University of Washington, Published by the American Physical Society.

Henderson, A. (1941), Consumer's Surplus and the Compensating Variation, *Review of Economic Studies*, 117-121.

Hicks, J.R. (1941), The Rehabilitation of Consumers' Surplus, *Review of Economic Studies*, 108-116.

IWW (1998), *Socio-Economic External Developments, Spatial Dynamics and Their Relation to Transport*, SCENARIOS Deliverable C1, Report for the European Commission DG VII, Karlsruhe.

Koblo, R. (1991), *The Visible Hand: Synergetic Micro-Foundation of Macroeconomic Dynamics*, Dissertation Thesis at IWW, University of Karlsruhe, Berlin.

Köhler, J., H. Pollitt, N. Raha, Y. Jin, and P. Cuthbertson (2003), *Results of the Combined SCENES/E3ME Model System Analysis*, Deliverable D4 of the TIPMAC project funded by the European Commission 5th RTD framework, Cambridge.

Krugman, P. (1991), *Geography and Trade*, Cambridge MA.

Lakshmanan, T.R. and W.P. Anderson (2002), *Transportation Infrastructure, Freight Services Sector and Economic Growth*, White Paper for the US DOT and the FHWA, Boston.

Mackie, P.J., J. Nellthorp, J. Kiel, W. Schade, and M. Nokkala (2001), *IASON Project Assessment Baseline*, Deliverable D1 of IASON project funded by the European Commission 5th RTD framework, TNO Inro, Delft.

Marshall, A. (1920), *Principles of Economics*, 1st edition 1890, 8th edition London.

Meadows, D.H. (1980), The Unavoidable a Priori, in: Randers, J. (Ed) *Elements of the System Dynamics Method*, Cambridge.

Nijkamp, P. and J. Poot (2003), Meta-Analysis of the Effect of Fiscal Policies on Long-Run Growth, *European Journal of Political Economy* 20, 91-124.

Oosterhaven, J. and J.P. Elhorst (2003), Indirect Economic Benefits of Transport Infrastructure Investments, in: Dullaert, W., B.A.M. Jourquin, and J.B. Polak (Eds) *Across the Border. Building upon a Quarter Century of Transport Research in the Benelux*, Antwerpen, 143-162.

Pfähler, W., U. Hofmann, and W. Bönte (1996), Does Extra Public Infrastructure Capital Matter? An Appraisal of Empirical Literature, *Finanzarchiv* 53, 68-112.

Ponti, M., S. Maffii, C. Borgnolo, E. Pastori, and G. Pasti (2002), *Common Assumptions and Scenarios*, Deliverable D1 of the TIPMAC project funded by the European Commission 5th RTD framework, Milan.

SACTRA – Standing Advisory Committee on Trunk Road Assessment (1999), *Transport and the Economy*, Report for the Department of the Environment, Transport and the Regions, 21.12.1999, http://www.roads.dft.gov.uk/roadnetwork/sactra/report99/index.htm.

Samuelson, P.A. (1954), The Transfer Problem and Transport Costs; II: Analysis of Effects of Trade Impediments, *The Economic Journal* 64, 264-289.

Schade, W. (2004), *Strategic Sustainability Analysis: Concept and Application for the Assessment of the European Transport Policy*, Dissertation thesis, Baden-Baden, publication forthcoming.

Schade, W., D. Fiorello, and A. Martino (2002), *ASTRA Model Update: Description of the ASTRA-T Model*, Deliverable D3 of the TIPMAC project funded by the European Commission 5th RTD framework, Karlsruhe.

Schade, W. and W. Rothengatter (2001), *Strategic Sustainability Analysis (SSA) – Broadening Existing Assessment Approaches for Transport Policies*, Transportation Research Record 1756, TRB, National Research Council, Washington, D.C., 3-11.

Schreckenberg, M. (1998), *Traffic and Granular Flow*, Singapore.

Schumpeter, J.A. (1934), *The Theory of Economic Development*, Cambridge MA.

Schuster, P., K. Sigmund, J. Hofbauer, and R. Wolff (1981), Selfregulation of Behaviour in Animal Societies, II: Games Between Two Populations Without Selfinteraction, *Biol. Cybernetics* 40, 17-25.

Simon, H. (1984), On the Behavioural and Rational Foundations of Economic Dynamics, *Journal of Economic Behaviour and Organization*, 35-55.

Sterman, J.D. (2000), *Systems Thinking and Modelling for a Complex World*, Boston.

Venables, A.J. and M. Gasiorek (1998), *The Welfare Implications of Transport Improvements in the Presence of Market Failure*, Report to the SACTRA Committee of the UK-DETR, London.

Wang, E.C. (2002), Public Infrastructure and Economic Growth: A new Approach Applied to East Asian Economies, *Journal of Policy Modeling* 24, 411-435.

Weidlich, W. and G. Haag (1999), *An Integrated Model of Transport and Urban Evolution*, Berlin.

Weidlich, W. and G. Haag (1984), *Concepts and Models of a Quantitative Sociology*, Springer Series in Synergetics, Berlin.

Traffic and Environment: Policy Maker's Response

Günter Hörmandinger

European Commission, Directorate General for Environment, Unit C.1 (Clean air and transport), 1049 Brussels, Belgium, guenter.hoermandinger@cec.eu.int

Keywords. *Transport, Environment, Economics, Policy*

JEL. *O13; O32; O33; O38; Q51; Q52; Q53; Q55; Q58; R40*

Abstract. The role of this intervention is to respond to the presentation of three authors in the session on transport and environment. The choice of areas for research proposed by these authors is generally supported. Five general areas for possible further research are highlighted: the real world as opposed to abstractions; the spatial aspects of transport costs and benefits; further research on environmental externalities; a more sophisticated approach to cost-benefit analysis; and the economic implications of transport innovations.

1 Introduction

This article is meant to provide a policy maker's response to the presentations made earlier in the session on transport and environment. Rather than going through the arguments made by the individual authors one by one, the approach of this paper takes its starting point from the environmental impacts of transport. References to the presentations in the session will be made as appropriate. This will then lead to a tentative formulation of areas that may be of interest for further study by economists. The opinions expressed in this article are those of the author and do not constitute a policy statement by the European Commission.

The paper by Schmutzler[1] sets the scene by spelling out an analysis of the environmental impacts of transport, distinguishing the emissions of harmful substances from each mode of transport by the modal shares and the overall volume of transport activity (**Fig.1**).

---

1 See contribution of Armin Schmutzler, Transportation and the Environment – Perspectives for Future Research, in this volume.

Fig. 1. A possible breakdown of the environmental impacts of transport

Emissions of type i:

$$e_i = f\sum_m \mu_{mF}\eta_{miF} + p\sum_m \mu_{mP}\eta_{miP}$$

m	– mode of transportation
f, p	– volumes of freight and passenger transport
μ_{mF} , μ_{mP}	– modal shares
η_{miF} , η_{miP}	– specific emissions of mode m

While this expression already contains a number of far-reaching simplifications (emissions are not the same as impacts; the spatial aspect of the emissions is not taken into account; not all impacts have the character of emissions, e.g. damage to the landscape or changes in lifestyles), it nevertheless usefully illustrates the generic intervention logic of environment policy, not only in transport policy but in relation to unwanted impacts of any human activity. Whenever such unwanted impacts are to be reduced, two types of response are possible in principle: the overall amount of that activity could be reduced, and/or it could be conducted in a different manner. Specifically in the field of transport, this has been spelled out in a research project called SPRITE that was undertaken on behalf of the European Commission[2] (**Fig.2**).

Fig. 2. Environmental intervention logic in transport policy according to SPRITE

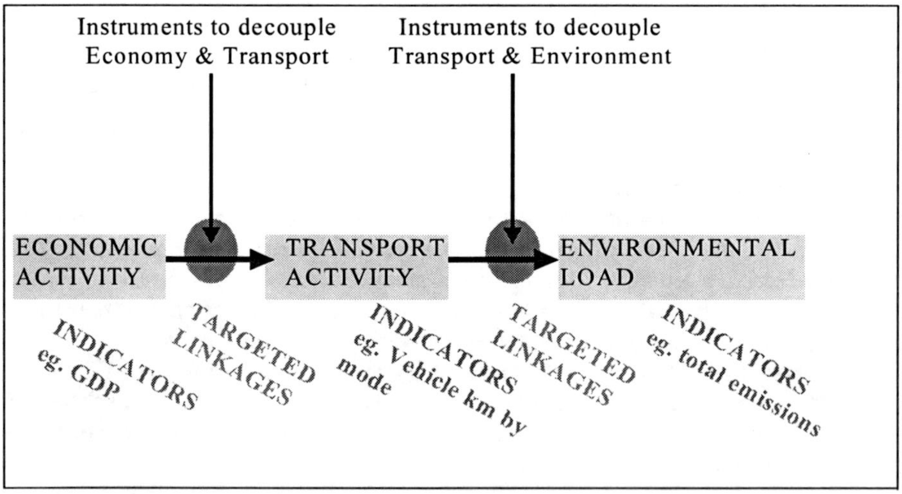

From the point of view of public policy, these alternatives have very different implications. The specific emission factors $\eta_{miF,P}$ denote (at least for road vehicles)

2 SPRITE (Separating the Intensity of Transport from Economic Growth). Project funded by the European Community under the Fifth Framework Programme for research, 'Competitive and Sustainable Growth' (1998-2002), http://www.its.leeds.ac.uk/projects/sprite/.

one of the success stories in terms of environmental policy intervention in the transport field, as cars have greatly improved their emissions over the past years. The reason for this appears to be both that there are technical solutions available and that the development and fitting of exhaust reduction technology fits into the normal product innovation cycle. To a certain extent, environmental policy thus went along with the main stream of the economy.

The same cannot be said about the modal shares $\mu_{mF,P}$. The trend in recent years has been a strengthening of road and air transport at the expense of the other modes. A combination of flexibility, reliability and a more seamlessly realised EU internal market in the field of road transport has acted to make road transport more attractive. Meanwhile aviation continues to grow at high levels. Policy intervention that aims at a reversal of this modal shift, including that pursued by the European Commission[3], is thus going against the mainstream of current trends, even though progress has been seen for example in EU railway policy. Trying to influence modal shares also involves persuading individuals – both in their private and professional lives – to change the way they organise and think about their transport. This is much harder to achieve than changing the characteristics of a product in ways that the final consumer never sees.

This last observation applies even more to transport volumes (f, p). Asking people to consider whether or not to travel is even more difficult than asking them to reconsider how to travel. Similar considerations hold for goods transport. It is therefore no surprise that transport demand management is politically difficult and that policy interventions with this goal are rare by comparison. The topic experienced a certain boost when the necessity of "decoupling" transport volumes from economic performance was highlighted at the European Council meeting in Gothenburg in June 2001, in the context of sustainable development. However, it should be noted that no major policy initiatives have so far followed this high-level pronouncement.

2 Environmental Impacts

In connection with the formulation of **Fig.1**, Schmutzler asks why there has been more success in improving some emissions (such as carbon monoxide) than others, notably CO_2. It is indeed worth distinguishing different types of environmental impact and look at them separately as they can be subject to quite different driving forces, linked to where the main intervention must take place in the formulation of **Fig.1**. The more prominent environmental impacts of transport are addressed in the following paragraphs.

---

3 European Commission (2001), European Transport Policy for 2010: Time to Decide, White Paper, COM(2001)370, http://europa.eu.int/comm/energy_transport/en/lb_en.html.

2.1 Air Pollution

Combating air pollution is one of the success stories of environmental legislation in the field of transport. This does not mean that all problems are solved. The air quality in the EU is in many respects still unsatisfactory, with many Member States currently unable to guarantee that the limit values for ambient air concentrations of all regulated pollutants will be met when they enter into force (e.g. 1 January 2005 for particulate matter and 1 January 2010 for oxides of nitrogen[4]). Several Member States will also have difficulties meeting their emissions ceilings under the corresponding Directive[5]. Nevertheless, the exhaust emissions from individual light-duty vehicles and heavy-duty vehicles have come down considerably since emission limit values have been introduced, and they are scheduled to decline further as the Euro-4 standards for light-duty vehicles enter into force on 1 January 2005[6], Euro-4 for heavy-duty vehicles from October 2005 and Euro-5 for heavy-duty vehicles from October 2008[7]. Work is currently under way to tighten these limit values further, with the aim of introducing Euro-5 standards for light-duty vehicles and Euro-6 for heavy-duty vehicles. Formal proposals to this effect are to be presented in the course of 2005.

It is worth noting that air pollution is not an intended activity. Nobody actually wants to pollute the air. Pollution is the unintended side-effect of fuel combustion, due to imperfect combustion and other technical shortcomings. The solution to this problem can therefore take the form of a "technical fix", meaning that the combustion process is improved and other technical innovations are being developed and deployed (better fuel quality, exhaust gas after treatment equipment). This activity goes in line with the existing trend, since new and improved generations of technology are developed and deployed as a matter of course in the normal cycle of product innovation. Having said that, it is by no means easy to develop and implement legislation that forces technical developments that would not otherwise take place. Experience shows that such legislation is introduced when the public concern about the environmental problem, and thus the political pressure to address it, is strong. Exhaust gas clean-up and the enforcement of fuel quality standards needed for its proper operation have now become commonplace features of modern road transport systems. The level of the clean-up rate is such that even with rising volumes of road traffic, the total amount of emissions is falling.

It should be noted that the number of actors directly concerned by this kind of regulatory activity is relatively small. It is limited to the industry whose products are being regulated and some of its suppliers, as well as a number of public authorities including those charged with vehicle type approval. The final customer is

---

4 Directive 1999/30/EC relating to limit values for NO_x, SO_2, Pb and PM_{10} in ambient air.

5 Directive 2001/81/EC on national emission ceilings for certain atmospheric pollutants.

6 Directive 1998/69/EC.

7 Directive 1999/96/EC.

never directly involved. Of course customers do bear the cost of the exhaust clean-up via the prices of new cars and of fuels, as they should do in an economic set-up that gives correct price signals. However, they do not see this cost directly, and they do not have to change any of their activities as a result. Also, the cost is relatively modest compared to the price of a new car. Thus, everybody keeps doing what they had been doing: Car makers produce cars, customers buy and drive them. No wide-ranging behaviour change or adaptation of habits or life styles is involved.

2.2 Climate Change

It has been asked why CO_2 emissions from road vehicles have not been reduced as effectively as those of air pollutants. CO_2 emissions are of course linked to transport volumes as mentioned above. But why has it not been possible to do what has been done for pollutants – breaking the link with transport volume growth? One may argue that this is simply a more recent problem that started to be addressed only in the late 1990s while emissions legislation dates back to 1970.

However, there is also a more fundamental issue. The emission of CO_2 is not an unwanted side effect that could be curbed by a technological fix. The energy that is chemically stored in the fuel can only be released by oxidising it (i.e. turning a hydrocarbon into CO_2 and water while releasing energy in the process). In that sense CO_2 is the intended main product of fuel combustion. It is possible to combust a fuel while avoiding to emit NO_x or CO or quantities of unburned fuel, but it is not possible to combust it without emitting CO_2.

What is technically possible, is to improve the efficiency with which the energy thus released is being used, and thus to reduce the overall amount of fuel that needs to be burned. There is indeed progress in improving technical efficiency, and this is where policy intervention can be (and indeed is) successful. Here again we are in sync with the mainstream of product evolution and improvement. It should be noted, however, that some of this progress is neutralised by counteracting tendencies. First, consuming less fuel reduces the cost of driving and thus encourages more driving (one example of the "rebound effect"). Even without this effect, travel volumes are rising generally, thus cancelling out some of the gains. Second, technology improvement can be used not only to reduce fuel consumption but also to boost performance, and the latter can be more attractive to the customer.

The only technical solution that will ultimately free us from CO_2 emissions consists in switching to non-fossil primary energy. However, this is more than a limited technology switch. It amounts to a large-scale system change. From an economic perspective, there is much that would be worthy of research here, linked to the various aspects of changes in the technical/physical systems that underpin the economy and society in general. An example would be the work by Carlota

Perez on techno-economic paradigm changes[8]. One of the lessons learned from that work provides sobering reading for anyone wanting to progress to a hydrogen economy – all of the paradigm changes identified so far were characterised by promises of massive cost reductions as compared to the established ways of doing things. It should be noted, though, that a massive change in the way energy is supplied to customers may not mean a strongly visible change to their lives. For example, alternative fuels for cars – even if produced from exotic sources – would imply no change at all from the drivers' perspective, except maybe small changes in handling the fuelling kit. Electricity from alternative primary energy sources would not imply any changes in households. The main change would be felt through the price of energy. This might facilitate economic studies.

It should be noted that ultimately some degree of behavioural adaptation by customers and economic actors may be inevitable as purely technological approaches may be too costly. This is supported by the outcome of the OECD project on Environmentally Sustainable Transport (EST)[9] . This project investigated three scenarios that would allow reaching a suitably defined sustainable transport system by 2020, one of them looking exclusively at technological options, the second one exclusively at non-technical options, and the third one at an optimal combination of both elements. It turned out that only the last scenario held any chance of realisation as the other two were not feasible in terms of costs or social acceptability. It has been mentioned earlier that measures that imply behaviour change pose greater difficulties to policy makers than other measures, which underlines even more the need to carefully research the options in this area.

2.3 Noise

The level of noise emitted as a result of transport activity is linked to the state of the technology used and the activity level. The actual noise nuisance is also strongly influenced by the spatial proximity of transport infrastructure and human habitations.

Technological progress is an important ingredient in a longer-term solution in addressing noise from transport, but on its own it is unlikely to be sufficient. Activities in areas such as demand management and land use planning will have to play a strong role as well.

---

8 Perez, C. (2003), Technological Revolutions and Financial Capital: The Dynamics of Bubbles and Golden Ages, Cheltenham.

9 http://www.oecd.org/document/58/0,2340,en_2649_34359_2346490_1_1_1_37465,00.html.

2.4 Land Use

There is a strong interaction between land use patterns and transport activity. Hence, spatial planning is a key influence for transport and all the environmental impacts linked to it.

The paper by Steininger and Molitor[10] highlights the important role that visions of town planning can have on the spatial structure of cities and hence, their transport systems. They trace the influence that early visions such as the one contained in the Charter of Athens in the early 1930s have had on present-day transport systems. This is quite convincing but it is important to highlight that these visions were not created in a vacuum. Instead, this author argues that these visions were merely the consequence of something else that came first. They were a reaction to the emergence of the mass-produced motor car, and served to explore its implications. We may be in need of a new transport paradigm today, in view of the environmental impacts of transport. But such a new vision can only make a real impact if it is based on some new, transport-relevant influence. This may be a new technology or energy source, a change in the character or organisation of society, or any other profound change in the determinants of transport activity. As long as the key drivers of transport remain the same, so will the dominant transport paradigm.

Steininger and Molitor conclude from the history of visions in spatial planning that more research is needed on the interaction between land use and transport. Despite the slight difference in interpretation referred to above, I would fully support this assessment. A key issue therein could be the interaction between systems of taxation, land use patterns and transport.

An interesting area for additional research would be the effect of new infrastructure on the economy. While it is generally agreed that large-scale public infrastructure projects should be fully economically assessed before their realisation, the practice sometimes does not live up to this ideal.

3 Some Issues for Research

What follows is necessarily a rather haphazard collection of topics that the author has chosen based on his own experience as well as inspiration taken from the papers that were submitted to the workshop. Its purpose is not to attempt completeness or authority, but to serve as one input among many to the academic community.

---

10 See K.W. Steininger and R. Molitor, Vision, Analysis and Future Pathways in Transport Research, in this volume.

3.1 The Real World

From a policy maker's perspective, it is important to obtain results that take into account the messy details of the "real world". This means that we need to go beyond some elegant and convenient assumptions that are often used as starting points, such as ideal markets. What is needed is information on the behaviour of real people in real decision-making situations. While there is considerable research already being undertaken in these areas, not all of it has yet penetrated the mainstream of economic policy advice in transport. It is a challenge to make this happen.

Schmutzler points to a certain reluctance on the part of some economists to touch an individual sector such as transport, both because this would lead to a loss of abstraction and generality, and because sector-specific considerations prevent cross-sectoral efficiency to be taken into account. He argues for an improvement of the existing research on the relative environmental performance of different modes, as well as more research into the potential for actually achieving modal shift. I would fully support that.

Examples of specific topics that are relevant in the transport field include oligopolistic or monopolistic situations; the characteristics of mature markets with increasingly tough competition and thin margins; the behaviour of individuals under conditions of incomplete information; incentives to cheat; the natural monopolies implicit in transport infrastructure provision; and network externalities.

The real world also requires us to go beyond the simpler versions of "homo oeconomicus" and allow for influences on human behaviour such as habits, perceptions and social driving forces to be taken into account.

Steininger and Molitor advocate research on the distributional impacts of transport policy. The present author would fully support that from a perspective of policy development, where policy makers are confronted with groups in society who have a strong interest to know whether they stand to gain or to lose out.

3.2 Spatial Aspects of Transport Costs and Benefits

The previous section did not only highlight topics for research; rather, it provided an overarching theme. One specific area, as already mentioned, concerns the spatial implications of transport. This becomes visible in situations of transit traffic, where the environmental externalities linked to transport activity become concentrated in a relatively small area along a transport corridor, while the economic benefits linked to this transport are located elsewhere, spread over the areas connected by this corridor (**Fig.3**). A simple comparison of costs and benefits of the overall situation could lead to the conclusion that the environmental costs located in the corridor were justified by the larger benefits linked to the large areas served by this traffic. The implied solution would be to ignore the environmental concerns in the corridor. This is politically not feasible and highlights the need to allow for spatial disaggregation of the analysis.

These arguments go in the same direction as those in the paper by Steininger and Molitor who also argue for a more explicit consideration of spatial aspects in transport economics.

Fig. 3. Spatial aspects of transport economics

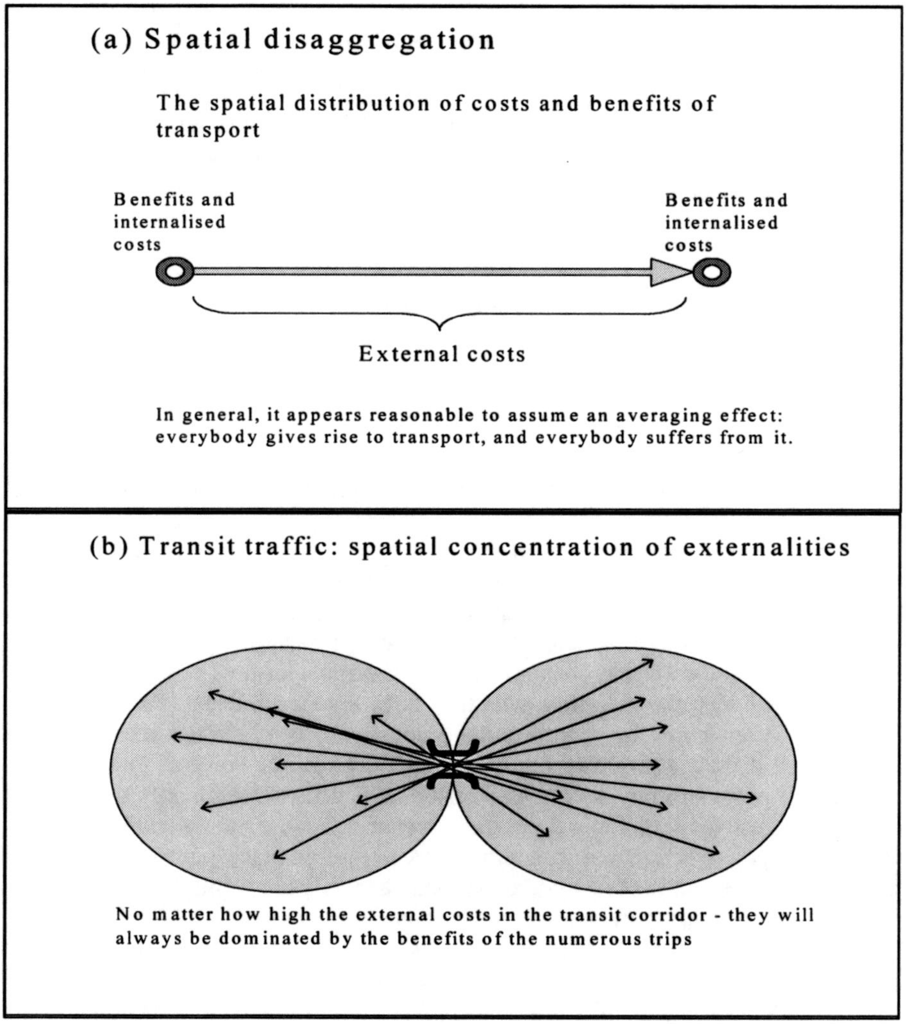

3.3 External Costs

There is a growing consensus that the likely impact of new policy proposals should be assessed before their finalisation. The European Commission has made its support for this tool clear in its Communication on impact assessment[11]. From an environmental perspective, a key to a successful assessment is to know the external costs linked to the environmental damage caused by an economic activity. There is a substantial body of research in this area and a certain consensus has been established on the values to use e.g. for the emission of certain substances. However, Schmutzler points to the tremendous uncertainties that still exist. There can be no doubt that it would be desirable to go further and establish these values more solidly. For example, we have practically no information on the variation of the marginal external costs of an activity as a function of the volume of that activity. It would also be useful to develop methods that go beyond purely numerical, monetary valuations that are not always possible in a meaningful way.

3.4 A More Sophisticated Approach to Cost-Benefit Analysis

From an economic perspective, the impact assessment of a policy proposal as referred to in the previous section comes down to establishing the costs and benefits to society of that proposal. Unfortunately there are some intrinsic difficulties linked to this task, as well recognised in the literature on the subject. This holds especially in the environmental field.

The costs of an action tend to be relatively well known, or at least well quantifiable, while the benefits of the same action are typically less well known or sometimes unknown. Costs tend to occur up-front while benefits come in later. When undertaking the cost-benefit analysis, the costs used in the analysis are of necessity those known at the time. Experience suggests that these values are often overestimated as subsequent progress in technology and manufacturing is not fully captured. Further, there is substantial information asymmetry: The only actors who really know about the costs of curbing a certain form of pollution are typically those causing the pollution, who thus have a vested interest. The costs of an action are often borne by a well-defined constituency of limited size while the benefits are diffuse and spread out over society. Thus, the voice of those bearing the costs is more strongly heard. And finally, it is difficult to identify the benefits ex post because they refer to a do-nothing scenario that did not materialise, assuming that the policy action in question was actually put in place[12]. In spite of all this, policy assessment is needed and cost-benefit analysis is a central tool in it. This points to the need to improve on all the aspects listed above.

Schade and Rothengatter[13] point to the avenues of further conceptual development in the models used for transport policy assessment. The present author would support this work in general, while adding two observations. First, with increasing complexity of models they tend to become obscure. It is vital to bear in mind what

11 Communication from the Commission in impact assessment, COM(2002)276.

12 It takes a trip to places such as Tehran or Caracas to appreciate what weak or absent pollution standards for cars mean in practice, for example.

13 See contribution of Wolfgang Schade and Werner Rothengatter, Research Issues in Transport Economics: Dynamics, Integration and Indirect Effects, in this volume.

the assumptions are that go into the models, and what original data is being used. Second, and even more importantly, it is necessary to highlight what is not in the models. There is a danger with numerical modelling, not just in economics but in general, that the focus shifts away from the real world and onto the model. This danger increases with increasing model complexity. Every effort must be made to overcome the dangers of being tied to closely to one's models. Both aspects – what is in the models and what is not – need to be highlighted in the clearest form possible to those who are the customers of the model output, notably when they are not economists or modellers but policy makers.

3.5 Economic Implications of Transport Innovations

It was argued before that the car-oriented visions of town planning as developed in the 1930s were not free-standing but motivated by the availability of the car which acted as an enabling factor. Today the search is on for an alternative vision of future transport. This requires new enabling factors. Candidates are being researched today, such as new types of fuels and drive technology (e.g. hydrogen and fuel cells), other technological advances (information and communication tools, robotics), new ways of organising transport (separating the ownership and use of cars, linking up different modes of transport), and new approaches that could eventually become socially accepted (such as universal road pricing). Each of these innovations has its own constituency of industries, developers and researchers. It is important to avoid wishful thinking and to analyse these new ideas in two ways: (i) what would be the criteria for this concept to succeed, and (ii) what would be the implications?

One of the innovations currently under development concerns the rising use of economic instruments in transport, notably road pricing. In this context it is fully justified that Steininger and Molitor propose to undertake research on behavioural changes due to significant transport price changes. Another subject for research in this area concerns the design of different types of incentives and the conditions under which they work or do not work properly.

4 Concluding Remarks

The above represents an attempt to highlight research needs in transport economics from an environmental perspective. Generally, it has been found that from a policy maker's perspective all the proposals made by the preceding authors can be supported. The preceding sections presented some additional flavours and qualifications to this. The result is largely illustrative rather than prescriptive. Researchers and those formulating research policies are called upon to form their own interpretations, in the context of their own work.

Liberalised Energy Markets – Do We Need Re-Regulation?

Michael Kraus

Fachhochschule Darmstadt (University of Applied Sciences), Hochschule für Wirtschaft und Technik, Fachbereich Wirtschaft, Haardtring 100, 64295 Darmstadt, Germany, kraus@fbw.fh-darmstadt.de

Keywords. *Electricity Market Liberalisation, Regulatory Economics, Benchmarking, New Regulatory Economics, Ex-Post-Impact Analysis*

JEL. *L5; L51; L43; K2; O13; N70*

Abstract. Against the background of energy market reforms and recent electricity market incidents and failures, the paper recalls the principles of economic regulation and highlights the methodological difficulties of any ex-post regulatory impact analysis. It synthesises theoretical contributions on regulation and describes the regulatory toolbox, with reference to the electricity market. After definitions and a discussion of the rationale of regulation, the various theories of regulation are described, distinguishing public-interest theories and private-interest theories. The normative regulatory concepts are divided up into the categories of price-based regulation, cost-based regulation (rate-on-return, sliding-scale and return-on-cost regimes), performance-based regulation (price-cap, revenue-cap, yardstick mechanism, Vogelsang-Finsinger and Sibley mechanisms, incremental surplus subsidy scheme), new regulatory economics and benchmarking. The paper reviews attempts in the literature to link electricity market reforms in the United Kingdom and particular market outcomes which reveal that methodological difficulties persist and comparatively little attention has been given to regulatory impact analysis. Notably, the ex-ante design of a potential ex-post impact analysis would be a useful addition to any new regulatory process.

1 Introduction

There is increasing debate whether energy liberalisation has met expectations and resulted in efficient electricity and gas markets. Notably the secure supply of electricity has been challenged by a series of major electricity market incidents worldwide. California went through an unprecedented energy crisis in 2002, and severe outages occurred in the United States and Canada in August 2003. The Enron case and illegal practices in energy trading in the US have shaken not only

North American energy markets. In 2003, extensive power blackouts occurred in Italy, Denmark, Sweden, and the United Kingdom. The French and German power sectors faced difficulties during the heat wave in the summer of 2003. And Norway experienced power problems in the same year related to its heavy reliance on hydropower.

These incidents have added to an increasingly critical stance toward energy liberalisation, and they raise difficult energy policy issues: Some critics link the recent problems to market liberalisation and poor market designs. Others want deregulation to be suspended or undone altogether.[1]

This paper does not try and provide the answers to these issues. Rather it attempts to put things into perspective and to highlight the difficulties and limits inherent in any regulation, including energy market regulation. To this end, the paper will focus on regulation in general rather than on energy market reform. It will (i) recall the principles of regulation, (ii) synthesise theoretical contributions on regulation, and (iii) describe the regulatory toolbox. It reviews attempts in the literature to link electricity market reforms in the United Kingdom and particular market outcomes. They reveal that methodological difficulties persist and comparatively little attention has been given to systematic regulatory impact analysis. Notably, the ex-ante design of a potential ex-post impact analysis would be a useful addition to any new regulatory process.

2 Principles of Regulation

2.1 Definitions

In its broadest definition, regulation is the employment of laws, rules or orders prescribed by an authority to regulate economic conduct in order to meet social or economic policy objectives and, therefore, is the opposite of "laissez-faire". Its purpose is to protect the public from the negative consequences of imperfect competition (Baumol, 1995: 255). Consequently, deregulation is a state's withdrawal of its legal powers to direct the conduct of economic players. There is no common definition of "re-regulation", a term that can mean unwinding an existing regulation (i.e. undoing it), or further developing or adjusting an already existing regulation.

A distinction is often made between structural regulation and conduct regulation (Kay and Vickers, 1990). While the former is used for regulation of market structure, like restrictions on entry and exit to marketplaces, issuing professional

1 Democratic presidential candidate Howard Dean proposed a comprehensive "re-regulation" of US businesses. After years of government deregulation of energy markets (and telecommunications, airlines and other major industries) he saw the need to reverse the trend towards deregulation in order to restore faith in scandal-plagued US corporations.

licences or unbundling of vertically integrated industries[2], the latter is used for regulation of the behaviour in the market, like price controls or provisions of minimum quality of service standards.

Furthermore, regulatory intervention can take the forms of ex-ante and ex-post regulation. Ex-ante regulation applies general rules of market entry and of conduct before market entry and is prescriptive in nature (i.e. laying down methods of calculation of prices). Ex-post regulation often takes place on a case-by-case basis, after market entry and conduct, with penalties in case of violation of applicable regulations or competition law. It can involve lengthy procedures, notably if the regulator can only intervene at the request of market participants and when other participants prolong the procedures.[3]

2.2 The Rationale for Regulation

Numerous reasons for market failure[4] can be found in the literature (see Aktan, 2003 and den Hertog, 2003) that justify government regulation, notably:

- economies of scale and natural monopoly (long-run average cost declining as firm size increases)
- excessive competition, external economies (consumption or production activities affecting the cost/benefit function of other economic units positively or negatively)
- information asymmetry (principle-agent situation)
- public goods (collective consumption goods versus pure or impure goods), trade-cycles
- protection of infant industries (i.e. administered renewable energy markets), bounded rationality

2 See for instance the EU Electricity Directive 2003/54/EC that in order to ensure non-discriminatory access to the network and to avoid conflicts of interest requires electricity utilities to separate the network business (natural monopoly) from those activities of vertically integrated companies which compete on the market, namely production and supply. The basic elements of the unbundling regime are a legal unbundling of the transmission system operator and distribution system operator from other activities not related to transmission or distribution; functional unbundling of the transmission operator and the distribution operator, in order to ensure their independence within the vertically integrated undertaking; accounting unbundling that requires to keep separate accounts for transmission and distribution activities.

3 Most European states apply an ex-ante regulation in their electricity sectors, except for the Nordic countries and Germany. The European gas markets, too, are predominantly regulated on an ex-ante basis; seven states apply ex-post regulation or variants of it (European Commission, 2003).

4 Examples for regulatory failures are the California energy debacle caused by market disruption due to deregulation, and also transmission problems and regional drought, and British Railtrack whose inadequate regulatory regime caused transportation quality to deteriorate substantially which eventually lead to the company's collapse.

- moral hazard (agents act in ways that incur cost which they do not have to bear)
- co-ordination problems
- transaction cost (to the extent consumers or producers incur costs for information about market opportunities, markets will not perform efficiently).

Government regulation can thus be viewed as aiming to correct imperfect competition, unbalanced market operation, missing markets and undesirable market results (den Hertog, 2003: 9). Regulatory regimes try to overcome market failures, notably efficiency loss or monopolistic rent, and, therefore, attempt to emulate functional competition.

Economic regulation is mainly exercised on natural monopolies and market structures with limited (or excessive) competition while social regulation consists of rules aiming to correct external economies, particularly those that impinge on health, safety, environmental and consumer protection (Aktan, 2003: 4).

3 Theories of Regulation

Regulatory theory can broadly be divided into the normative and the positive theory of regulation.[5] While the normative variant investigates which type of regulation is the most efficient, implicitly assuming that efficient regulation is desirable, the positive variant is directed to the economic explanation of regulation and the prediction of outcomes.

In practice it is difficult to consistently maintain a clear-cut distinction between the two approaches. Positive theories will explain and predict the behaviour of regulatory regimes but also assess the consequences of these regimes. To the extent that they formulate recommendations for the optimal design of regulatory regimes, they become normative. Conversely, normative theories will necessarily take account of the findings and principles of positive theories of regulation and will incorporate these.

The distinction between normative and positive is broadly identical with the distinction between (normative) public interest theories and (positive) private interest theory.[6]

Furthermore, as Joskow and Noll (1981) point out, a key problem of the public interest theory is that the evaluating, normative theory of economic welfare is used as a positive explanatory theory of regulation.

Ogus (2002) sees some ambiguity about what is to be regarded as a theory: *"It should not be confused with methodology which uncontroversially has a major*

---

5 A normative statement a judgement and states whether a situation is desirable or undesirable. Normative statements express what ought to be. It is, therefore, not possible to prove or to unprove such statements. Conversely, a positive statement is a statement about what is, and such statements, therefore, can prove wrong. Positive statements do not express approval or disapproval.

6 For an extensive treatment of public interest theory and private interest theory and the relation between the two, see den Hertog (2003: 7-40).

role to play in regulatory policy making. In any event, there has been no single economic theory; rather, several with different tools and with different implications. Further, while some of the theories are purely predictive, others combine prediction with normative evaluation. ... At the same time, economists have been too obsessed with finding a theory which will provide a complete explanation of the existence and incidence of regulation. The public interest approach, which assumes that law is made exclusively to generate aggregate social welfare is too naïve; and the private interest theory which relates it entirely to the furtherance of personal and group welfare is excessively cynical. Both sets of theories are nevertheless helpful in focussing attention on how the different institutions of regulatory decision making can be used either to advance the ostensible goals of regulation or else to subvert those goals to private ends."

3.1 Public-Interest Theory of Regulation

According to this traditional theory, economic regulation should be imposed when markets fail. The public-interest theory of regulation is normative in nature and based on neo-classical welfare objectives where the regulator maximises the total of the consumer and producer welfare.

Public-interest theory sees regulation as an arena of benevolent agents motivated by a desire to serve the public, and no unintended and unexpected consequences of regulatory actions arise in this view. The approach works on the premise that the regulator is fully informed, can implement regulation at no cost and has no own interests. Normative theories of regulation describe how governments ought to act, but do not explain why regulators act the way they do.

Recent research distinguishes a naïve period of public interest theory superseded in the 1980s by a more sophisticated one. The sophisticated variant does not require regulation to be perfect. It does, however, assume that market failure exists, that regulation is the most effective means of overcoming it and that regulation does not continue to exist once the cost exceed the advantages. According to the sophisticated theory, then, regulation can be accounted for as the efficient solution to market failure (den Hertog, 2001: 23-24).

The spectrum of normative regulatory regimes ranges from high-powered regimes, where regulatory rules provide strong incentives for performance improvement, to low-powered regulatory regimes, where low incentives induce the regulated agent to improve performance.[7] Burns and Estache (2003: 3) describe the regulatory and institutional ingredients of a low-powered regulatory regime as follows:

- Regulatory structures are bureaucratic, rigid and intrusive, implying a lack of flexibility and adaptability.
- Objectives devolved to management by the regulator are complex and contradictory.

---

7 For the respective taxonomy, see Laffont and Tirole (1993: 11).

- Prices are based largely on the firm's own costs, implying frequent profit confiscation (cost-plus or rate-of-return regime).

Accordingly, characteristics of a high-powered regime are:

- Managerial objectives are ring-fenced from public policy objectives, so that the running of the business is decentralised to the managers within a well-defined framework.
- Tarif controls are based on exogenous information and the business is able to retain the profits of improved efficiency (price caps).

Starkey and van Pelt (1995: 151-160) view regimes as high-powered if regulators do not consider increased profits of the regulated company as a failure of regulation itself. Burns and Estache (2003: 3-4) define the incentive power of a (normative) regulatory regime by the amount of control that is decentralised to the management, and by how far prices are decoupled from costs. They point out that while low-powered regimes might not be particularly efficient, high-powered ones might not proof sufficiently sustainable to deliver efficiency gains.

Newberry (1997: 2) rates cost-of-service or rate-of-return regimes lowest (power factor of 0) and price regulation where the utility receives all the benefits of cost reduction highest (power factor of 1).

In his seminal work on the principles of regulation, Kahn (1988: 325) depicts the limitations of the normative approach: *"Regulated monopoly is a very imperfect instrument for doing the world's work. It suffers from the evils of monopoly itself: the danger of exploitation, aggressively or by inertia, the absence of pervasive external restraints and stimuli to aggressive, efficient and innovative performance. Regulation itself tends to inherently be protective of monopoly, passive, negative and unimaginative".*

3.2 Private-Interest Theory of Regulation

A contrasting view is the private-interest theory, or public choice theory. Here, regulatory outcomes are seen as resulting from structures and processes and, therefore, need to be recognised explicitly in the design of regulatory regimes. For instance, the intervals of regulatory revisions, the interventions of different regulatory institutions or the communication within regulatory organisations will have an impact on the regulatory outcome. If these influences are not taken into account, the effective impact of regulatory outcomes will either be overestimated or underestimated. Regulatory agents are driven by the same motivations as private sector agents: self-interest. Private-interest theory assumes that the regulator maximises public welfare merely up to the point where its own interests are compromised. Behaviour is determined by the incentive structure, and a bad performance by regulation indicates a low-powered structure, rather than wrong motives. Under a positive regulatory regime, regulated companies have more discretion regarding conduct and try to gain influence over the regulator.

Traditionally, economists argue that regulation is the way to overcome market failure, while public choice economists hold the view that regulation does not effectively correct market failure because governments, or the regulator, also fail.

Notably, public choice theory argues that even though agents in the political marketplace like voters, politicians, lobbyists, or bureaucrats, may feel some compassion for others, their actions are also driven by self-interest. For instance, regulators benefit from higher budgets when negative events arise in the industries which they regulate. The tenet of public choice theory, therefore, is that regulators seek to maximise their self-interest rather than the public interest. Public choice theory is thus "*excessively cynical*" (Ogus, 2002). The theory received widespread attention through the seminal works of J. Buchanan and G. Tullock and has developed into various schools of thought.

According to the Chicago school, beneficiaries of regulation gain control of regulator and regulation protects interest groups ("capture theory of regulation"). Organised groups benefit more from regulation compared to less organised, diffuse groups, and notably the producers benefit at the expense of consumers. The Chicago school focuses mainly on the role of interest groups in the public policy process, and that school's major proponents Stigler, Posner, Peltzman, and Becker consider the contribution of interest groups to such policy formulation.

The central proposition of Stigler (1971) was that groups whose interests were concentrated would be better able to influence government than groups whose interests were diffuse. In his empirical work he showed that the main beneficiaries of regulation implemented in the consumer interest were not consumers but the regulated firms: "*Businesses and politicians are self-interested income-maximisers. They are not at all concerned with public interest and seek to maximise their votes or wealth*".

Peltzman (1976) points out that regulators, or political brokers, maximise a value function (interpreted as number of votes gained) that takes account of the utilities of consumers and of the producers. The latter seek to extort wealth from the consumers through regulation. Income is redistributed between the two groups to the point where the marginal loss in votes from consumers equals the marginal gain in votes from producers (Palda, 2002: 4).

Becker (1983) maintains that "*as political pressure increases, political influence increases and that it is competition between pressure groups for political influence which determines the equilibrium structure of regulatory measures like taxes, subsidies etc.*"

Adherents of the Virginia school of public choice are critical of the fact that the private interest theory is predictive, rather than normative, and that it is indifferent to the efficiency implications of the analysis (Ogus, 2002). This school proposes a (positive) theory of government failure as opposed to the theory of market failure. Agents will invest in the "regulatory market" in order to extract rents. When governments intervene in the market, individuals start seeking to influence them in order to transfer welfare to themselves. This act of spending resources in order to recoup them in the form of a transfer by the regulator is called rent-seeking. The Virginia school focuses mainly on rent-seeking by competing groups such as bureaucrats and politicians. The rents earned are important resources that bureaucrats and politicians devote to interest groups in order to attract their favour. There are deadweight losses associated with such rent-seeking that, therefore, constitutes a cost of regulation.

4 Regulatory Regimes

The normative regulatory concepts can be divided into the categories of price-based regulation, cost-based regulation, performance-based regulation, new regulatory economics, and benchmarking, the latter being a complementary category to others rather than a category of its own.

4.1 Price-Based Regulatory Regimes

Natural monopoly emerges in industrial sectors where economies of scale exist for a large range of output. This frequently occurs in capital-intensive industries, like the electricity industry, where a large proportion of cost is fixed cost.[8] In this case, the producer's cost function will be sub-additive, i.e. at some level of output it is cheaper for that producer[9] to produce all output than sharing the output among two or more companies. From a welfare-maximising viewpoint the first-best solution[10] is achieved if the (single) producer provides the output at uniform prices equal to marginal cost. Precisely because of the shape of its cost function, however, the producer's marginal cost is below average cost and, hence, the producer will never be able to break-even. He will incur losses and eventually be forced to quit the market.

A first-best solution applying marginal cost is not sustainable in monopolies unless the regulator provides the producer with a transfer payment, i.e. subsidy, in order to enable the producer recoup cost and make a profit. However, the regulator rarely disposes of all relevant information. For instance, in most jurisdictions, standard accounting is required on a yearly basis and not performed on a product unit basis. The producer has incentives to misreport costs in order to increase the subsidy and profits. Even if reported correctly, incurred cost may not be minimum cost of production, for instance, owing to inefficiencies or sub-optimal capacity choices.[11] Moreover, if the regulator provides transfer payments (i.e. subsidy) to the producer to cover its loss, distortions elsewhere in the economy will result. A first-best regulatory regime is, therefore, difficult to achieve in practice, and a departure from marginal cost and uniform pricing is necessary to recoup all costs.

---

8 For example, the fixed costs of building and operating an electricity distribution network or an electricity transmission grid is substantial while the cost of supplying one extra unit of distribution or transmission service is minimal.

9 Or service provider as in the case of electricity distribution network operators or transmission grid operators.

10 The first-best optimum is the best possible unconstrained solution that maximises welfare.

11 Leibenstein (1966) pointed to potential cost inefficiencies arising from a lack of effective competition within a market. These are known as X-inefficiencies and are often used as an argument in the case against pure monopoly.

In order for the monopolistic producer to recoup all the cost and to operate a sustained self-sufficient basis, a second-best solution[12] is required allowing the producer to set the price at average cost. This solution, however, is welfare inferior; and only in a one-good situation, the break-even requirement is sufficient to determine the second-best price. With more than one good many different price combinations are possible that all result in a break-even situation (Train, 1991: 116-117).

One approach frequently used in electricity utilities, still leading to a welfare-maximising first-best solution[13], is to allow the company, for instance, a network service provider, to impose a fixed charge for access to the service and a variable unitary price reflecting usage. Revenue through the fixed charge enables the company to recoup the loss, and revenue through the variable charge covers marginal cost. This is known as the two-part tariff pricing scheme.[14]

Another second-best solution regarding multi-good companies offers Ramsey pricing where prices are set at different levels for different customers, depending on their elasticity of demand. The overall constraint is that costs must be covered. It applies to any multi-good firm with substantial shared (fixed) costs.[15] Mark-ups on marginal costs are charged on users inversely related to the users' respective price elasticity for the products. Thus, if demand for product A is price-elastic, while demand for product B is not, then the price of product B should recover proportionately more of any shared cost than that of product A. Contrary to the prices with elastic demand, prices of products with inelastic demand will be above average cost. Ramsey pricing can be welfare-superior to average-cost pricing. However, regulatory regimes based on Ramsey pricing are difficult to implement in practice as they rely on demand-related information. For that reason, regulators often favour cost-related regimes over demand-related ones.

Under the Loeb-Magat scheme (Loeb and Magat, 1979: 399-404) that does not require the regulator to obtain cost information, the price the company charges is not directly regulated. Rather, the company receives a transfer payment (i.e. subsidy) equal to the consumer surplus generated at the selected price. The company will then choose a price equal to marginal costs.

---

12 The second-best optimum is the outcome subject to a constraint that violates one of the prerequisites for a first-best outcome.

13 This is called a Coase result (Train, 1991: 196f).

14 For a description, see Laffont and Tirole (1993: 144-152) and Berg and Tschirhart (1989); for an extension of two-part tariffs to multi-part tariffs (i.e. flat rates/block rates), see Knieps (2000), Vogelsang (1999), Train (1991).

15 Electricity utilities are multi-good companies as they distribute or transmit, for instance, high-voltage and low-voltage power as well as on-peak and off-peak power.

4.2 Cost-Based Regulatory Regimes

4.2.1 Rate-On-Return Regulation

Under this traditional regulation rate levels are set to provide an agent (i.e. utility) with the opportunity to cover all of its necessary costs, including a fair return on the capital employed. Although the utility may recover more or less than its full cost in the short run, its total cost should generally be equated with total revenues over a period of time. In order for the regulator to establish a permissible rate of return, the company provides detailed information on the cost incurred for providing its services. The company is allowed to recover this (reasonable) cost from its customers.

There are two main concerns with rate-of-return regulation. First, if the rate is set too high, the regulated company has an incentive to increase its capital expenditure inefficiently. Second, the regulated company has no incentive to reduce operating costs; if it does so, its revenue for the next year will be reduced by the same amount.

Averch and Johnson (1962: 1053-1069) demonstrated that regulated companies subject to rate-of-return regulation have an incentive to use inputs biased towards increased tangible assets (capital) and reduced labour.[16] [17]

A difficult task in practice is determining the asset base. It will be necessary for the regulator to decide the asset value and depreciation for the regulated company. A regulator can only overcome this problem if it can observe the cost and regulate the price directly. The rate of return will reflect the cost of debt and equity for the regulated company.

4.2.2 Sliding Scale Regulation

Sliding scale regulation is a derivative of the rate-of-return regulation. Under this scheme, sometimes termed rate-of-return bandwidth regulation or revenue sharing regulation, the agent is allowed a rate of return that varies as a result of other conditions. Usually, it is benchmarked against a reference range for the rate of return. During the regulatory period, the actual rate of return can vary within the range without causing regulatory review and rate adjustments. If the actual rate falls outside the range, it can trigger a pre-specified profit sharing mechanism or a rate review.

16 An effect known as Averch-Johnson effect; Train (1991: 19-67) points out that though the company will choose an inefficient mix of inputs, it will use the inputs that is has chosen efficiently.

17 Under any regulatory arrangement inducing companies to make savings against their expenditure projections, operating savings are more rewarding for the companies than comparable reductions in capital expenditure (Burns and Riechmann, 2004: 15-16).

4.2.3 Return-On-Cost Regulation

The return-on-cost regulation applies a similar principle as rate-of-return regulation. The firm is allowed a certain profit per unit of cost. It can increase costs by expanding output. While an expansion in output results in increasing revenue, the firm will increase its costs, since the revenue will help to offset the effect of the cost increase. The firm will expand output up until the point where demand becomes inelastic. If marginal revenue becomes negative, the firm will obtain better results by not expanding its output.

4.3 Performance-Based Regulatory Regimes

Performance-based regulation is a system that requires a compliance that is specified in terms of regulatory outcomes. It relies on financial incentives and disincentives to induce the desired behaviour of a regulated agent. The desired behaviours, or outcomes, are generally lower costs and improved quality of service. Regulated companies have some discretion in complying with these goals. The interest in performance-based regulation to some extent reflects dissatisfaction with cost-based regulation.

Performance regulation, also termed outcome regulation, is not necessarily synonymous to incentive regulation in the sense that performance-based standards do not per se offer any explicit incentive to go beyond the compliance level. In order to encourage further improvement, explicit incentives can be offered to the regulated agent.

4.3.1 Price-Cap Regulation

Under this type of regulation the price charged by the regulated agent is regulated rather than the profits. The initial price levels ("price caps") are set by the regulator based on present prices and revenues of the agent. The agent is allowed to increase its prices by the retail or consumer price index (RPI, CPI) less an efficiency improvement factor X. If the regulated company is more efficient than had bee assumed at the time when the X-factor was, it is allowed to retain excess savings as profits. Conversely, if the agent is less efficient than has been assumed at the time when the X-factor was, it will be at the expense of its profits. Provided there is no sharing mechanism in place, revenues and profits of the agent are not limited. Price-cap regulation thus encourages an agent to increase output in order to increase revenues and profits.

RPI-X regulation also provides the regulated agent with an incentive to cut costs beyond the projected levels underlying its revenue regulation. In principle, the X-factor could be set without reference to the costs of the agent. In practice, the regulator will require a good understanding of the costs of the regulated business and of their development over time. This requirement to understand projected costs, however, is the reason for major concerns about the price-cap regulation. The regulated agent necessarily will always have more information about its business than the regulator. Because of this information asymmetry, the agent might overstate the cost projections. This will notably be the case when productivity leaps are possible or when input prices decline significantly. In both cases, the agent could make excessive profits over a period of time. It would be counter-productive to try and re-negotiate or to impose a higher X-factor since only in the absence of any perceived regulator uncertainty incentives will be provided for the company to reduce its cost. Otherwise, the company faces a "hold-up problem" resulting in reduced efficiency increases. Similar issues arise with regard to the constant X-factor that will be reviewed at certain intervals to account for changes in the profitability of the agent ("regulatory lag").[18]

Price-cap regulation presents advantages over a rate-of-return regulation. Less information is required; apart from the negotiated X and the publicly available RPI, only information about prices and output are required, but no cost data. At the same time, no incentives are provided for inefficient factor inputs or cost inflation. Rather, there are incentives for the company to reduce cost, since any cost reduction will remain with the company. This is a concern, since the regulated company might reduce costs too much, impairing the quality of service. Both concerns may be offset through additional incentive schemes (separate licence condi-

---

18 Boes (2001: 18-19) describes a number of concerns in this respect: *"Lags in adjusting price caps give the profit-maximising utility incentives to improve productivity efficiency at the cost of allocative efficiency. Consider a regulator who has chosen a particular value of X and a regulated utility which reduces its costs to increase profits. The firm may retain this higher profit. However, at the next revision of X the prices are set so as to shift the gains from the efficiency increases from the producer to the consumers. The firm's incentive depends on the length of the regulatory lag. If the interval between the revisions is too short, there will not be many incentives for innovative activities of the utility. If the interval is too long, too much profit goes to the firm and the consumers are exploited. If the regulator is imperfectly informed about the costs, the firm will make strategic use of the regulatory lag. Let us assume that the manager of the firm knows that the regulator will choose X so as to siphon off the utility's profits. Insofar as cost-reducing innovations are reversible, the firm has an incentive to be a high-cost firm at the moment of the regulatory reviews, but a low-cost firm in between. A saw-tooth profile of the firm's cost-reducing innovations will result. The issue of the timing of productive-efficiency gains and price-cap reviews can be overcome (to a degree) by the use of "glidepath" and similarly lagged adjustments of the cap rather than loading all of the adjustments into current price. On the side of the firm, there may be imperfect information about the date of the next revision. If the manager of the utility knows some exogenous probability of the regulatory revision, he will act too cautiously in his innovation policy. A better result is achieved if the probability of revision is endogenised. This is the case if the manager knows that a revision becomes highly likely if the profit exceeds a particular level that is considered fair by the regulator. The regulation converges to prices where there is no excess of current over fair profit. Moreover, cost minimisation is achieved."*

tions) that reward companies for both accurate projecting and delivery of the desired quality of service.[19]

4.3.2 Revenue-Cap Regulation

Revenue-cap regulation is a modification of price-cap regulation. Under this regime the revenue of a regulated agent is capped rather than the price of the services it charges. The agent is allowed to increase revenues up to a predetermined level that is adjusted for efficiency with an improvement factor X. This form of regulation is frequently applied to electricity utilities in order to ensure that deliberate, politically desirable reductions in output, i.e. from demand-side management and energy conservation programmes ordered by regulators, will not reduce the utility's return. A disincentive of a utility with regard to politically imposed programmes is thus eliminated.

A drawback of this form of regulation is that a regulated agent with market power has an incentive to either raise prices or to stimulate demand to reach its revenue cap. Raising prices will both increase revenue and decrease output, translating in lower operating costs and higher profits.[20]

Two revenue-cap regimes can be distinguished. Under a fixed revenue-cap, the regulator fixes the revenue the company can earn in the first year. Revenues in subsequent years are adjusted according to the RPI-X formula. Hence, the revenue of the agent is independent of the level of output.

Under a variable revenue-cap regime the revenue is linked to further variables, such as, in the case of an electricity company, maximum demand on the power system or changes in the customer base. The national electricity regulator of South Africa (NER, 2003: 18) states two reasons why to apply a variable revenue-cap regime. First, it can reduce distortions created when customer-driven changes in costs cannot be recovered by the regulated business, and second, it can strengthen incentives for system growth.

Electricity transmission companies frequently apply revenue-cap regimes, since short-run transmission costs are largely independent of the total level of electricity transmitted through the grid. The transmission company is effectively provided with a guaranteed income regardless of the amount of electricity sold, and there is minimum risk. If cost can be lowered, the company increases its profits. In cir-

---

19 For a discussion of regulatory instruments and their effects on investment behaviour see Burns and Riechmann (2004: 24). They point out that as a result of the cyclical nature of regulatory proceeding, companies retain a greater share of the benefit of cost reductions made in early phases of a regulatory period, rather than later. The year in which savings are made in a regulatory review alters the period over which any benefit is retained by the company. In electricity distribution, for example, typical technical service attributes are long, short and transient non-planned supply interruptions, planned supply interruptions, voltage dips, voltage limits, harmonics, flicker etc.

20 A monopolistic electricity network operator, however, faces inelastic demand and has little means of stimulating the demand for network services.

cumstances where costs prove higher than anticipated at the time when the price is set, the business is provided with an incentive to reduce cost (NER, 2003: 19).

4.3.3 Yardstick Regulation

Yardstick regulation has been developed by Shleifer (1985) and can be applied in case several identical regulated agents exist, such as regional electricity distribution companies. It employs a mechanism by which a particular utility is regulated on the basis of the private information acquired from all remaining utilities. These constitute a benchmark (or "yardstick") against which the utility's potential can be assessed. The price that the utility charges, therefore, depends on the costs of other utilities. In return for the revelation of a utility's private information, the regulator uses that information exclusively for the regulation of the other utilities, not for the regulation of the utility revealing the information. Each utility knows that providing true information will not influence its own regulation. Hence, it has no incentive to give false information and will provide true information (Bös, 2001: 8).

Yardstick regulation implies little information requirement for the implementation of a first-best regulation. There are no adverse incentive effects for the regulated utility, and it pursues a profit-maximising strategy like under a first-best regulatory solution.

The mechanism, however, is not without drawbacks. For instance, it is vulnerable to collusion, since the profits of a utility depend on its own revelations. Yardstick regulation might be compromised in cases where single monopolistic utilities have been split up in a number of (privatised) utilities, as in the case of the British regional electricity distribution companies (Bös, 2001: 9).

In case of electricity transmission companies, yardstick regulatory regimes can raise problems because comparative analyses of transmission companies on an international basis are obscured by functional differences and different physical characteristics such as voltage levels and system services (NER, 2003: 20).

4.3.4 Vogelsang-Finsinger Regulation

Vogelsang and Finsinger (1979) proposed an iterative regulatory mechanism leading the regulated firm to gradually move to Ramsey prices and outputs.[21] In the first period of regulation, the regulated agent, a profit-maximising company, charges some price for each good, sells some quantity of each good, and incurs some cost for producing the outputs. The regulator, who is maximising welfare, observes these prices, outputs, and costs of the first period and constrains the company in its choice of prices in the second period. The company can charge any prices in the next period, provided the next period's price, when multiplied by the first period's quantities, does not exceed the first period's cost. Within this new regulatory set of prices, the company will in any given period choose prices that

---

21 For an extensive discussion of the Vogelsang and Finsinger mechanism see Train (1991).

are maximising profits. This iterative process continues until prices break-even with Ramsey prices.[22]

The main advantage of this regulatory adjustment process is the minimum information requirement for the regulator. In order to stipulate the regulatory set of prices, the regulator merely needs to know prices, quantities and total cost of the past period. Notably, no information on the shape of demand and cost functions is required, nor any information about the distribution of particular non-observable variables (Bös, 2001: 7).

Drawbacks of this type of mechanism are that the utility is induced to increase cost in the long run because present expenditure leads to a higher price level in the future, thereby increasing long-run profits. Demand and cost functions must remain unchanged until the Ramsey optimum is achieved, and this can only hold if the regulatory set of prices is frequently revised. Even annual revisions may not be frequent enough (Bös, 20001: 17) Concerns are reported particularly with regard to an application in the electricity industry which is capital-intensive and where long-run investment costs play a significant role. Kinnunen (2003: 46) points out that there is no inter-temporal connection between the cost functions of the different periods, nor is technological progress taken into account.

4.3.5 Self-Selecting Tariffs (Sibley Mechanism)

A self-selecting tariff scheme exists when a company offers the user the option to select one particular tariff of its choice. Economic theory suggests that a rational user faced with such an option will choose the tariff that maximises its individual consumer surplus. Self-selecting tariffs provide regulated companies and the regulator with a mechanism for increasing surplus. A self-selecting tariff scheme together with an existing scheme, where prices do not equal marginal costs, will produce increases in surplus. To enable the company to extract all the potential surplus gains, Sibley (1989: 393-404) proposes a mechanism that is applied separately to each user in situations where the users' demands differ. In each period the company is allowed to design a tariff for each user and to offer that tariff only to that user. For each user the regulator also designs a tariff that the company is required to offer to the user. The regulator's tariff consists of the per unit charge that the firm charged under its own tariff for the customer in the previous period; the fixed charge is the average operating profit per user that the company made in the previous period (Train, 1991: 264ff.).

4.3.6 Incremental Surplus Subsidy Scheme

Sappington and Sibley (1998) propose a regulatory mechanism called the incremental surplus subsidy scheme or ISS. It aligns social and private incentives with investment cycles and can be implemented also when the regulator has no information about the cost structure of the regulated company. The regulator only needs to share the agent's information of demand and to be able to observe expen-

22 For illustrating quantitative examples, see Train (1991: 149f.).

ditures of the agent. The scheme induces the agent to set prices at marginal cost in order to minimise production costs, and to undertake efficient investments. The company retains the social surplus created by the investment for one period. During that period, the company must bear the costs of the investment. In subsequent periods, the company is compensated for the actual costs of its investment.

4.4 New Regulatory Economics

The new economics of regulation views optimal regulation as a principal-agent situation where the company acts as an agent of the government in supplying third parties. The agent acts strategically, and the principal maximises social welfare accruing from the informational advantage of the agent. Regulatory activity is viewed as a control problem under incomplete information and attempts to reduce the information asymmetry. It gives incentives in the form of rewards and penalties in order to promote most efficient production.

The approach was first developed for the one-good firm by Baron and Myerson (1982); Laffont and Tirole (1993) examine the multi-good situation. Here, the regulator faces a choice between allocative efficiency, productive efficiency and distribution effects.

4.5 Benchmarking

In incentive-based regulation, efficiency of operations is a key element and almost invariably involves benchmarking or comparison of the actual with some reference performance. For example, the regulator can base a review under a RPI-X regime on industry-wide performance rather than company-specific performance.[23] This may involve explicit benchmarking between similar regulated companies.

Two techniques are commonly used when benchmarking companies: statistical (regression) analysis and data envelopment analysis (DEA).[24] [25] Statistical techniques attempt to establish a correlation between the inputs and the outputs of a

23 The term X-inefficiency, proposed by Leibenstein (1966) is not related to the term X in the RPI-X formula, the latter measuring productivity increases (Bös, 2001: 17).

24 In their survey of the use of benchmarking methods used by the electricity regulators in OECD and other countries, Jamasb and Pollitt (2001) find a notable preference for the non-parametric methods.

25 Electricity distribution companies in most cases can assess their relative efficiency on the basis of national cost comparisons. Transmission system operators, however, are frequently organised as legal national monopolies and, hence, need to look across national borders to obtain an indication of relative efficiency. One way of achieving this is to participate in international transmission system operator benchmark exercises together with regulators and transmission system operators from other countries.

company which then is used to determine the relative ranking of the companies in a sample group.[26]

DEA[27] is a linear programming-based technique to evaluate the efficiency of a number of producers that are referred to as a decision making unit (DMU). The relative performance of DMU is measured where the presence of multiple inputs and outputs makes direct comparisons difficult. A virtual producer is defined as a benchmark. Any company situated beyond this frontier is considered inefficient: If a given producer X is capable of producing a particular output with a certain input, other efficiently operating producers should also be able to do so. Similarly, if producer Y is capable of producing particular units of output with a certain input, again the other producers should be capable of doing the same. Producers X, Y and others are then combined to form the virtual producer with composite inputs and outputs. If that virtual producer is more efficient than the producer under study, because it can produce more with the same input or produce the same with less input, then the producer under study is inefficient.

Shuttleworth (1999) points out that despite its attractiveness in principle, benchmarking could be *"a long and winding path to a regulatory dead-end":* There is the risk that fundamental principles of economic regulation are violated, notably when operating cost and capital costs are benchmarked separately. Shuttleworth finds that the use of benchmarking is also inconsistent with conventional approaches for the estimation of the cost of capital (rate of return); efficient companies (on the frontier) will earn returns above the average. The principle that techniques for setting revenues should be as objective as possible is violated if estimates of cost and the manipulation of the frontier area remain entirely subjective. He concludes that benchmarking presents a number of methodological difficulties that, if not overcome, will rule out its use for regulation, because the results are intrinsically biased against cost recovery by regulated companies.

5 Electricity Market Reform and Regulatory Effectiveness

The value-chain of the electricity sector basically consists of four value-added activities: electricity generation, transmission (high, super-high voltage grids, i.e. 220-500 kV), distribution (low, medium, high voltage networks, i.e. 0.4-220 kV) and sales and wholesale and retail trading.

Only the activities of providing transmission grid and distribution network services are considered to be natural monopolies[28], barring competition in network

---

26 Jamasb, Nillesen, and Pollit (2003) study regulation benchmarking and show how strategic behaviour can result in inefficient behaviour by firms. They apply the DEA method on US utility data to examine implications of selected cases of strategic behaviour. Their results show that gaming can have significant effects on the measured performance and profitability of firms.

27 DEA has first been proposed by Charnes, Cooper, and Rhodes (1978).

28 Including the provision of regulating power and network congestion management.

services provision but also in upstream and downstream markets. Regulatory reform in the electricity market thus aims at removing barriers to competition in areas upstream of the grid, i.e. generation and imports, and downstream of the grids, i.e. sales and wholesale and retail trading.

The reform models observed worldwide differ by their specific blend of structural and conduct regulation. They feature various degrees of vertical integration (unbundling ranging from ownership and legal unbundling to formal accounting), different types of activities open to competition (i.e. generation, wholesale trading, retail trading), and different regimes of regulation transmission and distribution activities (Von Hirschhausen and Opitz, 2001: 3).

Kumka (1999: 14ff.) distincts the reform models as follows:

- Single Buyer: Under this regime, competition in generation and import takes place by way of negotiation between the single buyer and generators or importers. The single buyer acts thereby as a monopsonist upstream and a monopolist downstream.
- Electricity pool: Under this regime, an independent system operator is instituted, responsible for system operation and dispatching of the generating plants and imports. There is competition in generation and retail trading, while wholesale trading is organised through a compulsory pool and dispatching scheme. The system operator acts as a monopsonist upstream and a monopolist downstream.
- Third Party Access: Under this regime, the compulsory element in wholesale trading is removed and there is competition in generation, sales and wholesale and retail trading. The access to transportation and distribution grids is either regulated or negotiated. Vertical disintegration ranges from ownership, legal unbundling to formal accounting.
- Common Carrier: Under this regime, the value chain is fully unbundled and competition prevails at all levels. Transmission grids and distribution networks remain regulated monopolies.

It is difficult to pass judgement on the effectiveness and quality of an electricity market regulation. When can markets be considered efficient? In rare cases, like in the case of the sustained energy crisis in California, detrimental effects can directly be observed and attributed to features of the regulatory schemes. Though similar detrimental effects (sustained blackouts) had been observed in the Northern US and Canada, allegedly attributable to market reform, no objective link to market reform as the cause has been established yet. And the same holds true for the blackout in Italy.

The effects of regulation encompass a multitude of factors ranging from prices and profits to market structure and quality of service.[29] Given the overall regulation objective of maximising welfare, there is a temptation to reduce the analysis of regulatory impact to price surveys, accepting the price as the ultimate yardstick. Prices prior to regulation, or deregulation, of a particular market are compared with those after regulation, or deregulation. Lower prices are then attributed to increased efficiency of the sector and to a successful regulatory system. This is as

---

29 For a regulatory impact analysis, see OXERA (2001).

simple as misleading. A methodologically correct way of using price as a yardstick would be to measure prices observed after regulation against counter-factual prices, i.e. prices that would prevail had regulation, or deregulation, not occurred and the previous market framework persisted. Even in cases where counter-factual prices can been established, assessing the regulatory impact is not straight forward, as is illustrated by the following cases.

Bower (2002) analyses the electricity market reform of 1990 in the UK that was superseded by another reform in 1999 called New Electricity Trading Arrangements (NETA). He investigated the decline in prices after 1999. Had the fall in prices been caused by the regulator who was forcing the dominant duopoly of fossil fuel generators to divest coal-fired plants? Or have they occurred because the original Pool market mechanism was replaced with NETA? Backward regression analysis of functionally equivalent elements of day-ahead prices under the Pool and NETA indicates that changing the regulatory arrangements produced no statistically significant response (except for the removal of capacity payments). In contrast, coal plant divestment, increased imports of foreign coal, and overcapacity caused by the dash for gas, caused the majority of the price fall. Bower concludes, therefore, that direct system development costs, associated management costs, and increased operational risk of implementing NETA were unnecessary because industry restructuring, a result of the original reform, had already brought about a significant price reduction by March 2001.

Econometric analysis by Evans and Green (2003) on data from 1996 to 2002, however, implies support for two conflicting hypotheses. On a static view, increases in competition and the capacity reserve margin were chiefly responsible for the fall in prices. If, however, generators had been tacitly colluding before NETA, the impending change in market rules might have changed their behaviour a few months before the abolition of the Pool. That view implies that NETA resulted in reduced prices.

6 Conclusions

Expectations in respect to the potential results of energy market reforms and regulations were high and in some regards unrealistic. Recent energy market incidents are not likely linked to market reform. Regulatory impact and economic efficiency, though, are diffuse and hard to establish, and the benefits resulting from electricity market reform may not receive adequate recognition.

While economics places most of its effort on the complete explanation of the existence and incidence of regulation, comparatively little attention has been given to regulatory impact analysis. It would, therefore, be a useful addition to the regulatory process to consider the ex-ante design of a potential ex-post impact analysis.

References

Aktan, C.C. (2003), *(Im)Possibility of Rational Regulation*, Paper, 2nd International Conference of Japan Economic Policy Association.

Averch, H. and Johnson, L. (1962), The Behaviour of the Firm Under Regulatory Constraint, *American Economic Review.*

Baron, D. and R.B. Meyerson (1982), Regulating a Monopolist with Uncertain Costs, *Econometrica* 50, 911-930.

Baumol, W.J. (1995), Modified Regulation of Telecommunications and the Public-Interest Standard, in: Bishop, M., J. Kaye, and C. Mayer (Eds.), *The Regulatory Challenge*, Oxford.

Becker, G.S. (1983), A Theory of Competition Among Pressure Groups for Political Influence. *Quarterly Journal of Economics* 98, 371-400.

Berg, S.V. and J. Tschirhart (1989), *Natural Monopoly Regulation. Principles and Practice*, Cambridge.

Bös, D. (2001), *Regulation: Theory and Concepts*, Department of Economics, University of Bonn, Bonn Econ discussion papers.

Bower, J. (2002), *Why Did Electricity Prices Fall in England and Wales? Market Mechanism or Market Structure?* Economics Working Paper 0401008.

Burns, P. and C. Riechmann (2004), *Regulatory Instruments and Their Effects on Investment Behavior*, World Bank Policy Paper 3292.

Burns, P. and A. Estache (2000), *Information, Accounting and the Regulation of Concessioned Infrastructure Monopolies*, World Bank Workpapers 2000 series, wps 2034.

Charnes, A., W.W. Cooper, and E. Rhodes (1978), Measuring the Efficiency of Decision-Making Units, *European Journal of Operations Research* 2, 429-444.

den Hertog, J.A. (2003), *Public and Private Interests in Regulation: Essays in the Law and Economics of Regulation*, Proefschrift Universiteit Utrecht.

European Commission (2003), *Second Benchmarking Report on the Implementation of the Internal Electricity and Gas Market*, Staff Working Paper SEC(2003)448.

Evans, J. and R.J. Green (2003), *Why Did British Electricity Prices Fall After 1998?* University of Hull, Royal Economic Society, Annual Conference 2003 series no. 92.

Jamasb, T., P. Nillesen, and M. Pollit (2003), *Strategic Behaviour Under Regulation Benchmarking*, Department of Applied Economics, University of Cambridge, Cambridge Working Papers in Economics 0312.

Jamasb, T. and M. Pollitt (2001), *Benchmarking and Regulation of Electricity Transmission and Distribution Utilities: Lessons from International Experience*, Cambridge Working Papers in Economics, University of Cambridge.

Joskow , P. and R. Noll (1981), Regulation in Theory and Practice: An Overview, in: Fromm, G. (Ed.), *Studies in Public Regulation*, Cambridge MA.

Kahn, A.A. (1988), *The Economics of Regulation: Principles and Institutions*, Cambridge MA.

Kay, J.A. and J.S. Vickers (1985), Regulatory Reform: An Appraisal, in: *Deregulation or Re-Regulation*, London, 223-251.

Kinnunen, K. (2003), *Network Pricing in the Nordic Countries – an Empirical Analysis of the Local Electricity Distribution Utilities' Efficiency and Pricing*, doctoral dissertation, Department of Economics and Law, Oldenburg University.

Knieps, G. (2000), *Marktkonforme Infrastrukturbenutzungsgebühren: Zur Notwendigkeit eines mehrstufigen Tarifkonzepts*, Discussion Paper 70, Institut für Verkehrswissenschaft und Regionalpolitik, Freiburg University.

Kumkar, L. (1999), *Alternative Liberalisierungsmodelle für die Stromwirtschaft: Eine komparative Institutionenanalyse*, Kieler Arbeitspapier 92, Institut für Weltwirtschaft, Kiel.

Laffont, J.J. and J. Tirole (1993), *A Theory of Incentives in Procurement and Regulation*, Cambridge MA.

Leibenstein, H. (1966), Allocative Efficiency and X-Efficiency, *The American Economic Review* 56, 392-415.

Loeb, M. and W.A. Magat (1979), A Decentralized Method for Utility Regulation, *Journal of Law and Economics* 22, 399-404.

NER (National Electricity Regulator) (2003), *Economic Regulation of Transmission Using Incentive Based Regulation*, Consultation document, South Africa.

Newberry, D. (1997), *Rate-Of-Return Regulation Versus Price Regulation for Public Utilities*, Cambridge, UK.

Ogus, A. (2002), *W(h)ither the Economic Theory of Regulation? What Economic Theory of Regulation?, The Politics of Regulation*, Barcelona Workshop, Universitat Pompeu Fabra.

OXERA (Oxford Economic Research Associates) (2001), *Energy Liberalisation Indicators in Europe*, Final Report, Part 2.

Palda, F. (2002), *Interest Groups: A Survey of Public Choice Thinking*, École nationale d'administration publique, Montréal.

Peltzman, S. (1976), Towards a More General Theory of Regulation, *Journal of Law and Economics* 19, 211-240.

Posner, R.A. (1974), *Theories of Economic Regulation*, National Bureau of Economic Research Working Papers 0041.

Sappington, D.E.M. and D.S. Sibley (1988), Regulating Without Cost Information: The Incremental Surplus Subsidy Scheme, *International Economic Revue* 9/2, 297-306.

Shleifer, A. (1985), A Theory of Yardstick Competition, *RAND Journal of Economics*. 16/3, 319-327.

Shuttleworth, G. (1999), "Regulatory Benchmarking": A Way Forward or a Dead End?, *Energy Regulation Brief* 3, National Economic Research Associates, London.

Sibley, D. (1989), Asymmetric Information, Incentives, and Price-Cap Regulation, *RAND Journal of Economics* 20/3, 92-404.

Starkey, M. and J. van Pelt (1995), Productivity Measurement and Price Cap Regulation: Issues for Local Exchange Carriers in the USA, *Telecommunications Policy* 19/2, 151-160.

Stigler, G.J. (1971), The Theory of Economic Regulation., *Bell Journal of Economics and Management Science* 2, 137-146.

Tollison, R.D. (1998), The Interest-Group Theory of Government, University of Mississippi, *The Locke Luminary* 1/1, Part 4.

Train, K. (1991), *Optimal Regulation: The Economic Theory of Natural Monopoly*, Cambridge MA.

Vogelsang, I. (1999), *Price Regulation for Independent Transmission Companies*, Boston University Paper.

Vogelsang, I. and J. Finsinger (1979), A Regulatory Adjustment Process for Optimal Pricing by Multi-Product Firms, *Bell Journal of Economics* 10.

von Hirschhausen, C. and P. Optiz (2001), *Power Utility Re-Regulation in East European and CIS Transformation Countries (1990-1999): An Institutional Interpretation*, Deutsches Institut für Wirtschaftsforschung, Discussion Paper.

Energy Markets – Research Issues and Policy Needs

Christoph Weber, Alfred Voß

University of Stuttgart, Institut für Energiewirtschaft und Rationelle Energieanwendung, Pfaffenwaldring 31, 70569 Stuttgart, Germany, christoph.weber@ier.uni-stuttgart.de, av@ier.uni-stuttgart.de

Keywords. *Energy Markets, Energy Policy, Electricity, Stochastic Analysis, Robustness*

JEL. *Q40; Q41; Q48*

Abstract. The paper identifies three key challenges for current energy policies: Internalisation of externalities, efficient operation of markets and investment adequacy in liberalised markets. The corresponding research issues are then discussed, focusing on the simultaneous achievement of efficient market operation and investment adequacy in electricity markets. The paper points at the need for applied stochastic models in this field and provides some directions for the construction of such models. Furthermore it raises the question whether there is an underlying challenge: a trade-off between robustness and efficiency in the design of markets. Robustness as a control-theoretic concept is briefly sketched and its potential relevance is illustrated using several examples from environmental economics and beyond.

1 Introduction

"veritas adequatio rei et intellectu"

Applied research is at the crossroads of academics and real world and more than other disciplines it has therefore to face the quote attributed to Aristotle and cited in entry. It ascertains, if translated in an informal way, that truth is the matching of things and thinking. Or, expressed in a more dynamic, process-oriented perspective: (Applied) scientific knowledge is arising when the constructions of our minds – our models – and the real world are put into correspondence.

Energy market regulation and deregulation has always been inspired by contemporary economic thinking and has inspired in turn economic thinking – from the traditional "natural monopoly" idea to the concept of "contestable markets". But still we feel that economic thinking and economic models of energy markets have to evolve further to cope with the contemporaneous challenges of sustainability and globalisation.

2 Key Policy Challenges and Corresponding Research Needs

For some decades, energy policy in European countries has been marked by the triple objective of environmental protection, cost effectiveness and security of supply. And still today major policy challenges lie ahead in those three fields. They may be summarised through the following three key issues, related to the aforementioned traditional objectives:

1. Internalisation of externalities – environmental protection
2. Making markets work efficiently – cost effectiveness
3. Ensuring sufficient investments in liberalised markets – security of supply.

This policy needs also give rise to several research issues, which shall be briefly discussed in the following paragraphs. The next major paragraph is then devoted more specifically to the issue of reaching simultaneously efficient markets and sufficient investments in electricity markets.

2.1 Internalisation of Externalities

The quantification of externalities associated with energy and transport systems has been a topic now for more than a decade in the European Union and beyond (cf. e.g. Friedrich and Krewitt 1997). Recent advances notably include improved assessments of the externalities associated with noise and particle emissions and improved meteorological models. Nevertheless major scientific challenges await clarification:

- Huge uncertainties and methodological challenges still exist as far as the damage costs associated with climate change are concerned. Using mitigation costs instead of damage costs helps internalising the trade-off between various emission reduction policies. Yet it is clearly unsatisfactory for the more fundamental trade-off between climate change mitigation and adaptation, which has to be carried out when fixing European or rather world-wide emission reduction or stabilisation targets.
- Integrated assessment has been proposed as a unifying approach for dealing with environmental trade-offs in energy policy and beyond. But models and data need further improvement in order to provide reliable results.
- The implementation of external costs in concrete policies is still facing considerable reluctance and scientific research analysing the reasons for this reluctance may help overcome those barriers.
- The European Union is now about to implement an emission trading system for CO_2 and is thus relying on market-based instruments for climate change mitigation. However, applied research is lacking, which provides theoretically well-founded recommendations for the practical implementation of the trading system, e.g. on the primary allocation of certificates, on transfers of emission rights from old to new plants or on the advantages/inconveniencies of upstream, downstream or middlestream (as in the current EU-system) attribution of emission certificates.

– Besides the first-best instruments, being taxes and certificates, often also other policy instruments such as standards, subsidies or feed-in tariffs are applied in order to achieve energy efficiency and climate policy goals. Varying rationales are provided for justifying such policies, like information gaps among consumers or measurements/transaction costs for implementing first-best solutions. Also uncertainty, risk aversion and (partial) irreversibility of decisions could justify the use of second-best instruments. Some analyses have been done in that field (e.g. Gustafsson, 1998, Weber and Dicke, 2001) yet there is a need for more well-founded theoretical and empirical economic analyses, which could confirm or refute the validity of such arguments in the light of modern microeconomics and behavioural economics.

2.2 Making Markets Work Efficiently

Deregulation of electricity and gas markets has been a major political issue in Europe and worldwide during the 1990s. But still market opening is incomplete in many EU countries and at the same time the claims for more liberalisation have become less pressing all over the world and most notably in the U.S. after the California power crisis and the Enron debacle. The work and publications done in economics on the regulation of energy markets are impressive by their volume. Nevertheless in order to arrive at functioning and efficient energy markets, further research and applied models are needed, which should especially address the following issues:

– Interplay between physical system and (financial) markets
– Regional market power and workable competition
– Costs vs. benefits of unbundling.

In the first phase of the deregulated electricity business, many thought that electricity market mechanisms could simply be investigated and understood by transposing methods and concepts from finance mathematics and financial markets. For example, early publications on real options like Hsu et al. (1998) are mostly using the Margrabe (1978) model of cross-commodity options for valuing power plants. But more recent publications like Tseng and Barz (2002) take into account much more technical detail such as start-up costs, part-load efficiency or minimum operation times, when modelling power plants as real options. Similarly also for the description of markets and market dynamics, the technical characteristics of electricity – its non-storability and grid-dependency – have to be taken into account properly. For the Nordic, hydro-dominated electricity system this is less crucial than for the rest of Europe, since hydro-storage makes electricity markets behave almost like markets for storable commodities or equities. E.g. Lucia and Schwartz (2002) have developed a model for determining empirically the implicit market price of risk in electricity markets based on finance methods. They applied it to the Nordic power market and obtained reasonable results, with a market dominated by the risk aversion of buyers and consequently a negative market price for the risk associated with forward contracts. Conversely, Benatzky (2003) did not obtain consistent results when applying the same model to the German electricity market. This is, because in the German market there exists at best a convergence in probability between forward and spot market prices, whereas hydro storage in the Nordic market implies strong convergence since otherwise arbitrage possibilities would arise for hydro operators.

Also the issue of regional market power is intimately linked to the grid dependency of electricity and gas. Traditionally, the Hirschman-Herfindahl index is used frequently to measure market power in oligopolistic markets. But for grid-constrained markets it is unclear, whether it should be applied to single national markets or to the European market as a whole (cf. e.g. Ellersdorfer et al., 2003). And even if the issue of measuring market power correctly has been resolved, one has to ask, whether this market power is problematic or whether – perfect competition being out of reach due to economies of scale (notably in risk management) – the observed degree of competition corresponds to a workable competition or whether it rather constitutes an abuse of market power.

Fig. 1. Structure of a fully unbundled electricity industry.

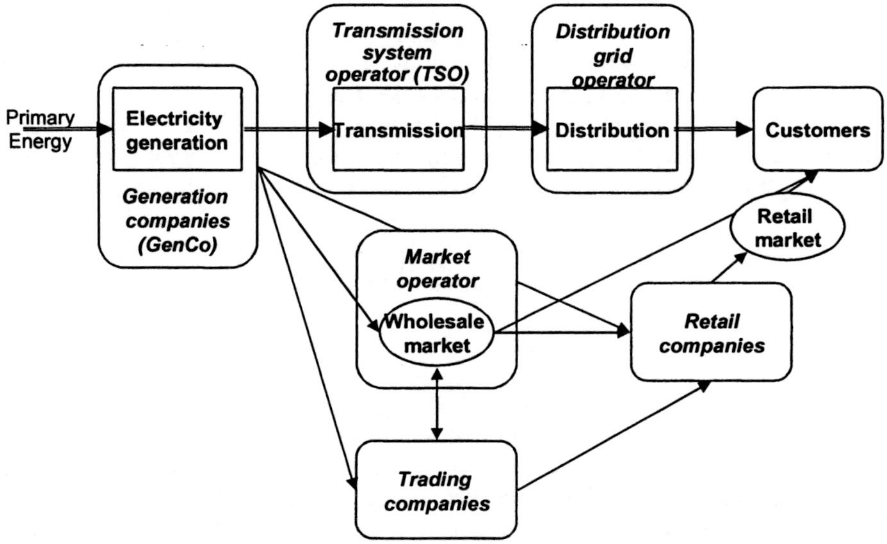

A fully unbundled electricity industry is depicted in **Fig. 1** (cf. Weber, 2004). Yet practice in most European countries to date is lacking far behind this theoretic model. And even one may wonder, whether such a full unbundling is really the welfare optimal solution. Especially the retail business (sometimes also called supply business) may generate in itself a rather limited value-added, whereas its separation from both distribution and generation implies considerable costs for data transfers, operation management and risk management. In this context, further applied economic research is needed to determine which market constellations are the most promising for obtaining market efficiency in the long term.

In the current political and market context, these general issues of market efficiency should be particularly investigated for the following three markets:

1. *Gas markets.* Here one key issue is finding workable trading arrangements in the presence of different gas qualities. Furthermore the value-added of the retail and trading business in itself being presumably also rather limited, the economic efficiency of various bundling alternatives should be analysed carefully.
2. *Regulating power markets.* Despite Europe-wide transmission grids, regulating power, which is key for system stability and security of supply, is traded at national or even sub-national level. The markets are fragmented and characterised by demand monopsons (cf. e.g. Swider and Weber, 2003). When generating capacities are scarce[1], regulating power and consequently security of supply will only be provided, if a substantial option premium is paid in advance. Here the impact of market structures and arrangements on market equilibria and prices has to be analysed carefully.
3. *Combination of renewables promotion and competitive electricity markets.* The integration of larger amounts of fluctuating renewables in the electricity system increases the volatility of the demand for conventional power and thus might decrease system stability. Moreover, the fluctuating patterns e.g. of wind energy are considerably different from the fluctuations in demand and thus pose new challenges for power plant operation, which have also implications for market prices and optimal market structure (e.g. two-hours-ahead spot market instead of day-ahead market). Furthermore, depending on the market arrangements for renewables production, considerable price effects may be expected on the conventional market. Here currently several research projects are under way, which analyse the integration costs, taking into account the stochastics of wind and other renewables (cf. RISOE, 2004, EEG, 2004), but further research is needed, focusing particularly on the market and long-term perspectives for the integration of renewables.

2.3 Ensuring Sufficient Investments in Liberalised Markets – Security of Supply

Security of supply certainly is a political subject with multiple facets, which do not all fall in the realm of applied economic research (e.g. protection against terrorist attacks). Yet it has also at least three aspects, which are challenges for applied economic research:

- Risk management in the longer run
- Oil and gas markets – production peak
- Capacity adequacy in electricity markets.

The third point will be taken up in some more detail in the following paragraph, but a few remarks on the first two are given beforehand.

---

[1] This occurs especially in thermally dominated markets – in hydro dominated markets like the Scandinavian ones usually energy is scarce, whereas capacity, defined as the maximum possible power output at one moment in time, is mostly not the limiting factor.

Risk management in companies (inside and outside the energy markets) has so far mostly focused on the short-term perspective – using notably measures like value-at-risk to evaluate the loss probabilities in the coming 1 to 10 days (cf. e.g. Pilipovic, 1998). For the electricity markets, the profit-at-risk methodology has been developed as a complement (cf. Henney and Keers, 1998), but it has remained so far rather unconnected to the general risk management literature. Weber (2004) describes an approach for combining the concepts of value-at-risk and profit-at-risk, considering also explicitly the incompleteness of markets. Incompleteness of markets is in contrast to the famous Arrow-Debreu framework, but is an empirical fact in almost all financial and commodity markets. It constitutes, however, a particular challenge in the case of electricity, given its non-storability. In this field further research is needed in order to get an improved understanding of market functioning and dangers of market failure, especially with respect to investment adequacy (cf. below).

Also in oil and gas markets, longer-term risks require increased attention. In recent years, the possibility of production peaking in the coming years has been put forward especially by geologists. Economists usually point in this debate at the substitution and technology improvement effects which will be induced by rising prices. Yet a tighter supply-demand balance is likely to induce more volatile prices, which in turn may substantially affect the world economy. Furthermore time lags in exploration and production development activities may induce medium-term shortages even if in the longer run production constraints are not binding. Applied economic research is needed in this situation, which looks carefully at the dynamics of world oil and gas prices resulting from the complex interplay of exploration activities, investment in new production facilities, production activities, forward market prices and politics. Thereby it seems crucial to abandon the a-priori assumption of general equilibrium and stability of the equilibrium and rather investigate the dynamics using recursive, stochastic models with various anticipation assumptions (from myopic expectations to perfect foresight, including also various forms of adaptive expectations). Also in this line of research, investigations on a possible trade-off between robustness and efficiency of markets (cf. below, Section 5) might be helpful.

3 One Key Challenge: Efficiency of Electricity Markets in the Longer Run

Electricity markets pose specific or/and more acute challenges to regulation than other energy markets given the fundamental physical characteristics of electricity: non-storability and grid-dependency. Moreover, electricity is considered almost as a primary need – at least in developed countries – and short-term price elasticity is traditionally very low, except perhaps for some large industrial users. In this context, ensuring the efficiency of electricity markets in the longer run, which means especially ensuring adequacy of generation capacities, is a serious challenge, as shall be demonstrated in the following paragraphs.

3.1 Problem Description

For maintaining security of supply in the medium and longer term, sufficient investments in new power plants are a necessary precondition. On the other hand, over-investment in generation capacities, as occurred in the former regulated electricity system, would reduce considerably the efficiency of the markets and reap the benefits of liberalisation for the customers. For the utilities, investments in new power plants are strategic and risky decisions, since they imply considerable sunk cost, which usually cannot be recovered for years. These investments, contrarily to the investments in transmission and distribution grids, have to be refinanced through revenues in competitive markets. The key issue in this context[2] is the question which has been labeled the *investment paradox:* How can long-term investments be refinanced in an energy market, where prices are almost all the time based on short-term marginal costs? (cf. Weber 2003)

The investment paradox may be summarised in six key theses. These are outlined in the following and justified briefly:

1. As long as sufficient generation capacity is available, electricity prices on an efficient (wholesale) market will not (or only little) be above variable generation costs.
2. When capacities become scarce, prices rapidly rise to extreme peaks.
3. First, capacity shortages only arise a few hours per year.
4. From one year to the following, the probability of capacity shortages increases dramatically
5. The revenues from capacity shortages, which could be taken to refinance investments, are extremely difficult to predict.
6. The first investor does not get any first-mover advantage.

Theses 1 and 2 are illustrated through **Fig. 2**. Prices at the German spot market have risen up to 100 €/MWh and more in a few hours of 2001 and 2003 but have been around 25 € on average. In principle, investments in power plants should be refinanced from the extra cash flow in the extreme hours, which is considerably above short-term marginal costs. This is also the theoretical solution proposed by conventional economic models of peak-load pricing (e.g. Boiteux, 1960, Chao, 1983, Oren, 2000). But the elements summarised in theses 3 to 6 make it unlikely that sufficient investment will take place if the market is organised – as in most European countries today – as energy-only market[3].

---

2 Another partly related issue is the appropriateness and the reliability of the political context for such investments.

3 Neuhoff and de Vries (2003) provide a micro-economic model of energy-only markets, where under-investment arises as a consequence of risk aversion and weather uncertainty.

Fig. 2. Price duration curve of German LPX spot market prices in 2001 and marginal generation costs of various technologies.

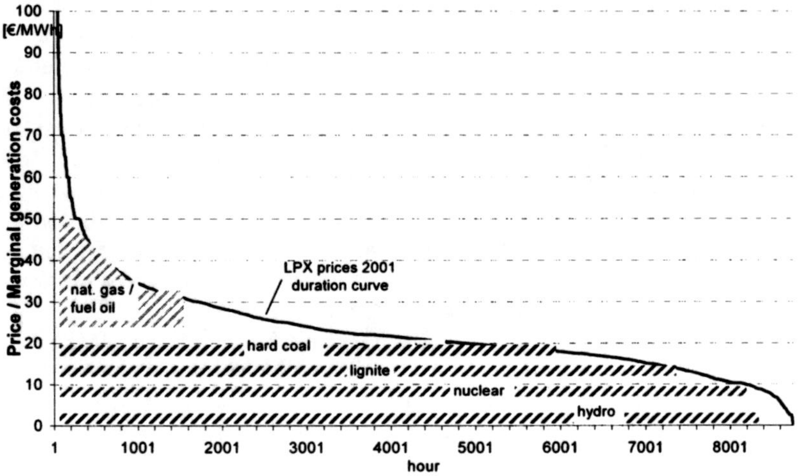

Fig. 3. Probability of capacity scarcity as a function of reserve margin and load uncertainty.

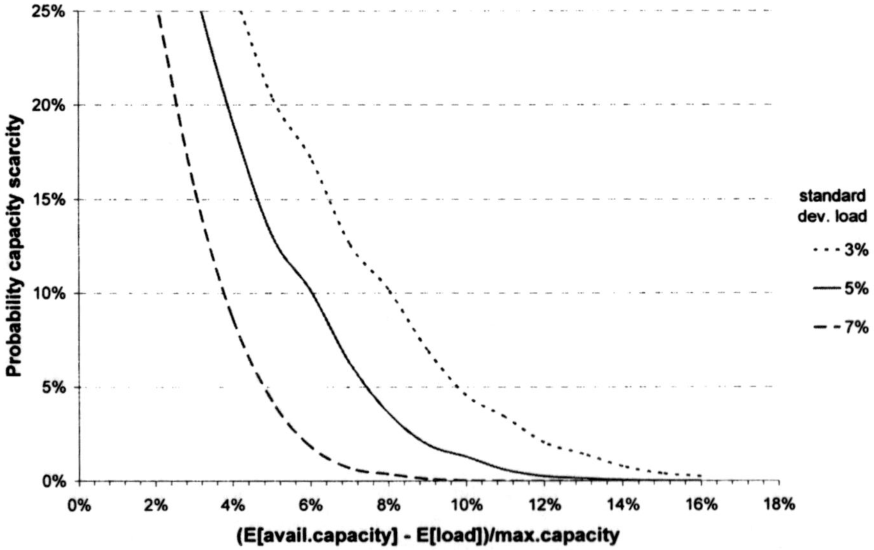

The time lag between an investment decision for a new power plant and its commitment is in Europe about two years for gas fired combined-cycle plants and up to five years for coal fired plants. It is extremely difficult to predict the revenues, which can be achieved as a consequence of capacity scarcities, even just for the first year after the commitment of the plant. If the predictions for the growth in demand or the reduction in installed capacities are false just by one percentage point, the revenues from capacity shortages will increase or decrease by a factor of 1.4 or more (cf. **Fig. 3**[4]). This holds, if the amount of the extra revenues is independent of the frequency of capacity shortages. In the (more likely) case of a positive correlation, the uncertainty on revenues is even higher.

So if the utilities or other potential investors have just slight misperceptions of the future development of the supply-demand balance, they may either over- or underinvest. And in the latter case, real capacity shortages may be observed.

3.2 Solutions Proposed

Facing this problem, two basic alternatives exist: Either one may rely on the existing energy-only markets and the utilities active therein or one may introduce new market elements, which of course should lead to a light-handed, as market-conform as possible regulation. In the first case, the following elements for ensuring long-term market efficiency may be envisaged:

- Increases in the market size and/or the market liquidity, e.g. through new transmission lines
- Increased use of Demand-Side-Management measures such as switchable loads
- Increases/decreases in the number of market participants
- Improved quantification of market uncertainties
- Further development of the mark-to-market valuation
- Creation/maintaining of a market structure with vertically integrated companies.

First elements for an assessment of these alternative proposals may be found in Weber (2003), yet further research is needed to investigate the prospects and limitations of the different approaches.

According to de Vries and Hakvoort (2003) major alternatives to a light-handed, market-conform reregulation of electricity markets are:

- Imposition of capacity requirements
- (Re-)Introduction of capacity payments[5]
- Use of capacity subscriptions
- Definition of mandatory reliability contracts
- Use of mothball reserve.

Again some elements for a comparative analysis have already been compiled (cf. de Vries and Hakvoort, 2003), but further research is needed, especially on the pros and cons of such reregulations vs. energy-only markets.

---

[4] The derivation of this figure is described in some detail in Weber (2003).

[5] Such capacity payments were in place in the former England and Wales pool system and are currently still practised in Spain.

4 One Key Research Need: Applied Stochastic Market Models

Given the non-storability of electricity, it should be clearly stated with any model used for the assessment of electricity market regulations, how it is dealing with stochastic fluctuations both in the demand-supply balance and in prices. This does not necessarily mean that all models have to be explicitly stochastic, one may also provide arguments why the use of expected values instead of full stochastic distributions is sufficient. Yet when deriving appropriate regulations for liberalised markets with increasing fluctuating supply stochastic models will certainly play a more and more important role (e.g. Weber, 2002, Barlow, 2002).

However the field of stochastic analysis is large and multiple alternative specifications could be employed. Here the following points seem worth retaining for directing the analysis and the model formulation:

1. *Non-normal distributions are important.* Empirical analyses of electricity market prices show that price changes are throughout non-normally distributed (cf. Cuaresma et al., 2004, Weber and Hoeck, 2003). Also GARCH-model specifications are usually not satisfactory, whereas switching-regime models provide an interesting alternative (cf. e.g. Elliott et al., 2000, Huisman and Mahieu, 2001, Weber, 2004). Wind power generation is another example of a non-normally distributed time-series. Here non-normality is a consequence of the non-linear power generation curve of wind turbines.
2. *Capacity constraints have to be considered.* They constitute a major cause of non-normal distributions of electricity prices, since price spikes are usually occurring when capacities get scarce. Furthermore, capacity adequacy is a key concern for energy market regulation in a longer-term perspective as discussed in Section 4.
3. *Multivariate distributions have to be modelled carefully.* E.g. the capacity credit attributable to wind energy converters strongly depends on the distribution of wind speeds (or rather generated wind power) in different sites (e.g. Lux et al., 1999, Norgard and Hottinen, 2004). For modelling the multivariate distributions of non-normal stochastic variables, the concept of copula (e.g. Nelsen, 1999, Embrechts et al., 2000) can be helpful.
4. *Long-term behaviour of stochastic processes is of key importance.* This is illustrated in **Fig. 4** through a comparison of the long-term behaviour of basic stochastic models often used in financial and energy market analysis. For the Wiener process (which is an integrated and thus non-stationary process in econometric terms), uncertainty steadily increases with the time horizon considered, whereas for the stationary mean-reversion process, uncertainty remains bounded. In practice, a combination of stationary and non-stationary processes is most promising when longer-term price developments have to be modelled (e.g. Karesen and Husby, 2002).

Fig. 4. Price uncertainty (measured as standard deviation of simulations) as a function of forecasting horizon in Wiener processes (Geometric Brownian motion) and mean reversion processes.

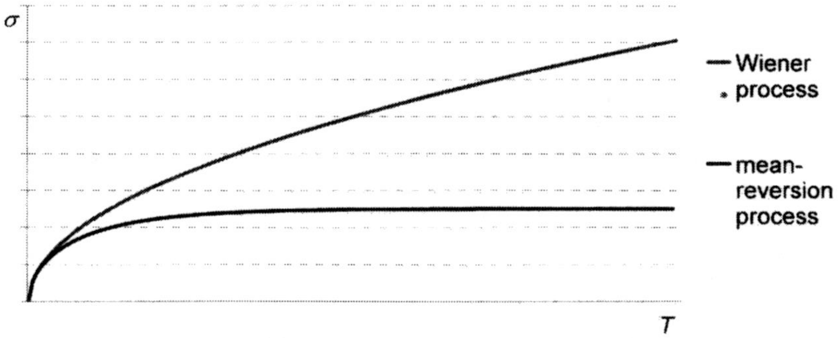

The usage of stochastic models will not guarantee in itself an adequate analysis. Rather, given the broad variety of possible models, it is even more important to bear Aristotle's saying in mind. A further key issue for successful applied models and for successful regulations is certainly the simultaneous consideration of physical and economic aspects. For example, the most successful scheme for electricity market operation in the U.S. is the Pennsylvania-New Jersey-Maryland (PJM) pool. And in this sophisticated scheme of "locational pricing", the prices at the different nodes in the electricity grid are determined using an economic model incorporating detailed electrical load-flow calculations.

The use of stochastic models should however not remain limited to the electricity markets. Also for oil and gas markets, stochastic models can provide useful insights into the dynamics of the market and the risks at hand. Therefore, Rehrl et al. (2004) propose to develop an explicitly stochastic model of the world oil and gas markets.

5 One Underlying Theoretical Challenge: Robustness vs. Efficiency?

In the previous paragraph, we have emphasised the necessity of employing stochastic models for analysing energy markets and related regulations. In this section, a related but more fundamental issue is raised: Is the objective of efficiency, which has guided most of the market reforms in the energy sector and beyond, sufficient? Or has it to be complemented by the objective of robustness?

Mathematical and engineering control theory has developed the concept of robust control in the last decades (e.g. Zhou and Doyle, 1998) and it has been shown that there is always a trade-off between the efficiency of a control system and its robustness (cf. e.g. Safonov, 1981, Doyle et al., 1988). The efficiency of the system describes its reactions to disturbance signals. The lower the integral loss function over the so-called transfer or sensitivity function, the less a system is affected by disturbances such as demand fluctuations, and the more efficient is the control. The economic equivalent clearly is the maximisation of welfare, which results in an efficient economic system.

Robustness by contrast is defined as stability of the control system in the presence of model uncertainty (deviations in the model parameters). So if the analogy holds, ascertaining that markets provide efficient, i.e. welfare-optimal solutions, implies that markets must have limitations with respect to robustness. *If* for example the true cost curve for electricity generation differs somewhat from the one assumed by the market, *then* an otherwise efficient market will produce instable results. This is true, even if the market (the control system) is welfare-optimal for coping with deviations in demand.

Deviations in demand are in this example stochastic disturbance signals, whereas deviations in the cost curve are deviations in the model parameters. And the essence of robust control is that there is a trade-off between the efficient treatment of external disturbances and the robustness with respect to uncertain (or false) model assumptions.

A full formal treatment of markets in a control-theoretic framework is beyond the scope of this paper. Yet a few examples may illustrate that the concept of robustness is also present in environmental and other economics – albeit so far hardly conceptualised as such[6].

As a first example taken from environmental economics, the issue of biodiversity is worth mentioning. In fact the value of biodiversity is at first sight in a conventional economic framework rather limited: species, which are not exploited so far in the economic system, are not part of the (presumably) efficient solution obtained by market economies. But the value of these species is that they provide robustness – insurance against uncertainties (or defections) in the production models employed currently by biotechnology firms, pharmaceutical labs and agriculture[7].

Also risk management, discussed earlier in the framework of energy markets, can be viewed as a strategy for coping with model uncertainties and increasing the robustness of an economic (sub-)system. The traders in a company are in permanent quest for efficient deals – providing the company with the maximum (expected) profit at the current information. Risk management, as a separate and independent function in the company, prevents the company from going bankrupt, if the (implicit or explicit) models of the market used by the traders happen to be wrong.

---

6 A few papers, notably by Hansen and Sargent (1995, 2003) and their co-workers (e.g. Andersen et al., 1998, Cagetti et al., 2002), but also by Onatski and Williams (2003) have already applied the control-theoretic concept of robustness in economics – notably in the context of risk aversion and in monetary economics.

7 Some concepts put forward in ecological economics such as resilience may indeed be rather close to the concept of robustness advocated here. However those have, at least to the knowledge of the authors, so far hardly been formalised in a welfare-optimisation framework.

As a final, more anecdotical example, the majors in Hollywood may be cited. For years they have been putting more and more money in the large blockbusters like Titanic or Lord of the Rings. This apparently is an efficient strategy if the films succeed with the public – as has been the case with the two aforementioned ones. But despite all efforts, the majors are still facing considerable model uncertainty with respect to consumer behaviour. And besides blockbusters, Hollywood is also producing a huge number of large budget productions, which yield almost as large negative commercial records. Therefore, currently Hollywood is (once again) turning towards small and independent producers and directors, increasing the robustness of its business by diversifying its production and giving the public also a broader variety of screenplays – even if they are on average not as profitable.

These examples of course do not prove in any rigorous way the necessity for including robustness as key objective in energy (and environmental) regulation. Yet we feel that both the issue of investment adequacy in electricity markets and the dynamics of world oil and gas markets could probably be better understood, if robustness of markets were addressed more explicitly. Also for the issues of sustainability in general, thinking in terms of trade-offs between efficiency and robustness might offer new perspectives. A considerable amount of theoretical and applied research will however be needed to identify the possibilities and the limitations of this novel line of thinking.

References

Andersen, E.W., L.P. Hansen, and T.J. Sargent (2003), A Quartet of Semigroups for Model Specification, Robustness, Prices of Risk and Model Deduction, *Journal of the European Economic Association* 1.

Barlow, M.T. (2002), A Diffusion Model of Electricity Prices, *Mathematical Finance* 12, 287-298.

Benatzky, J. (2003), *Stromfutures an der EEX: Ausgewählte Bewertungsmodelle und empirische Evidenz*, Diplomarbeit an der Universität Mainz, Lehrstuhl für Finanzwirtschaft.

Boiteux, M. (1960), Peak-Load Pricing, *Journal of Business* 33 (2), 157-179.

Cagetti, M., L.P. Hansen, and T.J. Sargent (2002), Robustness and Pricing with Uncertain Growth, *Review of Financial Studies* 15, 363-404.

Chao, H.P. (1983), Peak Load Pricing and Capacity Planning with Demand and Supply Uncertainty, *Bell Journal of Economics* 14, 179-190.

Cuaresma, J.C., J. Hlouskova, S. Kossmeier, and M. Obersteiner (2004), Forecasting Electricity Spot Prices Using Linear Univariate Time Series Models, *Applied Energy* 76.

de Vries, L. and R. Hakvoort (2003), *The Question of Generation Adequacy in Liberalized Electricity Markets*, Proceedings of the 26th Annual IAEE Conference, June 4-6, 2003. Prague.

de Vries, L. and C. Neuhoff (2003), *Insufficient Investment in Generating Capacity in Energy-Only Markets*, Working paper, University of Cambridge

Doyle, J., K. Glover, P. Khargonekar, and B. Francis (1988), State-Space Solutions to Standard H_2 and H_∞ Control Problems, in: IEEE (Ed.), *Preprints of 1988 American Control Conference*, 1691-1696.

EEG (2004), *The GreenNet Project*, cf. www.greennet.at.

Ellersdorfer, I., M. Blesl, T. Traber, U. Fahl, and A. Kessler (2003), Marktposition deutscher EVU im liberalisierten europäischen Elektrizitätsmarkt. – Analysen mit einem spieltheoretischen Modellansatz, *Energiewirtschaftliche Tagesfragen* 53.

Elliott, R.J., G.A. Sick, and M. Stein (2000), *Pricing Electricity Calls*, Working paper, University of Alberta, Calgliary, www.ucalgary.ca/~sick/Research/ElliottSickStein Electric5.pdf, accessed August 4, 2003.

Embrechts, P., F. Lindskog, and A. McNeil (2003), Modelling Dependence with Copulas and Applications to Risk Management, Rachev, S. (ed.): *Handbook of Heavy Tailed Distributions in Finance*, Amsterdam, 329-384.

Friedrich, R. and W. Krewitt (1997), *Umwelt- und Gesundheitsschäden durch die Stromerzeugung. Externe Kosten von Stromerzeugungssystemen*, Heidelberg.

Gustafsson, B. (1998), Scope and Limits of Market Mechanisms in Environmental Management, *Ecological Economics* 24, 259-274.

Hansen, L.P. and T.J. Sargent (2003), Robust Control of Forward Looking Models, *Journal of Monetary Economics* 3.

Hansen, L.P. and T.J. Sargent (1995), Robust Control and Model Uncertainty, *The American Economic Review: Papers and Proceedings.*

Huisman, R. and R. Mahieu (2001), *Regime Jumps in Electricity Prices*, Working paper, Energy Global, Rotterdam School of Management at Erasmus University Rotterdam. Rotterdam, also: http://papers.ssrn.com/paper.taf?abstract_id=271910 accessed August 4, 2003.

Hsu, M. (1998), Spark Spread Options Are Hot!, *Electricity Journal* 11, 28-39.

Karesen, K.F. and E. Husby (2002), A Joint State-Space Model for Electricity Spot and Futures Prices, NR *Norgsk Regnesentral report* 965, revised version May 13, 2002, also: http://www.nr.no/documents/samba/research_areas/BFF/JointElMod.pdf, accessed August 4, 2003.

Henney, A. and G. Keers (1998), Managing Total Corporate Electricity/Energy Market Risks, *The Electricity Journal* 11 (8), 36-46.

Lucia, J.J. and E.S. Schwartz (2002), Electricity Prices and Power Derivatives: Evidence from the Nordic Power Market, *Review of Derivative Research* 5, 5-50.

Margrabe, W. (1978), The Value of an Option to Exchange One Asset for Another, *Journal of Finance* 33, 177-186.

Nelsen, R.B. (1999), *An Introduction to Copulas*, New York.

Onatski, A. and N. Williams (2003), Modelling Model Uncertainty, *Journal of the European Economic Association* 1, 1087-1022.

Oren, S.S. (2000), *Capacity Payments and Supply Adequacy in Competitive Electricity Markets*, Presentation at VII SEPOPE, 7th Symposium of specialists in electric operational and expansion planning, 21 – 26 May 2000, Curitiba (PR) – Brasil.

Pilipovic, D. (1998), *Energy Risk*, New York.

Rehrl, T., C. Weber, and R. Friedrich. (2004), *Anticipating Economic Risks Associated with Tighter Oil and Gas Markets*, Project proposal for the EU 6th framework programme, Stuttgart.

RISOE (2004), *The Wilmar Project*, cf. www.wilmar.risoe.dk.

Safonov, M.G. (1981), Feedback Properties of Multivariable Systems: The Role and Use of the Return Difference Matrix, *IEEE Transactions on Automatic Control* 26, 47-65.

Lux, R., J. Sontow, and A. Voß (1999), *Systemtechnische Analyse der Auswirkungen einer windtechnischen Stromerzeugung auf den konventionellen Kraftwerkspark*, IER-Forschungsbericht Band 56, Institut für Energiewirtschaft und Rationelle Energieanwendung, Stuttgart.

Swider, D. and C. Weber (2003), Ausgestaltung des deutschen Regelenergiemarktes, *Energiewirtschaftliche Tagesfragen* 53, 448-453.

Tseng, C.L. and G. Barz (2002), Short-Term Generation Asset Valuation: A Real Options Approach, *Operations Research* 50, 297-310.

Weber, C. (2004), *Uncertainty in the Electric Power Industry: Methods and Models for Decision Support*, Springer.

Weber, C. (2003), *The Investment Paradox in Competitive Electricity Markets – Problem Formulation, Empirical Evidence and Solution Strategies*, Proceedings of the 26th International IAEE Conference, 4 – 6 June 2003, Prague.

Weber, C. and C. Hoeck (2003), *Methoden für das Risikomanagement kombinierter Erzeugungs- und Handelsportfolios*, Presentation at the 3. Internationale Energiewirtschaftstagung an der TU Wien, February 12 – 14, 2003, Vienna.

Weber, C. (2002), *Electricity Markets: Coping with Price Risk Through Integrated Bottom-Up and Financial Modelling*, IAEE Annual Conference, 26 – 29 June 2002, Aberdeen.

Weber, C. and N. Dicke (2001), *Innovation, Regulation and Market Penetration*, Energy Performance Regulations for Buildings in the European Countries, Internationaler Workshop ENPER, 12 November 2001, Paris.

Zhou, K. and J. Doyle (1998), *Essentials of Robust Control*, Prentice Hall.

An Agenda for Energy Policy – An Element of Innovation Policy

Eberhard Jochem

ETH Zürich, Centre for Energy Policy and Economics (CEPE), Weinbergstrasse 11, 8001 Zürich, Switzerland, and Fraunhofer Institute for Systems and Innovation Research (Fh-ISI), Breslauer Straße 48, 76139 Karlsruhe, Germany, e.jochem@isi.fraunhofer.de

Keywords. *Energy Policy, Innovation Policy, Energy Efficiency Policy, Material Efficiency, R&D Energy Policy*

JEL. *D62; E61; O32; Q41; Q48; Q55*

Abstract. Whereas the other contributions focused on regulatory issues of electricity and gas markets from the point of view of economic efficiency, this paper tries to broaden the view to the future context of all energy markets, or even all energy-related markets. It will not consider energy supply policies and specific market regulation or re-regulation needs, but it starts from the basic human needs leading to material and energy demand and the challenges humankind is likely to be increasingly faced during the next decade. These may influence not only energy research and policy agendas, but rather change its isolated policy understanding into a concept as part of innovation policy designed for sustainable development. Several suggestions are made to enlarge the R&D energy policy agenda as well as to improve the effectiveness of energy and climate policies, and analytical methods and tools are presented.

1 Energy Use – an Indirect Need – and Energy-Related World Challenges

Energy plays a central role in the economy of both industrialised and developing countries. Energy is used due to basic needs such as comfortable living, mobility, and services. These basic needs are satisfied by a certain status of technologies; most of them are highly inefficient viewed from both the first and second law of thermodynamics. The inefficiencies of energy use have many reasons: energy price levels that do not reflect full generating, transport and distribution cost or the cost induced by their use; classical market deficiencies such as lack of knowledge and market survey, investor-user dilemma, limits of credit lines etc. (DeCanio, 1993 and 1998; Frahm, 1997); other preferences of the investors due to social prestige, fashions, and group-specific value systems (DeGroot, 2001, Sorell et al., 2000; Kaufmann-Hayoz et al., 2001).

The inefficiencies do not only cover energy conversion and use (see below), but also inefficiencies of using materials and the capital stock (e.g. owning appliances, cars or plants with low yearly operating hours between 10 and 300 hours instead of pooling them). The inefficiencies may be justified by consumer preferences as long as they do not stay in conflict to principles of sustainable development. This condition is not met by today's energy use, particularly not in industrialised countries, as every country (and the world) faces three major energy-related challenges in this century and over the next decades, in particular:

- The share of fossil fuels in current primary energy use, amounting to 80% globally or in the EU, is likely to remain high during the next decades, given the economics and limited acceptance of nuclear power and the small economic potentials and present market shares for renewable energies. This situation conflicts with the pressing need to reduce energy-related CO_2 emissions which are driving global climate change. These emissions cannot be sufficiently absorbed by the geosphere and have thus increased the atmospheric CO_2 concentration by more than 100 ppm or 35% since 1880. The impacts of climate change are a major threat to mankind in this century according to the Intergovernmental Panel on Climate Change (IPCC, 2001). Today, first elements of adaptation cost already amount to billions of Euro per year in Germany, the EU, and world-wide.
- Recognising the role of crude oil as an energy price setter on world markets, energy policy will have to pay more attention to the peaking of oil production within the next two to three decades. With declining oil production, energy price levels are likely to increase substantially. This could induce high economic losses due to stranded investments of energy-intensive capital goods.
- Energy policy will also have to give greater consideration to diversity and security aspects given that global road, air and ship transportation is currently almost 100% dependent on oil; in addition: Two thirds of the remaining oil resources are concentrated in the Near East, a region of considerable political instability.

To meet these challenges, energy and technology policy must pursue improved efficiency in energy production and use as well as improved material efficiency and an increased use of renewable energies or nuclear energy as a substitute for fossil fuels, especially oil. Among these options energy and material efficiency is highly underestimated due to specific disadvantages in society where media play a major role (Jochem, 2003).

2 Today's Inefficient Energy System

Today, more than 400,000 PJ per year of global primary energy demand deliver almost 300,000 PJ of final energy to customers, resulting in an estimated 150,000 PJ of useful energy after conversion in end-use devices. Thus, 250,000 PJ or two thirds of primary energy demand are presently lost in energy conversion, mostly as low- and medium-temperature heat (UNDP/WEC/UNDESA, 2000). The largest conversion losses occur in road vehicles and thermal power generation (see **Fig 1**; looking from the viewpoint of the second law of thermodynamics, massive losses also occur in low temperature heat generation).

Fig. 1. Demand of energy services and induced energy demand along the energy chain, Germany 2002.

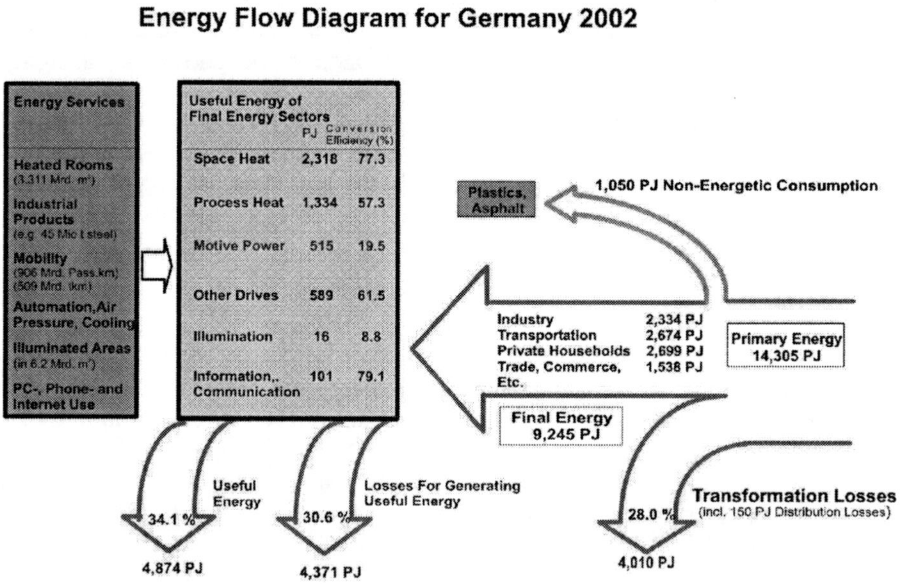

Source: Geiger and Wittke (2004)

Considerations of future improvements in energy efficiency often focus on energy-converting technologies and the distribution of grid-based energies, where the energy losses amount to some 60% of primary energy in most economies. But there are two additional areas for reducing future energy demand which are presently given little attention (see **Fig. 1**):

- Energy losses at the level of useful energy (currently about 39% of the German primary energy demand) could be substantially reduced or even avoided through such technologies as low-energy buildings, passive solar houses, membrane techniques or biotechnology processes instead of thermal processes, and lighter vehicles or the re-use of waste heat.
- The demand for energy-intensive materials could be reduced by recycling or substitution of those materials, by improving their design or material properties, and by intensifying the use of products, plants, and vehicles by pooling (e.g. car-sharing, leasing of machines).

First empirical and theoretical considerations suggest that the overall energy efficiency of today's industrial economies could be improved by some 80 to 90%

within this century (e.g. Enquete-Commission, 1991, Jochem et al., 2002). Given the above-mentioned challenges connected with energy use and the high potentials for efficiency improvements, the Swiss Board of the Federal Institutes of Technology (1998) promoted the vision of a 2000 Watt per capita society by the middle of the 21st century. This represents a reduction of present Swiss per capita primary energy use by two thirds while per capita income may increase by two thirds.

The challenges energy-related research is facing at the beginning of this century should not only be seen as threats. The technical and entrepreneurial solutions offer large opportunities for industries and service sectors, as the present intensive use of energy and materials will be substituted by capital goods and know-how. Furthermore, the new technologies may induce high export potentials for highly industrialised regions.

Countries and firms that invest in these technologies, related R&D and innovation policy are likely to boost their economies and make a significant contribution to the pressing problems of climate change and the imminent peaking of world oil production.

3 Plaidoyer for a Consistent Energy Policy

The intensity of the challenges of mankind's energy use seems to correlate with the inconsistency of the economic, energy and climate change policies in industrialised countries:

- High economic growth (more than 1.7% per year and capita) is asked for to cope with unemployment driven by ever increasing labour productivity (OECD countries since 1990: 1.6% per year). This growth is relatively unlikely given a linear per capita growth that has been prevailing for several decades and a rapidly ageing population.
- Low energy prices are one objective of energy policy to support economic growth and positive attitudes of the voters; in the light of the expected mid depletion point of oil production, the high increase in energy demand of developing countries, and major remaining oil resources in the Middle East (about 65%), the achievement of this objective is extremely unlikely.
- Greenhouse gases have to be substantially reduced (in Germany by 21% between 1990 and 2010 and in today's industrialised countries by some 60 to 80% until 2050), for the use of renewables a European target was set at 20% by 2020, and some lip-service goes to energy efficiency without any concise target and policy programme (where low energy price objectives are contradictory).
- The German Parliament had decided to phase out nuclear energy; this implies additional CO_2 emissions by 2030 of at least 60m tonnes. There is no specific additional programme for compensating these additional CO_2 emissions. No consistency of the German future energy supply is possible, if long-term CO_2 emission reduction targets will be maintained, except that no hard coal will be used and only little lignite by 2050 (or only zero CO_2 emission coal fired plants are built and operated) leading to high stranded investments in (conventional)

coal power plants and to high new investments in gas power plants and renewable energies (particularly if more efficient use of electricity and fossil fuels remains a forgotten option in the future).

This analysis demonstrates the urgent need for a consistent energy, climate and economic policy which needs a long-term view in order to evaluate the different options of efficient energy and material use, of energy conversion and CO_2 capture and storage. The Enquete Commission of the German Bundestag (2002) tried to draw those consistent visions, however, without analysing the cost involved and the impact on investments, the economy, structural changes, and society. The short attempt on consistency of present economic, energy and climate policies also demonstrates isolated policy making and a high level of lacking information on technical options of energy efficiency and material efficiency, but also on CO_2 capture and storage or future structures of electricity generation due to decentralised generating options.

4 More Emphasis on Efficiency Policy as Innovation Policy

The Board of the Swiss Federal Institutes of Technology (1998) promoted the vision of a 2000 Watt per capita society, i.e. a reduction of the per capita energy use by two thirds despite an increase of GDP by two thirds within the next 50 years. This vision has been checked by Swiss scientists since 2002 and the results are at least interesting: Synthesising the findings of all technological areas (i.e. converting primary energies to final and useful energies, reducing the losses of useful energies, increasing material efficiency, recycling and material substitution), it can be safely concluded that the *vision of the 2000 Watt per capita society is technically feasible* within some five decades as an absolute minimum of time (Jochem et al., 2002; Jochem et al., 2004a). This conclusion is based on the following observations and prerequisites:

- Not only improvements of energy conversion technologies (primary to final energy and final to useful energy) are needed, but larger options and potentials can be identified by reducing losses of useful energy (Romm, 1999), increasing material efficiency or material substitution (see below and **Fig. 1**).
- It is fortunate that the sector with the longest re-investment cycle, the buildings sector using about one third of final energy for heating, does not require as many additional successes of research and development as other sectors and technical areas (except for further cost reductions). However, the political acceptance in this field is presently far from sufficient to meet the targets of an efficiency potential of about 80% compared to the present building stock. Key technologies include new types of insulation and window systems, highly efficient low temperature heating and heat recovery systems, decentralised combined heat, cold, and power generation, integrated photovoltaic and solar thermal systems as well as ground-coupling systems for seasonal heat storage (Jakob et al., 2002).

- A major focus of R&D has to be the development of generic new technologies with low operating temperatures (e.g. membranes, absorption, biotechnology) and substantially improved efficiencies of energy and material use (e.g. changed properties of surfaces due to nanotechnology, feeding back brake energy by power electronics). Energy-intensive manufacturing equipment will undergo substantial changes through heat loss reduction and total process substitution (e.g. new physical, chemical, and biotechnological processes instead of conventional thermal separation and synthesis processes leading to energy savings up to 80% and 90%).
- With regard to transport, further advances in internal combustion engines and fuel cell technology, braking energy recuperation systems, light weight frames and new tyre materials are very promising. The performance of air planes can be considerably ameliorated by improved turbines, improved structural and aerodynamic efficiency as well as air traffic management techniques. Telematics offer helpful solutions to implement traffic and modal split management as well as freight logistics. New trans-shipment and container technology is important to make multi-modal freight traffic more efficient and attractive.
- More efficient material use, additional recycling of energy-intensive materials or substitution by less energy-intensive materials (e.g. biomass based polymers), greater re-use of products and improved material efficiency will all contribute to reducing the quantity of materials produced and, hence, the energy demanded (30% to 80%).
- Those foreseeable technical efficiency options at all levels of energy and material use are likely to be still insufficient for meeting the target. Entrepreneurial innovations will support these options and pooling (instead of owning) will intensify the use of machinery, plants, and vehicles.
- Structural changes to less energy-intensive production (partially induced by improved material efficiency or by saturation processes of energy-using appliances and infrastructures) will support the necessary efficiency gains. On the other hand, ever increasing mobility, particularly by aircraft, hedonistic lifestyles, or even climate changes resulting in higher summer temperatures inducing additional air conditioning demand are (or may be) compensating trends.

Politically, the feasibility may be at stake due to European societies' short-term decision horizons in the economy and the political system, a similar orientation and behaviour of many private households and the hesitant attitudes of many actors and responsible organisations. Many interest groups such as manufacturers, planners, product accompanying services, or the banking sector may not be aware of the opportunities and co-benefits offered by the shift towards greater resource efficiency (greater turnover, better competitiveness on world markets, higher product quality as a co-benefit for companies in industry and services, and new jobs, less external costs, eventually increased economic growth, fewer adaptation investments to climate change in the long term from a public point of view).

The transition to a 2000 Watt per capita society within half a century would imply a total turnover of the present capital stock of industrialised countries (and of a newly built highly efficient capital stock in developing countries anyway). The transition requires a fundamental change in the innovation system (e.g. research policy, education, professional training, technical standards, incentives, intermediates and entrepreneurial innovations). This system (illustrated for the institutional situation in Switzerland in **Fig. 2**) must be continuously extended, evaluated, and improved over the coming decades with the perspective that it will be integrated into the country's policy on innovation and sustainable development.

Fig. 2. Scheme of the Swiss energy and energy efficiency research and innovation system.

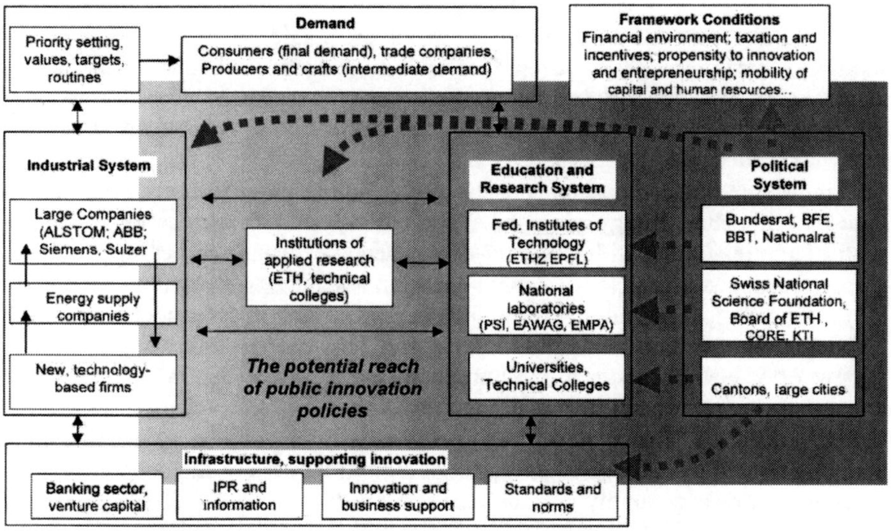

Source: Fh-ISI (2003)

In conclusion, the challenges of energy use at the global level become so demanding, that the portfolio of technical and entrepreneurial options has to be broadened and that energy policy has to be understood as part of an innovation policy which is substantially driven by aspects of sustainable development.

5 Implementation of R&D Visions Depends on Innovation Systems

Therefore, the research and innovation system of a country has to be analysed and the actors to be convinced by the new vision striving for a 2000 W per capita society. Research and innovation systems of a country encompass the "biotopes" of all those institutions (see **Fig. 2**; Smits and Kuhlmann, 2002) that are

- engaged in scientific research and the accumulation and diffusion of knowledge (i.e. research institutions, universities, technical colleges),
- engaged in education and professional training as well as the dissemination of new knowledge to broad audiences (educational institutions, media),

- developing and producing new technologies, processes, and products; and commercialising and distributing them (e.g. intermediates, infrastructure, technology producers, trade).

An innovation system also comprises the relevant policy institutions that set the economic, financial, and legal boundary conditions and regulatory bodies (standards, norms) as well as the public and private investments in appropriate infrastructure (Dosi, 1988). Every innovation system of a country (and even of a sector or a technological area within a country) is unique and develops its profiles and strengths only over decades. Each is based on stable exchange relationships among the institutions of science and technology, industry, commerce, and the political system. Since energy and material efficiency is dispersed over all sectors of the economy and the private households, the innovation system of resource efficiency is characterised by

- a high degree of compartmentalisation (e.g. buildings, road transportation, industrial branches, energy companies) and corresponding sectorisation of the political administration with low inter-departmental exchange and co-operation,
- non-interlinked arenas (corporatist negotiation deadlocks involving sovereignty of regions in federal states, e.g. cantons in Switzerland in cases such as building codes; co-generation using fossil fuels and heat pumps following a systems view, or of member states of the European Union) and related failed attempts at restructuring responsibilities in governments or at the EU level;
- dominance of a "linear model" of energy supply in political approaches (and among related technologists, energy economics researchers and consultants) focussing on energy supply options (such as costly renewables or fusion energy where technical and economic feasibility will be an open question for many decades to come) and neglecting opportunities at the useful energy and energy service level in most cases.

These characteristics of the innovation system of resource efficiency are general and almost independent of the country considered, but they are highly dependent on the ubiquity and heterogeneity of energy and material efficiency itself, and also on policies of neighbouring and trade-connected countries.

The weaknesses of under-coordinated innovation policy making, which seem to prevail in the energy and material efficiency field at the national and international level, should be analysed in more detail. Topics here include poorly articulated demand and weak networks which hinder fast knowledge transfer; legislation and market boundary conditions in favour of incumbent technologies (with high external costs), flows in the capital markets (focussing on large-scale technologies and players); and insufficiently organised actors in academia and industry at the national and international level.

Preconditions for success in realising the 2000 Watt per capita society include research on innovation-focussed and co-ordinating roles for government, addressing the large portfolio of technologies and innovations, reinforcing user-producer relations, supporting the building of new networks at the national and international level; stimulating learning and economy of scale effects, as well as the articulation of demand and prime movers. Research on these issues will involve evolutionary economics, sociology of organisation and science, political science, and management science.

6 Conclusions and Suggestions for a R&D Agenda

Besides the analysis of actors, their interests and role within the innovation system the following aspects should be on the research agenda:

- Developing an understanding of possible techno-economic options (e.g. efficiency options, renewables, material substitution, CO_2 capture and storage, pooling strategies and related entrepreneurial innovations;
- analysis of potentials at each stage of research, development, demonstration and market diffusion;
- analysis of the potentials of cost decreases by learning and economies of scale, but often more important: identification of co-benefits;
- analysis of actors in manufacturing, services and final users, their preferences, motivations and present or expected transaction cost (e.g. Ostertag, 2002);
- analysis of obstacles and market imperfections to identify needs of group-specific or technology-specific policies or business strategies.

The design of a possible *research and development agenda* in such a broad field of technological options and entrepreneurial innovations is without any doubt a major challenge and a huge task. Within the limited possibilities of such a paper, therefore, only a few general hints can be made:

- design possible policy options on the basis of available technical analyses (e.g. Jochem et al., 2002 and 2004a) and their economic perspectives which still have to be made in most cases;
- identify and communicate (even prefer) those options which should have imbedded flexibility regarding energy carriers, use of materials, and entrepreneurial options, given the fact of increasing uncertainties of available oil and gas resources, the mid-depletion point of oil production and depending energy price increases, the economic development of developing countries and their energy needs, and the need for limitation greenhouse gas emissions according to expected damages and adaptation cost (being still unclear at present);
- reflect these options and uncertainties under the aspects of the context of the European Union, the division of labour between national governments, the European Commission, and industrial research, the needs of developing countries and interests of European manufacturers and service companies as an opportunity on global markets.

In many cases, technologies or entrepreneurial options are available today (e.g. solar passive houses, reducing energy demand by 80 to 90%, three litres consuming cars, reducing fuel demand by 50%, variable speed drives reducing electricity demand by 30% to 50%, or car sharing reducing material demand by 80%). In these cases innovation policies are needed to take available technologies and know-how from the shelves. This may require some research to improve the *efficiency and efficacy of policy measures*:

- analyse and use the experiences of efficient policy measures in the EU member countries and other countries to design new policy activities at the national or EU level (or OECD level such as taxation of jet fuel); keep in mind efficiency aspects of policies such as regulation by technical standards: mass-produced products, regulation to improve market information: labelling. Or de-regulation of traditional rules, standards, ordinances, and laws hindering new technologies to penetrate into new markets may be needed;
- avoid and eliminate subsidies for energy production, distribution and use, if technology is mature; harmonise taxation schemes but also technical standards and informational standards among the European countries in order to enlarge homogenous markets and benefit from resulting potentials of economies of scale;
- try to internalise present and future externalities by economic mechanisms such as emission trading, taxes, or surcharges or by economic incentives such as reduced value added taxes or other tax deduction;
- use socio-psychological drivers among the actors (e.g. energy tables reducing transaction cost and stimulating priority shifts in companies at the local and regional level (Jochem et al., 2004b), television spots by popular stars inducing new shopping behaviour and value systems, etc., see Jochem et al., 2000).

Finally, several *methodological conclusions and recommendations* seem to be useful given the present limitations of analytical and prospective methods and the risk of too narrow interpretation of their results. There is a need to increase efforts to link process-oriented and macro models in a dynamic way in order to simulate policy-induced technical progress which at present is more or less limited to price policies in macro-economic models. In addition, existing process-oriented models having rather deterministic characteristics need less deterministic structures (reflecting more behavioural options of the relevant actors). This extension may only be achievable by involving more socio-psychological research and concepts in order to simulate behavioural and decision making aspects and the impact of changed policy design.

References

Board of Swiss Federal Institutes of Technology (1998), *Die 2000 Watt Gesellschaft – Modell Schweiz – Nachhaltigkeitsstrategie im ETH Bereich,* Wirtschaftsplattform, ETH Zürich.

DeCanio, S.J. (1998), The Efficiency Products: Bureaucratic and Organisational Barriers to Profitable Energy Saving Investments, *Energy Policy* 26, 441.

DeCanio, S. (1993), Barriers Within Firms to Energy-Efficient Investments, *Energy Policy* 21 (9), 906.

DeGroot, H.L.F. et al. (2001), Energy Savings by Firms: Decision-Making, Barriers and Policies, *Energy Economics* 23, 717.

Dosi, G. (1988), The Nature of the Innovative Process, in: Dosi, G. et al. (Eds.), *Technical Change and Economic Theory*, London, 221.

Enquête Commission (2002), *Sustainable Energy Supply Under the Conditions of Globalisation and Liberalisation*, German Bundestag (14/9400), Bonn.

Enquête Commission (1991), *Protecting the Earth – A Status Report with Recommendations for a New Energy Policy*, Bonn.

Frahm, T. et al. (1997), *Verhaltens- und Hemmnisforschung im Bereich Energie – Stand und Perspektiven*, Experten-Seminar des BMBF, Fraunhofer ISI, Karlsruhe/Bonn.

Geiger, B. and F. Wittke (2004), Die energiewirtschaftlichen Daten der Bundesrepublik Deutschland, BWK 1/2-2004, 41-46.

IPCC (Intergovernmental Panel on Climate Change) (2001), *Climate Change 2001 – Mitigation*, Contribution of Working Group III, Cambridge.

Jakob, M., E. Jochem, and C. Christen (2002), *Grenzkosten bei forcierten Energieeffizienzmaßnahmen in Wohngebäuden*, BFE Report, Bern.

Jochem, E., G. Anderson, D. Favrat, H. Gutscher, K. Hungerbühler, P.R. v. Rohr, D. Spreng, A. Wokaun, and M. Zimmermann (2004a), *Steps Towards a Sustainable Development – A White Book for R&D of Energy-Efficient Technologies*, CEPE/ETH and novatlantis, Zurich.

Jochem, E., E. Gruber, J. Letsch, K. Weissenbach, and K. Westdickenberg (2004b), *Modellvorhaben Energieeffizienz-Initiative Region Hohenlohe zur Reduzierung der CO_2-Emissionen – Endbericht Phase II*, Ministerium für Umwelt und Verkehr Baden-Württemberg, Stuttgart.

Jochem, E. (2003), Energie rationeller nutzen – Zwischen Wissen und Handeln, *GAIA* 11 (4), 9-14.

Jochem, E., D. Favrat, K. Hungerbühler, P.R. v. Rohr, D. Spreng, A. Wokaun, and M. Zimmermann (2002), *Steps Towards a 2000 Watt Society. Developing a White Paper on Research & Development of Energy-Efficient Technologies*, CEPE, ETH Zurich.

Jochem, E., J. Sathaye, and D. Bouille (2000), *Society, Behaviour, and Climate Change Mitigation, Advances in Global Change Research* 8, Dordrecht/London.

Kaufmann-Hayoz, R., C.S.B. Bättig, R. Defila, A. Di Giulio, P. Flury-Kleubler, U. Friederich, M. Garbely, H. Gutscher, C. Jäggi, M. Jegen, H.-J. Mosler, A. Müller, N. North, S. Ulli-Beer, and J. Wichtermann (2001), A Typology of Tools for Building Sustainability Strategies, in: Kaufmann, R. and H. Gutscher (Eds.), *Changing Things – Moving People: Strategies for Promoting Sustainable Development at the Local Level*, Basel, 33-107.

Ostertag, K. (2002), *No-Regret Potentials in Energy Conservation: An Analysis of Their Relevance, Size and Determinants*, Heidelberg.

Romm, J. (1999), *Cool Companies*, London.

Smits, R. and S. Kuhlmann (2002), *Strengthening Interfaces in Innovation Systems: Rationale, Concepts and (New) Instruments*, Report prepared on behalf of the EC STRATA Workshop 'New challenges and new responses for S&T policies in Europe', European Commission, Brussels.

Sorrell, S. et al. (2000), *Reducing Barriers to Energy Efficiency in Private and Public Organisations*, Final Report, University of Sussex, Brighton.

UNDP/WEC/UNDESA (2002), *World Energy Assessment*, UNDP, New York.

Energy Market Regulation: Impacts of EU Research

Domenico Rossetti di Valdalbero

European Commission, Directorate General Research[1], SDME 2/85,
1049 Brussels, Belgium, domenico.rossetti-di-valdalbero@cec.eu.int

Keywords. *Energy, Policy Making, EU Affairs*

JEL. *O3; Q4; Q5; C0; O2; H0; K0; L0; N7*

Abstract. European decisions in general, and in the energy field in particular, are often scientifically supported. Already before the formal "impact assessment", which has to accompany all the major policy initiatives launched by the European Commission since 2003, EU energy socio-economic research was used to develop tools and methods (models, software, database) able to evaluate scientifically the expected economic, social and environmental impacts of the proposed energy-related policy. This paper deals with empirical examples highlighting the role of the researchers in supporting EU policies regarding CO_2-emission trading, energy taxation, renewable electricity targets and energy efficiency potential.

1 Introduction

Energy – like water and information technologies – is a vital element for the development of modern societies. This is something which could be forgotten, especially as energy supply is relatively abundant and energy prices are relatively low. Energy is also a great source of wealth and an important sector of industrial activity on a global scale (oil) as well as on a regional scale (production and distribution of electricity and gas). Energy is not a simple consumer good. It comes with important challenges: security of energy supply, competitiveness, public service and protection of the environment (European Commission, 2000a). Furthermore, energy is in the heart of certain geopolitical tensions, of which the war in Iraq or the continuous tensions in the Middle-East are a demonstration. Energy, both by its production and its consumption, also causes "external costs", i.e. impacts on human health and the environment, which the energy market has not yet sufficiently taken into account.

---

1 The views presented in this paper do not necessarily reflect the European Commission official positions and the author alone assumes the responsibility for the contents. D. Rossetti would like to thank Ms. Nina Kajander for her help in formatting and proof-reading this paper.

For all these reasons, and in a Sustainable Development perspective, it is important that industry and public authorities act in a harmonised manner in order to prepare the energy options for the future. In this context, energy market regulation needs to be scientifically supported. The Communication Towards a European Research Area (ERA) (European Commission, 2000b) insists on "Developing the research needed for political decisions…" and the Communication "Making a reality of the ERA" (European Commission, 2000c) explicitly mentions the "Support for policy making and European scientific reference system…".

In the context of the European Union (EU), within the framework of the EU's various Research and Technological Development (RTD) Framework Programmes (FP), the energy socio-economic research assumes this role: Whether it is a renewable electricity target, an energy tax, a quantified objective to reduce greenhouse gases emissions, a voluntary agreement between public authorities and industries, a state aid exception for clean energies or a standard for energy efficiency, an evaluation of the impacts of the adopted measure is requested by policy makers. Impact assessment – "which identifies the likely positive and negative impacts of proposed policy actions, enabling informed political judgements" (European Commission, 2002a) – becomes a rule for all Commission major initiatives from 2003. EU researchers should therefore develop the tools and methodologies, scientifically agreed and peer-reviewed, that are able to make such assessments.

2 EU Energy Socio-Economic Research

In the various EU RTD Framework Programmes (FP1 from 1984 to 1987, FP2 from 1987 to 1991, FP3 from 1990 to 1994, FP4 from 1994 to 1998, FP5 from 1998 to 2002 and FP6 from 2002 to 2006), together with "technological" research, which includes hundreds of projects per FP aiming at promoting new and clean energy and environment technologies, improving quality of life, boosting growth, competitiveness and employment, "socio-economic research" in the energy field provides the scientific basis for energy and environment-related policy formulation, scenario-building and impact assessment. In particular, energy socio-economic research concerns the:

- development of tools and methods for energy strategy (modelling, forecasting and new paradigms for a low carbon energy sector; methods for the economic and environmental assessment of energy generation including externalities and security of supply; social acceptability, behavioural changes and international dimension related to sustainable energy RTD);
- elaboration of scenarios for energy supply and demand technologies and their interaction, and the analysis of cost effectiveness (based on full life cycle costs) and efficiency of all energy sources;
- analysis of social acceptability, behavioural changes and international dimension related to sustainable energy RTD.

The majority of the EU energy socio-economic research projects makes the links between energy and environment and addresses the issues of natural resources, economic growth and social needs, including both market competition and environmental constraints, top-down and bottom-up approaches. Among the main topics covered by the EU energy socio-economic research, it is worthwhile mentioning the Energy, Economy and Environment models and the energy external cost-related activities. The budget allocated to EU energy socio-economic research is estimated at around € 3 million per year. It should be reminded that the budget of the FP represents about 4% of the European Community's budget and approximately 6% of the EU's public civilian research investment.

In the FP6, a specific priority called "Scientific Support to Policies" (European Commission, 2002b), which includes the field of energy, has been launched. It has the objective to "underpin the formulation and implementation of Community policies, bearing on the interests of possible future members of the Union as well as the existing member states, and monitor their effects" (European Commission, 2002c). Directly related to energy, it concerns the "Development of tools, indicators and operational parameters for assessing sustainable transport and energy systems performance – economic, environmental and social" (European Commission, 2003a).

Some examples of models (energy bottom-up and macroeconomic) and tools (software and electronic database) developed by EU researchers in the various RTD FPs have been used in the EU's policy making process. This was particularly the case with the projects related to the energy and economic models (the so-called PRIMES, POLES, HERMES, E3ME and GEM-E3) and to the software and electronic database (the so-called SAFIRE and MURE).

3 Energy/Economic Models and Policy Applications

3.1 Energy Models

POLES and PRIMES (http://www.upmf-grenoble.fr/iepe/Recherche/Recha5.html and http://www.e3mlab.ntua.gr/manuals/PRIMsd.pdf), a world and European energy model developed from the beginning of the 1990s under the EU RTD FP, have been considered as part of the scientific references for the:

- EU energy and transport projections up to 2030 (European Commission, 2003b);
- World Energy, Technology and Climate Policy Outlook – 2030 (European Commission, 2003c);
- Energy cooperation with the developing countries (European Commission, 2002d);
- Impacts of fuel taxation on technology in the Green Paper on energy security of supply (European Commission, 2000a);
- Economic analysis of the effects of EU-wide emission trading in the Green Paper on greenhouse gas emissions trading within the European Union (European

Commission, 2000d); this document will be followed by a proposal for a directive and then a directive establishing a scheme for greenhouse gas emission allowance trading within the Community (European Commission, 2001a and 1996).

- Extended impact assessment on the "linking directive" (proposal for amending the directive establishing a scheme for greenhouse gas emission allowance trading) (European Commission, 2003d).

Fig. 1. Example of modelling results (PRIMES) used in EU policy making: The case of the EU emission trading scheme – Cost of reaching Kyoto target in 2010 (European Commission, 2000d).

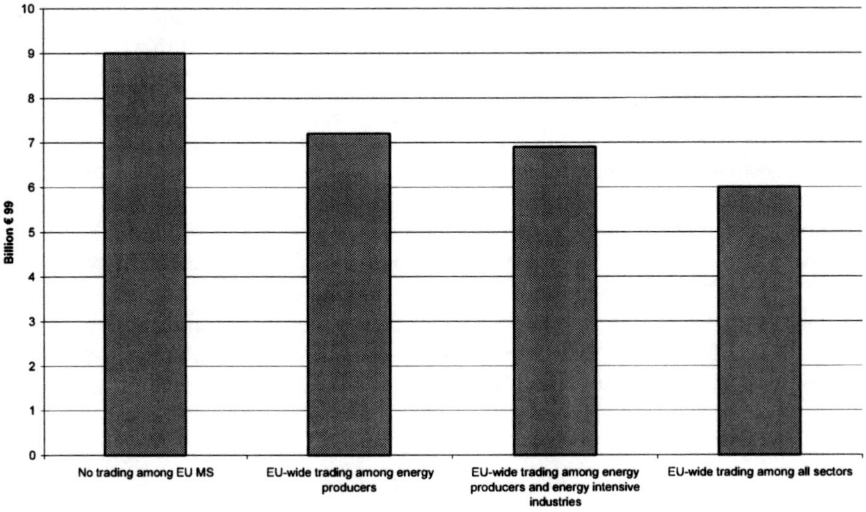

3.2 Macroeconomic Models

HERMES, GEM-E3 and E3ME, three macroeconomic models including an energy module, built and up-dated under the EU RTD FP, have provided the evaluation of the impacts of the proposed EU energy taxation on economy, energy and environment (European Commission, 1997a). The above mentioned proposal for a directive suggested to increase the minimum levels of indirect taxes (other than VAT) on fossil fuels (e.g. from 287 to 417 ECU/1000 litres for unleaded petrol) and on electricity consumption (to 1 ECU/MWh). The models also provided inputs to the Community competitiveness questions and to the national preoccupations (GDP variation in the different Member States).

The GEM-E3 computable general equilibrium model (http://gem-e3.zew.de/geme3ref.pdf) has also been used for illustrating the health related benefits of EU environmental policies (internalisation of external costs) and it is used to develop estimates of the macroeconomic impacts of improved air quality within the Clean Air for Europe programme (European Commission, 2001b).

Table 1. Example of modelling results (HERMES, GEM-E3, E3ME) used in EU policy making: The case of the Community energy taxation – Comparison of model results concerning Community energy taxation in 2005 (European Commission, 1997a).

	HERMES	GEM-E3	E3ME
GDP	+ 0.06%	+ 0.02%	+ 0.20%
Consumption price	+ 0.04%	+ 0.08%	- 0.08%
Employment EU15	+ 190,000	+ 155,000	+ 457,000
CO_2	- 1.6%	- 1.47%	- 0.50%

This table shows that the incidence of the proposed energy taxation is relatively limited and positive: an increase from 0.02% to 0.2% of GDP corresponding to ECU 1.6 to 16 billion from that time. A conclusion on the impact on inflation from the proposed measure cannot be made as one model expects a reduction and the two others a small increase. The effects on employment is limited but positive and the CO_2-emissions should be reduced in comparison to the reference case.

4 Software/Electronic Database and EU Policy Applications

4.1 Renewable Software Tool

SAFIRE, a computer based framework (http://www.esd.co.uk) developed under the EU research activities at the beginning of the 1990s, has provided the main quantified basis for setting EU and national targets for electricity from renewable energy sources. The objective is to double – from 6 to 12% – the share of renewables in the gross inland energy consumption by 2010, and to increase from 14% to 22% the electricity produced from renewable energy sources by 2010. These assessments were used in the:

- White Paper on renewable sources of energy based on the TERES II study (European Commission, 1997b);
- Proposal for a directive on the promotion of electricity from renewable energy sources (European Commission, 2000e);
- Directive on the promotion of electricity produced from renewable energy sources in the internal electricity market (European Commission, 2001c).

In addition to setting targets for renewable electricity, the directive allows the coexistence of various different national support schemes, expects that Member States ensure the guarantee of origin of electricity produced from renewable energy sources, reduce the administrative procedures and take the necessary measures to ensure the transmission and distribution of electricity produced from renewable energy sources.

Table 2. Example of software results (SAFIRE for the 2010 figure) used in EU policy making: The case of EU and Member States renewable electricity targets (European Commission, 2000e).

	RES-E % 1997	RES-E % 2010	RES-E % 1997 without large hydro	RES-E % 2010 without large hydro
Austria	72.7	78.1	10.7	21.1
Belgium	1.1	6.0	0.9	5.8
Denmark	8.7	29.0	8.7	29.0
Finland	24.7	35.0	10.4	21.7
France	15.0	21.0	2.2	8.9
Germany	4.5	12.5	2.4	10.3
Greece	8.6	20.1	0.4	14.5
Ireland	3.6	13.2	1.1	11.7
Italy	16.0	25.0	4.5	14.9
Luxembourg	2.1	5.7	2.1	5.7
Netherlands	3.5	12.0	3.5	12.0
Portugal	38.5	45.6	4.8	21.5
Spain	19.9	29.4	3.6	17.5
Sweden	49.1	60.0	5.1	15.7
UK	1.7	10.0	0.9	9.3
European Union	13.9 %	22.1 %	3.2 %	12.5 %

RES-E means electricity coming from renewable energy.

This table provides the figures of "green electricity", in percentage, in 1997 and the indicative targets for 2010. It also gives the renewable electricity figure "without large hydro", i.e. installations of more than 20 MW. The percentage for the EU is coming from the average renewable TWh consumed.

4.2 Electronic Database

MURE is an electronic database (http://www.isis-it.com/mure/), developed originally by European researchers and updated by energy specialists, which provides information on energy conservation measures that have been carried out in the EU Member States.

MURE has provided the basis for the figure firstly included in the energy efficiency communication (European Commission, 1998); secondly, in the action plan to improve energy efficiency in the European Community (European Commission,

2000f); and thirdly, in the proposal for a directive on the energy performance of buildings (European Commission, 2001d). The potential for energy efficiency has been estimated by MURE to be over 18% of the present energy consumption.

Finally, considering that household and tertiary sector (160 million buildings in the EU-15) are responsible for approximately 40% of the final energy demand (heating represents 70% of domestic energy consumption and 50% of commercial energy consumption) in the EU and that this sector has the highest potential, a Directive on energy performance of buildings has been adopted in 2003 (European Commission, 2003d). It deals with the integrated energy performance standards, application of these standards to new buildings and to certain existing buildings when they are renovated, certification schemes and specific inspection and assessment of boilers and heating/cooling installations.

Table 3. Example of electronic database results (MURE for the 2010 figure) used in EU policy making: The case of available economic energy efficiency potential in the EU (European Commission, 1998).

Sector	Final energy consumption, 1995 (Mtoe)	Available potential to 2010, percentage of 1995 consumption
Industry	268	17%
Transport	270	14%
Domestic and tertiary	358	22%
Total	896	18%

5 Conclusions

All the tools presented in this paper (PRIMES, POLES, HERMES, E3ME, GEM-E3, SAFIRE and MURE) and used to support various EU energy-related policies have been originally elaborated by researchers under various EU RTD Framework Programmes.

As far as the relation between the research work – accomplished by energy socio-economist researchers – and the policy applications is concerned, it is worth mentioning the following points:

- Specificity of energy: Before the current formal Commission "impact assessment" for all major policies (European Commission, 2002a), as demonstrated by the various examples in this paper, energy initiatives were already evaluated *a priori* (economic, energy and environmental impacts); this is probably due to the tradition of systematic analysis, quantification work and foresight activities in the energy field.

- Researchers' influence on the EU policy making: The tools (models, software, databases) developed by the socio-economic scientists play a key role in fixing targets (for renewables or energy efficiency) and in justifying policies (emission trading or taxation).
- Reference to the research work: In the EU legislative *iter* (generally a Commission communication, followed by a proposal for a directive and finally a directive), the reference to the scientific support is indicated in the first preparatory documents or in the accompanying information such as the Commission staff working document, but not as such in the final legally binding legislative act (directive).
- Timing period: Between five and ten years are generally needed between the starting of the research work (model development, data search, geographical coverage, etc.) and the policy applications (which take into account the scientific publications, the peer-review, the stakeholder validation, etc.). For example, HERMES was originally developed in 1989, MURE in 1991, PRIMES, SAFIRE, E3ME and POLES in 1992).

Energy has now a section in the EU Constitutional Treaty adopted in Brussels by the Heads of State and Governments (18 June 2004). The Union policy on energy shall aim to ensure the functioning of the energy market, ensure security of energy supply in the EU and promote energy efficiency and saving and the development of new and renewable forms of energy. It is most probable that the new EU energy-related initiatives will be more and more frequent in the future and that they will need to be assessed in-depth scientifically and quantitatively (European Commission, 2002e).

Researchers should therefore be prepared to elaborate new tools that are able to catch the increasing complexity of the world ("knowledge stock", geopolitical risks, human behaviour patterns, etc.), the very-long term problems (resource depletion, climate change, radioactive waste management, etc.) and the specific links between economy, energy, and environment (security of supply, externalities of energy, ecosystem damages, etc.).

References

European Commission (2003a), Work Programme for the Specific Programme for RTD&D "Integrating and Strengthening the ERA", Specific activities covering a wider field of research, Policy support and anticipating scientific and technological needs, 9/12/2003.

European Commission (2003b), European Energy and Transport – Trends to 2030, OPEC, Luxembourg, 2003.

European Commission (2003c), World Energy, Technology and Climate Policy Outlook 2030 (WETO), OPEC, Luxembourg, 2003.

European Parliament and Council (2003d), Directive 2002/91/EC on Energy Performance of Buildings, OJ, L1/65, 4/1/2003.

European Commission (2003d), Extended Impact Assessment on the Directive Amending Directive Establishing a Scheme for Greenhouse Gas Emission Allowance Trading

Within the Community, staff working paper, in Respect of the Kyoto Protocol's Project Based Mechanisms, SEC(2003)785, 23/7/2003.

European Commission (2002a), Communication on Impact Assessment, COM(2002)276, 5/6/2002.

European Commission (2002b), Sixth framework programme of the European Community for research, technological development and demonstration activities, contributing to the creation of the European Research Area and to innovation, Decision 1513/2002/EC, OJ, L 232/1, 29/8/2002.

European Council (2002c), Decision adopting a specific programme for research, technological development and demonstration: "Integrating and Strengthening the ERA (2002-2006), OJ, L 294/1, 29/10/2002.

European Commission (2002d), Energy Cooperation with the Developing Countries, COM(2002)408, 17/7/2002.

European Commission (2002e), Communication on the Collection and Use of Expertise by the Commission: Principles and Guidelines, COM(2002)713, 11/12/2002.

European Commission (2001a), Proposal for a Directive Establishing a Scheme for Greenhouse Gas Emission Allowance Trading Within the Community, COM(2001)581, 23/10/2001.

European Commission (2001b), Clean Air for Europe (CAFÉ) Programme, COM(2001)245, 4/5/2001.

European Commission (2001c), Directive on the Promotion of Electricity Produced from Renewable Energy Sources in the Internal Electricity Market, OJ, L 283/1, 27/10/2001.

European Commission (2001d), Proposal for a Directive on the Energy Performance of Buildings, COM(2001)226, 11/5/2001.

European Commission (2000a), Towards a European Strategy for the Security of Energy Supply, Green Paper, COM(2000)769, 29/11/2000.

European Commission (2000b), Towards a European Research Area, COM(2000)6, 18/1/2000.

European Commission (2000c), Making a Reality of the ERA, COM(2000)612, 4/10/2000.

European Commission (2000d), Greenhouse Gas Emissions Trading Within the European Union, Green Paper, COM(2000)87, 8/3/2000.

European Commission (2000e), Proposal for a Directive on the Promotion of Electricity from Renewable Energy Sources in the Internal Electricity Market, COM(2000)279, 10/5/2000.

European Commission (2000f), Action Plan to Improve Energy Efficiency in the European Community, COM(2000)247, 26/4/2000.

European Commission (1998), Energy Efficiency in the European Community, COM(1998)246, 29/4/1998.

European Commission (1997a), Proposal for a Directive Restructuring the Community Framework for the Taxation of Energy Products, COM(97)30, 12/3/1997 – Presentation of the new Community system for the taxation of energy products, Commission working staff document, SEC(97)1026, 30/7/1997.

European Commission (1997b), White Paper on Renewable Sources of Energy, COM(97)599, 26/11/1997.

European Commission (1996), Directive Establishing a Scheme for Greenhouse Gas Emission Allowance Trading Within the Community and Amending IPCC Council Directive 96/61/EC (24/9/1996), OJ, L 275/32, 13/10/2003.

Why Is Economic Theory Ignored in Environmental Policy Practice?

Friedrich Schneider

University of Linz, Department of Economics, Altenbergerstraße 69, 4040 Linz-Auhof, Austria, friedrich.schneider@jku.at

Hannelore Weck-Hannemann

University of Innsbruck, Institute of Public Finance, Universitätsstraße 15, 6020 Innsbruck, Austria, hannelore.weck@uibk.ac.at

Keywords. *Environmental Policy, Ecological Taxes, Tradable Permits, Voluntary Agreements, Road Pricing, Voting Behaviour, Public Bureaucracy, Interest Groups*

JEL. *Q00*

Abstract. In the past there was hardly any use of economic theory and instruments in environmental policy, mainly command and control measures dominated. More recently, ecological taxes became increasingly popular and have been proposed but not implemented with an ecological effect. Thus, the situation has not changed, and we must ask for the reasons of this situation and the prevailing non-acceptance of these instruments. The purpose of this paper is to give some answers on these questions using the Public Choice approach. The proposition of an ecological tax reform and road pricing measures are taken to discuss how actual environmental policy deviates from economic prescriptions.

1 Introduction

Today we are still far away from general acceptance and widespread policy application of market-based environmental instruments, and the situation has also not changed with respect to a successful environmental policy advice by economists. Hence, we should ask what are the reasons for this development and how a wider acceptance of policy advice by economists could be achieved. The purpose of this paper is to give some answers to these questions. To do so, we first present the main ideas of the Public Choice approach (Section 2). In Section 3 we discuss a recent suggestion of an ecological tax reform and its failure. In Section 4 pricing instruments in the transport sector are analysed with respect to their incentive mechanism and political chances to be implemented. Section 5 concludes with a summary and outlook.

2 The Public Choice Approach to Environmental Policy[1]

The usual way to proceed in the papers which follow the Public Choice approach is to single out the different (groups of) actors which are engaged in environmental policy making and to ask for their interests in the application of the different instruments which could be applied. Following Frey (1992: 133-140), typically, four groups of actors are considered: (i) the voters, (ii) the politicians, (iii) the public bureaucrats, and (iv) the 'economy', i.e. the owners, managers and employees of the industries which are to be regulated and their interest groups. In the following, we will give a short characterisation of the main interests of these four groups of actors in environmental policy.

2.1 The Voters

Over the last three decades, the sensitivity of voters with respect to environmental issues has certainly increased.[2] Thus, the approval of voters for ecologically sustainable policies should become more and more probable. However, it should be taken into account that ecological objectives 'compete' with other interests, especially with 'pure' economic objectives of the voters.

Assuming that the improvement of the environmental quality is a national (or, as in the case of the reduction of CO_2-emissions, even an international) public good, the most relevant question regarding the behaviour of voters is: Who will pay the costs? If the price elasticity of demand is low and/or if the supply elasticity is infinitely elastic, as in the case of mineral oil prices in small countries, where the consumer price of these products is determined by the prices on the international spot markets, the consumers have to bear the costs. This implies that the majority of voters directly pay for such a policy. But if price elasticity is high, only a small part of the burden of an environmental measure which increases the production costs of a good can be passed to the consumers. Thus, the producers, shareholders, managers as well as workers of these firms, have to bear the costs. Consequently, the resistance to environmental programs might be higher in regions with a high share of producer interests which oppose such a policy, because a higher burden can lead to reduced profits, wages and employment in these regions.

1 Elements of this chapter are taken from Kirchgässner and Schneider (2003) and Schneider and Volkert (1999).

2 See, e.g., the results of the IMAS-surveys for Austria (IMAS, 1995, 1996) or the results for Germany presented in Horbach (1992).

In Germany, empirical evidence for such a trade-off between the reduction of unemployment and ecological objectives was found. Horbach (1992) shows that in regions with a high unemployment rate the Green Party receives fewer votes in elections than in other regions. Moreover, he also shows that the more important the chemical and steel industries are in a certain region, the worse the election chances are for this party, because its ecologically oriented economic policy programme might weaken the position of these industries. Thus, citizens voting out of self-interest might be an obstacle for the approval of any kind of environmental policy. This implies that too little might be done, especially in those regions where environmental policy is needed most.

New arguments have emerged in the recent international discussion of the double dividend. The implementation of incentive-oriented environmental tax policies need not be accompanied by an increase, but by a shift in the tax burden. In such a case there is no immediate trade-off between fighting unemployment and enforcing stricter environmental policies. On the contrary, many simulations show that it might even be possible to have a small gain in employment.[3] As a study of the OECD (1997) shows a large number of winners among different economic sectors and firms might be generated, but with only small gains. On the other hand, there would be a few distinct losers among the firms whose economic position could deteriorate quite substantially. Thus, at first sight, politicians might be expected to enact such a tax alternative in response to the preferences of the majority of voters instead of caring for the minority of losers. However, as Public Choice theory tells us, "... a small concentrated identifiable, and intensely interested pressure group may exert more influence on political choice making than the much larger majority of persons, each of whom might expect to secure benefits in the second order of smalls ..."[4]. Thus, even if a double dividend allows to fight unemployment by enforcing stricter environmental policies in the economy as a whole there still can exist a political trade-off between fighting of unemployment in small, intensely interested, and highly influential pressure groups of potential losers and an incentive-based environmental policy.

However, the case of a double dividend where employment is rising with a stricter environmental policy is an exception in environmental policy making, which to a large extent depends on the existence of involuntary unemployment.[5] In most situations there is a trade-off between the production of better environmental quality and the production of consumer goods, i.e. the voters have to make a choice between better environmental quality and higher real income. In such situations, the decision of voters depends on the information of the citizens about the consequences of environmental problems, the lag between the time when the policy measure is taken and the time when the environmental situation is improved, and the discount rate of voters. Especially with respect to measures which are

3 See, e.g., the review of such studies in Kirchgässner (1998, 1999) or Schneider (1998) with results for Austria, Kirchgässner, Müller, and Savioz (1998) with results for Switzerland or Scholz (2000) and Bach et al. (2001) with results for Germany.

4 Buchanan and Tullock (1975: 142).

5 See, the corresponding simulation results in Kirchgässner, Müller, and Savioz (1998).

mainly to the benefit of future generations, self-interested individuals would generally not be willing to bear high costs. This is one of the main obstacles against efficient CO_2-reduction policies. But similar conditions hold in other areas of environmental policy making as well. Consequently, it can be expected that in many cases voters care more about the economic short-term development than about the environmental situation. This might delay or even prevent the approval of ecologically-oriented politics by the majority of voters. Even if a citizen is to some extent altruistic, well educated and informed it is not obvious that she/he as a 'rational' (even long-term oriented) voter will support ecologically oriented economic policies in elections or referenda.[6]

2.2 The Politicians

Politicians can be assumed to pursue a certain policy if – given that they achieve their objective – it is supported by a majority of voters, under the qualification that there is no considerable resistance either from the bureaucracy or from the interest groups. Insofar, if voters accept or even demand an undersupply of environmental policies, a government which wants to maximise its re-election probability gets no incentive from the voters to provide a better environmental quality.

However, even a democratic government is hardly ever only seeking re-election. According to the partisan hypothesis first developed by Hibbs (1977; see also 1992) and incorporated into the politico-economic models of Frey and Schneider (1978a, 1978b, 1979) re-election is more of a constraint which the government has to respect than an objective in itself. Thus, if a coalition government includes a 'green' party and/or if the dominating party of the government has a clientele which has an especially strong environmental orientation a government might provide a stronger environmental policy than it is demanded by the voters altogether (the median voter) as long as this does not endanger its re-election prospects. On the other hand, if the clientele of the government is more economically oriented it will hardly accept that the output of consumer goods is reduced in order to improve environmental quality. Thus, there might be a less strict environmental policy than it is demanded by the median voter.

Even if the level of environmental activities is (on the average) too low, the question again arises whether the remaining policies in this field are carried out in an efficient way. Again, if there is no pressure by the voters but if they are, instead, in favour of more visible but less efficient policies, it cannot be expected that there are pressures on the government from the side of the voters to pursue an efficient environmental policy. Thus, the use of bureaucratic instruments might be more in the interest of politicians than the use of economic instruments. However, there are two qualifications to be made. First, because the government should be better informed than the average voter, it should take into account that the higher efficiency of an environmental policy which uses economic instruments allows to

6 The role of altruistic/moral behaviour in such decisions is discussed in Kirchgässner (2000).

use resources for other purposes and – on this way – to satisfy more of the demands of the own clientele and/or to improve the re-election prospects. For this reason, the government should – ceteris paribus – be more in favour of applying economic instruments than the average voter.

Second, environmental taxes might have a special attraction for governments because they create revenue which can be used to cut other taxes and/or to finance additional projects. This can be advantageous for the government if the tax resistance against 'green taxes' can be expected to be lower than against other taxes. This holds especially if the clientele of the government is more environmentally oriented than the average voter.[7] On the other hand, as the opposition will try to use its chance and to make strong opposition against introducing or raising such visible taxes the leeway of a government to pursue such a policy is limited.

It is, moreover, possible to present environmental taxes as acceptable measures to the voters, if these taxes are characterised as 'punishment' for polluting the environment and if they are applied mainly to industrial polluters. Politically, it might be more difficult to sell the creation of a market for tradable permits to the voters because these can be considered as 'licences to pollute the environment' which – from a moral point of view – might be seen as morally unsound by those people who are especially strongly engaged for the natural environment.[8] Moreover, at least as long as grandfathering is used as the method for the original distribution of the emission rights, the government is much less interested in using tradable permits than in using ecological taxes.

Taking all these arguments together, the interests of the government might on the average lead to a less than optimal level of environmental policy, but – as with the voters – they can hardly be the reason why the use of market oriented environmental instruments was on such a low level in the past. Therefore, those who really oppose such a policy must be the public bureaucracy and/or private business, i.e. the regulated industries and their interest groups.

2.3 The Regulated Industries and Their Interest Groups

Officially, representatives of the industries which are to be regulated by environmental policy are much in favour of economic theory and hence the use of economic instruments. However, whenever the application of such instruments is discussed, they are at least very hesitant and in most cases in strong opposition to such a policy. If, e.g., ecological taxes are discussed, they argue against it and instead favour voluntary agreements which are just the opposite of an economic instrument of environmental policy, command and control policies or – at the most –

---

7 Acknowledging this, several opponents against the introduction of environmental taxes do not really argue against the use of environmental taxes per see but they are anxious that, given the less severe tax resistance, the government might be successful in increasing the total tax load. See, e.g., Zimmermann (1996).

8 For a discussion of ethical aspects of international emissions trading see Ott and Sachs (2000).

tradable permits.[9] For the latter, however, they demand grandfathering of the original distribution of the emission rights. Thus, if there are any economic instruments used at all, besides subsidies which are not discussed here, they prefer tradable permits which are distributed by grandfathering. In any case, they prefer a policy of command and control to a policy applying ecological taxes.

But why should the polluters, especially the industrial polluters, oppose the use of economic theory and of market oriented environmental policy instruments? After all, using these instruments the same ecological impact could be reached 'more cheaply' i.e. at lower costs, which finally should be in the interest of the relevant industrial sectors as well. It is obvious that the profit interest of any single producer which has a relevant amount of emissions is against any environmental regulation because it reduces its expected profits. But why is there a quite special opposition against economic measures of environmental policy?

The two main reasons for this opposition are probably the high efficiency of such a policy and distributional aspects.

- At the level of the economy as a whole, the high efficiency of economic instruments means that the aspired ecological objectives can be reached with minimal (social) costs. For the single firm, however, the situation is quite different. As long as a policy of command and control is pursued, it has a (sometimes considerable) leeway for negotiations with its environmental protection agency. In these negotiations it has an informational advantage; it knows the processes and the potential costs if the emissions have to be reduced by a certain amount, and it can threat with a reduction of employment or even with the displacement of the firm if the regulations are too strict. On the other hand, if environmental taxes are used, the firm can pollute as much as it wants, but it has to pay for it. Reductions of a tariff which has been fixed in the parliament and written into a law are much more difficult to negotiate than the extent of a regulation which is necessarily – more or less – individual for each firm. Thus, it can be expected that the regulation will – on the average – be less strict with a command and control policy than if economic instruments of environmental policy are used.
- There are also, however, important distributional consequences. Let us assume that the firm uses the same technology and has the same emission in both regimes, under a command and control and under an economically oriented environmental policy. Thus, at the margin everything is the same, the same technology, the same marginal costs, and the same prices of the goods produced. Moreover, the costs for reducing the emissions are the same. Inframarginally however, if taxes or tradable permits are used the firm has to pay for its (remaining) emissions while under a policy of command and control it gets it free. Thus to the extent of the legal emissions it gets an additional rent.[10] If wages are given, this rent can be appropriated by the owners. However, the employees (and/or their organisations, the trade unions) will realise that there is a possibility for a wage increase; they will demand their share of this rent. On the other

9 See Horbach (1992) who shows that two thirds of the German companies favour standards whereas only one third favours levies and taxes.

10 This argument has first been put forward by Buchanan and Tullock (1975).

hand, if taxes are used (and the revenue is used to cut other taxes, e.g.,) the general public benefits. Thus, shareholders (employers) as well as employees have an own interest to prevent the use of economic instruments.

A similar argument holds if we compare grandfathering with auctioning tradable permits. If there is competition, at the margin both systems lead to the same condition. That implies that the prices for the goods produced will be the same. If the permits are auctioned, there is additional revenue for the government which can be used to cut other taxes and which – in this way – may be to the benefit of the general public. If grandfathering is used, however, as, e.g., in the case of the sulphur dioxide allowance-trading program in the United States,[11] the existing firms get an additional rent. Moreover, they get a competitive advantage against newcomers in the market who do not get this rent because they have to pay for all the permits they need: Grandfathering of pollution rights creates a barrier to entry against new firms. Thus, it is no surprise that the existing companies as well as their interest groups favour the grandfathering of tradable permits.[12]

Given this situation and the at least partial conformity of employer and employees interest it is no surprise that the industries which are to be regulated generally oppose the use of economic environmental instruments, especially of ecological taxes.[13] Moreover, their organisations are well organised and they are important players in the political game. There are five main reasons why these interest groups are not only better organised than environmental interest groups but also better able to achieve their self-interested goals:

- In contrast to environmental interest groups, the respective industry and business associations usually have sufficient financial backing which is used for efficient lobbying.
- Producers themselves are closest to the origins of environmental problems in the production sector. This is the reason for substantial information asymmetries. Therefore, 'green' groups often have difficulties in getting information about pollution effects as well as about the feasibility of alternative technologies.
- Based on this information asymmetry, industry and business associations often have considerable influence on public opinion through their publications as well as through their impact on the media.
- The 'market power' of these interest groups is a crucial factor in the achievement of their objectives in the political arena. It is not only important in the

11 See Joskow, Schmalensee, and Bailey (1998: 671): "Allowances are given to existing electric generation units and those under construction, according to fairly complicated rules .... For our purposes here it suffices to note that essentially all of the allowances were allocated 'free' to incumbent sources." A more detailed description if the initial allocation is given in Joskow and Schmalensee (1998).

12 See for this also Svendsen (1999).

13 There seems to have been some change of the opinion in the United States. According to Svendsen (1999), private business interest groups are today more in favour of a grandfathered permit market, and no longer so much in favour of a command and control policy, but they still reject a tax policy.

goods and services markets but in the labour market as well, especially in the form of the threat of transferring production abroad.

- Quite often these associations gain personal representation in legislative institutions, in the parliament and its committees, which makes it possible to postpone or even reject environmental issues.

Taken together, representatives of industrial and business interest groups are able to influence legislative proposals in their early stages through active lobbying in hearings and in parliamentary committees. For that purpose, they provide detailed information about environmental measures. This has the effect of linking together lobbyists and members of the legislative bodies. As a result of this relationship, arrangements are made between the political administrative system and 'private' interest groups representing business interests. In Germany, such agreements have become common practise in more than 50 industrial committees and 'voluntary self-obligations' as well as in several hundred committees for the definition of the 'best available technology'.[14]

Compared to their counterparts of business and the economy, environmentally oriented interest groups are in a weak position. They have the possibility of organising spectacular actions, a strategy which is often used by Greenpeace which might be the best known of these groups. In doing so, in special situations they can have a strong impact on public opinion, influence private consumption and in this way influence the policy of single companies,[15] they might also have some impact on the decisions of voters, but they rarely have the same direct impact on the parliamentary system and the public bureaucracy economic interest groups have. Moreover, until the eighties the green interest groups were themselves in favour of command and control measures in environmental policy and against the use of economic instruments. Their main argument was that the natural environment should not be 'commercialised'. Against the combined pressure of economic and environmental interest groups, however, an efficient environmental policy using economic instruments had no chance at all.

2.4 The Public Bureaucracy

Already a cursory view at the available evidence tells us that – at least in Europe – many members of the public environmental bureaucracy are in strong opposition against using economic theory and the application of market-based instruments of environmental policy. They rather prefer the use of command and control. In most cases they favour, of course, policies which improve the situation of the natural environment; most members of the 'green bureaucracies' are highly motivated to

14 See Maier-Rigaud (1996) or Helbig and Volkert (1999).

15 The best known case is that in 1995 Greenpeace succeeded in preventing Shell from sinking the oil platform Brent Spar into the North See. See for this Huxham and Sumner (1999).

pursue this goal.[16] However, they do not necessarily favour efficient policies. More important for them is that a policy strengthens their personal position in the environmental policy game.

The empirical studies by Holzinger (1987) demonstrate that German environmental administrations have at least some leeway to follow their own interests, whereas objectives such as 'economic efficiency' or 'overall economic cost optimisation' are only of minor importance for them. They are vitally interested in environmental policy measures which are labour- and resource-intensive. As a result – and in accordance with the economic theory of bureaucracy as originally developed by Niskanen (1968, 1971) – they are able to increase their number of employees, and each year to have a larger budget at their disposal. The result of this is that the environmental administrations will try to implement those environmental policy measures which require high administrative controls. To increase their leeway they want the political authorities to regulate as little as possible so that they have the greatest possible leeway (and budget) for their own decisions.[17] Discretionary budgets are also necessary in order to meet the demands of those lobbies for which the different environmental sections of German ministries have become even more important than the parliament with its committees.

Economic instruments and especially environmental taxes are much less attractive for the public bureaucracy. While command and control policies can only exist with high labour costs and other expenditures, the use of taxes requires much less expenditure and less staff. Hence, a budget increase or a rise in the importance of environmental authorities is less likely than with the use of standards. Furthermore, a change from the current system of environmental standards to a system of taxes would require a high degree of flexibility in the environmental agencies.

Using taxes or tradable permits would of course reduce the information requirements of the public environmental bureaucracy considerably. Detailed information is only necessary for the tolerable total burden, for the 'correct' total emission amount derived from it, and – in the case of taxes – on the reactions of the industries to the taxes, which can be obtained in a kind of trial-and-error procedure by a gradual increase of the tax rate over a longer time span, but no detailed information about the prevention costs of different producers is needed, which is difficult to acquire. Thus, the efficiency of the bureaucracy could be increased considerably. But this is not necessarily also in the interest of the members of the bureaucracy, as the lower information requirements make it rather difficult to justify a large budget and a large staff.

Taking all arguments together, the industries which are to be regulated and the members of the environmental bureaucracy are the ones who are most in favour of command and control policies, and both have a strong impact on the design of the actual policy. Thus, it comes to no surprise that economic instruments like environmental taxes or tradable permits were hardly used up to now. On the other hand, with respect to the extent of the environmental program the interest of these

---

16 For a model which employs this assumption to explain the results of international climate protection policy see Congleton (1995).

17 See the results of the surveys described in Gawel (1994a, 1994b, 1995).

two groups of actors are quite opposite: While the bureaucrats favour a strict, most industries strive for a rather soft environmental policy. Thus, whether a policy is really strict or not depends mainly on the preferences of the voters (and of the clientele of the party (parties) in government). Taking into account the discounting behaviour of voters, the policy might be strict in those areas which today have a direct, noticeable impact on today's voters, but rather loose in those areas which would mainly benefit future generations. And this is exactly what we observe. There have been, e.g., considerable improvements in the water quality of our lakes and rivers, but up to today there is hardly any effective policy to prevent or even slow down global warming.

3 The Ecological Tax Reforms

3.1 General Remarks

The main theoretical as well as empirical argument in favour of an ecological tax reform is the hope for a double dividend: If taxes which cause distortions in one sector of the economy are reduced and at the same time taxes which reduce distortions in another sector of the economy are introduced instead, the efficiency of the whole economy should improve and – as a consequence – unemployment should be reduced. This idea, originally proposed by Binswanger et al. (1983) and strongly supported by Pearce (1991) could play a key role in reducing CO_2-emissions by the introduction of a general energy and/or CO_2 tax and – in this way – fighting global warming. In the last decade, it has become more and more popular in Europe, but not so much because of its environmental consequences but mainly because it seems to be an ideal method to solve the problems of many European labour markets without, e.g., having to introduce more flexibility into these markets. This belief is quite widespread despite the fact that the scientific discussion starting with Bovenberg and De Mooij (1994) has shown that with such a reform an increase of employment while not impossible is difficult to reach, and that it might improve the labour market situation somewhat, but not really solve the unemployment problem.[18] Thus, in many countries not only green but also other left-wing parties are today in favour of such a policy, and it is also supported by trade unions. This is insofar no surprise as there is quite a lot of evidence that left-wing parties are more active in fighting unemployment compared with right-wing parties which are more concerned about inflation.[19] Thus, the main interest in

---

18 See, e.g., the surveys in Goulder (1995), Kirchgässner (1998), and Bovenberg (1999). This is, of course, no argument against such a reform which still can make much sense; it is an argument against expectations of some of its proponents which are too high and which – with high probability – will prove to be wrong.

19 See, e.g., Hibbs (1977, 1992) as well as the politico-economic models of Frey and Schneider (1978a, 1978b, 1979) and the survey about political business cycles by Paldam (1997).

pursuing such a policy by left-wing (or green) parties is in many cases not a concern about the situation of the natural environment but about the labour market, even if the expectation is that it will help the environment more than the labour market: Such governments might help the environment 'for the wrong reason'.

On the other hand, as already mentioned above, environmental taxes have a special attraction for left-wing parties which traditionally aim for a higher government (tax) share because these taxes create revenue, which can be used to finance other projects, and the tax resistance against 'green taxes' might be lower than against other taxes.[20] This is important in a situation where the current social security system and its financing is not at all sustainable and – besides structural changes – new sources have to be found to finance it. Again, such governments might help the environment 'for the wrong reason'.

Thus, while these ecological tax reforms might be seen as a step in the right direction, taking into account the motives of the politicians in enforcing such a reform one has to conclude that this new development is far away from indicating a change in the general perception about the relative merits of command and control versus economic instruments of environmental policy and of the political acceptance of the latter. We still have the situation that – in principle – nearly everybody supports the use of incentive orientated economic instruments for ecological reasons, but when it comes to their application there is strong resistance by important political actors. At best, they will be introduced for other (non-environmental) reasons and/or in a way which is not very helpful for the environment. But, on the other hand, it is a step in this direction and one might hope that over time citizens become more familiar with such instruments and their advantages which might – in the long run – increase their acceptance in the electorate.

3.2 Example: An Ecological Tax Reform Suggested in 2003 and Its Failure

In order to strengthen our argument of the small effect and influence of economists using their theory in environmental politics we would like to give a concrete example. For Austria, an ecological tax reform has been suggested in 2003 which, in principal, should have a chance to be implemented but most probably will not due to public choice reasons. The key elements of such an ecological tax reform – having been developed in a study by Schneider and Proidl (2003) – are the following[21]:

1. In order to reduce CO_2-emissions, taxes on non-renewable energy sources are introduced in such a way that there is a positive ecological effect, i.e. a significant reduction of CO_2-emissions should occur.

---

20 For the discussion of this argument see, e.g., Zimmermann (1996) or Schneider (1997, 1998).

21 This study contains first a lot of information about ecological taxation in small open countries which can be compared to Austria. Then in the study a detailed suggestion and model of an ecological tax reform is presented.

2. All revenues from this tax are immediately spent in a revenue neutral way. One part of this additional revenue is used for the subsidisation of renewable energy investments, another part is spent to reduce the burden of taxes and social security payments on labour income, and a third part is used for subsidising middle and lower income households in order to partly compensate for the increased spending on gasoline and other energy sources.
3. This means that there are no additional tax revenues for the minister of finance but every cent of this new revenue is spent in the economy, or redistributed to the households.
4. For planning this ecological tax reform, a long time horizon is considered: The fossil energy tax starts with a value of 0.44 cent/kwh in the year 2004 and would end in 2013 with a value of 1.45 cent/kwh, i.e. a yearly increase of about 0.11 cent/kwh with a final rate of 1.45 cent/kwh in the year 10.
5. It is estimated that in total, i.e. aggregated over the 10 years, additional tax revenues of 31bn EUR would be achieved and the ecological steering effect would be a 10% reduction of fossil energy use. As already argued, the aggregated sum of 31bn EUR would be spent for different purposes: It would be used for subsidising investments for renewable energy sources up to an amount of 6.7bn EUR so that the use of renewable energy sources would increase by 5%. Another 10.9bn EUR would be used to reduce the burden of the direct income tax of low and middle income earners so that they would be almost fully compensated. The final amount (13.4bn EUR) would be dedicated to reduce the tax and social security burden on labour income, from which all labour intensive enterprises will profit most. This would mean that almost all enterprises would make a net-profit because the burden of taxes and social security payments per year on labour income would be reduced by 3.69% per year (over the 10 years) so that the overall production costs will not increase with the exception of only a few energy intensive enterprises.
6. If one undertakes a dynamic simulation with the help of a macro-econometric model estimated for Austria one can demonstrate that if such a tax reform would be implemented an additional increase of 2.3% of the GNP over these 10 years would result and employment would rise by about 0.5%.

Hence, one can clearly demonstrate that with such an ecological tax reform two major political concerns could be avoided. First, every increase of indirect taxation is disadvantageous for low and middle income earners because they are net losers. Thus, without compensation politicians realistically will have no chance to realise it. This has been avoided in the proposal of Schneider and Proidl (2003). According to their type of compensation most low and middle income people would even win and have somewhat more money, only those who have a long way from home to work (if they drive more then 40.000 km per year) could not be fully compensated. Second, industry quite often claims that due to increased energy costs, they will shift production out of the country. This threat can not be put forward because the compensation in reducing tax and social security burden on labour income is by far bigger for most industries so that they will also make a net profit. In addition, the overall economic development is slightly positive. Due to additional investments in renewable energy sources, even a small positive increase of gross national product and of employment is to be expected.

According to this design the ecological tax reform as suggested by Schneider and Proidl (2003) should have chances to be realised as the main reservations are overcome from a politico-economic perspective. However, the latest suggestions of a tax reform by the Austrian government actually intend lower direct and corporate tax rates in a very traditional way without any ecological effect. It seems that the opportunity to implement an ecological tax reform which would be politically attractive will be missed once again. Whether the political benefit of an ecological tax reform has so far not been realised or the political benefit of a traditional tax reform lowering income taxes and corporate taxes can be better sold in the political arena/market has to be left open at this time.

4 Pricing Road Use: Politico-Economic Considerations

With respect to the negative externalities associated with private transportation – either congestion in urban areas or environmental damages more generally – economists have extensively explored the role that economic incentives might play in bringing about a more efficient allocation of road space and natural resources. The idea that road users should be charged their marginal external costs is a widely accepted principle in the economic as well as in the transportation literature.[22]

However, while analysts see road pricing as an attractive policy tool, most attempts to introduce economic incentives of this type in the transport sector have failed. These failures may partly be due to the technical difficulties of introducing the appropriate price incentives but more importantly, politico-economic reasoning suggests that road pricing is rarely adopted because the public does not support these policy measures.[23]

Previous work that studied the political difficulties of using economic incentives to allocate road space and natural resources sought to compensate those who lose when road pricing is used with the help of revenues generated by road pricing programs.[24] However, as is argued by Oberholzer-Gee and Weck-Hannemann (2002), a wider notion of what the public perceives to be the 'cost' of using economic incentives is adequate. Politico-economic reasoning suggests that voters as consumers and/or producers (employers/employees) in the industries affected have to pay the costs and thus will not be enthusiastic about such a policy. In addition,

22 See, e.g., Button and Verhoef (1998).

23 For evidence of these failures see, e.g., Jones (1998). More recently, the introduction of road pricing measures in Germany seems to have failed due to technical difficulties indeed. Austria, in contrast, was successful with implementing a road pricing scheme in 2004, but the measures hardly differentiate as to ecological characteristics and in addition, the revenues are earmarked exclusively for financing road infrastructure.

24 For such an argument see, e.g., Common (1989), Small (1992), or Rietveld and Verhoef (1998).

while economists universally embrace the allocation of resources via markets, the general public often appears to be much more sceptical of pricing instruments. There is ample evidence that pricing is not considered to be a fair allocation mechanism whether in situations to eliminate excess demand or in public good contexts. Moreover, economic incentives have the potential to crowd out intrinsic motivation which implies that pricing measures become less effective and, in addition, there may be negative spillovers to other areas where no (monetary) incentives for environmental protection exist.

Political economists view the policy measures that governments and parliaments adopt as outcomes of exchange processes. This implies that, in practice, voter preferences are not directly translated into politics. Elected officials supply the policies that voters and interest groups demand, and in exchange for regulation, politicians receive votes, money and information. From a political economy perspective, it is useful to think about the negative externalities of private transportation as transfers to specific groups which are allowed to make use of resources without bearing the full opportunity costs. The introduction of road pricing then increases transfers to some groups (for instance, those who primarily consume environmental amenities) and decreases the transfers to others (e.g., low-income drivers). Whether or not it is possible to devise a road pricing program that will find political acceptance not only depends on the changes in welfare brought about by pricing – the approach taken generally in the transportation and the welfare-oriented economic literature – but also on the relative influence of groups in the political game.

Once the influence of groups is taken into account, the set of environmental policy instruments that is actually employed in politics can deviate significantly from the theoretical optimum.[25] As is argued in public choice theory, policy makers favour instruments that weaken the government's budget constraint. In this respect, environmental taxes recommend themselves because they generate additional funding. If road pricing revenues ought to be returned to citizens, lawmakers can still try to channel these funds toward their own constituencies. Road pricing revenues could also be used to compensate those who lose when economic incentives are introduced. Goodwin (1990) and Small (1992) have identified important interest groups and made suggestions how the revenues from road pricing schemes can be used to overcome their political opposition. In such exercises, the analyst should keep in mind that expected welfare changes are a necessary, but not a sufficient condition for political mobilisation to occur. If groups are not already organised – existing carpool users are an example for a group that would mostly benefit from road pricing – it is unlikely that they will exercise decisive influence in any road pricing debate. In contrast, automobile associations, public transport unions and environmental groups can be counted on to exert considerable influence.

Road users are certainly the best organised group whose members are likely to lose when road pricing is introduced. This is an argument to target revenues from road pricing to projects that benefit drivers. There is some empirical evidence that

---

25 Buchanan and Tullock (1975), Hahn (1989) or Schulze and Ursprung (2000).

indeed, taxes can be introduced if they are channelled back to the transportation sector. As Rivlin (1989: 113) states "(T)here is one apparent exception to the tax rule: taxes held in trust funds and earmarked to specific purposes can be raised. There was no perceptible backlash when the gasoline tax was raised (in the United States) in 1983, presumably because the increase was thought necessary to fix the roads." Kimenyi, Lee and Tollison (1990) show for the US in general that, in comparison to general fund financing, earmarking leads to increased tax revenues. Similar arguments apply to the 1993 popular referendum in Switzerland that approved an increase in gasoline taxes. Earmarking the revenues for the purpose of maintaining and improving the road infrastructure apparently convinced some drivers that the increase in taxes was in their best interest.[26]

Previous research comparing the relative effectiveness of compensation mechanisms shows that increases in road investments are by far the most popular measure while in comparison, using road pricing revenue to reduce income taxes is highly unpopular.[27] In other words, these studies suggest that reduced accessibility to roads ought to be compensated with improvements of the road network instead of a reduction in general taxes. In view of the progressivism of many tax systems, these attitudes may reflect a preference not to combine a regressive policy measure such as road pricing with a reduction in general taxes that would also mainly benefit higher-income groups. In addition, this evidence underlines the principle that compensating those who lose is easier if compensation remains in the same 'dimension' as the losses.[28]

Nevertheless, road pricing programs are still politically problematic not only when compensation of losers is deficient but also in another respect. Politicians are inclined to favour policies whose costs are difficult to see and, on the contrary, whose benefits should be highly visible and attributable to their programs. As the negative externalities of private transportation vary geographically and over time, the prices for road usage will have to vary as well to be economically efficient. Charging drivers different amounts at different points in time keeps the costs of using roads highly visible, reminding voters of the policy every time they stop at toll booths or look at their electronically generated charges. Thus, the costs remain highly visible while the benefits of the policy – better environmental quality and reduced congestion – are much less salient, at least in the long run. The benefits are hard to see, for instance, because the counterfactual – how prevalent asthma or how much congestion would be without road pricing – is hard to assess.

In summarising this discussion it can be concluded that road pricing measures as other incentive-based instruments in environmental policy are difficult to implement but have better chances to be realised when their design deviates from the ideal. The question posed in the subtitle of the seminal paper by Hahn (1989: 96) "How the patient followed the doctor's orders" can be answered in the way – here once again – that the actual use of incentive-based instruments in environmental policy departs "from the role which economists have conceived for them".

---

26 See Kirchgässner (1993).

27 See Verhoef, Nijkamp, and Rietveld (1997).

28 For a discussion of this argument see Oberholzer-Gee and Weck-Hannemann (2002).

5 Concluding Remarks

There are many possible reasons why incentive-based instruments as a means to internalise external costs have been rarely applied in environmental policy in the past. Public choice theory suggests that there are good reasons why politicians, voters, bureaucrats and representatives of well organised interest groups are rather reluctant to favour price instruments on a large scale. It is argued that incentive oriented instruments are neither in the interest of the decision makers on the supply side nor they are favoured by the most influential groups of voters on the demand side on the political market.

However, pricing instruments may have a chance to be implemented if they are introduced in such a way that well-organised groups are benefiting most and the costs are spread to less influential and latent interest groups. Earmarking of revenues in this case may be an essential feature to achieve the respective aim on the part of politicians and most powerful interest groups. Beyond that, the opposition to environmental measures – either incentive-based instruments like taxes or tradable permits as well as command-and-control instruments – may be mitigated by accepting exceptions and allowances. If, for instance, taxes are fixed at a relatively low rate and thus avoidance costs in the case of emission standards exceed the tax burden, this solution is in effect favourable for polluters. If likewise exemptions are made for the most polluting sectors, e.g. the energy intensive producing industries in the case of CO_2 taxes, this implies that resistance of those producers who produce most emissions can be weakened. On the other hand, such a procedure aiming at increasing the political chances to implement such measures at the same time reduces the environmental impact and economic efficiency of such a policy significantly.

Altogether, it has to be concluded that either there is still limited support of the use of incentive-based instruments in environmental policy or the application of such instruments in many respects deviates from the ideal lowering their economic and ecological impact. Public choice theory as a positive science contributes to explain these facts as was tried to elaborate in this paper. On the other hand, public choice theory as a normative approach and, more specifically, constitutional economics gives hand to try to overcome this situation. One way is to think about adequate institutional conditions contributing to improve the chance that incentive-based instruments as the most efficient means in environmental policy are implemented in a right way in the political decision making process. Referring to a process-oriented approach, it may be argued that the political process itself has to ensure that all relevant arguments have a chance to be considered in the discussion resulting in efficiency to be reached endogenously, i.e. via the process. All the pros and cons have to enter in the political process without distortion. This may be better guaranteed if voters have a direct say in political matters and can act as agenda setters as is the case with institutions of direct democracy and the right of initiative. In this case it is expected that politicians are forced to be more responsive to voters' interests than in a system of representative democracy where principal-agent problems are more pronounced. Moreover, when the principles of fiscal equivalence and institutional congruence are realised spillovers in external effects may be overcome and all relevant benefits and costs are more adequately taken into consideration in the political decision making process.

Finally, the caveat that the interests of future generations are neglected remains. This argument is especially relevant in the discussion about sustainable development and environmental policy. However, there is no way out of this dilemma except to rely on the present generation and living individuals to pay regard to these interests though not in a comprehensive way but least partially. This is another argument besides political failure that political decisions deviate from the economic ideal considering the welfare of the general public, including present and future generations.

References

Bach, S., M. Kohlhaas, B. Meier, B. Praetorius, and H. Welsch (2001), *Auswirkungen und Perspektiven einer ökologischen Steuerreform in Deutschland: Eine modellgestützte Analyse*, mimeo, University of Osnabrück.

Binswanger, H.C., H. Frisch, and H.G. Nutzinger et al. (1983), *Arbeit ohne Umweltzerstörung*, 2nd edition, Frankfurt.

Bovenberg, A.L. (1999), Green Tax Reforms and the Double Dividend, *International Tax and Public Finance* 6, 421-443.

Bovenberg, A.L. and R.A. de Mooij (1994), Environmental Levies and Distortionary Taxation, *American Economic Review* 84, 1085-1089.

Buchanan, J.M. and G. Tullock (1975), Polluters' Profits and Political Response: Direct Controls Versus Taxes, *American Economic Review* 65, 139-147.

Button, K.J. and E.T. Verhoef (1998) (Eds.), *Road Pricing, Traffic Congestion and the Environment: Issues of Efficiency and Social Feasibility*, Cheltenham.

Common, M.S. (1989), The Choice of Pollution Control Instruments: Why Is So Little Notice Taken of Economist's Recommendations? *Environment and Planning* A21, 1297-1314.

Congleton, R.D. (1995), *Return to Rio: On the Political Economy of Environmental Treaties*, Universität Konstanz, Sonderforschungsbereich "Internationalisierung der Wirtschaft", Diskussionsbeitrag Nr. 280, Serie II.

Frey, B.S. (1992), *Umweltökonomie*, 3rd edition, Göttingen.

Frey, B.S. and F. Schneider (1979), An Econometric Model with an Endogenous Government Sector, *Public Choice* 34, 29-43.

Frey, B.S. and F. Schneider (1978a), An Empirical Study of Politico-Economic Interaction in the United States, *Review of Economics and Statistics* 60, 174-183.

Frey, B.S. and F. Schneider (1978b), A Politico-Economic Model of the United Kingdom, *Economic Journal* 88, 243-253.

Gawel, E. (1995), Bürokratie, Theorie und Umweltverwaltung: Ökonomische Einsichten in verwaltungsrechtliches Handeln im Umweltschutz, *Zeitschrift für Angewandte Umweltforschung* 8, 79-89.

Gawel, E. (1994a), *Zur politischen Ökonomie von Umweltabgaben*, Tübingen.

Gawel, E. (1994b), Umweltpolitik zwischen Verrechtlichung und Ökonomisierung, *ORDO* 45, 63-103.

Goodwin, P.B. (1990), How to Make Road Pricing Popular, *Economic Affairs* 10, 6-7.

Goulder, L.H. (1995), Environmental Taxation and the Double Dividend: A Reader's Guide, *International Tax and Public Finance* 2, 157-183.

Hahn, R.W. (1989), Economic Prescriptions for Environmental Problems: How the Patient Followed the Doctor's Orders, *Journal of Economic Perspectives* 3, 95-114.

Helbig, J. and J. Volkert (1999), *Freiwillige Standards im Umweltschutz*, Heidelberg.

Hibbs, D.A. (1992), Partisan Theory After Fifteen Years, European *Journal of Political Economy* 8, 361-373.

Hibbs, D.A. (1977), Political Parties and Macroeconomic Policy, *American Political Science Review* 71, 1467-1487.

Holzinger, K. (1987), *Umweltpolitische Instrumente aus der Sicht der Bürokratie: Versuch einer Anwendung der ökonomischen Theorie der Bürokratie*, München.

Horbach, J. (1992), *Neue politische Ökonomie und Umweltpolitik*, Frankfurt.

Huxham, M. and D. Sumner (1999), Emotion, Science and Rationality: The Case of the Brent Spar, *Environmental Values* 8, 349-368.

IMAS (1996), *Umfrageberichte von IMAS-International*, Linz.

IMAS (1995), *Umfrageberichte von IMAS-International*, Linz.

Jones, P.M. (1998), Urban Road Pricing: Public Acceptability and Barriers to Implementation, in: Button, K.J. and E.T. Verhoef (Eds.), *Road Pricing, Traffic Congestion and the Environment: Issues of Efficiency and Social Feasibility*, Cheltenham, 263-284.

Joskow, P.L., R. Schmalensee, and E.M. Bailey (1998), The Market for Sulphur Dioxide Emissions, *American Economic Review* 88, 669-685.

Joskow, P.L. and R. Schmalensee (1998), The Political Economy of Market-Based Environmental Policy: The U.S. Acid Rain Program, *Journal of Law and Economics* 41, 37-84.

Kimenyi, M.S., D.R. Lee, and R.D. Tollison (1990), Efficient Lobbying and Earmarked Taxes, *Public Finance Quarterly* 18, 104-113.

Kirchgässner, G. (2000), Die Bedeutung moralischen Handelns für die Umweltpolitik, *GAiA* 9, 41-49.

Kirchgässner, G. (1999), Wirtschaftliche Auswirkungen von Energiesteuern auf kleine offene Volkswirtschaften: Theoretische Überlegungen und Simulationsergebnisse, in: Schneider, F. (Ed.), *Internationale Strategien und Erfahrungen zur Neuorientierung der EU-Energiewirtschaft*, Linz, 153-181.

Kirchgässner, G. (1998), Ökologische Steuerreform: Utopie oder realistische Alternative, in: Krause-Junk, G. (Ed.), *Steuersysteme der Zukunft*, Berlin, 279-319.

Kirchgässner, G., U. Müller, and M.R. Savioz (1998), Ecological Tax Reform and Involuntary Unemployment: Simulation Results for Switzerland, *Schweizerische Zeitschrift für Volkswirtschaft und Statistik* 134, 329-353.

Kirchgässner, G. (1993), Akzeptieren die Bürger Steuererhöhungen? Einige Bemerkungen im Zusammenhang mit der Erhöhung des Treibstoffzolls, *Aussenwirtschaft* 48, 153-174.

Maier-Rigaud, G. (1996), Für eine ökologische Wirtschaftsordnung, *Jahrbuch für Ökologie*, 71-79.

Niskanen, W.A. (1971), *Bureaucracy and Representative Government*, Chicago.

Niskanen, W.A. (1968), The Peculiar Economics of Bureaucracy, *American Economic Review, Papers and Proceedings* 58 (2), 293-305.

Oberholzer-Gee, F. and H. Weck-Hannemann (2002), Pricing Road Use: Politico-Economic and Fairness Considerations, Transportation Research Part D, *Transport and Environment* 7, 357-371.

OECD (1997), *Environmental Policies and Employment*, Paris.

Ott, H.E. and W. Sachs (2000), *Ethical Aspects of Emissions Trading*, Wuppertal Institute for Climate, Environment and Energy, Paper No. 110, Wuppertal.

Paldam, M. (1997), Political Business Cycles, in: Mueller, D.C. (Ed.), *Perspectives on Public Choice: A Handbook*, Cambridge (UK), 342-370.

Pearce, D.W. (1991), The Role of Carbon Taxes in Adjusting to Global Warming, *Economic Journal* 101, 938-948.

Rietveld, P. and E.T. Verhoef (1998), Social Feasibility of Policies to Reduce Externalities in Transport, in: Button, K.J. and E.T. Verhoef (Eds.), *Road Pricing, Traffic Congestion and the Environment: Issues of Efficiency and Social Feasibility*, Cheltenham, 285-308.

Rivlin, A.M. (1989), The Continuing Search for a Popular Tax, *American Economic Review* 79 (2), 113-117.

Schneider, F. and H.M. Proidl (2003), *Ökonomische Aspekte für eine österreichische ökologische Energiebesteuerung*, Energieinstitut an der Johannes Kepler Universität Linz, Linz.

Schneider, F. and G. Kirchgässner (2003), On the Political Economy of Environmental Policy, *Public Choice* 115, 369-396.

Schneider, F. and J. Volkert (1999), No Chance for Incentive-Orientated Environmental Policies in Representative Democracies? A Public Choice Analysis, *Ecological Economics* 31, 123-138.

Schneider, F. (1998), Induzieren ökologische Steuerreformen einen Lenkungseffekt oder nur volle Staatskassen?, *IAW-Mitteilungen* 26.

Schneider, F. (1997), Einige Bemerkungen zu den Umsetzungsproblemen ökologisch-orientierter Wirtschaftspolitik aus der Sicht der Neuen Politischen Ökonomie, in: Schmid, H. and T. Slembeck (Eds.), *Finanz- und Wirtschaftspolitik in Theorie und Praxis*, Bern, 467-486.

Scholz, C.M. (2000), *Environmental Tax Reforms and the Double Dividend: A Theoretical and Empirical Analysis for Germany*, Tübingen.

Schulze, G. and H.W. Ursprung (2000), Economic Integration and Environmental Policy: A Survey of the Politico-Economic Literature, in: Vosgerau, H.-J. (Ed.), *Institutional Arrangements for Global Economic Integration*, London, 161-186.

Small, K.A. (1992), Using the Revenues from Congestion Pricing, *Transportation* 19, 359-381.

Svendsen, G.T. (1999), U.S. Interest Groups Prefer Emission Trading: A New Perspective, *Public Choice* 101, 109-128.

Verhoef, E.T., P. Nijkamp, and P. Rietveld (1997), The Social Feasibility of Road Pricing: A Case Study for the Randstad Area, *Journal of Transport Economics and Policy* 31 (3), 255-276.

Zimmermann, K.W. (1996), Zur politischen Ökonomie von Ökosteuern, *ORDO* 47, 169-194.

On the Political Economy of Economic Policy Advice – With Applications of Environmental Policy

Gebhard Kirchgässner

University of St. Gallen, Swiss Institute for International Economics and Applied Economic Research, *CES*ifo, and Leopoldina, SIAW-HSG, Bodanstrasse 8, 9000 St. Gallen, Switzerland, gebhard.kirchgaessner@unisg.ch

Keywords. *Economic Policy Advice, Environmental Policy*

JEL. *H89; Q48*

Abstract. It is a hardly disputable fact that one can get scientific reports in favour of (and against) nearly every policy a government wants to perform. One of the reasons for this is that economic theory is in many relevant cases so weak that it is possible for different economists to defend pretty contrary positions with the claim of scientific truth. This makes empirical research necessary. However, using the ecological tax reform as an example, it is shown that researchers can often easily obtain their 'desired' empirical results without (obvious) violations of the rules of scientific work. To detect such manipulations, a critical discussion of theoretical approaches and empirical results is necessary. Finally, we discuss how it is possible that despite all these problems the process of policy advice may lead to something like 'objectivity', why even economists who are not corrupt in most cases promote the objectives of their clients, and why economic policy advice is demanded at all.

1 Introduction

Let me start with three examples of scientific policy advice:

- In 1993, the Swiss government planned to introduce an energy and/or CO_2-tax. This was based on a study by Prognos (1993) which indicated that considerable employment gains could be realised with an appropriate repayment to the taxpayers. On behalf of the Society for the Promotion of the Swiss Economy, Erdmann (1997) wrote a report which warned against large employment losses which might result from such an 'ecological tax reform'. A study, financed by the Swiss National Science Foundation, came to the conclusion that small employment gains might be realised.[1]

- The state of Berlin is – more or less – bankrupt. The Senate (state government) decided that the budget of the universities has to be cut by about 200 bn EUR. It asked Roland Berger, the most famous German consulting firm, for a report, and – without visiting the universities – they also came to the conclusion that 200 bn EUR could be saved and showed how this might be achieved.[2]
- In Switzerland, 19 cantons have public monopolies on fire and natural (elementary) damage insurance, while private insurance companies are working in the other cantons. The private insurers demand that (as in Germany) the public monopolies should be abolished. To defend their position, the public monopolies asked Thomas von Ungern-Sternberg, professor of economics at the University of Lausanne, for a report. He showed that the public monopolies are cheaper (1994, 1995). Then, the private insurers asked Bernd Schips, professor of economics at the Swiss Federal Institute of Technology in Zürich, for an opposing report. He concluded that the private insurers are cheaper (1995). In 1998, the Swiss Supreme Court 'decided' that von Ungern-Sternberg is right: the public monopolies are cheaper.[3]

These three examples suggest that when asking for a report you can get whatever you want. This might sound cynical, but many other examples could be added which impart the same impression. And especially the third example is provoking. It is obvious that it is difficult to evaluate the possible effects of tax reform. Different theoretical assumptions might lead to quite different results. And that a commercial consulting firm is behaving in the way Roland Berger did is in line with the opinions many people share today. But that two professors of economics come to opposing answers on the relatively simple question whether the cantonal monopolies or the private insurers are cheaper creates severe doubts on the validity of such reports in particular and – quite generally – on the purpose of economic policy advice.

They also clearly contradict the traditional approach to the theory of economic policy advice as developed, e.g., by Tinbergen (1956), which – in an admittedly somewhat simplifying matter – may be characterised in the following way: Politicians, elected in a democratic process, try to maximise social welfare; they behave like benevolent dictators. They lack, however, knowledge, in two respects. First, they need information about the preferences of the people. Second and more important, they lack information about their political possibilities: the instruments

---

1 See Meyer zu Himmern and Kirchgässner (1995) or Kirchgässner, Müller, and Savioz (1998).

2 See R. Köhler, Hochschulen: Finanzsenator lässt uns ausspionieren, Berliner Morgenpost 12/03/2003 (http://morgenpost.berlin1.de/archiv2003/030312/berlin/story590318.html (25/05/04)), J. Kaube, Ansichtsrat: Roland Bergers Sparvorschläge für die Berliner Universitäten, Frankfurter Allgemeine Zeitung 15/03/2003, (http://www.hu-berlin.de/presse/zeitung/archiv/02_03/num_6/seite1.shtml (25/05/04)).

3 Bundesgerichtsentscheid 124 I 25, Lausanne, 27/02/1998.

which are available and especially the (expected) economic outcomes if the instruments are used in a specific way. Policy advisors, on the other hand, also behave like benevolent dictators. They have the duty to provide the politicians with this information. Some perform opinion polls to find out the preferences of the population. Others, economic policy advisors, have to provide the information about the (economic policy) instruments and their effects on the economy. In many situations, such advice can be provided solely based on economic theory. In other situations, empirical research is needed to find out the 'correct' policy measures. Economic research institutes, be they publicly financed as the major institutes in Germany or privately as those in the United States, have the objective to perform such empirical research in an objective and unbiased manner.

This traditional approach has several severe shortcomings. First of all, the assumption of the government as a benevolent dictator has to be questioned. Though it is still often used in theoretical economic models,[4] over the last fifty years, public choice theory has effectively destroyed the belief in this assumption. First of all, Arrow (1951) has shown that it is highly problematic to talk about something like 'social welfare' with respect to a democratic system. For a democracy, the social welfare function which (implicitly or explicitly) is assumed to exist whenever this term is used in discussions about public policy, does not exist in general. Moreover, following Schumpeter (1942), Downs (1957) and Buchanan and Tullock (1962), public choice has re-invented the notion that there is not only market failure but also government failure. The latter results not so much from informational problems but mainly from the fact that politicians – like all other individuals too – mainly strive for their own utility and much less for social welfare, whatever this might be. Thus, public choice considers politicians like all other individuals as self-interested, rationally acting utility maximisers.

Taking this into consideration, the task of economic policy advice becomes much more difficult. To transmit information to the politicians on what is to be done in a specific situation to reach a certain objective is not the only problem the policy advisor has to solve. In addition, the information has to be presented in such a way as to create incentives for the politicians to actually use this information. Thus, the process of transforming scientific advice into economic policy has to be taken into consideration as well.[5]

Though papers about economic policy advice in the public choice tradition fully recognise this point, they fall (as all others, too) into a second fallacy: Economists are – like probably all other people – rather uncritical towards themselves, and whenever they give policy advice, they see themselves as benevolent dictators. They do not only often believe that they have lots of information, much more than they actually do, but they also consider themselves as being objective and standing above the daily political discussions and political ideologies. The latter they derive

---

4 Today, this still holds for a large part of modern public finance like, e.g., the theory of optimal taxation. See for this the dispute between Richter and Wiegard (1993, 1994) on the one side and Blankart (1994) on the other side.

5 See for this, e.g., Meier and Mettler (1986).

from their authority as scientific economists.[6] However, economists are in the same way self-interested, rationally acting individuals like all other human beings, too. This also holds when they give policy advice. The money they earn, e.g., if they produce reports that are used by their clients to strive for their objectives is not necessarily a sign of corruption. However, it can hardly be denied that scientists are often paid for producing exactly the statements their clients want to hear, a fact they are aware of and put up with.[7] It does not help to argue – often mainly for the pacification of their own conscience – that this money is spent on a good purpose (according to their opinion). In addition, they often do not want to be reminded later on what they have written in earlier reports.[8]

The general public has a more realistic picture of economists as policy advisors than they have themselves. The same economic agents, who in modern economic theory are usually assumed to have rational expectations, which implies that their expectations are on average correct, accuse economists who are policy advisors to be biased and sometimes even to be corrupt. They certainly have a point and are not totally wrong. As the examples above show, today it is possible to find a professor of economics willing to write a scientific report in support of nearly any political position.[9]

When asked, economists who are engaged in political debates nearly always claim that their statements are purely scientific and that their clients did not influence their results at all. This may be true in many cases. However, it would be just the opposite of the usual economic procedure if we strongly believed in such affirmations. Economists usually take into account the behaviour of economic agents and not their verbal statements, and they try to draw conclusions about the preferences of the individuals from their *actual* behaviour.[10] The reason for this is that talk is in many cases cheap, but acting is costly. Thus, in general, individuals are more honest when acting than when talking. This holds for economists as for all other human beings, too. If we judge by behaviour and not by verbal statements, the impression of biasedness can, however, not be put aside easily.

The third problem connected with the traditional economic approach to policy advice is that it almost exclusively focuses on the advice to the government. This

6 See, e.g., Hesse (1994: 18).

7 It often does not need very much to cause economists (and other scientists) to act in the interest even of organisations which have nothing to do with economics as a science at all. E.g., conferences organised as well as books edited by and with contributions of prominent economists have been financed by the 'Professors World Peace Association', an organisation financed by the Mun-Church, which has as its main purpose improving the public image of this organisation. (See for this also Blankart, 1987: 669).

8 In accordance with the traditional innocence assumption which economists apply on themselves there are only very few theoretical papers of the advisory process that allow for biased experts. Such an exception is, e.g., Krishna and Morgan (2001).

9 See, e.g., further examples in Kirchgässner (1996).

10 The basic paper (with respect to the theory of consumer behaviour) is Samuelson (1948).

might, however, be only a minor part of the actual advice. Much of the advice is either directly given to interest groups, or to the parliament or the government on behalf of interest groups. The latter holds, e.g., whenever the interest groups are able to nominate experts for political hearings. Moreover, especially but not exclusively in a direct democracy, a considerable part of the advice is also directed to the general public, if economists, e.g., write columns in newspapers. In many cases economists are free to write what and about which subject they want, the only problem being whether it will be published or not, but it is often also the case that economists are asked by the editors of a newspaper to write about a certain subject. In a direct democracy this can be, e.g., before a referendum, and at least sometimes the advisors are asked to write in support of or against a certain proposal which is at stake.

If all three problems are to be taken up seriously, the analysis of the advisory process has (at least) to be amended by stating (and answering) several new questions. While it is still possible to ask how far the patient followed the doctor's order, as, e.g., Hahn (1989) did with respect to environmental policy, it also has to be asked why the doctor made his prescriptions. The recourse to scientific knowledge, be it a theoretical or empirical one, is not sufficient, because economic theory rarely gives us clear cut answers on policy questions, and empirical results are often contradicting. Moreover, they might be manipulated quite easily. Thus, not only the question what happened after a specific advice has been given is interesting, but also the question: What happened before it was given? Thus, we also have to analyse the process of economic advising itself, and – as economists – we should employ the economic approach of behaviour.

In doing so, we have to dissociate from the picture of the ideal scientist which is in most of our minds and apply the economic model of behaviour on ourselves as well. That is, we must assume that economists are self-interested rationally acting utility maximisers, too. Economic theory supposes that this is a useful assumption for analysing human behaviour. There is no reason to except economists from this assumption.[11] This does not only imply that their information is limited as well, but also (and more importantly) that strong monetary incentives can cause economists to defend (nearly) any, even arbitrary political position.

In the following, some steps in this direction are taken. In Section 2 it is shown that economic theory is in many relevant cases so weak that it is possible for different economists to defend pretty contrary positions with the claim of scientific truth. This makes empirical research necessary. However, using the ecological tax reform as an example, it is shown in Section 3 that researchers can often obtain their 'desired' empirical result by manipulating the empirical results without (ob-

11 There is empirical evidence that economists behave even more in accordance with this model than the average individual, especially, that economists are stronger self-interested and less altruistic than others. Experiments with the ultimatum game show, e.g., that students of economics show much stronger free rider behaviour (as predicted by economic theory) than other students. See for this Carter and Irons (1991). Frey and Meier (2003) explain this by a selection effect.

vious) violations of the rules of scientific work. To detect such manipulations, a critical discussion of theoretical approaches and empirical results is necessary. Thus, in Section 4, we discuss how it is possible that despite all these problems the process of policy advice may lead to something like 'objectivity' and why even economists who are not corrupt promote in most cases the objectives of their clients.

2 On the Power of Statements of Economic Theory

Whenever economists give an advice how to solve current economic problems, they typically give answers which imply changes in relative prices. To reduce unemployment it is demanded, e.g., that trade unions make moderate wage claims and that taxes and charges on labour are reduced in order to reduce the price of and increase the demand for labour.[12] And to reduce air and water pollution ecological taxes and/or tradable permits are the usual prescription in order to impose a positive price on environmental media.

There are two basic assumptions behind such proposals:

1. *Stability:* The economic system is stable in the following sense: small changes of policy instruments lead only to small changes of the economic objectives.
2. *Substitution:* Increases (reductions) of the (relative) price of a good lead to reductions (increases) in the (relative) demand for this good and increases (reductions) in the demand for other goods: The good which is now (relatively) more expensive will be (partially) substituted by goods which are now (relatively) cheaper.

Whether the economic system is stable in this sense is quite independent of the question whether this system tends to reach full employment or not. Equilibria with (involuntary) unemployment can be stable in this sense as well. The assumption of stability stated above is much weaker, it only excludes chaotic behaviour of the economic system. If we had to take into account chaotic behaviour, economic policy would be a gamble: Small changes of government expenditure or even an infinitesimally small change of a single tax rate could lead to a massive recession, but also to a strong economic upswing.[13]

The assumption of substitutability implies that the (aggregate) demand functions for individual goods have a negative slope: An increase (reduction) of the price leads to a reduction (increase) of the quantity demanded. This assumption is so fundamental for economic theorising that von Weizsäcker speaks of the "confidence in the working of the substitution principle" as the basic common conviction of economists (1976: 69, own translation).

---

12 See, e.g., Sachverständigenrat (2003: 361ff.).

13 For the relevance of chaos theory for economics see, e.g., Baumol and Benhabib (1989).

Is this basic common conviction covered by economic theory? This question may sound ridiculous. One should assume that economists who give policy advice take into account the relevant results of economic theory. Until about thirty years ago, it was possible to assume (with more or less bad conscience) that these assumptions are without problems. Since then, however, it has been shown that these assumptions are not necessarily covered by economic theory. Thus, the question whether it is possible to give economic policy advice based on economic theory is no longer trivial. Why this is the case is first explained in general and then illuminated with two examples.

Let us first ask whether aggregate demand functions have a negative slope. Somewhat more precisely the question is whether we get aggregate demand functions for individual goods with a negative slope if all economic agents behave 'rationally' in the sense of the economic model of behaviour. A general answer to this question cannot be derived from partial analyses but, if the feedback of the actions of individual actors is to be taken into account, by the theory of general equilibrium. This was the question Sonnenschein (1972, 1973) asked in the early seventies. He has shown that employing the usual assumptions about the individual preferences in an exchange economy the demand function for an individual good can (locally) have any slope.[14] To exclude this possibility rather restrictive assumptions about individual preferences are necessary. This also holds if one tries, as Hildenbrand (1983) did, to impose restrictions on the possible distributions of preferences (and initial endowments).

With respect to the assumption of stability it has been shown that such economies can have multiple equilibria. If such multiple equilibria exist they cannot be globally stable, and some equilibria are not even locally stable: Small deviations from one equilibrium can lead to a totally different new equilibrium.[15] This implies, however, that the two basic assumptions about the structure of the economic system which are typically employed whenever policy advice is given are not covered by general equilibrium theory.

Thus, the attempt to derive univocal results about the basic structure of exchange economies which extend the existence and optimality conditions of equilibria but are only based on the general primitives of economic analysis has failed. If one takes into account these 'non-results', then it is no surprise that it is possible to derive nearly any result by employing the corresponding assumptions. This is shown by the following examples:

1. Since the seminal work of Pigou (1920) it is well known among economists that it is possible to internalise external effects using (Pigou-)taxes. Today, the most important and threatening external effects relate to the situation of our natural environment. As mentioned above, for a pretty long time economists have requested the introduction of ecological taxes. This demand is based on the idea

14 See for this Ingrao and Israel (1987: 315ff.) as well as Balasko (1988: 120f.). – Further work in this area and generalisations of the results of Sonnenschein are given by Mantel (1974), Debreu (1974), and Mas-Colell (1977).

15 See for this Ingrao and Israel (1987: 329ff.).

that the imposition of a positive price for the private usage of nature would reduce pollution and, therefore, improve the situation of the natural environment. However, Braulke and Endres (1985) have shown that this is not necessarily the case. The introduction of ecological taxes is logically consistent with an extension of pollution. Thus, the theoretical basis for the introduction of such taxes seems to disappear.
2. To preserve the stocks of non-renewable natural resources an extension of recycling activities is generally requested. Jäger (1976), however, has shown that, because of declining prices, extended recycling might even lead to an increased exploitation of natural resources.

These examples show that despite the factual consensus between most economists, economic theory is unable to provide a robust theoretical foundation for policy advice.[16] Thus, economic theory seems to be at best of limited help for economic policy. This even holds for microeconomics, where there is a large consensus among economists: The validity of the dominating theory is hardly disputed. How much less help can we expect from macroeconomics where the basic consensus which lasted up to the beginning of the seventies has long ago broken apart?[17]

But even if it is assumed that stability is given and the substitution principle holds, we are still far from an ideal situation. Many economic policy measures have income and substitution effects which go in opposite directions. The overall effect is theoretically open. In such a situation economists – following the statement of von Weizsäcker (1976) – usually argue for the dominance of the substitution effect. There are, e.g., two effects to be considered with respect to the impact of wage increases on unemployment in Europe today. One of the reasons for low employment might be the weakness of domestic demand.[18] The income effect of a wage increase strengthens domestic demand which leads – ceteris paribus – to an increase of employment. On the other hand, a wage increase raises labour costs, which leads to a (partial) substitution of labour by other production inputs. At the same time, the costs of domestic compared to foreign production increase, which also leads to a substitution process. These two processes cause a reduction of demand for labour and, therefore, also a reduction in employment. Thus, the overall effect of a wage increase on employment is theoretically open. If one believes in the disposable income argument of wages usually employed by trade unions, the income effect dominates, employment increases and unemployment is reduced. Most economists, however, believe (as the employer organisations do) that the substitution effect dominates: A wage increase raises – ceteris paribus – unemployment.

Thus, whenever the income and the substitution effects go in opposite directions it is possible that different economists make opposite statements without violating the rules of the scientific game. Because it is theoretically open which effect domi-

16 This is claimed, e.g., by Friedman (1985: 3).

17 The situation of Macroeconomics is described, e.g., by Mankiw (1990).

18 See for this, e.g., OECD (1997: 20ff.).

nates, we need empirical research. But how much can we rely on the empirical results which are presented, based on simulations with different models which have been validated with different methods, like econometric models or computable general equilibrium models?

3 On the Use of Empirical Methods in Economic Policy Advice: The Ecological Tax Reform as an Example

There is hardly any measure in environmental policy which has been more debated in recent years than the 'ecological tax reform'. This holds for the popular but for the scientific debate as well. The main question was and is: Does a 'double dividend' exist, i.e. can such a reform improve the situation of our natural environment and in this way provide a 'green dividend', and, by using the revenue to cut distortionary labour taxes, at the same time improve the economic situation of a country, especially increase employment (or reduce unemployment, respectively), which might be the 'blue dividend'. The reason why this was expected is very simple: In both cases we come closer to the conditions for Pareto-optimality. Using this consideration, an ecological tax reform, i.e. introducing environmental taxes and cutting labour taxes while keeping government revenue constant, has long been demanded, already at the beginning of the eighties by Binswanger, Frisch, Nutzinger et al. (1983), and in the nineties most forcefully by Pearce (1991).

Starting with the seminal paper of Bovenberg and de Mooij (1994a), a second round of the double dividend debate has started. This round, which is dominated by the work of Bovenberg together with several co-authors,[19] destroyed some of our earlier beliefs. Using optimal taxation theory and general equilibrium models, the main message of this work is that it is more likely that environmental taxation reduces employment and especially economic welfare, if narrowly defined, i.e. if ecological effects are not taken into account. Moreover, in most cases where economic efficiency gains can be reached, there are other tax instruments which lead to even larger economic efficiency gains. Thus, an ecological tax reform might be appropriate from an ecological point of view, but one should be very cautious to expect (large) employment gains from such a reform.

The basic theoretical problem is the one mentioned above, that income and substitution effects work in opposing ways. A (partial) switch from a labour to an energy tax makes labour cheaper and energy more expensive. Thus, the substitution effect leads to an increase in the demand for labour. On the other side, the shrinking of the tax base increases the dead-weight loss of taxation and – by this way – leads to a negative income effect, which reduces the demand for labour. The ques-

---

19 See, e.g., Bovenberg and de Mooij (1994a, 1994b) and Bovenberg and van der Ploeg (1994, 1996). Overviews of this discussion are given in Kirchgässner (1998), Bovenberg (1999), Bovenberg and Goulder (2002) as well as Schöb (2003). For a discussion highlighting the employment effects see also Bovenberg (1995).

tion is which effect outweighs the other one. As mentioned above, economists normally tend to believe that the substitution effect is stronger. In most of the models of L.A. Bovenberg, however, the income effect dominates. Thus, the ecological tax reform might lead to an improvement of the situation of the natural environment, but the economic situation will – under these assumptions – deteriorate.

A major problem with many of these models is that they assume full employment which implies that they only know voluntary unemployment. Besides the fact that outside the economists' profession hardly anybody believes that such an assumption makes sense, especially in the European situation of mass unemployment, this assumption has the drawback that hardly anything can be said about the development of unemployment, at best about the development of employment. Moreover, the policy proposals in favour of an ecological tax reform are based on the conviction that current unemployment is mainly involuntary. Models, which do not take this into account are hardly able to answer the relevant policy questions. But it is tricky to model involuntary unemployment in an equilibrium setting, and models in which this is tried often do not lead to totally different results.

However, there are also theoretical models which predict a positive impact on employment by such a reform.[20] Thus, it is finally an empirical question what the effects of such a reform are. What we need is a simulation model which is based on as much empirical evidence as available. There are two main lines to answer such questions which have been followed in the last three decades. On the one hand, econometric models have been used for such simulations which are estimated using time series of economic variables. On the other hand, computable general equilibrium models have been developed. They usually use data of one year for calibrating the model. The assumption behind this is that the economy was in an equilibrium situation in that year.

Both concepts have been used to evaluate the effects of ecological tax reforms. As mentioned above, in Switzerland, the government started this discussion in the nineties with a proposal to introduce an energy and/or CO_2-tax, based on a report by Prognos (1993) on behalf of the Swiss Federal Department of Home Affairs. This report used econometric estimates and predicted large employment gains. G. Erdmann (1997), without using any model, warned about possible large employment losses. The studies supported by a programme of the Swiss National Science Foundation used computable general equilibrium models and came to the conclusion that small but positive employment gains were to be expected.

In Germany, the situation was quite similar. The largest positive employment effects have been demonstrated in a study produced by the German Institute for Economic Research (1994) which was financed by Greenpeace. They assumed an annual increase of real mineral oil prices by seven percent, and predicted that this would cause between 300,000 and 700,000 additional employed people, despite the fact that economic growth is reduced by about 0.2% per year. Similar results are produced by Meyer and Ewerhart (1996).[21] Both results are based on demand

20 See, e.g. Koskela and Schöb (1999) or Koskela, Schöb, and Sinn (2001).

21 See also Meyer (2000) and the references given there.

oriented econometric models. On the other hand, the earliest computable general equilibrium models for Germany by Conrad and Schröder (1991, 1993) or Welsch and Hoster (1995) predicted no increase or even a reduction of employment as a result of such a reform.

The basic theoretical difference between the econometric models and the computable general equilibrium models for the Federal Republic of Germany is that the former are more demand side and the latter more supply side driven. Moreover, the former generally assume that there is involuntary unemployment while most of the latter (in the neo-classical style) assume full employment. While this corresponds in some respect with the traditions in which these models have been developed, these are not necessary properties of such models; it is possible to employ both assumptions in both kinds of models. Nevertheless, as can be shown with two examples, different labour market assumptions can make a lot of difference for the generated result.

The first example are simulations for Switzerland which are based on a computable general equilibrium model presented in Kirchgässner, Müller, and Savioz (1998). The model was calibrated for the year 1996 where the unemployment rate was about five percent. Under the assumptions of (i) involuntary unemployment and (ii) that the new tax revenue is used to reduce contributions for the old age pension system, the model predicts that the introduction of a CO_2-tax of CHF 36,- per ton would reduce the unemployment rate (in the long run) from five to four percent, which corresponds to about 30,000 people additionally employed.

A basic assumption employed in this simulation is that nominal wages remain constant; workers have to pay higher energy prices, but they are (at least partially) compensated by lower social security contributions. Thus, at least the real gross wage rate is reduced. However, trade unions do not necessarily have to accept this. They might try to get a compensation for the price increase by a corresponding increase in gross wages. Whether they succeed or not depends on the resistance of the employers. To show the effects of such policies, we present simulations with no adjustment of gross wages, with full adjustment and with a partial adjustment of 50%.

Table 1. Results of trade union strategies (Switzerland)

Trade union strategy	Reduction of CO_2-emissions (%)	Change of GDP (%)	Unemployment rate (%)
Constant nominal wage	- 8.5	+ 0.5	4.0
Partial adjustment of the real wage	- 8.6	+ 0.2	4.6
Constant real wage	- 8.7	- 0.2	5.3

The results of the CO_2-emission and of GDP are deviations from the benchmark.

Table 1 shows the simulation results.[22] The trade union strategy has hardly any effect on the CO_2-emission. Insofar, the ecological objective is reached quite independently of their strategy. On the other hand, it has a considerable impact on the general economic development, and, therefore, also on employment. If the real wage remains constant, GDP is somewhat reduced and unemployment slightly increased. Thus, the economic objective of this policy is missed. If there is only a partial adjustment, unemployment is slightly reduced and GDP slightly increased. Only in the case of no adjustment do we get a considerable reduction of unemployment.

Similar simulations have been performed for the Federal Republic of Germany by the Centre for European Economic Research in Mannheim.[23] Also employing a computable general equilibrium model, they asked for the effects of the first step of the German ecological tax reform which took place in 1999. In this step (as in later steps) energy prices have been increased and social security contributions reduced.[24] For the trade unions they assumed three different strategies, that the reduction of the employees' social security contributions are totally taken into account in the wage negotiations between employer organisations and trade unions, that they are not taken into account at all, and that there is partial adjustment.

Table 2 shows the results. Qualitatively, they are similar to the Swiss results. If the reduction of the social security contributions is fully taken into account (no adjustment), GDP and employment increase at least slightly. If they are not taken into account at all (full adjustment), GDP and employment are slightly reduced. If there is only partial adjustment, hardly anything happens.

Table 2. Results of trade union strategies (Germany)

Trade union strategy	Reduction of CO_2-emissions (%)	Change of GDP (%)	Employment (%)
No adjustment	- 0.88	+ 0.74	+ 1.30
Partial adjustment	- 1.29	+ 0.01	+ 0.09
Full adjustment	- 1.45	- 0.27	- 0.37

This example shows that with different assumptions about trade union behaviour but the same class of models, quite different results can be obtained. Of course, assumptions about trade union behaviour are not the only ones which have

22 For more details of these simulations see Kirchgässner (1999).

23 See Koschel, Wünsche, and Eckerle (1999).

24 The major components have been the introduction of a tax on electric energy of DM 0.02 per kWh as well as an increase of the mineral oil tax for gasoline by DM 0.04 per litre, for light heating oil by DM 0.04 per litre and for natural gas by DM 0.32 per kWh. These increases came into effect on April 1, 1999. At the same time social security contributions for the old age pension system have been reduced by 0.8 percentage points to 19.5 %. See for this *Gesetz zum Einstieg in die ökologische Steuerreform* of March 3, 1999, FÖS-Mitteilungen Nr. 15, March 1999 as well as Jacobs et al. (1998).

an impact on the results; different assumptions about government behaviour might, e.g., have similar implications.[25] Moreover, these assumptions do not have to be explicitly stated; it is possible to derive them from more general assumptions about trade union or government behaviour. In addition, econometric models are no less prone to such 'manipulations' than the computable general equilibrium models which today are mostly used to evaluate programs of environmental policy.[26] And all this is possible without violating scientific standards.

4 On the Process of Policy Advice

Thus, we are in a situation where we can find economists providing scientific (and empirical) support for nearly every political position. Apart from other factors, this is possible because economic theory is compatible with nearly all (factual) statements and because the necessary empirical research can lead to rather different results. But, under such conditions, for what is economic policy advice useful, why is it demanded and can we expect that (besides ideology) information is transmitted in the process of economic policy advice? Or do we have to assume that (most) economists in this business are corrupt, because they deliver results demanded by their clients?

To get a (at least partially) satisfactory answer one has to take into account that science is not the business of separate (especially honourable) individuals but that it is a process, in which some scientists make conjectures and others criticise those. This holds for the social sciences equally as for the natural sciences. As Karl R. Popper (1962: 95) states:

> *"It is a mistake to assume that the objectivity of a science depends on the objectivity of the scientist. And it is a mistake to believe that the attitude of the natural scientist is more objective than that of the social scientist. ... the objectivity of science is not a matter of the individual scientists but rather the social result of their mutual criticisms, of the friendly-hostile division of labour among scientists, of their co-operation and also of their competition."*

Thus, some of the conjectures will (at least temporarily) survive criticisms and be taken as approved hypotheses, while others will be refuted because of logical deficiencies or incompatibility with the available empirical data. It is not decisive whether the individual scientist is objective or not, but that the scientific discourse takes place in a climate where criticisms are not only allowed but even desired. Only criticisms of our conjectures enable us to detect their weaknesses and to proceed to better conjectures. In this respect, there is no difference between natural

25 See, e.g., the results for Austria reported in Kirchgässner (1999).

26 In Kirchgässner (2001) it is shown how regression results about the relation between the government's share and economic growth or unemployment in a country can be 'produced'.

and social scientists. If we had to rely on the objectivity of the individual scientist to reach scientific progress, then the possibilities for progress would be rather limited, because scientists – like all other human beings – are generally biased in favour of their own ideas. Whether scientific progress is possible or not in a society depends much more on the (rational) organisation of the scientific process than on the intentions of the individual scientists. Nevertheless, in an open discourse, scientists have strong incentives to strive for objectivity in order not to be refuted (too swiftly) by other participants. This is the only way to acquire reputation and – in this way – also to pursue their other (individual) objectives.[27]

What holds for the (pure) scientific process, holds for the process of policy advice as well. If information (too) is to be transmitted in this process it must be ensured that the discussion is public and that the respective material is publicly available. As to empirical questions, this includes the exact specification of the data employed as well as their sources. Only under these circumstances competing interest groups as well as the general public have the possibility to critically discuss different statements. This discussion is, however, necessary to enable participants in the political discourse to distinguish between factual statements and political (ideological) positions. Of course, both have their legitimate place in this discourse, but it should always be possible to differentiate between them, irrespective of how difficult this might seem to be in a concrete situation. Insofar, the concept which assumes that the public discourse and not the individual motivation of scientists is crucial to get 'objective' information is fully based on the principle of 'freedom from value judgements' as proposed by Weber (1919), Albert (1956, 1963), and others.

With respect to economic policy recommendations, it is safe to say that in most cases experts have a personal interest to obtain (nearly) exactly those results they actually achieve, which implies that they are biased in favour of their clients. This contradicts the notion of the ideal scientist, whose only objective is to find 'truth'. It is a fact that clients (often very carefully) look for (potential) experts who can be expected to produce exactly the results desired by the clients. Because experts know of these expectations it can be assumed that the results sought by the customer are at least not completely contrary to the experts' own ideological views. In the end, they have to identify themselves with these positions if their report is published.

That experts come to different conclusions does, on the other hand, not imply that the results are casual or arbitrary. Even if the statements of experts are quite different, a critical discussion is still possible which uncovers mistakes and tricks of individual experts and, therefore, allows a more objective evaluation of the

---

27 This is in analogy with the role of the (self-interested) entrepreneur in the market and his contribution to the social result. As Adam Smith already wrote: "It is not from the benevolence of the butcher, the brewer, or the baker, that we expect our dinner, but from their regard to their own interest. We address ourselves, not to their humanity but to their self-love, and never talk to them of our own necessities but of their advantages." (1776: 27).

situation from the outside. The main purpose of such a discussion is to show how the different arguments are related to specific interests even if they are garnished with the rhetoric of social welfare. Such a clarifying discussion is certainly not for the benefit of all participants but it can help other independent people or the political authorities to make 'reasonable' political decisions. This holds more in a direct than in a (purely) representative democracy, because the public political discourse is of greater importance if people have (the possibility of) the final decision.[28]

Moreover, it can even be helpful for the political discourse and the following decision if the experts of both sides try to make their points very strong. Lakatos (1970) argues that it can be detrimental for the scientific progress if a theory is withdrawn 'too fast' in a scientific discourse. The same holds for the political discourse. Thus, it makes sense that all sides present all their arguments in such a discourse. Only then do voters (and their representatives in the parliament) really know about what they have to decide on.

It might be taken for granted that in many cases scientists strive for truth and that this is their only motivation. In addition, governments (clients) at least sometimes are really interested in objective (scientific) results. Moreover, economists as experts not always write what their clients expect. All this is not to be denied. But it can also not be denied that, besides truth, scientists often strive for quite other objectives and that their reports made on behalf of special interest groups usually reflect what those groups expect. What follows from this for the concept which is presented here?

First, it has to be taken into account that the incentives of scientists depend on the environment in which they operate. Other conditions hold in the 'scientific game' than in the 'political game' or the 'policy advice game'. Generally, the scientific game is more transparent and has a more long-run perspective. Thus, the strive for objectivity is stronger in (purely) scientific activities than in the policy advice game, but it can exist in the latter as well. Moreover, there are many arguments in the utility functions; (monetary) income is a very important one, but only one among many arguments.

Reputation in the scientific community plays certainly an important role for scientists, and they are usually not willing to risk this reputation because of negligible financial rewards. Thus, it would not be rational even for self-interested scientists to be corruptible for small amounts of money and to produce results which can easily be rejected.[29] This holds the more, the more intense the information spills over from the political to the scientific area, i.e. the easier other scientific colleagues get knowledge of political advice statements which are scientifically not sound. Thus, striving for objectivity can be generated by self-interest, even if it might appear or be interpreted differently: as intrinsic motivation. On the other hand, among scientists (as among other people) there is also genuinely non-self-

28 See for this Kirchgässner, Feld, and Savioz (1999, Chapter 3).

29 On the other hand, it is really astonishing how little money is often necessary to make economists (but also other scientists as well as politicians) risk their reputation (and their future career).

interested (altruistic, intrinsically motivated) behaviour. In some situations, such behaviour can even be very relevant for society.[30]

Nevertheless, in order to find answers to the question how the process of policy advice has to be organised so that not only ideology but also information is transmitted, it makes sense to follow the concept of constitutional economics and assume self-interested behaviour of all participants. This holds even if the majority of scientists were purely intrinsically motivated and solely striving for objective knowledge.[31] In analogy to the constitutional considerations of Popper (1945: 121) the relevant question is: How can we organise the institutions of scientific policy advice in such a way that bad or incompetent experts can be prevented from doing too much damage? A somewhat nicer formulation for this is: The rules of the policy advice game should be built in such a way that even those scientific experts who are more interested in their own (monetary) income than in truth will produce objective knowledge. As shown above, a precondition for this is the open discussion of research methods and results: A critical discussion has to be possible.

In (non-experimental) empirical economic research this implies, e.g., that equations from published papers should more often be re-estimated by others than it is done today.[32] To be able to do this, it is necessary that the data which are employed are available for others. In this sense, already today there are some journals which demand that the data which are used in the papers published in the journal are made publicly available (e.g., via the internet).[33] This should cause no problems as long as only data are used which are provided by public institutions. Problems can arise if the data are collected by private firms for commercial reasons. But also if scientists have collected their own data they will hardly be willing to make them publicly available as long as they did not make full use of them. In both cases, however, it can be demanded that the data are made available to the public after a certain period of time.[34]

With respect to the question of the objectivity of scientific reports it has additionally to be taken into account that scientific experts who get their mandate from interest groups are in many cases neither able nor willing to do anything else than to support the political objectives of their clients. This holds even if they are in no way corrupt. First, a report not in support of the political objectives of the client will – with high probability – never be presented to the general public. This alone ensures that the published reports are (largely) supporting the objectives of the cli-

30 See G. Kirchgässner (2003).

31 On the position of constitutional economics see, e.g., Buchanan (1987a, 1987b).

32 As the results of the 'Journal of Money, Credit, and Banking-Project' show, it is very often impossible to replicate the results exactly. See for this Dewald, Thursby, and Anderson (1986) as well as Anderson and Dewald (1994).

33 This holds, e.g., for the *Journal of Applied Econometrics*, the *Journal of Human Resources*, or the *Journal of Business and Economic Statistics*, as long as there are no problems of data protection.

34 An additional problem arises if opinion poll data are used which can – for technical or financial reasons – not be reproduced. See for this Kirchgässner (1992: 16f.).

ent. Second, an expert who presents results which contradict the objectives of his/her client might get no further mandate. Consequently, the selection of the experts by clients leads to a substantial convergence of interests of clients and experts. We observe a similar process in the market for scientific reports as, following Adam Smith (1776), it has already been described by Alchian (1950) and Friedman (1953): (i) The self-interest of the experts provides incentives for them to help their clients to reach their political objectives. (ii) Even if all experts only support those political objectives of which they are personally convinced and which they believe to be justified (in a moral way), the selection mechanism generates an assignment between clients and experts such that finally the political objectives of clients and experts are largely corresponding. In this game all experts may survive, but only under the protection of specific clients. 'Objectivity' in this game can only be reached approximately and only by a public discourse.

5 Concluding Remarks

But if all this is the case, why is economic policy advice demanded at all? What is the benefit a political party or an interest group can get if it pays for a report which (at least to a large extent) has the content which is demanded? If, as economic theory supposes, people have rational expectations, they will see through the game and will hardly be impressed by such reports. But if they have no effect, why is there a demand for such reports, why are governments, political parties and interest groups paying quite a lot of money for them? If they also have rational expectations, should they not dispense with them?

The possibility mentioned above that by the exchange of arguments a (socially) better solution can be reached does not play a role here because we face the situation of the production for a public good for which rational individuals (under the usual assumptions) hardly make considerable voluntary contributions. Moreover, especially with respect to interest groups, the assumption of altruistic behaviour seems to be extremely implausible. This also holds for NGOs or for groups of environmentalists. Especially if they 'know' what has to be done, they might (and often actually do) make contributions to the public good itself (or what they presume that the public good is), but they would hardly waste money on reports if they believe that these would have no effect. Thus, spending money for reports does not seem to be compatible with rational expectations of the clients as well as of the general public. This holds at least as long as the purpose of these reports is to have an impact on the decisions of the general public and/or their elected representatives, i.e. as long as these are not (purely) technical reports.

Such an argument overlooks, however, that interest groups have a strong demand for good and convincing arguments. (This holds especially in the direct democracy, but at least to some extent also in a purely representative democratic system.) A rationally enlightened general public knows cui bono an argument is presented, and it also takes into account that arguments supported by scientists are weapons in the battle of interests. Nevertheless, it is able to distinguish between 'good' and 'bad', more or less convincing arguments. While the former are perhaps able to change their convictions, the latter ones surely cannot. Scientists, however, are – or are at least supposed to be – specialists in producing 'good' arguments. Therefore it makes sense that interest groups and political parties demand scientific advice. And if one side presents scientific reports, the other side has hardly any other possibility than to do the same.

This also implies that the clients have an interest in advice of high quality: The arguments which are put forward by the scientists should be convincing in the political discourse. Thus, when selecting experts, parties and/or interest groups do not only consider their (assumed) political ideology but also their reputation. This reputation does not only depend on their former advisory activities but also on their scientific (and possibly also their rhetoric) reputation. Thus, the clients have self-interest in demanding scientifically sound reports which increase the chances to find 'good' solutions, if this holds for (nearly) all parties involved in the political discourse.

How such a process might work can be illustrated with our example of the ecological tax reform. Scientific reports have been financed by different interested parties, and the results – especially with respect to labour market effects – were quite different and more or less in line with the interests of the clients who paid for them. The discussion in the meantime showed that, first of all, such a reform might help to reduce unemployment somewhat, but that it is neither the panacea of Europe's labour market problems nor the job killer which has been announced it will be. On the contrary, most simulations show that the labour market effects are rather modest. Second, the discussion has shown that the effects which are finally to be expected depend on quite a lot of details which have to be taken into account. The German realisation of the ecological tax reform is, e.g., certainly not the ideal one.[35] But the discussion of this project which took place in Europe within the last ten years has, at least in my opinion, definitely brought many valuable new insights. Insofar, this is an example of how economic policy advice can – besides all ideological disputes – improve our (still very limited) knowledge about how the world works and how an effective and sustainable environmental policy might look like.

References

Albert, H. (1963), Wertfreiheit als methodisches Prinzip, in: Beckerath, E.v., H. Giersch, and H. Lampert (Eds.), *Probleme der normativen Ökonomik und der wirtschaftspolitischen Beratung*, Berlin, 32-63.

Albert, H. (1956), Werturteil und Wertbasis: Das Werturteilsproblem im Lichte der logischen Analyse, *Zeitschrift für die gesamte Staatswissenschaft* 112, 410-439.

[35] See, e.g., Böhringer and Schwager (2003).

Alchian, A.A. (1950), Uncertainty, Evolution, and Economic Theory, *Journal of Political Economy* 58, 211-221.

Anderson, R. G. and W. G. Dewald (1994), Replication and Scientific Standards in Applied Economics a Decade After the Journal of Money, Credit, and Banking Project, *Federal Reserve Bank of St. Louis Review* 76 (6), 79-83.

Arrow, K.J. (1951), *Social Choice and Individual Values*, New York (2nd edition 1963).

Balasko, Y. (1988), *Foundations of the Theory of General Equilibrium*, Orlando.

Baumol, W.J. and J. Benhabib (1989), Chaos: Significance, Mechanism, and Economic Applications, *Journal of Economic Perspectives* 3, Winter, 77-105.

Binswanger, H.C., H. Frisch, H.G. Nutzinger et al. (1983), *Arbeit ohne Umweltzerstörung*, Frankfurt (2nd edition 1988).

Blankart, C.B. (1994), 'Neue Finanzwissenschaft': Eine alternative Sicht, *Zeitschrift für Wirtschafts- und Sozialwissenschaften* 114, 245-254.

Blankart, C.B. (1987), Review of: G. Radnitzky and P. Bernholz (Eds.), *Economic Imperialism: The Economic Method Applied Outside the Field of Economics*, (Paragon House, New York 1987), *Zeitschrift für die gesamte Staatswissenschaft (JITE)* 143, 669-673.

Böhringer, C. and R. Schwager (2003), Die ökologische Steuerreform in Deutschland: Ein umweltpolitisches Feigenblatt, *Perspektiven der Wirtschaftspolitik* 4, 211-222.

Braulke, M. and A. Endres (1985), On the Economics of Effluent Charges, *Canadian Journal of Economics* 18, 891-897.

Bovenberg, A.L. and L.H. Goulder (2002), Environmental Taxation and Regulation, in: Auerbach, A.J. and M. Feldstein (Eds.), *Handbook of Public Economics*, Vol. 3, Amsterdam et al., 1471-1545.

Bovenberg, A.L. (1999), Green Tax Reforms and the Double Dividend, *International Tax and Public Finance* 6, 421-443.

Bovenberg, A.L. and F. van der Ploeg (1996), Optimal Taxation, Public Goods and Environmental Policy with Involuntary Unemployment, *Journal of Public Economics* 62, 59-83.

Bovenberg, A.L. (1995), Environmental Taxation and Employment, *De Economist* 143, 111-140.

Bovenberg, A.L. and R.A. de Mooij (1994a), Environmental Levies and Distortionary Taxation, *American Economic Review* 84, 1085-1089.

Bovenberg, A.L. and R.A. de Mooij (1994b), Environmental Taxes and Labor Market Distortions, *European Journal of Political Economy* 10, 655-683.

Bovenberg, A.L. and F. van der Ploeg (1994), Environmental Policy, Public Finance and the Labor Market in a Second-Best World, *Journal of Public Economics* 55, 349-390.

Buchanan, J.M. (1987a), The Constitution of Economic Policy, *American Economic Review* 77, 243-259.

Buchanan, J.M. (1987b), Constitutional Economics, in: *The New Palgrave, A Dictionary of Economics*, London, Vol. 1, 585-588.

Buchanan, J.M. and G. Tullock (1962), *The Calculus of Consent: Logical Foundations of Constitutional Democracy*, Ann Arbor.

Carter, J.R. and M.D. Irons (1991), Are Economists Different, and If So, Why?, *Journal of Economic Perspectives* 5 (2), 171-177.

Conrad, K. and M. Schröder (1993), Choosing Environmental Policy Instruments Using General Equilibrium Models, *Journal of Policy Modeling* 15, 521-543.

Conrad, K. and M. Schröder (1991), An Evaluation of Taxes on Air Pollutant Emissions: An Applied General Equilibrium Approach, *Schweizerische Zeitschrift für Volkswirtschaft und Statistik* 127, 199-224.

Debreu, G. (1974), Excess Demand Functions, *Journal of Mathematical Economics* 1, 15-21.

Dewald, W.G., J.G. Thursby, and R.G. Anderson (1986), Replication in Empirical Economics: The Journal of Money, Credit, and Banking Project, *American Economic Review* 76, 587-603.

Downs, A. (1957), *An Economic Theory of Democracy*, New York.

Erdmann, G. (1997), *Volkswirtschaftliche Auswirkungen von Lenkungsabgaben auf Energieträger in der Schweiz*, Bern.

Frey, B.S. and S. Meier (2003), Are Political Economists Selfish and Indoctrinated? Evidence from a Natural Experiment, *Economic Inquiry* 41, 448-462.

Friedman, L.S. (1985), *Microeconomic Policy Analysis*, New York.

Friedman, M. (1953), The Methodology of Positive Economics, in: Friedman, M. (Ed.), *Essays in Positive Economics*, Chicago, 3-43.

German Institute for Economic Research (Ed.) (1994), *Wirtschaftliche Auswirkungen einer ökologischen Steuerreform*, Berlin.

Hesse, H. (1994), Als Wissenschaftler in der Politik?, in: Universität Hannover (Ed.), *Vorträge im Fachbereich Wirtschaftswissenschaften*, Vol. 20, Hannover, 17-37.

Hahn, R.W. (1989), Economic Prescriptions for Environmental Problems: How the Patient Followed the Doctor's Orders, *Journal of Economic Perspectives* 3 (2), 95-114.

Hildenbrand, W. (1983), On the Law of Demand, *Econometrica* 51, 997-1019.

Ingrao, B. and G. Israel (1987), *La mano invisibile*, Rome; English translation: *The Invisible Hand, Economic Equilibrium in the History of Science*, London, 1990.

Jacobs, O.H. et al. (1998), *Stellungnahme zur Steuerreform 1999/2000/2002*, ZEW Dokumentation No. 98-10, Mannheim.

Jäger, K. (1976), Eine ökonomische Theorie des Recycling, *Kyklos* 29, 660-677.

Kirchgässner, G. (2003), *On Minimal Morals*, mimeo, University of St. Gallen.

Kirchgässner, G. (2001), Ökonometrische Schätz- und Testergebnisse, empirisch gehaltvolle Aussagen über die Wirklichkeit und wirtschaftspolitische Beratung, *Konjunkturpolitik* 47, 103-138.

Kirchgässner, G. (1999), Wirtschaftliche Auswirkungen von Energiesteuern auf kleine offene Volkswirtschaften: Theoretische Überlegungen und Simulationsergebnisse, in: Schneider, F. (Ed.), *Internationale Strategien und Erfahrungen zur Neuorientierung der EU-Energiewirtschaft*, Linz, 153-181.

Kirchgässner, G., L.P. Feld, and M.R. Savioz (1999), *Die direkte Demokratie: Modern, erfolgreich, entwicklungs- und exportfähig*, Basel/München.

Kirchgässner, G. (1998), Ökologische Steuerreform: Utopie oder realistische Alternative, in: Krause-Junk, G. (Ed.), *Steuersysteme der Zukunft*, Berlin, 279-319.

Kirchgässner, G., U. Müller, and M. R. Savioz (1998), Ecological Tax Reform and Involuntary Unemployment: Simulation Results for Switzerland, *Schweizerische Zeitschrift für Volkswirtschaft und Statistik* 134, 329-353.

Kirchgässner, G. (1996), Ideologie und Information in der Politikberatung: Einige Bemerkungen und ein Fallbeispiel, *Hamburger Jahrbuch für Wirtschafts- und Gesellschaftspolitik* 41, 9-41.

Kirchgässner, G. (1992), *Wissenschaftstheorie und Wissenschaftsbetrieb: Einige einführende Bemerkungen*, Diskussionspapier Nr. 68 der Volkswirtschaftlichen Abteilung der Hochschule St. Gallen.

Koschel, H., A. Wünsche, and T. Eckerle (1999), Was bringt die ökologische Steuerreform der deutschen Wirtschaft?, *ZEW Konjunkturreport* 2 (1), 6-9.

Koskela, E. and R. Schöb (1999), Alleviating Unemployment: The Case for a Green Tax Reform, *European Economic Review* 43, 1723-1746.

Koskela, E., R. Schöb, and H.-W. Sinn (2001), Green Tax Reform and Competitiveness, *German Economic Review* 2, 19-30.

Krishna, V. and J. Morgan (2001), A Model of Expertise, *Quarterly Journal of Economics* 116, 747-775.

Lakatos, I. (1970), Falsification and the Methodology of Scientific Research Programmes, in: Lakatos, I. and A. Musgrave (Eds.), *Criticism and the Growth of Knowledge*, Cambridge, 91-195.

Mankiw, N.G. (1990), A Quick Refresher Course in Macroeconomics, *Journal of Economic Literature* 28, 1645-1660.

Mantel, R.R. (1974), On the Characterization of Aggregate Excess Demands, *Journal of Economic Theory* 7, 348-353.

Mas-Colell, A. (1977), On the Equilibrium Price Set of an Exchange Economy, *Journal of Mathematical Economics* 4, 117-126.

Meier, A. and D. Mettler (1986), Einfluss und Macht in der Wirtschaftspolitik, *Schweizerische Zeitschrift für Volkswirtschaft und Statistik* 122, 37-59.

Meyer, B. (2000), Zur Abschätzung der Wirkungen umweltpolitischer Maßnahmen auf Umwelt und Wirtschaft durch den Einsatz makroökonomischer Modelle, *Allgemeines Statistisches Archiv* 84, 171-189.

Meyer, B. and G. Ewerhart (1996), *Modelling Towards Eco Domestic Product*, Institut für empirische Wirtschaftsforschung der Universität Osnabrück, Working Paper No. 48.

Meyer zu Himmern, A. and G. Kirchgässner (1995), Umweltschutz und internationale Wettbewerbsfähigkeit, in: Jochimsen, M. and G. Kirchgässner (Eds.), *Schweizerische Umweltpolitik im internationalen Kontext*, Basel, 43-76.

OECD (1997), *Études économiques de l'OCDE 1996-1997: Suisse*, Paris.

Pearce, D.W. (1991), The Role of Carbon Taxes in Adjusting to Global Warming, *Economic Journal* 101, 938-948.

Pigou, A.C. (1920), *The Economics of Welfare*, London.

Popper, K.R. (1962), Die Logik der Sozialwissenschaften, *Kölner Zeitschrift für Soziologie und Sozialpsychologie* 14, 233-248; quoted from the English translation: The Logic of the Social Sciences in: Adorno, Th. W. et al., *The Positivist Dispute in German Sociology*, New York 1976, 87-104.

Popper, K.R. (1945), *The Open Society and Its Enemies, Vol. I: The Spell of Plato*, London.

Prognos (1993), *Bewertung der wirtschaftlichen Auswirkungen einer CO_2-Abgabe*, Bericht im Auftrag des Eidgenössischen Departements des Innern, Basel.

Richter, W.F. and W. Wiegard (1994), Erwiderung zu den Kommentaren von Charles B. Blankart und Fritz Söllner, *Zeitschrift für Wirtschafts- und Sozialwissenschaften* 114, 255-266.

Richter, W.F. and W. Wiegard (1993), Zwanzig Jahre 'Neue Finanzwissenschaft', Teil II: Steuern und Staatsverschuldung, *Zeitschrift für Wirtschafts- und Sozialwissenschaften* 113, 337-400.

Sachverständigenrat (2003), *Jahresgutachten 2003/04: Staatsfinanzen konsolidieren – Steuersystem reformieren*, Wiesbaden.

Samuelson, P.A. (1948), Consumption Theory in Terms of Revealed Preference, *Economica* 15, 243-253.

Schips, B. (1995), *Ökonomische Argumente für wirksamen Wettbewerb auch im Versicherungszweig 'Gebäudefeuer- und Gebäudeelementarschäden'*, St. Gallen.

Schöb, R. (2003), *The Double Dividend Hypothesis of Environmental Taxes: A Survey*, CESifo Working Paper No. 946, Munich.

Schumpeter, J.A. (1942), *Capitalism, Socialism and Democracy*, New York.

Smith, A. (1776), *An Inquiry into the Nature and Causes of the Wealth of Nations*, London; quoted from the new edition: Clarendon Press, Oxford.

Sonnenschein, H. (1973), Do Walras Identity and Continuity Characterize the Class of Community Excess Demand Functions?, *Journal of Economic Theory* 6, 345-354.

Sonnenschein, H. (1972), Market Excess Demand Functions, Econometrica 40, 549-563.

Tinbergen, J. (1956), *Economic Policy: Principles and Design*, Amsterdam.

Ungern-Sternberg, Th. v. (1995), *Kritische Überlegungen zu dem Gutachten von Professor Schips über die kantonalen Gebäudeversicherungsmonopole*, Cahiers de recherches économiques No 9502, Département d'économétrie et économie politique, Université de Lausanne.

Ungern-Sternberg, Th. v. (1994), *Die kantonalen Gebäudeversicherungen: Eine ökonomische Analyse*, Cahiers de recherches économiques No 9405, Département d'économétrie et économie politique, Université de Lausanne.

Weber, M. (1919), *Wissenschaft als Beruf*, München/Leipzig.

Weizsäcker, C.C. v. (1976), Die Welt aus der Sicht der Ökonomen, in: H. Körner et al. (Eds.), *Wirtschaftspolitik: Wissenschaft und politische Aufgabe*, Bern, 67-83.

Welsch, H. and F. Hoster (1995), A General Equilibrium Analysis of European Carbon/Energy Taxation, *Zeitschrift für Wirtschafts- und Sozialwissenschaften* 115, 275-303.

Insights in Political Processes on the Ecological Tax Reform from a Ministerial Perspective

Kai Schlegelmilch[1]

Federal Ministry for the Environment, Nature Conservation and Nuclear Safety, Alexanderplatz 6, 10178 Berlin, Germany, kai.schlegelmilch@bmu.bund.de

Keywords. *Economic Policy Advice, Environmental Policy, Economic Environmental Policy Approaches, Economic Environmental Policy Instruments, Tax Policy, Ecological Tax Reform*

JEL. *H23; Q48; Q50*

Abstract. Firstly, the paper describes and compares the evolution – in theory – and the application in practice of various market-based approaches and instruments, inter alia the Ecological Tax Reform (ETR). Secondly, it provides insights in the history and the more than 20 years of debate on a potential ETR in Germany. Thirdly, the design and the phase of implementation of the ETR in Germany from 1999 on are described and analysed. Fourthly, the manifold and ambivalent experiences with the ETR are presented. Finally, conclusions for political considerations, design, implementation and marketing aspects are drawn.

1 Introduction

This contribution refers to the two articles from a) Gebhard Kirchgässner and b) Friedrich Schneider/Hannelore Weck-Hannemann in this volume. These articles aim at describing the political economy of the Ecological Tax Reform (ETR) from a mainly theoretical point of view and comprise illustrative elements from practice. In what follows, these articles are contrasted with experiences and practices the author has gathered during more than a decade. Half of the time he spent at the Wuppertal Institute, partly also at the European Environment Agency, himself as policy advisor on that topic. For the last six years, however, he worked with the German Federal Ministry for the Environment, Nature Conservation and Nuclear

[1] I am most grateful for very valuable comments from my colleague Astrid Harnisch on a draft version of this paper. Florian Keppler also kindly made helpful remarks on a draft version.
This article is written on the author's private capacity and must not be associated to any institution.

Safety (www.bmu.de). There he is Assistant Head of Division in the Working Group on Environment and Energy, Climate Protection Programme of the Federal Government and responsible for the ETR. He has been very much involved in the discussion, design, decision making, implementation and marketing of the ETR in Germany, introduced in April 1999, half a year after the change of government towards a red/social-democratic-green one.

Yet, as policy advisor at the Wuppertal Institute he had already been involved in advising the previous conservative-liberal government in 1995. Together with Ernst Ulrich von Weizsäcker, Henner Ehringhaus, Anselm Görres and others he founded the association Green Budget Germany (Förderverein Ökologische Steuerreform – www.eco-tax.info) back in 1994 to promote and accelerate the implementation of an ETR in Germany, since 2001 he is Vice-President. The following article is written on his personal capacity.

This article presents several experiences with the ETR in Germany, partly taking into account other countries' experiences, highlighting interesting examples in the context of political advice and political economy. The history and the experiences with the implementation of an ETR demonstrated that there were different waves of public debate and also of policy approaches and instrument choices. Industry successfully delayed effective government actions as soon as its initially own demand for more market-based instruments came too close to implementation. It followed a policy approach hopping from one instrument to another mostly just before implementation became serious. The policy sequence started from command-and-control with ordinances and regulations, going on with environmental agreements and taxes and finally emissions trading. However, not accepting industry's own target under the environmental agreement when it came to nailing down a target for the emissions trading caused enormous damage to the credibility of environmental agreements. Given this experience, it remains to be seen to what extent governments are still willing to accept such agreements.

Policy advice on ETR was particularly critical in the phase of gaining political support before its implementation, but also after its implementation when further improvements had to be made. However, given the brain drain after the change of government, and the many studies beforehand made government less dependant on policy advice in the implementation phase in this special case. It is not easy to generalise the process and explore the lessons learned in order to help other countries which are also working on the implementation of economic policy instruments. Every country has a very special set of actors including the influence of certain people as it is explained for the German case in this paper. It is, however, important to really bring together different actors from the political parties, the bureaucracies, scientific institutions, industries and environmental NGOs with their counterparts in other countries to allow for creating a good network and for ensuring that the same "language" is spoken by the stakeholders. Such a transfer e.g. was agreed between the Czech Ministry for the Environment and the German Ministry for the Environment back in 2002. This successful approach is about to be enlarged to other countries.

2 Comparison of Policy Approaches and Instruments

In current climate policy at least four seemingly competing policy approaches and instruments[2] are often discussed and implemented, although at partly different stages and times: ordinances/regulations as an element of a traditionally dominating command-and-control policy, environmental agreements, emissions trading and ETR. All of them are often part of overarching policy programmes, such as the climate protection programme. Several countries have introduced different approaches and implemented different instruments to various degrees. The evolution, in theory and practice, of these approaches and instruments is yet very different and it is of practical and theoretical interest to compare these different paths of development. In the following I will therefore first of all explore the use of policy approaches in Germany regarding climate change taking into account sequences and mixes of different policies. More concrete data and examples are provided in the next chapter on the historical aspects.

Traditionally, since the launch of active environmental policies in the late 1960s, environmental policies have been dominated by more or less strong regulations and can therefore be characterised as command-and-control policies. Environmental agreements were introduced at a later stage. They were basically invented by the bureaucracy and the political decision makers, more or less jointly with industry. First introduced in the 1970s for some particular, relatively clear cut problems, they were also used from the late 1980s, early 1990s on to combat global problems such as the depletion of the ozone layer and climate change. The following remarks refer basically to agreements on climate change. Before they were implemented there was hardly any theoretical economic literature on such agreements providing a rationale for their application. Also, policy advice virtually was not existing, given there was no real theory about different policy approaches in this area. So why did bureaucracy invent and apply such an instrument unknown or at least neglected in theory?

One may argue the instrument reflects some features of the Coase Theorem (Coase, 1960) given the element of seemingly voluntary negotiations. This may be true to a certain extent, but here it is government itself as one of the stakeholders and not two other subjects of society. And would bureaucracy really care about Coase and theories? The thesis presented here is that bureaucracy invented this instrument, because the phase of pure command-and-control policy was gone while an increasingly stronger demand for so-called market based instruments had emerged. In fact, it was industry itself which claimed that there should be less command-and-control environmental policies, but more market-based instruments in order to achieve targets cost-efficiently according to market mechanisms. This claim was made during more than a decade in the 1980s and early 1990s without substantial changes in the real instrumental mix.

However, there was one important exception which is the waste water charge. The idea for this instrument first came up in Germany around 1971, (BMI, 1974),

---

2 The terms policy approach and instrument are partly used synonymously.

following examples of then Czechoslovakia, the then German Democratic Republic, France, the Netherlands, Poland and Hungary (Lühr, 1989: 432). They had adopted this instrument, still some only on paper. In 1974, the German government drafted a law, which was adopted in 1976, and entered into force in 1978. Still, the first payment of the charge was due only in 1981, progressively increasing to its initially agreed full amount until 1985 – quite a long way from the first draft law to its interim final full rate. Later on further increases were made.

Apart from this exception, it took some time until finally in the mid-1990s industry's demands were taken more seriously and market-based instruments such as the ETR were intensively discussed, designed and gradually became more likely to be implemented. And just as a market-based approach became more concrete and at the edge of implementation, industry changed its positions and asked for more flexible approaches and instruments. This appears a bit surprising, although not really if the real interests are considered. With such instruments emerging on the political horizon, practically most of the negotiation power of industry would have gone which industry had during the mostly comfortable times of command-and-control; or at least of command and the attempt to control. One could even question who is commanding and who is controlling – depending on the counterfactual, since this kind of policy requires capacities and information for monitoring, controlling, enforcing and eventually applying sanctions, if existing at all. And it is exactly the partial lack of such capacities and information which offers large negotiation power to industry.

At the same time, in the late 1980s and early 1990s, international negotiations developed and conventions and protocols on global problems such as the Montreal Protocol on the depletion of the ozone layer and the United Nations Framework Convention on Climate Change (UNFCCC) were adopted. Given learning processes within companies and increasing international pressure, different industries per se became more interested in shaping policy instruments regarding the environment also in order to establish comparative advantages. Presumably organisations like the World Business Council on Sustainable Development (WBCSD) facilitated, if not accelerated, such a learning process. Environmental catastrophes and mismanagement and/or insufficient communication related to such disasters contributed to this process. On the national level, organisations of progressive companies were founded – BAUM, future and Unternehmensgrün being the most important in Germany.

Coming back again to the national agenda, allowing for the application of market-based instruments appears to endanger industry's power since it would be the market forces that push industry towards a certain behaviour and investment. And – as entrepreneurs know very well – you cannot run counter market forces for a longer time. These forces are too strong. Industry's negotiation power would have gone. In Germany, there was not only the demand for market-based instruments, but at the same time a proposal for implementing a waste heat ordinance was put forward in the early 1990s, an element of a strengthened command-and-control policy, though intending to ask for implementing only profitable energy saving measures. This aimed at unveiling all energy saving potentials in industry by gathering and making available a bulk of information, so far only in industry's hands.

Furthermore the international public was looking more closely at Germany as the first Conference of the Parties (COP 1) of the United Nations Framework Convention on Climate Change (UNFCCC) was to take place in Berlin in 1995. Apart from the German government setting ambitious national targets (-25% CO_2-reduction by 2005 against 1990-levels) expectations were high that German industry should contribute to greenhouse gas emissions reductions. Against this multiple challenge industry moved a step out of the pressure of expectations and potential instruments by launching a self-commitment in March 1995 (BDI, 1995a) which was updated in 1996 though without substantial improvements (BDI, 1996). It was prepared in a joint effort of industry and bureaucracy (Ministry for Environment and Ministry for Economic Affairs) – basically to avoid the other instruments discussed.

Here it becomes evident that these environmental agreements were not at all voluntary, but only a somewhat forced reaction on the pressure emerging through the discussion of alternative instruments (Fischedick et al., 1995 and Rennings, 1996). Hence, the term voluntary is not used here – besides in line with the official terminology of the European Commission (1997 and 1996) and the European Environment Agency (1997).

After the change of the German government in 1998 – by the way, the first time ever in Germany that the population voted directly for a change; before the government changed during a legislative period –, the ETR was implemented in Germany from April 1999 on, and industry had apparently lost the battle against this market-based instrument as such. Still, industry had tremendous impact on the design of the ETR as described in more detail below.

Finally, an even more market-based instrument was emerging on the EU horizon: emissions trading. Emissions trading is a theoretical environmental concept developed decades ago, though basically applied in the USA. EU Member States hardly have experience with that. Ironically, it was the USA that insisted on emissions trading during the negotiation of the Kyoto Protocol which they now refuse to ratify themselves. German industry in particular succeeded in delaying and fighting against emissions trading for general reasons and a lot of misperceptions. It almost succeeded, strangely enough at least, to isolate Germany in the EU, the country often perceived as frontrunner. Thanks also to the support of some big global players like BP and Shell who had experienced the enormous economic and environmental advantages of emissions trading due to the implementation of these instruments within their own company, the German position became eventually positive, though never enthusiastic (BMU and BMWI, 2002).

However, in the end the EU emissions trading directive was adopted (on EU level) and the national implementation plans were due by the 31st of March 2004 (BMU, 2004a,b). In fact, Germany, as one of the very few Member States of the EU, succeeded to deliver its National Allocation Plan (NAP) just in time on that day. But the price was high from an environmental point of view. Whereas the Environment Minister proposed to take the above mentioned environmental agreement on climate change (together with a subsequent agreement on the increase of cogeneration) and the therein mentioned overall target respectively commitment of emission reductions as base line for the emissions trading allocation, industry opposed strongly. Industry fought heavily against this objectively fair approach, although it did not ask for more than industry itself had promised to reduce voluntarily anyway. In the end, industry succeeded in almost escaping any reduction commitment in the first budget period (2005-2007). The thesis of many economists that these environmental agreements would not comprise any additional measure compared with the business as usual was more than confirmed. In fact, apparently they even had less substance given the fact that their target was not accepted as basis for emissions trading (BUND, 2004).

The initial claim for an increased use of market-based instruments by industry apparently was just a means to delay or avoid additional regulation (in the meaning of policy) – independent of the kind of instrument. Strangely enough, the bargaining for the allocation of emission credits and the final targets set for industry demonstrated impressively that even within such an instrument there can be strong negotiation power. In fact, in such a way, even market-based instruments can get very close to command-and-control policy, including an inefficient allocation. However, this is the case for the first allocation/target setting, but less likely for the operational phase of emissions trading.

But what role did policy advice play? The thesis here is that for the implementation of an ETR most aspects had been well examined beforehand – minor exceptions are presented in the chapter on the design and implementation of an ETR in Germany. Thus particular policy advice was hardly needed. For the emissions trading such advice was not available in the Ministry. Given a very tough time schedule, it was necessary to get policy advice in every day's processes. To that end, several researchers were asked to work as closely with the Ministry partly even in house, as possible to allow for immediate comments on any emerging aspects.

Concluding on these policy approaches and instrumental developments and the varying claims for instruments, industry's position could be considered as "instrument hopping" or it is like "zapping from one instrument to another" – always ahead of implementation. It became fairly clear that from an industry point of view, voluntary agreements are the preferred way to go. The attempts of combining a cap and trade approach with environmental agreements, has been widely seen as unnecessary state intervention, although the idea clearly is to reduce emissions in an economically efficient manner and to provide a secure framework for potential investments. Claims for market-based instruments appear to serve the purpose of delaying and avoiding any action. And by not accepting the initial targets for emissions trading on the basis of the environmental agreement industry succeeded in ruining the credibility of the instrument of environmental agreements – ironically the one once favoured so much by itself.

3 History of ETR

The conclusions of the previous chapter also apply to the ETR. For more than 20 years protagonists discussed ETR, publications were made much more than on any other instrument (except for command-and-control). Actually, it was back in 1983 that the Swiss economist Hans-Christoph Binswanger, together with Hans Nutzinger and Heinz Frisch (Binswanger et al., 1983), had invented the ETR. This idea was picked up by others, such as the leader of the Institute for European Environmenal Policy (IEEP), Ernst von Weizsäcker. Environmental organisations like the German section of Friends of the Earth or BUND, worked on it more in depth. Parties started to getting interested. However, the first larger round of public debate was triggered in 1988 by an unconventional proposal laid down in a study by the Heidelberg based Environment and Prognosis Institute (UPI, 1988): All conventional taxes should be replaced by different kinds of environmental taxes. Given the increasing debate, the Federal Association of German Industry (Bundesverband der Deutschen Industrie – BDI) had also commissioned a study to explore the value of an ETR. Very likely against its expectations, the study by the Institute for Fiscal Research Studies at the University of Cologne found that it made indeed sense. At least BDI was fair enough to allow for the publication of the study (BDI, 1995b). Though the issue was picked up by Environmental Parties and Social Democrats the unification of the two German states made environmental issues drop down the political agenda – including the issue of ETR. This study reminded one of the study that BDI had asked from the economist Werner Meißner at Frankfurt University back in 1978 (Meißner and Hödl, 1978). He should examine the overall job impacts of advanced environmental policies. Industry was likely considering environmental protection as a job killer, searching for arguments to underline its thesis. But in fact he found that the balance is positive. This demonstrates the importance of independent policy advice. Other stakeholders were, of course, very interested in these results.

A second round of public debate was initiated by a study of the German Institute for Economic Research (DIW, 1994), commissioned by Greenpeace and published in 1994. For the very first time it simulated an ETR in Germany and its overall impacts on growth, employment and energy consumption. Its findings confirmed the so-called double dividend thesis as up to 800,000 additional jobs were predicted until 2005, while CO_2-emissions would drop by 14%. Now, policy started to get very excited about ETR. Practically all parties were somewhat in favour of it (Schlegelmilch, 1995). In February 1995, the Leader of the conservative group in the Parliament, Wolfgang Schäuble, asked his deputy, Hans-Peter Repnik, to develop a concept for an ETR, even if Germany had to go this path alone. All at a sudden, the Greens felt "their" issue and idea would be occupied by the conservatives and a competing race between the parties started following the line "who is first to present a concept for an ETR which could be implemented in Germany". And, in fact, the conservatives soon had an internal paper drafted, to which one could have subscribed. But finally, it was the Greens and the Social Democrats winning this race. But the internal paper of the conservatives from May 1995 (CDU, 1995) was watered down within the party, mainly by the agricultural lobby and Bavaria. The outcoming official paper of the conservatives in November 1995 comprised no longer ambitious energy tax proposals as yet in the internal paper to which one could have subscribed. But it contained lots of subsidies for environmentally-friendly behaviour and investments. Where the money should come from to finance that remained unsolved. By the end of 1995, it was found out later (Krebs and Reiche, 1997), a meeting between Chancellor Helmut Kohl, Jürgen F. Strube, the Chief Executive Officer of BASF, the large chemical company (in which Helmut Kohl once made his training as student), and the President of the Federal Association of German Industry, Hans-Olaf Henkel, had taken place in which Helmut Kohl promised that as long as he would be Chancellor no ecotax would be introduced. With that turning point, the protagonist of an ETR, Wolfgang Schäuble had to withdraw from his idea which he in fact did publicly at the end of 1995. As a consequence the debate was bogged down in the policy arena afterwards again.

This discussion and development was certainly also negatively influenced by the fact that the DIW study from 1994 had not calculated any exemptions for business. Hence a few energy-intensive sectors would have been hit quite strongly. This was likely the moment when industry started to fight ETR more offensively and changed its more or less neutral or vaguely positive attitude. This is somewhat hard to understand given that the majority of industry would be winning.

On the evening of the 8th of November 1994, Green Budget Germany (GBG – Förderverein Ökologische Steuerreform – FÖS) was founded by ETR protagonists. The intention was to bridge the way for industry to agree to an ETR since the DIW study had apparently impacted the opposite. Ever since it is a small, but partly influential association with good political contacts and the scientific capacity to analyse features appropriately. GBG, however, did not succeed in getting industry agree to ETR, but at least clarified that it all depends on a good design and that it is not a question per se as to whether to condemn an ETR or as to whether to praise an ETR.

Another study by the Rhine-Westphalian Institute for Economic Research in 1996 (RWI, 1996) created confusion. In an unusual way it had presented preliminary findings in a press conference. It should demonstrate that overall there would be substantial job losses in the energy-intensive industry, particularly in North-Rhine-Westphalia. Numbers were mentioned which seemed to show that. But the reaction from the then Minister President (now Federal Minister of Economic Affairs) Wolfgang Clement was such that a government would never design an ETR in such a way that there would be such substantial job losses. Apparently, the design was considered crucial, while the idea as such was still attractive (Luhmann, 1996). When looking closer at the short version of the RWI study published quite some time afterwards, one was struck by the results. In a table one could find the negative job balance (-400,000) – and in the text one could find statements like: "There are also positive job impacts in other sectors" and "the overall impact is not necessarily positive". However, the positive impacts have not been quantified and put in the same table as the losses. Tricky idea one could argue. The impression that remains in the public is that the overall impact is negative. But serious science and helpful policy advice looks different. Furthermore, the announced comprehensive study has never been published – at least not until mid 2004. The suspicion is that this was an attempt to bring down enthusiasm for an ETR – and it succeeded, at least for some time.

In the run up to the elections in 1998, the German Association of Natural Protection (Deutscher Naturschutzring – DNR) started a campaign, funded by the Heinrich-Böll-Foundation, closely linked to the Green Party, in which it promoted an ETR and gathered support from 80 scientists, 200 companies, trade unions and many more (DNR, 2004). A general book on ETR was also published for this campaign (Krebs et al., 1998). Generally, one could look back at a broad coalition of stakeholders in favour of ETR. This is important to remember when considering the further development and acceptance. In March 1998, the Green Party had (again – as several times before) adopted its position to increase transport fuel taxes up to 5 DM, about 2.56 €, per litre until 2010. This claim had been put forward initially by the Council on Environmental Advisers several years before. However, this scientifically sound and justified demand was considered as a big threat by the public since the time span until 2010 was more or less neglected, potentials for structural changes and a large fleet of low-consuming cars were not taken into account. The public debate almost made the Greens stumble.

Another danger emerged from the Federal Association of German Industry (BDI) in summer 1998. One of its committees planned to launch a brochure on the job losses if an ETR was to be implemented. Likely BDI intended to publish this in a large number of issues in many companies and disseminate it to their employees. Somewhat by chance, this campaign fortunately never took off the ground. In a drafting stage, protagonists of an ETR received an informal hint. The draft leaflet was full of unproven statements and potential horror scenarios – all based only on the thesis that an ETR would in any case imply tremendous reallocations and thus job losses. However, several countries had already introduced an ETR successfully whilst improving their employment situation (Schlegelmilch, 1999). The only way to prevent a similar debate as in spring 1998, but now just before the elections was to make BDI's supposed intention public and to show that these statements were superfluous and based on wrong assumptions. Otherwise one could well imagine that the debate would have been timed just before the elections triggering an irrational debate influencing the public opinion in a way that facts could hardly have time to reach people's attention. Hence, the author decided to go ahead and unveil this plan (Schlegelmilch, 1998) – still risking to be on the black list of BDI ever since.

However, they did not only survive this difficult period, but the Greens and Social Democrats then even formed the first red-green government in Germany. In fact, in terms of numbers another constellation would have been feasible, too. The Social Democrats could have chosen – as before in the 1970s until 1982 – the Liberal Democrats as partners. Besides, the Liberals in Germany are – unlike their partners in the United Kingdom – much less environmentally progressive. But, maybe because Oskar Lafontaine as party leader had substantial influence at that time, the Greens, his preference, were chosen. In addition, there were similar constellations in the important Land North-Rhine-Westphalia. Equivalent structures on the federal level would make politics easier. This was likely the crucial decision which helped the ETR to come on the agenda for implementation.

4 Design and Implementation of the ETR in Germany

Major parts of the design, the implementation and the environmental impacts are well described and laid down in detail in a paper from the German Federal Ministry for the Environment, Nature Conservation and Nuclear Safety (BMU, 2004c). Hence, it is generally referred to and only very briefly summarised here. In a nutshell, energy taxes were introduced or increased in overall five small steps, announced ahead. The revenue was used to lower social security contributions to the pensions fund, a minor part of more than 10% were used to favour environmental fuels, techniques and behaviour. Overall about 2% of total taxes and levies were shifted from labour towards energy/resource use in an almost revenue neutral way. In the following, aspects of policy advice are at the core of debate, and in the next chapter, the focus is on environmental impacts and experiences with public reactions. When the government and others reflected on how to best implement the ETR, it turned out that basically three issues had not yet been solved from the policy advisor side:

- How to exempt electricity from renewables from the electricity tax?
- How to treat and possibly differentiate business?
- How to take social aspects better into account?

Here, although Germany has had a debate of about 15 years and several dozens of studies, at least one dozen being of some practical use, good advice that could now be implemented as the window of opportunity had come, was missing. Since the implementation in 1999, at least better ideas have been developed on how to answer those questions, though only partly been implemented. Even though researchers and policy advisors were closely involved in the design phase of the ETR no real valuable idea for answering these questions was put forward that could have been implemented. Overall three hearings took place in the Finance Committee of the German Bundestag to receive advice from all kinds of stakeholders. In several parts, also a kind of brain drain was visible were protagonists of an ETR now came into positions in the government or parliament which allowed for directly influencing the process and decision making.

5 Experiences with the ETR in Germany

As mentioned in the last chapter, experiences are described and laid down in detail in a paper from the German Federal Ministry for the Environment, Nature Conservation and Nuclear Safety (BMU, 2004c). In the following, some particular aspects are selected and discussed, clearly more informal than it could be done in an official paper. The experiences were very ambivalent. The idea of an ETR was not well understood, particularly the fact that revenues were put into the pensions fund and were not used for environmental purposes. Many did not even realise that their social security contributions to this pensions fund had been reduced. Furthermore, the acceptance was only moderate since people did not like paying higher energy taxes while the world oil price increase was pushing gasoline prices up at the same time. Some even argued that spending more money on the pensions fund would delay any serious reforms in Germany's pension system. In fact, it turned out later that this had been a major motivation for some influential political leaders.

There were always two schools of how to use the revenues: One argued one should not increase total influence of the state and thus reduce other more distorting taxes and levies. This was dominant in the 1990s and also adopted by the broad majority of protagonists, and clearly also from environmental NGOs where this position would not seem self-evident. Others argued that one should use the money for financing structural changes in transport, energy, agriculture and other sectors. This would imply an increase of the state quota, but ensure an acceleration of the structural change and hence the target would likely be reached earlier. The former school eventually succeeded, but for acceptance reasons, the extent to which the latter school gained influence increased over time. The latter found its way to implementation by an increased spending for modernising the buildings stock from 2003 on.

In fact, it turned out that the political agreement to spend major parts for reducing labour costs was absolutely essential for the ETR to survive the major public debate in 2000. Had there been no planning and announcement to use the revenues for lowering the pensions fund contribution and had the lowering of the high unemployment in Germany not been the absolute top priority, the ETR would have been stopped very likely by Chancellor Schröder in autumn 2000. He would not have continued the ETR making his government unpopular if the revenues were basically spent for some prestigious environmental projects. Only a strong fiscal driver can ensure the political survival of an ETR in critical situations.

In autumn 2000, when the world oil prices had quadrupled within the last 18 months, some tabloids blamed the increase of about 60 pfennigs (or around 0.30 €) on the ecotax, although only one quarter, 12 pfennigs (0.06 €) could seriously be attributed to the ecotax. The other part was due to the increasing world oil price and exchange rate of the US-dollar. Even worse, major parts of the opposition, and even protagonists of an ETR from the conservatives in the mid-1990s, including the former Environment Minister and now party leader of the conservative party, Angela Merkel, used the political situation to blame high fuel prices on the government as well. This situation did not make it easier for the government to communicate the facts and apparently given this debate the public is still influenced and there is no broad acceptance, but this varies around 30-50%. Somewhat encouraging is the general acceptance for lowering taxes for those who burden the environment less as polls show.

It was a bit schizophrenic that on the one hand the government offered a market-based instrument where the decision where, when, how and whether to save energy was left up to every individual's decision to allow for maximum flexibility and freedom and thus a very cost-efficient approach – as often claimed. But on the other hand, people always and still do claim that the "good" government would certainly know best how to spend the money for the environment and thus it should also do accordingly, but not use it for something else like the pensions fund, implying a higher state influence, opposed in general. People expected environmental impacts to stem from the use of the revenues, whereas the government expected environmental impacts to stem from the tax incentive itself.

Reality finally confirmed the government's point of view. The environmental impacts became clearly visible – although hardly any money was used for environmental purposes. According to figures from the Federal Statistical Office, fuel consumption in road traffic (in each case, figures are based on amounts of mineral oil taxed in Germany) has been decreasing continually, with decreases of 2.8% in 2000, 1.0% in 2001, 2.3% in 2002 and 3.5% in 2003. The biggest contribution to this development was petrol sales, which fell by 4.5% in 2000, by 3.0% in 2001, by 3.3% in 2002 and by an additional 4.3% in 2003. In 2000, 2002 and 2003, sales of diesel fuel decreased by 0.7, 1.2 and 1.6%, respectively. A slight increase was registered for diesel fuel in 2001, although this increase, at 1.4%, was much smaller than that seen in 1999 (+4.7%). The reasons given for this decrease include efficient, more reserved driving habits and overall mileage reductions, due to the higher petrol prices, and the lower specific mileage fuel consumption of new vehicles.

Goods transports on roads have also decreased in the past few years. The Federal Statistical Office reports that tonnage in road transport of goods decreased by 2.9% in 2001, 4.3% in 2002 and 1.5% in 2003. Decreases in railway goods transport levels, at 1.6% in 2001 and 1.1% in 2002, were smaller than in the road transport sector. In 2003, railway goods transports actually increased by 4%. Transport companies are responding to the increased adaptation pressures by using their vehicles more and more efficiently. Pursuant to the Federal Office for Goods Transports, total no-load mileage of German trucks, as a percentage of total mileage, has continued to decrease, while the percentage share of with-load kilometres has increased further – in 2000, somewhat more strongly than in the years before: With-load kilometres as a percentage share of total kilometres increased from 71.4% in 1995 to 73.4% in 1998, to 74.1% in 1999 and to 75.3% in 2000.

In addition, in recent years the numbers of passengers travelling by public transport have begun increasing again. Following a downward trend in the numbers of passengers using local public transport up to 1998, these numbers again registered constant increases over five consecutive years. According to the Federal Statistical Office, the numbers of people using local public transportation have grown continuously since 1999: +0.4% in 1999; +0.8% in 2000; +0.8% in 2001; +0.5% in 2002 and +1.5% in 2003.

According to CarSharing, a nation-wide umbrella association of car-sharing providers, the numbers of people who are members of car-sharing agencies and who use their services increased by 26% in 2000, by 22% in 2001, by 8% in 2002 and by 15% in 2003 (in each case, the increases are with regard to the previous year).

The climate, the environment, the job market and innovative enterprises all benefit from the ecological tax reform, as the reform makes it possible to reduce automobile traffic, with its high external costs; replaces automobile transports with more environmentally sound modes of transport; and reduces energy consumption and the related environmental pollution by promoting use of alternative fuels. These positive trends need to be reinforced via a reliable framework; a reliable planning framework is one of the keys to energy-saving investments, which can take a number of years to pay off.

The Environmental Protection Agency has just released a report on the empirical impacts of the ETR. It finds that, in reality, the impacts of the ETR are often much better and brought about more benefits than generally perceived. It particularly demonstrates several concrete companies, large and small ones, which clearly benefited from the ETR (Umweltbundesamt 2004).

Strictly scientifically, not all of those phenomena can be attributed fully to the ETR, and some is certainly also due to the high oil price. However, given people's perception that most of the fuel price increases is due to ETR (though e.g. in 2000 only a quarter was attributable to that), it could be justified to argue that the environmental dividend as just described could also be claimed by the ETR protagonists. And perceptions are facts and can have strong influences which justifies a rather cheeky approach. Nevertheless the message is very clear: Prices matter – and this has to be enlarged to "Prices and perception/awareness matter". This is all that market-based approaches have to proof, either triggered by higher demand as seen in 2004 or by ecotaxes as implemented in Germany and other countries.

The positive impacts of the ETR in Germany were also confirmed by a study in 2001 by four institutes, led by DIW (Bach et al., 2002). For the transport sector it said that CO_2-emissions would be reduced by 3.84% until 2010 against 1998. Here policy advice helped to get more rationality in the public debate, though this was basically a study for interested stakeholders. However, the government used the findings to underline the appropriateness of the ETR.

6 Conclusions

The major conclusions that can be drawn are:

1. Different waves of public debate on ETR led to an ever increasing chance for implementation.
2. However, industry successfully delayed implementation of effective market-based instruments by instrument hopping and by changing policy approaches just as appropriate to that end.
3. The likely rationale behind this is that once such market-based instruments such as ETR are implemented in a more or less text book form, industry would be dependant almost completely to market forces. Though often claimed to be good, this should, of course, rather never apply to one's own company as one knows the radical effectiveness of market-based instruments. Hence, negotiations on the design of an ETR and e.g. emissions trading became very important.
4. A fiscal driver appears to be crucial for the survival of an ETR in crisis situations, environmental arguments alone will not be sufficient. Fiscal and environmental stakeholders should become more aware of their joint interests and thus "natural" alliance to exploit their full potential for the sake of the environment and the budget.

5. The usefulness of policy advice depends heavily on the phase of the political process, the stakeholders and the way it is provided.
6. It is not easy to generalise the process and explore the lessons learned in order to help other countries which are also working on the implementation of economic policy instruments. Every country has a very special set of actors including the influence of certain people as it is explained for the German case in this paper. It is, however, important to really bring together different actors from the political parties, the bureaucracies, scientific institutions, industries and environmental NGOs with their counterparts in other countries to allow for creating a good network and for ensuring that the same "language" is spoken by the stakeholders. Such a transfer e.g. was agreed between the Czech Ministry for the Environment and the German Ministry for the Environment back in 2002. This successful approach is about to be enlarged to other countries such as Poland in 2004.

References

Bach, S., et al. (2002), The Effects of Environmental Fiscal Reform in Germany: A Simulation Study, *Energy Policy* 30, 803–811.

BDI (1996), *Updated and Extended Declaration by German Industry and Trade on Global Warming Prevention*, Cologne.

BDI (1995a), *Declaration by German Industry and Trade on Global Warming Prevention*, Cologne.

BDI (1995b), *Beurteilung ökologischer Steuerreformvorschläge vor dem Hintergrund des bestehenden Steuersystems*, Berlin.

Binswanger, H.C., H. Nutzinger, H. Frisch, et al. (1983), *Arbeit ohne Umweltzerstörung*, Frankfurt/Main.

BMI (Bundesministerium des Innern) (Ed.) (1974), *Umweltgutachten 1974 des Rates von Sachverständigen für Umweltfragen*, Bundestags-Drucksache 7/2802, Bonn, XI f.

BMU (Federal Ministry for the Environment, Nature Conservation and Nuclear Safety) (2004a), German cabinet agrees on basis for the start of emissions trading, press release, No. 087/04, Berlin, see: http://www.bmu.de/en/800/js/news/pressrelease 040331/, accessed 30.08.2004.

BMU (Federal Ministry for the Environment, Nature Conservation and Nuclear Safety) (2004b), Nationaler Allokationsplan für die Bundesrepublik Deutschland 2005-2007, Berlin, see: http://www.bmu.de/files/nap_kabinettsbeschluss.pdf.

BMU (Federal Ministry for the Environment, Nature Conservation and Nuclear Safety) (2004c), The ecological tax reform: introduction, continuation and development into an ecological fiscal reform, http://www.bmu.de/files/oekost_en.pdf, accessed 30.08.2004.

BMU (Federal Ministry for the Environment, Nature Conservation and Nuclear Safety) and BMWA (Federal Ministry of Economics and Labour) (2002), Federal Government Reaches Breakthrough in Emissions Trading, joint press release, No. 291/02, Berlin, http://www.bmu.de/en/800/js/news/pressrelease021204/.

BUND (2004), BUND-Analyse des nationalen Zuteilungsplans für den europäischen Emissionshandel (Kabinettsbeschluss vom 31. März 2004, BUND-Analysis of the national allocation plan of 31st March 2004), Berlin.

CDU-/CSU-Fraktion (1995), "Konzept 2000", Entwurf, 03/05/1995.

Coase, R.H. (1960), The Problem of Social Cost, *Journal of Law and Economics* 3.

DNR (Deutscher Naturschutzring) (2004), http://www.foes-ev.de/4fakten/index.html, here 2. Deutschland and „Klare Befürworter der Ökologischen Steuerreform, Aufruf von BUND und DNR von 1998", accessed 30/08/2004.

DIW (Deutsches Institut für Wirtschaftsforschung) (1994), Ökosteuer – Königsweg oder Sackgasse, Berlin.

European Commission (1997), *Communication on Environmental Agreements*, Brussels.

European Commission (1996), *Communication on the Use of Environmental Agreements as an Instrument for the Implementation of Environmental Policy in the Community*, COM(96) 561, Final Report, Brussels.

European Environment Agency (1997), *Environmental Agreements*, Copenhagen.

Fischedick, M. et.al (1995), *„Erklärung der deutschen Wirtschaft zur Klimavorsorge": Königsweg oder Mogelpackung?*, Wuppertal Papers No 39, Wuppertal.

Görres, A., H. Ehringhaus, and E.U. v. Weizsäcker (1994), The Way Towards an Ecological Tax Reform – Less Pollution and More Employment, in: *The Memorandum of Green Budget Germany – GBG*, Munich, see: http://www.foes-ev.de.

Krebs, C., D.T. Reiche, and M. Rocholl (1998), *Die Ökologische Steuerreform. Was sie ist, wie sie funktioniert, was sie uns bringt,* edited by Deutscher Naturschutzring (DNR), Naturschutzbund (NABU), and Bund für Umwelt und Naturschutz Deutschland (BUND), Berlin, Basel, Boston.

Krebs, C. and D.T. Reiche (1997), Wie die Ökologische Steuerreform beerdigt wurde, *Blätter für deutsche und internationale Politik* 7/97 (documented in: Frankfurter Rundschau on 27/08/1997).

Luhmann, J. (1996), RWI Presents Contradicting Study to DIW/Greenpeace, *Wuppertal Bulletin zur Ökologischen Steuerreform* 3, 12f.

Lühr, H.-P. (1989), Die Abwasserabgabe – Grundlagen und Auswirkungen, *WSI-Mitteilungen* 8, 432-438.

Meißner, W. and E. Hödl (1978), *Auswirkungen der Umweltpolitik auf den Arbeitsmarkt*, Bonn.

Memorandum junger Abgeordneter des Deutschen Bundestages zur Klimakonferenz in Berlin, Juni 1995.

Rennings, K. (1996), *Negotiated Agreements in Environmental Protection: No Free-Market Instrument*, Centre for European Economics Research (ZEW), Mannheim.

RWI (Rheinisch-Westfälisches Institut für Wirtschaftsforschung) (1996), *Regionalwirtschaftliche Wirkung von Steuern und Abgaben auf den Verbrauch von Energie – Das Beispiel NRW*, Essen.

Schlegelmilch, K. (Ed.) (1999), *Green Budget Reform in Europe. Countries at the Forefront*, Heidelberg.

Schlegelmilch, K. (1998), Auf zum letzten Gefecht. Wie der BDI mit einer unsachlichen Kampagne gegen Ökosteuern in den Wahlkampf eingreifen will, *Die ZEIT*, 02/07/1998, 25.

Schlegelmilch, K., (1995), Parteien im Wettstreit. Welche Partei hat die beste Ökologische Steuerreform (ÖSR)?, *ÖkologiePolitik* 70, 9f.

Umweltbundesamt (2004), Quantifizierung der Effekte der Ökologischen Steuerreform auf Umwelt, Beschäftigung und Innovation, http://www.umweltbundesamt.de/uba-info-presse/hintergrund/index.htm, Berlin.

UPI (Umwelt- und Prognose Institut) (1988), *Ökosteuern als marktwirtschaftliches Instrument – Vorschläge für eine ökologische Steuerreform*, UPI-Report No. 9, Heidelberg.

Printing and Binding: Strauss GmbH, Mörlenbach